# ARCTIC 8 POLICY:
## REASSESSING INTERNATIONAL RELATIONS

# ARCTIC 8 POLICY
## REASSESSING
## INTERNATIONAL RELATIONS

Edited by
Ferdi Güçyetmez
Jared R. Dmello

TRANSNATIONAL PRESS LONDON
2024

POLICY SERIES: 16

Arctic 8 Policy: Reassessing International Relations

Edited by Ferdi Güçyetmez and Jared R. Dmello

Copyright © 2024 Transnational Press London

First Published in 2024 by Transnational Press London in the United Kingdom, 13 Stamford Place, Sale, M33 3BT, UK.
www.tplondon.com

Transnational Press London® and the logo and its affiliated brands are registered trademarks.

Requests for permission to reproduce material from this work should be sent to: sales@tplondon.com

Paperback
ISBN: 978-1-80135-271-0
Digital
ISBN: 978-1-80135-272-7

Cover Design: Nihal Yazgan
Cover Photo by Willian Justen de Vasconcellos on unsplash.com

Transnational Press London Ltd. is a company registered in England and Wales No. 8771684.

# CONTENTS

# PREFACE

When we initiated this book project, our planned purpose was to emphasise that the Arctic is a large and promising area. However, as the research and analyses deepened, we found that the importance of this region has been a recurring theme across time across various dimensions. These findings consist of statements considered important in terms of geopolitics and geography as well as history and climate, with implications for national and international security. We observed new geopolitical opportunities by combining the knowledge brought by history with the geography changed by the climate. The role of the region has transformed across the centuries. When we examine a historical perspective from the 1800s, the Arctic was seen as just a huge ice mass. Yet, by the 1900s and into the 2000s, it played a leading role in the power scenarios of geopolitical theories, evolving into the intervention area of powerful states. We thought that investigating the Arctic region only with states and politics would cause us to make comments with incomplete information. For this reason and in line with contemporary, non-traditional theorisation approaches to security studies, we felt the need to explain this study not directly based on the policies of the countries, but with the climate change crisis that has shaped this process today. With climate change and emerging technologies driving both incremental and innovative change, we have designed this analysis of the political order developing in the largely impassable glaciers of the Arctic from a multidisciplinary perspective, uniting multiple scholarly and applied disciplines, such as political science, geography, history, public policy, and security studies. This book, the culmination of research efforts by many talented scholars from around the globe, provides new insight into explaining the behaviour of Arctic countries, which are geopolitical powers and key stakeholders in the region and beyond, in terms of climate, energy and security more broadly. We present this body of work in two parts; first, we identify the risks and implications for the Arctic region as a whole, followed by country-level analyses.

In this context, we divided the book into two sections and 12 chapters. In the first section, we analysed the actual and phenomenal issues in the Arctic region in 4 chapters. Specifically, before examining the Arctic policies of the countries, we need to understand the geopolitical position, energy availability, climate change and security policies in the Arctic. In the second section, we analysed the Arctic countries directly included in the Arctic Circle under 8

1

headings.

The first section begins with Ferdi Güçyetmez's exploration by providing an introductory overview of Arctic geopolitics, defining the Arctic Circle and elucidating its geographical features. Following this, Alina Bykova delves into the realm of security dynamics within the Arctic, shedding light on NATO's evolving security policies and their implications for the region. Anna Soer further contributes to this discourse by dissecting the complexities surrounding energy dynamics in the Arctic, exploring the interplay between energy resources, transformations, and environmental considerations. Lastly, Rabia Kalfaoğlu conducts an in-depth analysis of the Arctic's vulnerability to global climate change, with a particular focus on the impact of climate shifts on the region's glaciers.

In the second section, the book shifts its focus towards country-level analyses. Aslıhan Genç scrutinizes the Arctic policies of the United States, tracing their evolution from historical perspectives to contemporary geopolitical realities. Jackson Walling follows suit by dissecting Canada's Arctic policies and its diplomatic relations within the circumpolar north. Ebru Caymaz offers insights into Russia's strategic maneuvers in the Arctic, shedding light on the country's policies and their implications for regional dynamics. Yeliz Albayrak explores Finland's Arctic strategies and its diplomatic engagements with other Arctic nations, while Emre Sipahioğlu provides a historical perspective on Sweden's Arctic policies, analyzing their evolution and regional impact over time. The exploration continues with Allison G. Kondrat delving into Norway's geopolitical interests and security considerations in the Arctic, followed by Jared R. Dmello and Bianca Acosta's examination of Iceland's Arctic policies from a strategic standpoint. Veysel Babahanoğlu and Elif Miray Yazıcı conclude this section by scrutinizing Denmark's Arctic relations, shedding light on its geopolitical engagements with Arctic nations.

Editors

Ferdi Güçyetmez[1] and Jared R. Dmello[2]

---

[1] University of Bern, Department of Political Science, Geopolitical Studies, Switzerland.
E-mail: ferdigucyetmez26@gmail.com, ORCID: 0000-0003-1204-2606.
[2] Senior Lecturer of Criminology, University of Adelaide, Australia. E-mail: jared.dmello@adelaide.edu.au, ORCID: https://orcid.org/0000-0001-8805-1061.
**Acknowledgements:** We would like to thank Prof. Dr. Ibrahim Sirkeci for helping with the publication of the book. We would like to thank Anna Soer for her contributions and suggestions during this process.

# SECTION I

# IDENTIFYING SIGNIFICANT RISKS IN THE ARCTIC

# CHAPTER 1

# INTRODUCTION TO ARCTIC GEOPOLITICS

Ferdi Güçyetmez[1]

'Every act of creation is an act of destruction': This dialogue, which first emerged in Eastern philosophy, laid the foundation for the concept of "war for peace" that would follow years later. New concepts have emerged as war has gained perspective, and multidisciplinary disciplines have since been involved in examining the causes, conduct, and termination of conflicts. However, is it only weapons that are necessary for war? From the first nomadic societies where acts of warfare emerged to the era of war theorists, such as Thucydides, Thomas Aquinas, Carl von Clausewitz, Niccolò Machiavelli, or Helmuth Karl Bernhard von Moltke, there was another action that was as effective as weapons throughout history: strategy. Strategy is a broad and deep subject, with strategic studies having emerged as a scholarly discipline in its own right, but the depth that concerns us for the purpose of this text is geopolitics and geography because from these dimensions, all other components of security and society can be examined.

## The Origins of Geopolitics

Taking an etymological look at the origin of the term, the word "geopolitics" is derived from the words "géo" (land) and "politique" (politics). In other words, it has emerged as a combination of geography and politics; in other words, it is the politicisation of geography. If one speaks of politics, it inevitably involves a struggle for power and authority. The relationship between geography and politics is not only a simple connection but also a complex interaction, involving a wide variety of stakeholders and encompassing many different social and physical constructs. Geopolitics is, thus, a multi-cornered space, where power, geography, and international relations intersect. It emphasises the importance of geographical factors in shaping the strategic decisions, borders, and national interests of states and international actors. Geopolitics provides strategic ideas about the future by utilising the geographical structure of countries and is important for

[1] University of Bern, Department of Political Science, Geopolitical Studies, Switzerland.
E-mail: ferdigucyetmez26@gmail.com, ORCID: 0000-0003-1204-2606.

understanding international relations.

The concept of geopolitics is not restricted to warfare alone, but also includes attributes, such as territorial expansion and conflict between states. Geopolitics is a broad system of thought that affects the strategic decisions of states with factors such as geographical location, natural resources, climate, and population. Systematic analyses of geopolitical conditions can help us better understand international power balances and regional conflicts of interest. For example, conflicts of interest in a strategic region can cause tensions and conflicts in international relations. Countries that are important due to their geographical location could be exposed to competition from other states and be forced to pursue a strategic balance policy. These analyses help us understand the foreign policy preferences of states and their role in the international system. While geographical factors influence the strategic decisions of states, they play a major role in determining the balance of power and conflicts of interest in international relations.

State policies that do not take geography into account have often resulted in strategic failures. In the struggle for regional dominance, geography can offer opportunities according to the position of countries. These opportunities are also an area of struggle for other countries. States, such as the United States of America, surrounded by oceans, England as an island country, and Switzerland surrounded by the Alps are under the natural protection of their geography. The historical record provides a plethora of examples where natural geography made a lasting contribution on state security. For example, in 1805, Napoleon failed against England in the Trafalgar Sea Battle. Later, in 1940, Hitler could not reach England due to the natural barrier of the English Channel. In 1941, Hitler invaded the Soviet territories with Operation Barbarossa and had to retreat with a great defeat because he did not take natural conditions into account. The German army, which set out with a geopolitical objective (Lebensraum), was defeated because it ignored the geography of the region. Similarly, the history of Africa changed with the arrival of European countries such as England, Italy and France to North Africa with the increase in maritime dominance.

The term geopolitics was first used by the German geopolitician Friedrich Ratzel in the late 19th century. Ratzel argued that the survival and growth efforts of states depend on geographical factors. According to him, expansion and territorial gains are necessary for the strengthening of states. Ratzel's ideas formed the basis of Germany's territorial expansion policies;this school of thought was influential in Germany in the early 20th century.

Geopolitical theories, generally originating from the 19th and early 20th centuries, focus on the influence of geographical factors on the power and expansion objectives of states. Ratzel defends the principle of "either you grow or you perish". According to this idea, geographically expanding states tend to be more powerful than other states.

Halford Mackinder is a geopolitical theorist who's approach focused on geographical determinism. He emphasised the strategic importance of the Eurasian continent, which he calls the "World Island"[2]. According to him, states that control Eurasia are closer to achieving world domination. Mackinder's "Heartland" theory argues that Central Asia is the centre of power, and the control of this region is decisive in ensuring global hegemony.

Another classical geopolitical approach is that of Nicholas Spykman, who is known for his "Rimland" theory.[3] According to him, the Eurasian coastline facing the sea is a strategic region for world power. Control of this region provides a significant advantage for world domination. Spykman argues that the United States should control the Rimland by using its naval power. The Rimland Theory advocates important approaches to the geopolitics of the Arctic. The Arctic region is considered an area of strategic importance according to Nicholas Spykman's "Rimland" theory. According to Spykman, the sea-facing coastline of Eurasia is an important region for world power. Control of the Arctic coast offers geostrategic advantages, including access to natural resources and the opening of sea routes. Therefore, rivalry and conflicts between the great powers may arise in the Arctic region.

The Arctic region is strategic in terms of the Rimland theory. The Arctic coast is located at a geostrategically critical point and has energy resources, opening of sea routes, and natural resource potential. Control of the Arctic coast can affect the access of geographically expanding states to the seas and the rivalry between global powers. This situation may cause geopolitical rivalry between the great powers and requires the development of policies for the protection of their strategic interests in the Rimland region.

The Rimland approach works in the same way as the "great power rivalry" theory: The Arctic region is the scene of geopolitical competition between great powers. The opening of Arctic Sea routes, access to energy resources,

---

[2] Britannica, T. Editors of Encyclopaedia. "Eurasia." Encyclopedia Britannica, January 11, 2024. https://www.britannica.com/place/Eurasia.

[3] Meinig, Donald W. "Heartland and Rimland in Eurasian History." The Western Political Quarterly 9, no. 3 (1956): 553–69. https://doi.org/10.2307/444454.

and the potential of undersea resources make the region attractive. In particular, countries such as Russia, the United States, Canada, Norway and Denmark (Greenland) pursue various policies to protect their strategic interests and defend their rights in the Arctic region. Within this theoretical perspective, additional engagement by actors in the region increases the likelihood of tension or conflicts to empower one entity to achieve its objectives or enhance its political interests.

## Arctic Geopolitics

The Arctic is a region around the North Pole, including most of the North Ice Sea and the Arctic Ocean. The Arctic region includes parts of countries such as North America, Russia, Canada, Greenland, Norway, Sweden, Finland and Iceland. These regions are generally characterised by cold climates, glaciers, mountainous terrain and large bodies of water. The Arctic region is known for its extremely cold climate. Winters are very long and harsh and summers are short and cool. In winter, temperatures can drop to -50 °C, while in summer average temperatures range between 0-10 °C. The climatic conditions in the region cause large glaciers to form and sea ice to cover large areas.

When considering Arctic geopolitics, a few key areas are readily identifiable:

- Arctic Geography: Based on geopolitics, we emphasise the influence of Arctic geography on issues such as national security, borders, access routes, and resources. A country's geographical location can greatly influence its relations with other countries.

- Strategic Position of Arctic Countries: The geographical location of a country is geo-strategically important. A country located at the crossroads of seas, near important trade routes, or bordering neighbouring countries may have a strategic advantage in international relations.

- Arctic Access Routes: Geopolitics focuses on Arctic countries'access to transport routes such as seas, rivers, and airspace. These access routes are critical for maintaining trade and military activity.

- Arctic Resources: Geography also determines the distribution of natural resources. Geopolitical analyses can provide new insight into how the control of resources such as energy resources, water resources, minerals and agricultural land affects international competition.

- Arctic Borders: A country's geographical boundaries shape its relations with other countries. The determination of borders, territorial disputes, and strategies to protect borders are among the geopolitical issues. Of note for this region, how countries bordering the Arctic engage with each other and other would-be actors impacts the geopolitical calculus.

- Arctic and International Relations: Geopolitics examines a country's relations with its geographical environment. This includes relations with international organisations and neighbouring countries, alliances, and competition. Arctic Geostrategy: Geostrategy, a sub-branch of geopolitics, focuses on military strategies and power projection. A country's geographical location affects its defence doctrines and military operations.

Geopolitics plays a fundamental role in international relations and is important for understanding the causes of conflicts between countries and how national interests can be protected. Therefore, geopolitical analysis is considered a factor in shaping the foreign policy decisions of states. In the Arctic region, new sea routes opened by melting glaciers and developing icebreaker technology connect the Pacific and Atlantic Oceans and facilitate transportation between Europe, the Americas, and Asia. Four key routes should be of strategic interest based on their likelihood of shaping the geopolitics of the region.

1. The Northern Sea Route (NSR) connects the Atlantic and Pacific Oceans through the northern coast of the Russian Federation, starting from the Bering Strait. By using the Northern Sea Route instead of the Indian Ocean and the Suez Canal, the journey from Hamburg to Shanghai was more advantageous in terms of safety, distance, time, and fuel consumption.

2. The Northwest Passage (NWP), which has a similar route as the Northern Sea Route, starts from the eastern coast of Russia and extends to the coasts of Finland, Sweden, and Norway (Northwest Europe), connecting the Bering Strait to the Pacific Ocean. Like the Northern Sea Route, the Northwest Passage reduces the distance between Europe and the Far East.[4] This Passage connects the Arctic

---

[4] Michael Byers, "Crises and International Cooperation: An Arctic Case Study", *International Relations* 31, no. 4 (2017): 381.

Ocean to the Pacific Ocean through the waterways around the northern coast of North America and the archipelago north of Canada. Like other sea routes, the Northwest Passage shortens the distance between continents. For comparison, the sea route between London and Yokohama is 21,200 kilometres (km) via the Suez Canal and 23,300 km viathe Panama Canal, yet only 15,700 km via the Northwest Passage and 13,481 km via the Northeast Passage.[5]

3.  The Arctic Bridge crosses the southern coast of Greenland and connects Canada's Churchill Harbour with Russia's Murmansk Harbour. The Arctic Bridge can be used for transport for four months of the year, with the first successful crossing occurring in 2007.[6]

4.  The Transpolar Sea Route runs through the centre of the Arctic Ocean and connects the Bering Strait to the Atlantic Ocean. Since the glaciers around the North Pole have not completely melted, the Transpolar Sea Route is not in use today.

The increase in the possibility of transport routes in the Arctic Ocean has led to an increase in disputes between coastal states regarding their sovereignty claims over the sea routes. These claims will lead to significant challenges in the future, both in terms of geopolitics and from a legal perspective. Thus, states are trying to preemptively open new paths for themselves, both militarily in the field and legally in the international arena.

With the purchase of Alaska from Russia in 1867, the United States gained a foothold in the region as a coastal Arctic neighbour. The United States bought the territory for 7.2 million dollars, i.e. 2 cents per acre. In 1867, the dollar exchange rate was 1.60 rubles. Russia sold Alaska for 11.520 million rubles. England was the architect of the sale. With the outbreak of the Crimean War in 1853, Britain, France and Türkiye united against Russia. Given this alliance and the multiple conflict fronts, it was clear that Russia could not also defend Alaska. All sea routes, even the gold mines, were controlled by the ships on the other side. Russia feared that Britain would annex Alaska. For this reason, instead of giving the region to England, it agreed to transfer it to a country with which it had good relations at the time, and as a result of negotiations with America for Alaska, the parties agreed on

---

[5] Guy Emmanuel ve Lasserre, Frédéric. "Commercial Shipping in the Arctic: New Perspectives, Challenges and Regulations," Polar Record 52, no. 264 (2016): 294-304.

[6] Trude Pettersen, "Russia, Canada to Resume Arctic Bridge", Barents Observer, (November 2011), https://barentsobserver.com/en/topics/russia-canada-resume-arctic-bridge

30 March 1867 in Washington. At first, people reacted with "What will America do with this ice floe?" but 140 years later, this region is more than an ice floe. This strategic decision on Russia's part plays into the long-term geopolitical calculations for power balancing in the region.

Map 1. Major Arctic Shipping Routes[7]

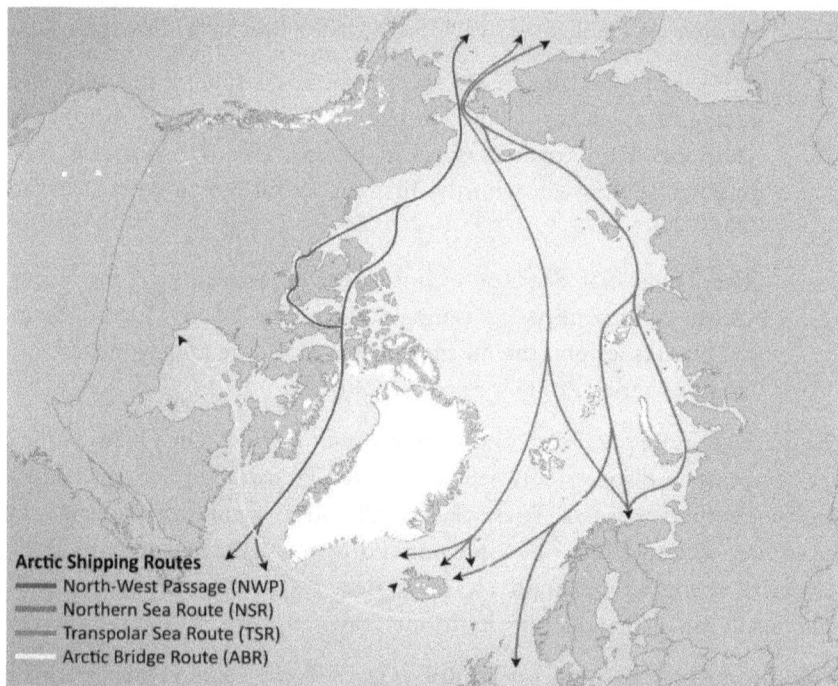

**Arctic Shipping Routes**
— North-West Passage (NWP)
— Northern Sea Route (NSR)
— Transpolar Sea Route (TSR)
— Arctic Bridge Route (ABR)

*Source: The Arctic Portal*

According to estimates, half of the world's remaining oil lies under the ice in the northern part of the Arctic Circle, opening another area for conflict and assertion of political interests. As a result of its studies in an area of 1800 km, Russia says that there are 10 billion tonnes of crude oil under the Lomonosov Hills[8]. In addition, it is thought that there is also oil accumulation under the Ross Sea in the Antarctic Continent where the South Pole is located. However, an agreement was made not to carry out economic activities in the region for 35 years. According to the latest findings in the Arctic region, 90 billion barrels of oil, 47.3 trillion cubic metres of natural gas and 44 billion

---

[7] "The Arctic Portal," The Future of Arctic Shipping, accessed May 5, 2022, The future of Arctic Shipping - Arctic Portal .

[8] Bieliszczuk, Bartosz, (2018), Northern Sea Route: Economic and Political Significance for Russia, accessed January, 10, https://pism.pl/publications/Northern_Sea_Route__ Economic_and_ Political_ Significance_for_Russia.

barrels of natural gas liquids have been found in the region[9]. In other words, this ratio is 44 times the 1.1 trillion cubic metres of natural gas energy reserves found in the Mediterranean Leviathan region, 6 per cent of the world's oil reserves and approximately 25 per cent of the world's natural gas reserves. The future importance of this issue should not be underestimated. This means that the Arctic plays a major role in geopolitical competition. The United States keeps huge icebreakers permanently stationed in the region and continues to work on nuclear-powered systems, an indication of its readiness to exert its political dominance in the territories near the Arctic.

Another problem in the region is that the decrease in permanent sea ice has exposed the coastal borders more and economic activity has become easier, a higher-order byproduct of climate change in the region. Scientific research data reports that the glaciers in the region will melt by 2058. The melting of glaciers means new trade routes for the countries in the region. From 2006 to 2018, the Pentagon observed at least 12 Arctic ice extensions in satellite imagery records[10]. These findings show that the Pentagon, which detects Arctic shipping routes with satellite images, closely follows the strategic transport routes in the region.

Overall, the Arctic ice passages are an important geographical feature that affects several areas such as trade, energy, fisheries, tourism, and geopolitical competition. The opening of these passages creates new opportunities and challenges for the states of the region and the international community. Therefore, the Arctic region is of increasing importance in international relations. Arctic ice passages refer to waterways that offer significant geopolitical and economic opportunities arising from the melting of glaciers in the Arctic region and the opening of sea routes. Arctic ice passages connect the North Sea and the North Atlantic, creating shortened sea routes. These routes can greatly shorten maritime transport from Asia to Europe and America.

The Northern Sea Route along the east coast of Siberia and the Northwest Passage north of Canada are particularly important in this perspective. Short and reliable sea routes can speed up international trade and reduce costs, returning long-term benefits to the parties that control them. When Arctic ice passages become a more attractive option for trade vessels, this can

---

[9] USGS, Circum-Arctic Resource Appraisal: Estimates of, accessed January 8, Undiscovered Oil and Gas North of the Arctic Circle, https://translate.google.com/?sl= en&tl=tr& op=translate.
[10] IPPC Report (2019), Sea Ice and Polar Oceans: Changes, Consequences and Impacts, accessed January 10, https://www.ipcc.ch/srocc/chapter/chapter-3-2/.

increase trade volumes and provide economic opportunities. The Arctic region contains significant energy resources. Ice passages can facilitate the transport of energy products and the development of energy projects. Oil and natural gas reserves in the Arctic seabeds are particularly important in this perspective. Arctic waters have rich fishing grounds. Glacier passages can promote the fishing industry by facilitating access for fishing vessels. Opened Arctic Sea routes can attract tourists to the region. This provides new opportunities for the tourism industry. Arctic ice passages can become an area of geopolitical competition. Various countries may compete to control or utilise these passages. Increased military presence in the region and border disputes could further complicate this geopolitical competition. The opening of Arctic ice passages could raise environmental concerns. Increased maritime traffic and industrial activities could cause environmental impacts and affect ecosystems in the region.

## Conclusion

The Arctic region is a geography of increasing geopolitical importance. The strategic location of the region causes the Arctic to become an important player in the international arena. The issues that increase the importance of the geography in the Arctic region are diverse. This diversity underpins the concept of Geopolitics. Namely, climate changes in the Arctic region, melting of glaciers and the opening of sea routes have eased both access to energy resources and the progress of merchant ships from Asia to Europe, making the region more attractive for trade routes. This has led to a change in geographical patterns and made it perhaps the most valuable region in the next century. Thus, competition between the Arctic countries and other great powers has moved to the 90 degrees north latitude line.

As a result, Arctic geopolitics has become an area of overlapping strategic interests and potentially high conflict at the global level. This region is an important factor affecting international relations not only in terms of energy resources, but also in issues such as maritime transport and environmental protection. It is uncertain how the geopolitical dynamics in the Arctic region will evolve in the future, but the region will continue to play an influential role in global politics and economy. Therefore, it is important for the international community to closely monitor developments in the Arctic region and develop appropriate strategies.

## Bibliography

Byers, Michael, "Crises and International Cooperation: An Arctic Case Study",

*International Relations* 31, no. 4 (2017): 381.

Guy, Emmanuel and Lasserre, Frédéric. "Commercial Shipping in the Arctic: New Perspectives, Challenges and Regulations," *Polar Record* 52, no. 264 (2016): 294-304.

Trude Pettersen, "Russia, Canada to Resume Arctic Bridge", *Barents Observer,* (November 2011), https://barentsobserver.com/en/topics/russia-canada-resume-arctic-bridge

"The Arctic Portal," The Future of Arctic Shipping, accessed May 5, 2022, The future of Arctic Shipping - Arctic Portal .

IPPC Report (2019), Sea Ice and Polar Oceans: Changes, Consequences and Impacts, accessed January 10, https://www.ipcc.ch/srocc/chapter/chapter-3-2/.

Bieliszczuk, Bartosz, (2018), Northern Sea Route: Economic and Political Significance for Russia, accessed January, 10, https://pism.pl/publications/ Northern_ Sea_ Route__ Economic_and_Political_Significance_for_Russia.

Britannica, T. Editors of Encyclopaedia. "Eurasia." Encyclopedia Britannica, January 11, 2024. https://www.britannica.com/place/Eurasia.

Meinig, Donald W. "Heartland and Rimland in Eurasian History." *The Western Political Quarterly* 9, no. 3 (1956): 553–69. https://doi.org/10.2307/444454.

USGS, Circum-Arctic Resource Appraisal: Estimates of, accessed January 8,

Undiscovered Oil and Gas North of the Arctic Circle, https://translate.google.com/?sl= en&tl=tr&op=translate

# CHAPTER 2

# WHAT THE ARCTIC MEANS TO NATO

## Alina Bykova[1]

### Introduction

The Arctic is warming four times faster than the rest of the world. The region is warming four times faster than the rest of the world.[2] Once considered a zone of peace and exceptionalism that was relatively sheltered from global politics, the Arctic has progressively (re)entered the forum of international affairs over the last decade, both due to interests in northern natural resources now made more accessible by the climate emergency, and Russia's unprovoked invasions of Ukraine in 2014 and 2022.

While NATO has no official Arctic policy, the organization has been concerned with the Arctic space since the first days of its inception. Cold War militarisation of the Arctic brought the region into the immediate fold of NATO's security agenda. Considering that NATO's chief adversary was the large northern nation of the Soviet Union, and is arguably Russia today, its continued focus on the Arctic space is unsurprising. Today, NATO must make important decisions about how to manoeuvre in an increasingly tense and securitised region, one that is dominated by a belligerent and unpredictable adversary in the form of Russia, which holds sovereignty over more than half of the Arctic coastline and has extensively developed and militarised its northern regions over several centuries.

This chapter examines the past, present, and future of NATO involvement in the Arctic, at a time when Arctic affairs have become increasingly unstable and further, are existentially threatened in the immediate future by devastating changes to the very topography and geography of the region driven by rampant global warming.

[1] Alina Bykova is a PhD candidate in history at Stanford University and the editor-in-chief at The Arctic Institute.
[2] Fraser Alex. "On the Front Lines of Climate Change in the World's Northernmost Town." Reuters, 3 September 2019. https://www.reuters.com/article/us-climate-change-svalbard-wideimage/on-the-front-lines-of-climate-change-in-the-worlds-northernmost-town-idUSKCN1VO19M.

## The Formation of NATO

The North Atlantic Treaty Organization is a military and political alliance comprised of 32 states, including two new members, with Finland having joined in April 2023, followed by Sweden in February 2024. Initially founded in 1949 with the purpose of promoting security and cooperation in Europe after World War II and countering growing Soviet influence, NATO was originally made up of only nine members, five of which are Arctic states (Canada, the United States, Iceland, Denmark and Norway). This fact, and the organization's general focus on the North Atlantic, naturally brings the Arctic into the fold of the Treaty's sphere of interests.

NATO emerged from a divided post-war Europe that was characterized by wartime destruction and trauma, and Western concerns regarding Soviet belligerence. Historian Lawrence S. Kaplan argues that NATO's inception was driven by a British desire for unity and cooperation among Western nations to both rebuild and defend themselves, and American willingness to join the Alliance because its experience in WWII had eroded the previous policy of American isolationism. European "economies could not be rebuilt without massive American support, and their defense capabilities could not cope with the aggressive Soviet Union without an American commitment to counterbalance the Communist adversary," writes Kaplan.[3] Coupled with the Marshall Plan for US economic support to Europe, the newly articulated Truman Doctrine policy of containing the Soviet threat further reinforced cooperation between European and North American allies, which led to US "military entanglement" and "integration" with Europe, and directly contributed to the formation of NATO.[4]

Although the United States, Britain, and the USSR fought as allies in the Second World War, ideological differences and Western worries that the Soviet Union, led by Joseph Stalin, would not honour the promises of cooperation and non-aggression that were made at the Yalta and Potsdam wartime conferences in 1945 led to tension in the immediate post-war period and a breakdown of relations by the end of the decade. At Yalta and Potsdam, American presidents, Franklin Delano Roosevelt and Harry Truman, and British prime minister Winston Churchill made agreements with Stalin that the Soviets would not impose authoritarian rule in East/Central Europe. However, as early as 1945, Stalin was already, following Marxist ideology,

---

[3] Lawrence S. Kaplan, "Origins of NATO: 1948-1949, Emory Int'l Literature 34 no.11 (2019): 11-12.
[4] Kaplan, "Emory," 13.

denouncing Western ideology as dangerous.[5] The Soviet incursion into Eastern and Central Europe in the years following 1945 under the guise of liberation, and the progressive destruction of civic and political liberties there, made matters untenable for the West.[6] Historian Odd Arne Westad argues that the Cold War began in Poland after the imposition of strict Soviet control in the country. "Britain had gone to war with Germany over the fate of Poland in 1939, and it would be hard for any British government to accept Soviet occupation and dictatorship in that country," Westad writes.[7] Ultimately, the allied relationship between the United States, Britain, and the Soviet Union forged in the wartime years of 1941-1945 could not overcome prior decades of ideological opposition and competition which had existed since the Russian Revolution.

The United States and the United Kingdom were not the only concerned parties contending with the possibility of Soviet aggression. Norway had reasons to fear the Soviet Union after WWII as well, which ultimately drove it to become one of the founding members of NATO. In the aftermath of the war, a Soviet effort, pushed forward by foreign affairs minister Vyacheslav Molotov, was made to renegotiate the Svalbard Treaty. Established in 1920 largely as a result of World War I, the Treaty placed the Svalbard archipelago under Norwegian jurisdiction, something that the Soviet leadership contested immediately and vehemently due to the claim that Russia had a historical presence on the islands dating back centuries.[8] Eventually, the Soviet Union recognized the treaty in exchange for Norway's acknowledgement of the Soviet Union as an official state, and began to mine coal on the islands under the conditions of the treaty. By the 1940s, the Soviets had recognized the strategic importance of Svalbard as a key piece of territory that would help determine the fate of the Soviet Northern Fleet, based in the Kola Peninsula. For this reason, Soviet leadership, represented on the international stage by Molotov, was eager to pressure Norway to renegotiate the Svalbard Treaty and give the Soviet Union a piece of the

---

[5] Hershberg James. "The Cuban Missile Crisis," Chapter. In The Cambridge History of the Cold War, edited by Melvyn P. Leffler and Odd Arne Westad, (Cambridge: Cambridge University Press, 2010), 57 doi:10.1017/CHOL9780521837200.005.

[6] Norman Naimark and Leonid Gibianskii (eds.), The Establishment of Communist Regimes in Eastern Europe, 1944-1949, (Boulder: Westview Press, 1997).

[7] Odd Arne Westad. The Cold War: A world history, (London: Penguin Press, 2017), 60.

[8] Dadykina Margarita, Alexei Kraikovski, and Julia Lajus, 2015. "Hunting Activities of Russian Pomors on Spitsbergen in the 18th Century: New Evidences in Transnational Perspective." HSE Working Papers. December (2015).

islands that they saw as rightfully theirs.[9]

The Soviets made several proposals to Norway, including both a treaty for the joint management of Svalbard and a joint defence agreement. Under the 1920 Svalbard Treaty, article 9 prohibited using the islands for "warlike purposes," effectively banning militarisation of the archipelago. The Soviets hoped to nullify this rule to use Svalbard to their advantage.[10] While Norway was initially amendable to the renegotiation of the Svalbard Treaty and felt pressured to entertain the Soviet proposal, the Soviets eventually abandoned the effort on their own after realising that any expansion into the Atlantic Arctic would prompt retaliation from Western states such as the United States, which already had a military presence in Greenland and Iceland, and could even build bases on the Norwegian part of Svalbard if the treaty were negotiated and the non-militarisation clause were removed.[11]

Ultimately, Norwegian leadership decided that trusting the Soviets in these matters was unreliable, especially after being invaded by Germany in 1940. Soviet aggression in what would become its East and Central European satellite states led Norway to let go of decades of neutrality policy and become a founding member of the Alliance, as well as one of the closest Western allies of the United States.[12] In January 1949, Soviet diplomatic correspondence to Norway called into question their effort to join NATO and the purpose of the "Atlantic Union" itself: "In spite of the fact that the sponsors of this Union declare that it shall serve defensive purposes, the Soviet Government has good grounds for the assertion that the Union in preparation cannot serve to strengthen the peace of the world, but on the contrary will be a grouping of states pursuing aggressive ends, which is confirmed by the fact that the Atlantic Union is being established outside and apart from the United Nations Organization," wrote the Soviet ambassador in Oslo to the permanent under-secretary of state at the Norwegian Ministry of Foreign Affairs on January 29th.[13] A few days later, the Norwegian government issued a statement to the Soviet government in which it outlined its position on potentially joining several regional defence unions, and stated

---

[9] Sven Holtsmark, "A Soviet Grab for the High North? USSR, Svalbard, and Northern Norway 1920-1953," Norwegian Institute for Defense Studies. 7, no. 14. (1993).
[10] Holtsmark, 21.
[11] Holtsmark, 49.
[12] Wegge Njord, "The Strategic Role of Land Power on NATO's Northern Flank." Arctic Review on Law and Politics 13 (2022): 94–113. https://www.jstor.org/stable/48710660 .
[13] NATO archives, D-D(51)166, June 26 1951, "Exchange of notes between Norway and the USSR in connection with Norway joining the Atlantic Pact" https://archives.nato.int/exchange-of-notes-between-norway-and-ussr-in-connection-with-norway-joining-atlantic-pact

that:

> "The Norwegian Government asks the Soviet Government to rest assured that Norway will never become a party to a policy of aggression. It will never allow Norwegian territory to be used in the service of such a policy. The Norwegian Government will not enter into any agreement with other states by which Norway incurs the obligation to open bases on Norwegian territory to the armed forces of foreign powers, as long as Norway has not been attacked or is not being threatened by an attack. Norway and Russia have been living peacefully together as neighbouring states since time immemorial, and the Norwegian Government feels certain that the Soviet Government knows our country's unbroken tradition in the work for peace and our wish to maintain peaceful relations with all peace-loving peoples."[14]

The Soviets continued to protest the Norwegian move in subsequent exchanges, claiming that entry into NATO could in fact affect Norway's security negatively. "Far from promoting Norway's security, Norway's inclusion in the above grouping may, on the contrary, lead to Norway's being embroiled in the policy of a certain grouping of Powers pursuing far-reaching aggressive aims," wrote the Soviet ambassador to the Norwegian Foreign Minister on February 5, stating that the Soviet government found Norway's promises of non-aggression insufficient and that they were worried about the formation of air and naval bases on Norwegian territory which could be used against them. The letter concludes with a Soviet acknowledgement of the "good neighbourly relations between the USSR and the Soviet Union", in which the ambassador proposed a non-aggression pact between the two states, "in order to remove any doubt whatsoever" about the good intentions of the Soviet Union.[15]

Norway responded on March 3 with a cautious statement that its entry into NATO had been approved by the Norwegian parliament and that it would proceed with its initial plan to join the Alliance, and would participate in multilateral talks to draft a defence agreement with the other NATO founding members.[16]

Up to this point, various efforts to establish an alliance between Western Europe and the United States were unsuccessful until 1948, as interested

---

[14] Exchange of notes between Norway and the USSR in connection with Norway joining the Atlantic Pact, 3.
[15] Exchange of notes between Norway and the USSR in connection with Norway joining the Atlantic Pact, 4.
[16] Exchange of notes between Norway and the USSR in connection with Norway joining the Atlantic Pact, 5-6.

parties failed to achieve diplomatic consensus and domestic support. "The movement toward America's entanglement with Europe was restored less by diplomacy than by a series of repressive acts on the part of the Soviet Union," Kaplan writes.[17] The Soviet coup in Czechoslovakia in February 1948, followed by the Berlin Blockade starting from May 1948, solidified European concerns about a potentially expansionist Soviet aggressor. The Brussels Pact, created in March 1948, was a defensive alliance between Britain, France, Belgium, Luxembourg, and the Netherlands. In the summer of that year, talks were held with American representatives about what US military cooperation with the Brussels Pact states could look like, and it was during this time that the language of NATO's famous Article 5 was drafted, which states that an attack against one of the alliance members would be considered an attack against all parties. "The North Atlantic Treaty would not become a reality for another six months, but its substance was in place by September of 1948," Kaplan says.[18] In the following months, Italy, Portugal, Denmark, and Norway were added to the agreement, giving rise to the modern manifestation we are accustomed with today.

The speed with which NATO was created was more than anything a symptom of Western European and American military weakness, Westad argues. "The advice President Truman had got from the Joint Chiefs of Staff was clear: US troops could not defend continental western Europe against the Red Army, even if atomic bombs were to be used…The Soviets were in a position to establish full control of all of Europe within less than two months, the Joint Chiefs reported," he writes, noting that US military planners were worried about the potential for a real war with the Soviet Union from mid-1948 onwards.[19] The North Atlantic Treaty was signed on April 4, 1949, and continues to define diplomatic relationships and the geopolitical status quo of Europe more than 70 years later.

## NATO in the Cold War Arctic

World War II led northern nations to realise the strategic importance of the Arctic for both military and civilian purposes, leading Arctic states to establish scientific and military bases in the region and causing the north to become one of the most militarised spaces of the Cold War.[20] Meteorological

---

[17] Kaplan, 20.
[18] Kaplan, 25.
[19] Westad, 119.
[20] Daniel Heidt and Whitney Lackenbauer, The Joint Arctic Weather Stations: Science and Sovereignty in the High Arctic, 1946-1972. (Calgary: University of Calgary Press, 2022), 11.

data from the north was invaluable for weather predictions in the south, a fact that the Nazis knew when they occupied Svalbard during WWII to establish weather stations there.[21] The advent of nuclear weapons and the development of modern military technology irrevocably changed the region as well. As Western and Soviet military strategists found in the 1950s and 1960s, the quickest way to hit targets in enemy countries was to fly bombers and later intercontinental ballistic missiles (ICBMs) over the Arctic.[22]

Due to centuries of involvement in the Arctic and massive Soviet industrialisation policies enacted under Joseph Stalin, the Soviet north had become the most militarised, industrialised, urbanised, and populous Arctic region in the world and was also home to a formidable Soviet nuclear arsenal, as well as hundreds of warships, icebreakers, nuclear submarines, and ballistic weapons based in the Kola Peninsula, which represented a direct threat and challenge to the West and NATO.[23] This massive build-up of advanced technologies and forces effectively in NATO's backyard and basically a stone's throw away from Norway, which was considered the keeper of NATO's northern flank, led the High North to become a central feature of NATO's security strategy as the Cold War went on.[24] Military scholar and colonel of the Royal Norwegian Air Force, Gjert Lange Dyndal, argues that the 1960s saw the Arctic change from a northern flank of a Central front to an "independent theatre of war."[25] Dyndal states that the advent of ballistic missile submarines in the late 1960s is what solidified the perception of the High North as a pivotal Cold War battleground and caused military strategists to raise alarms about the danger posed by the military and naval build-up in the Kola region.[26]

Even prior to these developments, the Soviet Northern Fleet was a formidable concern for the Organization. A 1953 report from the NATO

---

[21] John A. Kington and Franz Selinger. Wekusta: Luftwaffe Meteorological Reconnaissance -Units and Operations 1938-1945. (Flight Recorder Publications: 2006).

[22] Townsend, Jim and Andrea Kendall-Taylor. "Back to the Future: The Origins of Great-Power Competition in the Arctic." Partners, Competitors, or a Little of Both?: Russia and China in the Arctic. Center for a New American Security, 2021. http://www.jstor.org/stable/resrep30199.5.; Mathieu Landriault & Adam MacDonald. "Debating Arctic Security through a Media Lens – The Case of NATO's Trident Juncture Operation." Accessed October 20, 2023. https://arcticyearbook.com/arctic-yearbook/2019/2019-scholarly-papers/306-debating-arctic-security-through-a-media-lens-the-case-of-nato-s-trident-juncture-operation.

[23] Bruno Andy, and Ekaterina Kalemeneva. "Creating the Soviet Arctic, 1917–1991." In The Cambridge History of the Polar Regions, edited by Adrian Howkins and Peder Roberts, 462–86. (Cambridge: Cambridge University Press, 2023). doi:10.1017/9781108555654.019.

[24] Dyndal Gjert Lage, "How the High North Became Central in NATO Strategy: Revelations from the NATO Archives." Journal of Strategic Studies 34, no.4 (2011): 557–85. doi:10.1080/01402390.2011.561094.

[25] Dyndal, 561.

[26] Dyndal 572.

military representatives committee about the Soviet bloc's strength and capabilities indicates that the Alliance was well aware of this fact, as the document outlined a list of naval and military installations and support centres across various regions, including information on the Northern Fleet based out of the Kola area. The detailed report listed the estimated number of ships and equipment held at the Black Sea, Baltic and Northern fleets, and information about supply logistics and potential for mobilization, as well as estimated combat efficacy. The document further stated that further resources would likely be devoted to expanding the Northern fleet and building more Arctic bases in subsequent years.[27]

NATO archival documents show that the organization was aware that uninhabited and remote Arctic and maritime spaces could be used for surveillance activities in the 1950s and that the Treaty sought to take measures to mitigate these perceived threats. According to a 1950 NATO report, the Arctic was one of the prime locations where hostile naval and submarine forces, weather and radar stations, and shipping and supply stations could be established and concealed, especially in the Arctic Ocean surrounding Norway and Iceland, as well as Greenland and the Northwest Territory of Canada. Three of the four threat areas listed in the document are in northern regions.[28] A report issued the following year by the NATO International Planning team to the standing group of the Military Committee[29] continues in the same vein, iterating that the northern maritime regions surrounding Norway must be frequently patrolled, and that this activity would be best taken on by Norwegian and British forces. However, the document noted, Norway's unwillingness to station military forces on its territory in an effort to placate the Soviet Union, coupled with difficult Arctic weather conditions, made surveillance of the region challenging. The report suggested that NATO was most concerned about the possibility of "a convoy carrying assaulting forces to Norway, Spitzbergen or Iceland," and "large numbers of submarines westbound." The document also suggested that reconnaissance forces of about 300 men based in Bodø, northern Norway, would be beneficial, and that local forces might have a better chance at navigating in

---

[27] "NATO archives," SG 161/3-FINAL REV, September 30, 1953, "Soviet bloc strength and capabilities." 32. https://archives.nato.int/soviet-bloc-strength-and-capabilities .

[28] "NATO archives," MCM-0022-1950, November 6 1950, "Reconnaissance of uninhabited regions and maritime areas." 3. https://archives.nato.int/reconnaissance-of-uninhabited-regions-and-maritime-areas

[29] The Military Committee is the highest military authority in NATO and the principal advisor to the North Atlantic Council, as well as a delegator to subordinate NATO groups related to military-strategic issues.

difficult conditions, compared to employing foreigners.[30]

The defence of Norway was a major concern for NATO and the country itself. According to political scientist Andreas Østhagen, "military planning since the 1940s has been dominated by concerns over Russian military activity in the North – both as an extension of Russia's broader strategic plans and more recently in terms of other types of interference and destabilising measures vis-à-vis Norway's northernmost regions."[31] The Organization was aware that Svalbard could not be militarized and adhered to Article 9 of the Svalbard Treaty, and the Alliance was concerned that Norway could be one of the first places that the USSR attacked due to its proximity to the Northern Fleet and strategic importance to the Western allies. More than a decade after its inception, the NATO Military Committee was concerned about its ability to defend Norway in the case of a Soviet attack. A 1965 document reflected on the conditions in northern Norway, and concluded that:

> "The present forces stationed in Norway cannot prevent by the use of military means the Soviet forces stationed in the Kola Peninsula from seizing Finnmark. In the event that the Soviets are not deterred from preparing for an attack against North Norway, reinforcements would have to be sent into the area…Based on the information provided in the study, the Military Committee would like to stress that the most effective method of avoiding a surprise attack on North Norway is to continue to convince the Soviets of the fact that any such initiative by them would bring about the implementation by the Alliance of timely counter-measures."[32]

One way to bolster NATO security was to hold frequent exercises in difficult terrain. NATO's northern preparedness included Arctic defensive exercises on a regular basis. One of the most prominent hosts of the exercises was Norway, where exercises involving tens of thousands of soldiers from numerous member countries have been held since the 1950s[33] for allies to "learn how to operate together" in rough terrain and cold conditions.[34]

Various NATO members responded to the Soviet threat in individual,

---

[30] NATO archives, SG 135/2, October 26 1951, "The reconnaissance in peacetime of the Arctic approaches to Norway" https://archives.nato.int/reconnaissance-in-peacetime-of-arctic-approaches-to-norway-2

[31] Østhagen, Andreas, "Norway's Arctic Policy: Still High North, Low Tension?" The Polar Journal 11, no. 1 (January 2, 2021): 75–94. doi:10.1080/2154896X.2021.1911043.

[32] "NATO archives," MCM-0142-1965, October 10, 1965, "Contingency Study, Northern Norway" https://archives.nato.int/contingency-study-northern-norway-3 .

[33] NATO. "Norway and NATO - 1949." NATO. Accessed September 20, 2023. http://www.nato.int/cps/en/natohq/declassified_162353.htm.

[34] NATO. "Exercise Cold Response 2022 – NATO and Partner Forces Face the Freeze in Norway." NATO. Accessed September 20, 2023. https://www.nato.int/cps/en/natohq/news_192351.htm.

bilateral, and multilateral ways. For example, in 1958, Canada and the United States established the North American Aerospace Defence Command (NORAD) to serve as an early warning and defence system for North America against Soviet bombers and ballistic missiles. NORAD functioned in conjunction with NATO and involved the placement of long and short-range radar systems and air defence systems across the continent, and the establishment of a joint command structure and information-sharing between Canadian and American forces.

> "The Canada-United States region is an integral part of the NATO area. In support of the strategic objectives established in NATO for the Canada-United States region and in accordance with the provisions of the North Atlantic Treaty, our two governments have, by establishing the North American Air Defence Command (NORAD), recognized the desirability of integrating headquarters exercising operational control over assigned air defence forces. The agreed integration is intended to assist the two Governments to develop and maintain their individual and collective capacity to resist air attack on their territories in North America in mutual self-defence,"

wrote the Canadian delegation to a North Atlantic Council meeting on May 14, 1958 at the Palais de Challiot in Paris.[35]

The defence of Norway, Canada, and the United States was not NATO's only concern in the Arctic. NATO archival documents indicate the essential role of Iceland and Greenland in North Atlantic defence and specifically the protection of the Greenland-Iceland-UK (GIUK) gap, an essential naval chokepoint. A 1950 report from the Organization, titled "The position of Iceland with the NATO structure," outlined the paramount importance of Iceland's position for NATO security:

> "It has been demonstrated twice in the past, and is well recognized for the future, that in any general war the sea lines of communication between Western Europe and North America will be of vital important and will be overburdened with shipping. Just as certainly the air lanes will be equally vital and equally overburdened with traffic. Iceland's geographic position is such as to draw her inescapably into the vortex of any struggle for the control of these vital lines of communication. She closely flanks the great circle route, and the guards the only approach from the Soviet arctic bases to the Atlantic. Her terrain and hydrography conduce to the establishment of large and efficient bases for the support and economical operation of

---

[35] NATO archives, C-R(58)35, May 14 1958, "Record of meeting," 14 https://archives.nato.int/record-of-meeting-915

both the sea forces and the air forces which will be necessary in that area...We have no reason to suppose, nor even to hope, that the Soviets have failed to appreciate either the extreme dependence of the North Atlantic Treaty Powers on their lines of communication, or the vital position of Iceland in the defense of those lines...It thus becomes apparent that, in case of war, the Soviet Union must make every practicable effort at least to deny the use of Iceland to the North Atlantic Treaty Powers, if not actually to occupy the islands and secure its use to herself."[36]

Further NATO communications from the early 1950s indicate great attention to the status of the island and the possibility of Soviet attempts to gain control of the territory. Documents mention the necessity to maintain a presence of 500-600 American soldiers in the country, as well as sixty-day minimum stockpiles of food and supplies for troops. NATO pushed for even more soldiers on the island, arguing that several hundred was not nearly enough to thwart a potential Soviet coup and that a minimum of 1,000 peacetime troops were needed.[37] A 1950 document written by a commander of the US Navy Reserve to the NATO Standing Group for international working teams, titled "Peacetime security forces for Iceland," raised questions about how long US forces should be stationed on the island and in what number, whether there was a need to install an air warning system with numerous stations, and how the initiative was to be financed.[38]

The issue was complicated by the fact that Iceland had (and still has) no military of its own and was unable to finance the defence measures proposed by NATO and the United States, which resulted in an American contingent being stationed there until 1994. Allied troops had maintained a presence in Iceland since 1940, when British forces arrived on the island to pre-empt a German attempt to take over. Following the signing of a bilateral defence agreement between Iceland and the United States in 1951, an air base for US and NATO forces was developed at Keflavik, which included air defence, maritime surveillance, and early warning systems. NATO documents from the 1950s indicate that agreements were made that allowed for the allied use of Keflavik Air Base, the Reykjavik Port and Air Base, and the Hvalfiord Anchorage. "The vital importance of taking security measures in peacetime

---

[36] NATO archives: SGM-0341-50, September 15 1950, "The position of Iceland within the NATO structure," 4-5 https://archives.nato.int/position-of-iceland-within-nato-structure
[37] NATO archives, SG 047/3-FINAL, December 29 1950, "Security provisions and defence measures for Iceland," 9. https://archives.nato.int/security-provisions-and-defence-measures-for-iceland-2
[38] NATO archives: SGM-0601-50, December 14 1950, "Peacetime security forces for Iceland," https://archives.nato.int/peacetime-security-forces-for-iceland

to ensure the integrity of this area must, therefore, be stressed," a Standing Group report from 1950 stated, stressing that all measures had to be taken to safeguard the area from a potential Soviet invasion or "local Communist saboteurs." The document also recommended that the "Arctic Ocean approaches" to Iceland be kept under constant surveillance.[39] The Keflavik Air Base hosted American and NATO troops throughout the Cold War and was closed down in 2006 following a reassessment of the US-Iceland defence agreement, only to be reopened again in 2016.[40]

Greenland was likewise vital to NATO's strategic interests and security in the North Atlantic, especially for the defence of North America and the capability to strike targets in the USSR, as evidenced by military build-up in the 1950s and 1960s. On April 27, 1951, the United States and Denmark signed a joint defence agreement for Greenland, which allowed the US to establish bases in Greenland for NATO defence activities and gave them the green light to effectively operate without restrictions in large parts of the territory.[41]

The agreement allowed for the construction of several American bases on the island, including Thule air base, which housed many bomber planes and later a massive radar station. A Distant Early Warning system (DEW) was built across Greenland in the late 1950s as an extension of the Canadian infrastructure, which was meant to intercept Soviet bombers.[42] According to a 1953 NATO report, Greenland's geographical position made it a critical base in the case of a war with the USSR, and this consideration led the United States to open three large bases on the island. The report also said that Danish forces in Greenland were patrolling parts of the east coast of the island regularly to make sure that Soviet enemy intruders were not establishing weather stations there, as the Germans had tried to do during WWII. "The reason why the island is so important to the NATO is that the Russians when carrying out air-attacks on America will have to pass Greenland. Opposite the Americans could use their air bases in Greenland as starting points for

---

[39] NATO archives, SG 047/3-FINAL, December 29 1950, "Security provisions and defence measures for Iceland," https://archives.nato.int/security-provisions-and-defence-measures-for-iceland-2
[40] Iceland and the US. Accessed October 20, 2023. https://www.government.is/diplomatic-missions/embassy-of-iceland-in-washington-d.c/iceland-and-the-us/ , The Independent Barents Observer. "U.S. military returns to Iceland." Accessed October 20, 2023. https://thebarentsobserver.com/ru/node/437.
[41] NATO archives, SGM-2518-52, November 14 1952, "The defence agreement between Denmark and the United States," https://archives.nato.int/defence-agreement-between-denmark-and-united-states
[42] Petersen Nikolaj, "The Iceman That Never Came: 'Project Iceworm', the Search for a NATO Deterrent, and Denmark, 1960-1962." Scandinavian Journal of History (Trykt Utg.) 33 no 1, (2008): 75–98.

air-attacks on Russian territory," the report said.[43]

The 1950s also saw the increased relevance of the GIUK gap, a concept that was articulated in the First and Second world wars to reduce German attacks on Allied shipping routes in the North Atlantic.[44] GIUK, for Greenland, Iceland, and the UK, denoted a naval chokepoint that was critical for NATO security. Keeping control of Greenland and Iceland was essential to the West, as this would help prevent the passage of Soviet submarines from bases in the Kola Peninsula into the Atlantic Ocean where they could strike targets on the American East Coast and disrupt shipping and communication lines with Europe.[45] The GIUK Gap was essential to the Soviet Union as well, as monitoring the gap would alert them to potential NATO warships heading towards USSR territory. In response, NATO states expended considerable effort to monitor the region: "Maritime patrol aircraft from the UK, Norway, and the U.S. (Navy P-3s, flying from Keflavik) covered the area from above, while nuclear and conventional submarines lurked below the surface. The choke points were also monitored by an advanced network of underwater sensors installed to detect and track Soviet submarines," states an article from the US Naval Institute.[46] British defence specialists called this initiative an effort "to mind the gap" and "contain the Soviet Union at sea."[47] The strategy lost relevance after the fall of the Soviet Union but has re-emerged as a potential problem area over the last decade due to Russian aggression and increased activity in the north.

As evidenced in the above section, NATO has operated in the Arctic since its very inception and has seen it as a strategic region of interest to deter and combat a potentially hostile Soviet or Russian force. With the resurgence of Russian military activity in the Arctic in the 21st century, old NATO concerns about Arctic security are being raised once more, and the region has been subject to increased tension in recent years.

---

[43] NATO archives, SGM-1666-53, July 31 1953, "Meeting of the chairman of the Standing Group with the Danish chief of defence," https://archives.nato.int/meeting-of-chairman-of-standing-group-with-danish-chief-of-defence-31-july-1953

[44] Tossini Vitor. "The GIUK Gap The Chokepoint in Britain's Backyard," UK Defence Journal. accessed January 21, 2023. https://ukdefencejournal.org.uk/the-giuk-gap-the-chokepoint-in-britains-backyard/.

[45] Vasquez Orbaiceta Gonzalo, The Resurgence of the GIUK Gap´s Strategic Significance. Opinion Paper IEEE 49/2023. https://www.ieee.es/Galerias/fichero/docs_ opinion/2023/DIEEEO49_ 2023_GONVAZ_Artico_EN G.pdf

[46] CDR Salamander. "Once More into the GIUK Gap," April 20, 2016. US Naval Institute. https://blog.usni.org/posts/2016/04/20/once-more-unto-the-gap

[47] Tossini.

## NATO in the Present-Day Arctic

Soviet leader Mikhail Gorbachev's Murmansk Speech in 1987 and the fall of the Soviet Union in 1991 ushered in an era of "Arctic exceptionalism," a two-decade period of stability and cooperation in Arctic relations[48] that transformed the area into a "zone of peace."[49] The Arctic Council was founded in 1996 in accordance with these values.[50] Western states helped Russia clean up and decontaminate vast swaths of territory affected by nuclear waste dumping and pollution, and sent aid to treat outbreaks of tuberculosis in the north.[51] Until the mid-aughts, the region did not experience any notable geopolitical competition.

The unfolding climate emergency changed the status quo in many ways. In 2007, Russia planted its flag on the seabed under the North Pole, triggering what journalists have termed a "scramble for the Arctic" and ushering in a renewed period of increased tension and rivalry.[52] Russia, which in the 1990s and early 2000s was still a toothless relic of the collapsed Soviet empire, found its legs again and began rapidly developing its northern regions, primarily for the exploitation of valuable northern resources.[53] Indeed, 80 percent of Russia's gas production and 20 percent of crude oil production come from the Arctic,[54] and Arctic resources make up 10 percent of the Russian GDP.[55] Additionally, the warming north and retreating sea ice began to open access to Russia's Northern Sea Route (NSR), which could substantially reduce shipping times between Europe and Asia, and Russia progressively began to

---

[48] Åtland Kristian. "Mikhail Gorbachev, the Murmansk Initiative, and the Desecuritization of Interstate Relations in the Arctic." Cooperation and Conflict 43, no. 3 (2008): 289–311. http://www.jstor.org/stable/45084526 .

[49] Mathieu Boulègue and Duncan Depledge, "It Is Time to Negotiate a New Military Security Architecture for the Arctic." The Wilson Center. April 16, 2021. Accessed October 20, 2023. https://www.wilsoncenter. org/blog-post/no-5-it-time-negotiate-new-military-security-architecture-arctic.

[50] Arctic Council. "The History of the Arctic Council." Accessed October 20, 2023. https://arctic-council.org/about/timeline/.

[51] Wilson Rowe Elana, "Health and Human Security: Communicable diseases in the post-Soviet Arctic" in Gjørv, Gunhild Hoogensen, Bazely, Dawn R., Goloviznina, Marina, and Tanentzap, Andrew J., eds. Environmental and Human Security in the Arctic. (Routledge, 2014).

[52] Kraska, James, ed. Arctic Security in an Age of Climate Change. Cambridge: Cambridge University Press, 2011. doi:10.1017/CBO9780511994784.

[53] Helge Blakkisrud, "Governing the Arctic: The Russian State Commission for Arctic Development and the Forging of a New Domestic Arctic Policy Agenda." NUPI. Accessed October 20, 2023. https://www.nupi.no/publikasjoner/cristin-pub/governing-the-arctic-the-russian-state-commission-for-arctic-development-and-the-forging-of-a-new-domestic-arctic-policy-agenda.

[54] IEA. "Energy Fact Sheet: Why Does Russian Oil and Gas Matter? – Analysis." Accessed October 20, 2023. https://www.iea.org/articles/energy-fact-sheet-why-does-russian-oil-and-gas-matter.

[55] Stronski, Eugene Rumer, Richard Sokolsky, Paul. "Russia in the Arctic—A Critical Examination." Carnegie Endowment for International Peace. Accessed October 20, 2023. https://carnegieendowment.org/ 2021/03/29/russia-in-arctic-critical-examination-pub-84181.

increase its presence in the north, reopening old Soviet military bases that had been abandoned after the USSR's collapse and establishing new ones.[56] In 2012, Vladimir Putin resumed the presidency of the Russian Federation, after vacating the post to Dmitry Medvedev briefly for four years, solidifying Western fears that Russia was sliding back into authoritarianism.[57]

These events, however, were not the tipping point in Arctic affairs. Despite adding tension to the situation in the north, not even the Russian invasion of Ukraine and annexation of Crimea in 2014 could shake the relative stability of Arctic relations. While Europe was in crisis following Russia's incursion onto Ukrainian territory, the members of the Arctic Council maintained good relations and cooperation continued in various regional organizations throughout the north. The tradition of Arctic exceptionalism continued under the popular moniker of "High North, low tension."[58]

The watershed moment came in February 2022, when Russia launched a full-scale invasion against Ukraine. In the weeks and months that followed, the Arctic Council members issued a statement that they would pause work with Russia,[59] and Sweden and Finland negated decades of neutrality policy when they petitioned to become NATO members.[60] Finland was admitted to the Alliance in April 2023, followed by Sweden in February 2024. Today, seven out of eight Arctic states are NATO members, a shift that will undoubtedly lead to profound changes in Arctic politics. Clearly, Russia's unprovoked violence in Ukraine has irreparably changed the security landscape of both Europe and the north.[61] The breakdown of relations has been far-reaching, affecting major intergovernmental bodies such as the Arctic Council, but also regional partnerships such as the Barents Euro-Arctic Council (BEAC), which Russia dropped out of in September 2023 after stating that Western

---

[56] Kjellén Jonas, "The Russian Northern Fleet and the (Re)militarisation of the Arctic". Arctic Review on Law and Politics, 13 (2022): 34-52. https://doi.org/10.23865/arctic.v13.3338.

[57] Gessen, Masha. The man without a face: the unlikely rise of Vladimir Putin. (London: Granta, 2012).

[58] Minna Ålander. "High North, High Tension: The End of Arctic Illusions." Foreign Policy Research Institute. Accessed October 20, 2023. https://www.fpri.org/article/2023/05/high-north-high-tension-the-end-of-arctic-illusions/.

[59] Boulègue Mathieu. "Exploring Military Security Issues in the Arctic." Chatham House, January 12, 2023. https://chathamhouse.soutron.net/Portal/Public/en-GB/RecordView/Index/202842.; Dickie, Gloria, Timothy Gardner, Gloria Dickie, and Timothy Gardner. "Arctic Council in Upheaval over Russia as Climate Change Transforms Region." Reuters, March 3, 2022, sec. World. https://www.reuters.com/world/arctic-council-countries-halt-meetings-over-russias-invasion-ukraine-2022-03-03/.

[60] Wall Colin and Njord Wegge. "The Russian Arctic Threat: Consequences of the Ukraine War," Center for Strategic and International Studies, January 25, 2023. https://www.csis.org/analysis/russian-arctic-threat-consequences-ukraine-war.

[61] Khorrami Nima. "By Merely Entertaining NATO Membership, Sweden Has Changed | Wilson Center." The Wilson Center. Accessed October 20, 2023. https://www.wilsoncenter.org/article/merely-entertaining-nato-membership-sweden-has-changed.

hostility was to blame for the lack of cooperation.[62] Indigenous groups in and out of Russia also report the difficulty in carrying out important initiatives to strengthen Indigenous rights and monitor environmental problems in the north.[63] Despite its isolation, Russia remains a formidable force in the north, with jurisdiction over 53 percent of the Arctic coastline. Contrary to what some journalists have argued, Russia has not "lost the Arctic to NATO,"[64] considering that the Russian Arctic is the most populated and industrialised northern region in the world, and that it has a substantial head start on Arctic military build-up and infrastructure development compared to most other Arctic states.[65]

Chinese influence in the Arctic has grown in recent years as well. China has been an observer at the Arctic Council since 2013, and in 2018, it released a national plan for northern regions and proclaimed itself a "near-Arctic state."[66] China has also been investing in extractive industries in Canada and Greenland,[67] and has interest in the region due to its development of the Polar Silk Road, a part of its Belt and Road Initiative. Russia's isolation from the West in Arctic affairs since its full-scale invasion of Ukraine has opened new avenues for cooperation with China,[68] and the Russian government has recently said that they plan to open a BRICS research facility on Svalbard to counterbalance the majority-Western research bases in Ny-Ålesund.[69] All of this considered, along with China's efforts to construct a major icebreaker

---

[62] Edvardsen Astri. "Russia Withdraws from the Barents Cooperation." High North News. Accessed October 20, 2023. https://www.highnorthnews.com/en/russia-withdraws-barents-cooperation.

[63] Last John. "The Ukraine War Is Dividing Europe's Arctic Indigenous People." Foreign Policy, June 27, 2022. https://foreignpolicy.com/2022/06/27/russia-ukraine-war-saami-indigenous-arctic-people-norway-sweden-finland/.

[64] Sharpe, Tom. "Russia Has Permanently Lost the Arctic to NATO." The Telegraph, July 3, 2023. https://www.telegraph.co.uk/news/2023/07/03/russia-nato-arctic/.

[65] Danoy Jim, and Marisol Maddox. "Set NATO's Sights on the High North." Atlantic Council, October 14, 2020. https://www.atlanticcouncil.org/content-series/nato20-2020/set-natos-sights-on-the-high-north/.

[66] Kopra Sanna. "China and Its Arctic Trajectories: The Arctic Institute's China Series 2020." The Arctic Institute - Center for Circumpolar Security Studies, March 17, 2020. https://www.thearcticinstitute.org/china-arctic-trajectories-the-arctic-institute-china-series-2020/.

[67] Pezard Stephanie, et al. "China's Strategy and Activities in the Arctic: Implications for North American and Transatlantic Security." RAND Corporation, December 23, 2022. https://www.rand.org/pubs/research_reports/RRA1282-1-v2.html.

[68] Rehman Maria. "Changing Contours of Arctic Politics and the Prospects for Cooperation between Russia and China." The Arctic Institute - Center for Circumpolar Security Studies, August 23, 2022. https://www.thearcticinstitute.org/changing-contours-arctic-politics-prospects-cooperation-russia-china/.

[69] Braw Elisabeth. "Arctic Harmony Is Falling Apart." Foreign Policy, May 15, 2023. https://foreignpolicy.com/2023/05/15/russia-china-arctic-cooperation-svalbard/.

fleet,[70] China stands to become a significant Arctic player in the near future.

While Norway has been one of the few NATO states to have consistently invested in Arctic development over recent decades, and indeed has named northern development and security as its most important priority, most other Arctic states, and NATO itself, have only just awakened to the fact that the balance of power in region is currently in favour of Russia. The Canadian government has faced criticism throughout the 2010s for not doing enough to modernise and engage with its Arctic regions,[71] and the United States has only recently started to release updated policy documents and strategies concerning the Arctic.[72] Some experts have argued that Arctic security was very much on the backburner of American strategic priorities up until the Trump administration.[73]

NATO currently has no official Arctic policy, nor a command devoted solely to northern affairs, a fact that some experts have called problematic due to the possibility that this will impede NATO's ability to "adequately navigate revived strategic competition in the region."[74] Yet over the past 15 years, NATO officials have consistently pushed against ideas of developing a dedicated body to oversee Arctic projects. In 2009, NATO Secretary General Jaap de Hoop Scheffer stated that a Joint Force Command (JFC) for the Arctic was untenable because it would lead to regionalisation in the Organization, which would undermine its core principals:

> "There are many regions – but there is only one NATO. And we must ensure that, as we look today at the High North, and perhaps in the future at other regions, we do not get drawn down the path of regionalisation – because that is the path to fragmentation. And that is a path we must avoid at all costs."[75]

This attitude was upheld in 2020, when Camille Grand, NATO's assistant

[70] Greenwood, Jeremy. "The Polar Silk Road Will Be Cleared with Chinese Icebreakers." The Brookings Institute, November 24, 2021. https://www.brookings.edu/articles/the-polar-silk-road-will-be-cleared-with-chinese-icebreakers/.

[71] Edwards Kyle. "The N.W.T. Premier Has a Sweeping Vision for Canada's North. Is He Dreaming?" Macleans, May 31, 2019. https://macleans.ca/news/canada/the-n-w-t-premier-has-a-sweeping-vision-for-canadas-north-is-he-dreaming/.

[72] Lanteigne Marc. "NATO Review - The Changing Shape of Arctic Security." NATO Review, June 28, 2019. https://www.nato.int/docu/review/articles/2019/06/28/the-changing-shape-of-arctic-security/index.html.

[73] Lanteigne Auerswald David. "NATO in the Arctic: Keep Its Role Limited, For Now." War on the Rocks, October 12, 2020. https://warontherocks.com/2020/10/nato-in-the-arctic-keep-its-role-limited-for-now/.

[74] Buchanan Elizabeth. "Cool Change Ahead? NATO's Strategic Concept and the High North." NATO Defense College, April 14, 2022. https://www.ndc.nato.int/news/news.php?icode=1680.

[75] NATO. "Speech by NATO Secretary General Jaap de Hoop Scheffer on Security Prospects in the High North." NATO, January 29, 2009. http://www.nato.int/cps/en/natohq/opinions_50077.htm.

secretary for defence investment said that a separate JFC for the Arctic was considered unnecessary at the time:

> "In the NATO political structures, we don't have committees that deal with the south, the north, the Mediterranean and so forth. So the issues are dealt with through our normal processes for planning, for operations and for political debates. We have not established a working group on any region. Sometimes it will take the form of a dedicated paper or strategy. I don't think we are there yet with the High North."[76]

In recent years, a debate has arisen among Arctic scholars and commentators about whether there should be a separate Arctic command. At this time, the closest thing to a northern command in NATO is JFC Norfolk. Established in 2019, this command is based in the United States and oversees the United Kingdom and Norway, covering the strategic GIUK gap.[77] Experts have pointed out that a greater NATO presence in the Arctic would potentially not be welcome by all members, firstly because some Arctic states such as Canada would see the shift as diluting their sovereignty and control in the North, and secondly because southern NATO states may be opposed to stretching their resources to a region that does not concern them and draining money and weapons from other priority locations such the Baltic and Mediterranean regions.[78] Arguments against having an increased presence in the north also state that a strong NATO presence in the region would do nothing but aggravate Russia, which already sees the Alliance as hostile and considers its encroachment close to Russian borders as an existential threat.[79] Political scientists Julie Wilhelmsen and Anni Roth Hjermann point out that Russia typically casts itself as a force for peace and stability in the Arctic, while painting NATO presence as a dangerous and provocative catalyst for potential conflict in the region.[80] In 2017, a member of the NATO Committee on Transatlantic Relations himself recommended that NATO

---

[76] Sprenger Sebastian. "NATO's Camille Grand on the Alliance's Arctic Tack." Defense News, May 12, 2020. https://www.defensenews.com/global/europe/2020/05/11/natos-camille-grand-on-the-alliances-arctic-tack/.

[77] Baudu Pauline. "Navigating Melting Ice and Eroding Exceptionalism: Theory-Driven Policy Pathways for NATO's High North Commitment." IRIS, July 22, 2022. https://www.iris-france.org/168952-navigating-melting-ice-and-eroding-exceptionalism-theory-driven-policy-pathways-for-natos-high-north-commitment/.

[78] Pincus Rebecca. "NATO North? Building a Role for NATO in the Arctic." War on the Rocks, November 6, 2019. https://warontherocks.com/2019/11/nato-north-building-a-role-for-nato-in-the-arctic/.

[79] Behrmann John, Lon Strauss, and Njord Wegge. "Getting the Joint Force and NATO Ready to Defend the Arctic." The Kingston Consortium on International Security (KCIS), December 7, 2022. https://www.thekcis.org/publications/insights/insight-211.

[80] Wilhelmsen, Julie, and Anni Roth Hjermann. "Russian Certainty of NATO Hostility: Repercussions in the Arctic." Arctic Review on Law and Politics 13 (2022): 114–42. https://www.jstor.org/stable/48710661.

should maintain situational awareness in the Arctic but must do so in a "non-provocative" way "without the deployment of military assets in the High North."[81] Experts arguing for a greater NATO presence in the Arctic say that it is needed to unequivocally demonstrate to Russia that NATO has its eye on the region and act as a deterrent to further Russian aggression, especially in the wake of Russia's full-scale invasion of Ukraine.[82] Commentators taking this stance argue that this is especially important in light of Russia's increased military exercises in the region, with more than 8,000 soldiers in August 2023 and continuous sea and air patrols with the Northern Fleet in the Arctic,[83] as well as Russia's ongoing pattern of hybrid warfare tactics against numerous European states, often including Norway, by way of cyber-attacks, radar jamming, and illegal photography, perhaps as a show of force and a complaint about NATO activities near its borders.[84]

Despite the lack of an official Arctic position, NATO and its member states have taken a greater interest in Arctic affairs in recent years, and especially following the second invasion of Ukraine. This is likely partially motivated by the possibility for resource extraction in previously ice-bound areas, exacerbated by retreating sea ice, and of course by the evolving security situation in the north both before and after February 2022. NATO exercises in the Arctic have become more frequent, and some of the largest exercises in recent years, including Trident Juncture in 2018 and Cold Response in 2022, have been held in northern Norway (Norway hosts Cold Response every two years). Approximately 50,000 soldiers from all NATO states and partner countries participated in Trident Juncture, and 30,000 in the latest iteration of Cold Response,[85] with the objective "to ensure that NATO forces are trained, able to operate together, and ready to respond to any threat from any direction," according to NATO press resources.[86] At the same time, NATO states' warships and submarines have been making port calls more often in northern Norway and operating in nearby waters as part of NATO

---

[81]NATO and Security in the Arctic, https://www.nato-pa.int/document/2017-nato-and-security-arctic-connolly-report-172-pctr-17-e-rev1-fin .

[82] Evers Zachary Mason. "A Changing Security Landscape: NATO and Russia in the Arctic." The International Affairs Review. Accessed October 20, 2023. https://www.iar-gwu.org/print-archive/ fl2h wo 38rikirjykl1w8lguqhmt2ub.

[83] Edvardsen Astri. "Den russiske Nordflåten på lengre tokt i Arktis." High North News, August 18, 2023. https://www.highnorthnews.com/nb/den-russiske-nordflaten-pa-lengre-tokt-i-arktis.

[84] Østhagen Andreas, Otto Svendsen and Max Bergmann. "Arctic Geopolitics: The Svalbard Archipelago." Center for Strategic and International Studies, September 14, 2023. https://www.csis.org/ analysis/arctic-geopolitics-svalbard-archipelago.

[85] NATO. "Exercise Cold Response 2022 – NATO and Partner Forces Face the Freeze in Norway." NATO, March 25, 2022. https://www.nato.int/cps/en/natohq/news_192351.htm.

[86] NATO. "Trident Juncture 18 - Media Resources." NATO, October 31, 2018. https://www.nato.int/ cps/en/natohq/news_158620.htm.

missions and in cooperation with the Norwegian Armed Forces.[87] In September 2023, a French nuclear submarine made a first-ever port call in Tromsø. Commander Sébastien Chatelain, Military Attaché at the French Embassy in Norway, said that, "[t]his short port call allowed a long-term deployment in the Northern Atlantic of the two ships. Their deployment show Allied commitment to security in Northern Europe and France's desire to gain better knowledge of the area. France conducts more than 20 port calls per year in Norway, with ships operating for the surveillance of critical undersea infrastructures, for NATO operations, or bilateral cooperation with the Norwegian Armed Forces." [88]

Svalbard continues to pose a problem as NATO's "Achilles Heel,"[89] as it did during the Cold War, since military forces and weapons cannot be present on Svalbard due to Article 9's non-militarization provision, but the archipelago remains a strategic point that may be used to "project power" in the GIUK-N (Greenland, Iceland, UK, Norway) gap which Russia may attempt to claim in a war situation,[90] so experts argue that there needs to be a strong amphibious force on the Norwegian mainland that can intervene if necessary.[91]

An important policy shift in regard to NATO in the north has come from Canada, which has increasingly welcomed NATO exercises in its territory and stated in its recent Arctic policy that it is committed to supporting information sharing with NATO and strengthening situational awareness in the Arctic. While Canada still relies more on its relationship with the United States in the scope of NORAD rather than NATO, this encouraging language towards NATO cooperation "indicates a significant shift in Canada's official position."[92] Montreal, Canada will also be the host of the new NATO Centre of Excellence for Climate Change and Security, which

---

[87] Edvardsen Astri. "Frequent Submarine Calls in Tromsø – New US Nuclear Submarine on Logistical Stop." High North News, October 4, 2023. https://www.highnorthnews.com/en/frequent-submarine-calls-tromso-new-us-nuclear-submarine-logistical-stop.

[88] Edvardsen Astri. "'Security in the Arctic Is of Greatest Interest to France,' Says French Commander." High North News, September 29, 2023. https://www.highnorthnews.com/en/security-arctic-greatest-interest-france-says-french-commander.

[89] James Wither, "Svalbard: NATO's Arctic 'Achilles' Heel'." RUSI Journal 163, no. 5 (2018): 28-37. doi:10.1080/03071847.2018.1552453.

[90] Baudu Pauline, "Minding the Archipelago: What Svalbard Means to NATO." Arctic Review on Law and Politics 14 (January 6, 2023): 76–82. doi:10.23865/arctic.v14.5197.

[91] Østhagen et al.

[92] Lackenbauer Whitney and Alexander Sergunin, "Canada's and Russia's Security and Defence Strategies in the Arctic: A Comparative Analysis." Arctic Review on Law and Politics no.13 (2022): 232–57. https://www.jstor.org/stable/48710668.

was announced in summer 2023.[93] An August 2022 visit by NATO Secretary General Jens Stoltenberg was another positive sign regarding Canada-NATO relations. The visit was directly relevant to Arctic affairs, as Stoltenberg visited the Canadian north with Prime Minister Justin Trudeau and stated that NATO must step up its presence in the Arctic. "The Arctic is the gateway to the North Atlantic, hosting vital trade, transport and communication links between North America and Europe. Ensuring freedom of navigation and unfettered access is essential to keep our economies strong and our people safe," the Secretary General said.[94]

Efforts to boost cooperation and defence are ongoing in other parts of the north. Even prior to Russia's full-scale invasion of Ukraine and Finland and Sweden's bids to join NATO, the Nordic states discussed forming a joint Nordic air force to improve communication and defence between Norway, Denmark, Sweden and Finland.[95] According to journalists and military sources, the project has received even more support since the events of 2022.[96] High North News pointed out in summer 2023 that there is a larger than normal military presence of both American and NATO forces in Iceland,[97] and that Norway is working on developing an air command centre in northern Norway in collaboration with the United States and United Kingdom.

Since the events of 2022, discussions are being held in NATO circles about the role of Nordic countries in safeguarding NATO's northern flank. In September 2023, NATO's defense chiefs met in Oslo for a conference on NATO's Military Committee. Norwegian Defense Minister Bjørn Arild Gram made a speech in which he emphasised that "NATO is the north," a clear indication of the importance of NATO for geopolitics. "The Nordic areas' relevance as a stage for global competition is constantly increasing. A large part of Russia's nuclear capabilities are located on the Kola Peninsula... Our deterrent positioning in the region will grow stronger as we welcome Finland and Sweden into the alliance. The allies in the region have a special

[93] NATO. "Environment, Climate Change and Security." NATO, July 24, 2023. https://www.nato.int/cps/en/natohq/topics_91048.htm.
[94] NATO. "NATO Is Stepping up in the High North to Keep Our People Safe." NATO, August 25, 2022. https://www.nato.int/cps/en/natohq/opinions_206894.htm.
[95] Reuters. "Nordic Countries Plan Joint Air Defence to Counter Russian Threat," March 24, 2023, sec. Europe. https://www.reuters.com/world/europe/nordic-countries-plan-joint-air-defence-counter-russian-threat-2023-03-24/.
[96] Bye Hilde-Gunn, "Luftforsvarssjefen tar initiativ til et arktisk luftoperasjonssenter." High North News, August 15, 2023. https://www.highnorthnews.com/nb/luftforsvarssjefen-tar-initiativ-til-et-arktisk-luftoperasjonssenter.
[97] Edvardsen Astri. "Sterkere alliert militært nærvær på Island." High North News, September 7, 2023. https://www.highnorthnews.com/nb/sterkere-alliert-militaert-naervaer-pa-island.

responsibility for developing NATO's deterrence in the northern areas," Gram said.[98]

The military rivalry in northern Europe will not be going away any time soon, as NATO announced in September 2023 that it would hold its largest ever exercise since the Cold War in 2024, with 40,000 troops coming together in Germany, Poland, and the Baltic states. "Never before have NATO and national defence plans been so closely interlinked… A new era of collective defence is upon us," said the Chair of the NATO Military Committee, Rob Bauer, at the meeting of the Military Committee in Chiefs of Defence Session in Oslo. Following Bauer's speech, Norwegian Chief of Defence Eirik Kristoffersen agreed with the sentiments expressed by Bauer and added that 2024 would also see the largest exercise held in the Nordic region, called Nordic Response, during which the new joint Nordic air defence would be tested.[99]

NATO exercises in Europe continue regularly in the present moment. A press statement on the nuclear exercise Steadfast Noon held on October 16, 2023, states that NATO will remain a nuclear alliance as long as nuclear weapons exist and that this is a routine exercise, but is meant to show that the Alliance is committed to defending all of its allies. As with many NATO press documents of the last year and a half, there is a focus on transparency. The statement mentions that the exercise was "long-planned" and is not linked to current world events. Held in the southern Mediterranean region, the exercise is happening more than 1,000 kms from Russian border, the statement says.[100]

Russia also shows no signs of slowing its Arctic ambitions. The country is building thirty floating nuclear power plants to supply remote settlements along the NSR with power. Some of these stations are already complete and in place in the Arctic, despite protests from critics that their development will amount to a "floating Chernobyl."[101] Analysing Arctic trends over the past

---

[98] Edvardsen Astri. "Forsvarsministeren: Utforming av avskrekking i nordområdene er et særlig nordisk ansvar." High North News, September 20, 2023. https://www.highnorthnews.com/nb/forsvarsministeren-utforming-av-avskrekking-i-nordomradene-er-et-saerlig-nordisk-ansvar.

[99] NATO. "Joint Press Conference by Chair of the Military Committee, Admiral Rob Bauer and the Norwegian Chief of Defence, General Eirik Kristoffersen Following the Meeting of the Military Committee in Chiefs of Defence Session, Oslo, Norway." NATO, September 16, 2023. https://www.nato.int/cps/en/natohq/opinions_218279.htm.

[100] NATO. "NATO Holds Long-Planned Annual Nuclear Exercise." NATO, October 13, 2023. https://www.nato.int/cps/en/natohq/news_219443.htm.

[101] Josephson Paul, The Conquest of the Russian Arctic. Cambridge, MA and London, England: Harvard University Press, 2014. 335. https://doi-org.stanford.idm.oclc.org/10.4159/harvard.9780674419827.

decade, a 2022 government report from Finland concluded that following the events of 2014, and especially 2022, coupled with general increased military activity in the north, geopolitics have arrived on the scene in the Arctic and that the region is fundamentally changed by these facts. "If the current power regime in Russia maintains its position, it seems likely that hard security tensions in the Arctic will become more complicated," says the report.[102] Despite these difficulties, some hope remains for regional cooperation. The Arctic Council has recently resumed activities with Russia in a limited capacity.[103] Russia is also cooperating with other Arctic states in fisheries management.

In the immediate future, NATO must contend with the climate emergency. NATO itself has pointed out that climate change is a "threat multiplier" and a potential driver for future conflict in the north.[104] The Arctic is warming four times faster than the rest of the planet. Some areas, such as Svalbard, are now several degrees Celsius hotter on average than they were fifty years ago.[105] Many parts of the north are already in crisis, brought on by retreating sea ice, thawing permafrost, eroding coastlines, and raging wildfires. While these developments open opportunities for the extraction of valuable natural resources in the north, they also have a devastating impact on remote settlements and Indigenous communities, which are at the forefront of the climate catastrophe. A lot of attention has been paid to securitising northern regions, but the Organisation has not sufficiently consulted Indigenous groups in the north.[106] First and foremost, NATO must strive to include Indigenous communities at the table, as this is a fundamental feature of the United Nations Declaration on the Rights of Indigenous Peoples and the key principle of Free Prior and Informed Consent, both of which are guidelines for equitable and lawful engagement with Indigenous communities.

The inability to constructively work with Russia poses major challenges in this area, both for continued work on Indigenous rights, and on research collaboration that can shed light on the ongoing impacts of climate change.

---

[102] Koivurova Timo, et al. "Arctic Cooperation in a New Situation : Analysis on the Impacts of the Russian War of Aggression." Muu julkaisu, December 21, 2022. https://julkaisut.valtioneuvosto.fi/ handle/ 10024/164521.

[103] Edvardsen Astri. "Light at the End of the Tunnel for the the Arctic Council." High North News, September 12, 2023. https://www.highnorthnews.com/en/light-end-tunnel-arctic-council.

[104] Baudu.

[105] Fraser.

[106] Jonassen Trine. "Arctic Indigenous Leaders: We Did Not Shut Down." High North News, March 31, 2023. https://www.highnorthnews.com/en/arctic-indigenous-leaders-we-did-not-shut-down. ; Reid, Julian. "Indigenizing NATO." Turkish Policy Quarterly, June 19, 2023. http://turkishpolicy.com/ article/ 1201/indigenizing-nato.

In the present situation, it is clear that the Arctic is a region undergoing profound changes, both to its political order and geopolitical position, but also to its very geography. The rapidly unfolding situation makes the path forward murky and means that NATO will have important decisions to make for its future in the region and the future of Alliance security.

## Conclusion

Over the last decade, tensions in the Arctic have risen to levels unseen since the days of the Cold War. Once again, the Arctic is becoming a militarised and securitised space, and it seems that the days of Arctic exceptionalism are soon to be in the distant past. While the Arctic remains a region of relative cooperation and stability today, the conditions remain for the possibility of conflict in the future. Cold War rhetoric is at a forefront once again, with military strategists and defence experts discussing the GIUK gap, Arctic missile placements, and increased military exercises in the north. While NATO does not have an official Arctic policy or command centre, it is very much present in the region, both through its historic guardian of the northern flank, Norway, and its newest members, Finland and Sweden.

In recent years, countless newspaper articles with headlines shouting about a "new Cold War" in the north have been published. Some experts, in fact, argue that the Cold War never ended in the Arctic, considering that most of the military installations in the region remained ready to blast their opponents into oblivion even when the region was regarded as a "zone of peace" in diplomatic circles.[107] While the unique ideology that defined Cold War rivalry, namely Communism, is largely a thing of the past, today a rivalry between authoritarian hydrocarbon empire Russia and more than thirty NATO states is underway. Nonetheless, the Arctic remains a relative zone of peace. There is currently no open conflict in the region, and no major flashpoints that risk spilling into conflict in the foreseeable future. The few territorial disputes that exist are either at an impasse or are being adjudicated in court proceedings.[108]

A lot of speculation has come from the current situation, especially about what the NATO response to Arctic military build-up ought to be. On the one hand, it would be imprudent for NATO to contribute to further

---

[107] Huebert Rob, "A New Cold War in the Arctic?! The Old One Never Ended!" Arctic Yearbook, 2019. https://arcticyearbook.com/arctic-yearbook/2019/2019-commentaries/325-a-new-cold-war-in-the-arctic-the-old-one-never-ended.

[108] Østhagen Andreas, "Fish, Not Oil, at the Heart of (Future) Arctic Resource Conflicts." Arctic Yearbook, 2020. https://arcticyearbook.com/arctic-yearbook/2020/2020-scholarly-papers/341-fish-not-oil-at-the-heart-of-future-arctic-resource-conflicts.

militarisation of the Arctic, as it will undoubtedly aggravate the situation with Russia. While it is necessary for NATO to formulate an Arctic policy and continue monitoring the developments in the region closely, going further by potentially opening Arctic bases, creating a new Arctic command, or stationing new weaponry there may contribute to rising tensions. On the other hand, Russia has proven numerous times in Moldova, Georgia, and Ukraine, that it does not respect the territorial integrity of sovereign states, and has behaved in increasingly aggressive and unpredictable ways in recent years, meaning that a strong defensive posture, especially in the Arctic, which is a key region of strategic interest for the Russian Federation, may be needed to indicate that there will be a swift response if boundaries are violated in the north.

In the coming years, NATO leaders and Alliance members will have to make difficult decisions on how to proceed with Russia. What is clear is that the Arctic is once again re-entering centre stage in the realm of Atlantic geopolitical rivalry, and this development will undoubtedly have far-reaching consequences in the European and global security order. For too long, the Arctic has been considered a remote and peripheral region that is irrelevant to global processes. Today, more than ever, it is evident that what happens in the Arctic does not stay in the Arctic, both politically and environmentally, and that regional events and global processes have an irrevocably interconnected relationship that will likely be amplified in the coming years and decades.

## Bibliography

Ålander, Minna. "High North, High Tension: The End of Arctic Illusions." *Foreign Policy Research Institute.* May 11, 2023. https://www.fpri.org/article/2023/05/high-north-high-tension-the-end-of-arctic-illusions/.

Åtland, Kristian. 2008. "Mikhail Gorbachev, the Murmansk Initiative, and the Desecuritization of Interstate: Relations in the Arctic." *Cooperation and Conflict* 43 (3): 289–311.

Auerswald, David. 2020. "NATO in the Arctic: Keep Its Role Limited, For Now." *War on the Rocks.* October 12, 2020. https://warontherocks.com/2020/10/nato-in-the-arctic-keep-its-role-limited-for-now/.

Baudu, Pauline. 2022. "Navigating Melting Ice and Eroding Exceptionalism: Theory-Driven Policy Pathways for NATO's High North Commitment." *IRIS.* July 22, 2022. https://www.iris-france.org/168952-navigating-melting-ice-and-eroding-exceptionalism-theory-driven-policy-pathways-for-natos-high-north-commitment/.

———. 2023. "Minding the Archipelago: What Svalbard Means to NATO." *Arctic Review on Law and Politics* 14 (January): 76–82. https://doi.org/10.23865/arctic.v14.5197.

Behrmann, John, Lon Strauss, and Njord Wegge. 2022. "Getting the Joint Force and

NATO Ready to Defend the Arctic." *The Kingston Consortium on International Security (KCIS)*. December 7, 2022. https://www.thekcis.org/publications/insights/insight-211.

Blakkisrud, Helge. "Governing the Arctic: The Russian State Commission for Arctic Development and the Forging of a New Domestic Arctic Policy Agenda." *NUPI*. Accessed October 20, 2023. https://www.nupi.no/publikasjoner/cristin-pub/ governing-the-arctic-the-russian-state-commission-for-arctic-development-and-the-forging-of-a-new-domestic-arctic-policy-agenda.

Boulègue, Mathieu. 2023. "Exploring Military Security Issues in the Arctic." *Chatham House*. January 12, 2023. https://chathamhouse.soutron.net/Portal/Public/en-GB/Record View/Index/202842.

Boulègue, Mathieu, and Duncan Depledge. n.d. "No. 5 | It Is Time to Negotiate a New Military Security Architecture for the Arctic." *The Wilson Center*. https://www.wilsoncenter.org/blog-post/no-5-it-time-negotiate-new-military-security-architecture-arctic.

Braw, Elisabeth. 2023. "Arctic Harmony Is Falling Apart." *Foreign Policy*. May 15, 2023. https://foreignpolicy.com/2023/05/15/russia-china-arctic-cooperation-svalbard/.

Bruno, Andy, and Ekaterina Kalemeneva. 2023. "Creating the Soviet Arctic, 1917–1991." In *The Cambridge History of the Polar Regions*, edited by Adrian Howkins and Peder Roberts, 1st ed., 462–86. Cambridge University Press. https://doi.org/ 10. 1017/ 9781108555654.019.

Buchanan, Elizabeth. 2022. "Cool Change Ahead? NATO's Strategic Concept and the High North." *NATO Defense College*. April 14, 2022. https://www.ndc.nato.int/ news/news. php?icode=1680.

Bye, Hilde-Gunn. 2023. "Luftforsvarssjefen tar initiativ til et arktisk luftoperasjonssenter." *High North News*. August 15, 2023. https://www.highnorth news.com/ nb/ luftforsvarssjefen-tar-initiativ-til-et-arktisk-luftoperasjonssenter.

Dadykina, Margarita, Alexei Kraikovski, and Julia Lajus. 2015. "Hunting Activities of Russian Pomors on Spitsbergen in the 18th Century: New Evidences in Transnational Perspective." SSRN Scholarly Paper. Rochester, NY. https://doi.org/10.2139/ ssrn.2707082.

Danoy, Jim, and Marisol Maddox. 2020. "Set NATO's Sights on the High North." *Atlantic Council* (blog). October 14, 2020. https://www.atlanticcouncil.org/content-series/nato20-2020/set-natos-sights-on-the-high-north/.

Dickie, Gloria, Timothy Gardner, Gloria Dickie, and Timothy Gardner. 2022. "Arctic Council in Upheaval over Russia as Climate Change Transforms Region." *Reuters*, March 3, 2022, sec. World. https://www.reuters.com/world/arctic-council-countries-halt-meetings-over-russias-invasion-ukraine-2022-03-03/.

Dyndal, Gjert Lage. 2011. "How the High North Became Central in NATO Strategy: Revelations from the NATO Archives." *Journal of Strategic Studies* 34 (4): 557–85. https://doi.org/10.1080/01402390.2011.561094.

Edvardsen, Astri. 2023a. "Den russiske Nordflåten på lengre tokt i Arktis." *High North News*. August 18, 2023. https://www.highnorthnews.com/nb/den-russiske-nordflaten-pa-lengre-tokt-i-arktis.

———. 2023b. "Sterkere alliert militært nærvær på Island." *High North News*. September 7, 2023. https://www.highnorthnews.com/nb/sterkere-alliert-militaert-naervaer-pa-island.

———. 2023c. "Light at the End of the Tunnel for the the Arctic Council." *High North News*. September 12, 2023. https://www.highnorthnews.com/en/light-end-tunnel-arctic-council.

———. 2023d. "Forsvarsministeren: Utforming av avskrekking i nordområdene er et særlig nordisk ansvar." *High North News*. September 20, 2023. https://www.highnorth news. com/nb/forsvarsministeren-utforming-av-avskrekking-i-nordomradene-er-et-saerlig-nordisk-ansvar.

———. 2023e. "'Security in the Arctic Is of Greatest Interest to France,'Says French Commander." *High North News*. September 29, 2023. https://www.highnorthnews. com/en/security-arctic-greatest-interest-france-says-french-commander.

———. 2023f. "Frequent Submarine Calls in Tromsø – New US Nuclear Submarine on Logistical Stop." *High North News*. October 4, 2023. https://www.highnorthnews. com/en/frequent-submarine-calls-tromso-new-us-nuclear-submarine-logistical-stop.

———. n.d. "Russia Withdraws from the Barents Cooperation." *High North News*. Accessed October 20, 2023. https://www.highnorthnews.com/en/russia-withdraws-barents-cooperation.

Edwards, Kyle. 2019. "The N.W.T. Premier Has a Sweeping Vision for Canada's North. Is He Dreaming?" *Macleans*. May 31, 2019. https://macleans.ca/news/canada/the-n-w-t-premier-has-a-sweeping-vision-for-canadas-north-is-he-dreaming/.

"Energy Fact Sheet: Why Does Russian Oil and Gas Matter? – Analysis." n.d. *IEA*. https://www.iea.org/articles/energy-fact-sheet-why-does-russian-oil-and-gas-matter.

Evers, Zachary Mason. n.d. "A Changing Security Landscape: NATO and Russia in the Arctic." *The International Affairs Review*. Accessed October 20, 2023. https://www.iar-gwu.org/print-archive/fl2hwo38rikirjykl1w8lguqhmt2ub.

Gessen, Masha. 2012. *The Man without a Face: The Unlikely Rise of Vladimir Putin*. New York: Riverhead Books.

Greenwood, Jeremy. 2021. "The Polar Silk Road Will Be Cleared with Chinese Icebreakers." *The Brookings Institute*. November 24, 2021. https://www.brookings. edu/articles/the-polar-silk-road-will-be-cleared-with-chinese-icebreakers/.

Heidt, Daniel, and P. Whitney Lackenbauer. 2022. *The Joint Arctic Weather Stations: Science and Sovereignty in the High Arctic, 1946-1972*. Northern Lights Series, no. 20. Calgary, Alberta, Canada: University of Calgary Press.

Holtsmark, Sven. 1993. *A Soviet Grab for the High North? USSR, Svalbard, and Northern Norway 1920-1953*. Vol. 14. Forvarstudier 7. Norwegian Institute for Defense Studies.

Huebert, Rob. 2019. "A New Cold War in the Arctic?! The Old One Never Ended!" *Arctic Yearbook*. 2019. https://arcticyearbook.com/arctic-yearbook/2019/2019-commentaries/ 325-a-new-cold-war-in-the-arctic-the-old-one-never-ended.

"Iceland and the US." n.d. Accessed October 20, 2023. https://www.government.is/ diplomatic-missions/embassy-of-iceland-in-washington-d.c/iceland-and-the-us/.

Jonassen, Trine. 2023. "Arctic Indigenous Leaders: We Did Not Shut Down." *High North News*. March 31, 2023. https://www.highnorthnews.com/en/arctic-indigenous-leaders-we-did-not-shut-down.

Josephson, Paul R. 2014. "The Conquest of the Russian Arctic." In *The Conquest of the*

*Russian Arctic.* Harvard University Press. https://www.degruyter.com/ document/ doi/ 10.4159/harvard.9780674419827/html.

Kaplan, Lawrence. 2019. "Origins of NATO: 1948--1949." *Emory International Law Review* 34 (January): 11.

Khorrami, Nima. n.d. "By Merely Entertaining NATO Membership, Sweden Has Changed | Wilson Center." *The Wilson Center.* Accessed October 20, 2023. https://www.wilsoncenter.org/article/merely-entertaining-nato-membership-sweden-has-changed.

Kington, John, and Franz Selinger. 2006. *Wekusta: Luftwaffe Meteorological Reconnaissance Units & Operations 1938 - 1945.* 1. publ. in Great Britain. Ottringham: Flight Recorder Publ.

Kjellén, Jonas. 2022. "The Russian Northern Fleet and the (Re)militarisation of the Arctic." *Arctic Review on Law and Politics* 13 (2022): 34. https://doi.org/10.23865/ arctic.v13.3338.

Koivurova, Timo, Markku Heikkilä, Johanna Ikävalko, Stefan Kirchner, Sanna Kopra, Harri Mikkola, Riina Pursiainen, Susanna Sepponen, Matleena Moisio, and Adam Stepien. 2022. "Arctic Cooperation in a New Situation : Analysis on the Impacts of the Russian War of Aggression." Muu julkaisu. December 21, 2022. https://julkaisut.valtioneuvosto.fi/ handle/10024/164521.

Kopra, Sanna. 2020. "China and Its Arctic Trajectories: The Arctic Institute's China Series 2020." *The Arctic Institute - Center for Circumpolar Security Studies.* March 17, 2020. https://www.thearcticinstitute.org/china-arctic-trajectories-the-arctic-institute-china-series-2020/.

Kraska, James, ed. 2011. *Arctic Security in an Age of Climate Change.* 1st ed. Cambridge University Press. https://doi.org/10.1017/CBO9780511994784.

Lackenbauer, P. Whitney, and Alexander Sergunin. 2022. "Canada's and Russia's Security and Defence Strategies in the Arctic: A Comparative Analysis." *Arctic Review on Law and Politics* 13: 232–57.

Lanteigne, Marc. 2019. "NATO Review - The Changing Shape of Arctic Security." *NATO Review.* June 28, 2019. https://www.nato.int/docu/review/ articles/ 2019/ 06/28/the-changing-shape-of-arctic-security/index.html.

Last, John. 2022. "The Ukraine War Is Dividing Europe's Arctic Indigenous People." *Foreign Policy* (blog). June 27, 2022. https://foreignpolicy.com/2022/06/27/russia-ukraine-war-saami-indigenous-arctic-people-norway-sweden-finland/.

MacDonald, Mathieu Landriault & Adam. n.d. "Debating Arctic Security through a Media Lens – The Case of NATO's Trident Juncture Operation." *Arctic Yearbook.* Accessed October 20, 2023. https://arcticyearbook.com/arctic-yearbook/2019/2019-scholarly-papers/306-debating-arctic-security-through-a-media-lens-the-case-of-nato-s-trident-juncture-operation.

NATO. 2009. "Speech by NATO Secretary General Jaap de Hoop Scheffer on Security Prospects in the High North." *NATO.* January 29, 2009. http://www.nato.int/ cps/en/natohq/opinions_50077.htm.

———. 2018. "Trident Juncture 18 - Media Resources." *NATO.* October 31, 2018. https://www.nato.int/cps/en/natohq/news_158620.htm.

———. 2022a. "Exercise Cold Response 2022 – NATO and Partner Forces Face the

Freeze in Norway." *NATO*. March 25, 2022. https://www.nato.int/cps/ en/ natohq/ news_192351.htm.

———. 2022b. "NATO Is Stepping up in the High North to Keep Our People Safe." *NATO*. August 25, 2022. https://www.nato.int/cps/en/ natohq/ opinions_ 206894.htm.

———. 2023a. "Environment, Climate Change and Security." *NATO*. July 24, 2023. https://www.nato.int/cps/en/natohq/topics_91048.htm.

———. 2023b. "Joint Press Conference by Chair of the Military Committee, Admiral Rob Bauer and the Norwegian Chief of Defence, General Eirik Kristoffersen Following the Meeting of the Military Committee in Chiefs of Defence Session, Oslo, Norway." *NATO*. September 16, 2023. https://www.nato.int/cps/ en/ natohq/ opinions_218279.htm.

———. 2023c. "NATO Holds Long-Planned Annual Nuclear Exercise." *NATO*. October 13, 2023. https://www.nato.int/cps/en/natohq/news_219443.htm.

———. n.d. "Exercise Cold Response 2022 – NATO and Partner Forces Face the Freeze in Norway." *NATO*. Accessed October 20, 2023a. https://www.nato.int/cps/en/ natohq/news_192351.htm.

———. n.d. "Norway and NATO - 1949." *NATO*. http://www.nato.int/cps/en/ natohq/ declassified_162353.htm.

Østhagen, Andreas. 2020. "Fish, Not Oil, at the Heart of (Future) Arctic Resource Conflicts." *Arctic Yearbook*. 2020. https://arcticyearbook.com/arctic-yearbook/ 2020/2020-scholarly-papers/341-fish-not-oil-at-the-heart-of-future-arctic-resource-conflicts.

———. 2021. "Norway's Arctic Policy: Still High North, Low Tension?" *The Polar Journal* 11 (1): 75–94. https://doi.org/10.1080/2154896X.2021.1911043.

Østhagen, Andreas, Otto Svendsen, and Max Bergmann. 2023. "Arctic Geopolitics: The Svalbard Archipelago." *Center for Strategic and International Studies*, September. https://www.csis.org/analysis/arctic-geopolitics-svalbard-archipelago.

Pezard, Stephanie, Stephen J. Flanagan, Scott W. Harold, Irina A. Chindea, Benjamin J. Sacks, Abbie Tingstad, Tristan Finazzo, and Soo Kim. 2022. "China's Strategy and Activities in the Arctic: Implications for North American and Transatlantic Security." *RAND Corporation*. https://www.rand.org/pubs/research_reports/RRA1282-1-v2.html.

Pincus, Rebecca. 2019. "NATO North? Building a Role for NATO in the Arctic." *War on the Rocks*. November 6, 2019. https://warontherocks.com/2019/11/nato-north-building-a-role-for-nato-in-the-arctic/.

Rehman, Maria. 2022. "Changing Contours of Arctic Politics and the Prospects for Cooperation between Russia and China." *The Arctic Institute - Center for Circumpolar Security Studies*. August 23, 2022. https://www.thearcticinstitute.org/changing-contours-arctic-politics-prospects-cooperation-russia-china/.

Reid, Julian. 2023. "Indigenizing NATO." Turkish Policy Quarterly. June 19, 2023. http://turkishpolicy.com/article/1201/indigenizing-nato.

*Reuters*. 2019. "On the Front Lines of Climate Change in the World's Northernmost Town," September 3, 2019, sec. Environment. https://www.reuters.com/article/us-climate-change-svalbard-widerimage-idUSKCN1VO19M.

———. 2023. "Nordic Countries Plan Joint Air Defence to Counter Russian Threat,"

March 24, 2023, sec. Europe. https://www.reuters.com/world/europe/nordic-countries-plan-joint-air-defence-counter-russian-threat-2023-03-24/.

Sharpe, Tom. 2023. "Russia Has Permanently Lost the Arctic to Nato." *The Telegraph*, July 3, 2023. https://www.telegraph.co.uk/news/2023/07/03/russia-nato-arctic/.

Sprenger, Sebastian. 2020. "NATO's Camille Grand on the Alliance's Arctic Tack." *Defense News*. May 12, 2020. https://www.defensenews.com/ global/europe/ 2020/ 05/11/natos-camille-grand-on-the-alliances-arctic-tack/.

Stronski, Eugene Rumer, Richard Sokolsky, Paul. n.d. "Russia in the Arctic—A Critical Examination." *Carnegie Endowment for International Peace*. March 29 2021. https://carnegieendowment.org/2021/03/29/russia-in-arctic-critical-examination-pub-84181.

"The History of the Arctic Council." n.d. *Arctic Council*. https://arctic-council.org/ about/ timeline/.

Tossini, J. Vitor. 2023. "The GIUK Gap – The Chokepoint in Britain's Backyard." *UK Defence Journal*. January 21, 2023. https://ukdefencejournal.org.uk/the-giuk-gap-the-chokepoint-in-britains-backyard/.

Townsend, Jim, and Andrea Kendall-Taylor. 2021. "Back to the Future: The Origins of Great-Power Competition in the Arctic." Partners, Competitors, or a Little of Both? *Center for a New American Security*. https://www.jstor.org/stable/resrep30199.5.

"U.S. military returns to Iceland." n.d. *The Independent Barents Observer*. Accessed October 20, 2023. https://thebarentsobserver.com/ru/node/437.

Wall, Colin, and Njord Wegge. 2023. "The Russian Arctic Threat: Consequences of the Ukraine War," January. https://www.csis.org/analysis/russian-arctic-threat-consequences-ukraine-war.

Wegge, Njord. 2022. "The Strategic Role of Land Power on NATO's Northern Flank." *Arctic Review on Law and Politics* 13: 94–113.

Westad, Odd Arne. 2017. *The Cold War: A World History*. First edition. New York: Basic Books.

Wilhelmsen, Julie, and Anni Roth Hjermann. 2022. "Russian Certainty of NATO Hostility: Repercussions in the Arctic." *Arctic Review on Law and Politics* 13: 114–42.

Wither, James K. 2018. "Svalbard: NATO's Arctic 'Achilles'Heel'." *The RUSI Journal* 163 (5): 28–37. https://doi.org/10.1080/03071847.2018.1552453.

# CHAPTER 3

## ENERGY IN THE ARCTIC: COMPLEXITY AND THINKING IN A SOCIAL DYNAMICAL SYSTEM

### Anna Soer[1]

Over 99% of energy production and consumption in the Arctic comes from fossil fuels. This dependence on fossil fuels triggers a wide range of security and health concerns. Firstly, the dependence of fossil fuels within households has been shown to cause detrimental health effects from respiratory illnesses to cancers – especially targeting women and children. These health concerns bleed into other structural issues from the lack of secure and sound housing to the difficult access to healthcare for remote and urban Arctic communities, especially so in Arctic Canada. Secondly, concerns surrounding the dependence on fossil fuels pose complex and compound risks from environmental security risks to national security risks linking politics with economics with human security. The concept of human security has gained momentum in recent decades – becoming central to global development agendas propelled by international organizations such as the United Nations Development Program (UNDP) – and has framed and complexified the notion of security to become more holistic. In this perspective of holism, complexity itself deserves a center stage in this chapter on energy-based issues in the Arctic. Complexity, in between order and chaos, defines the difficult task ahead of drafting a resilient and sustainable future for the region. Similarly, thinking in systems – to quote the title of Donella H. Meadows'work (2008) – entails the understanding of the 'what': defining these issues goes beyond listing elements but flows into an understanding of the "interconnected set of elements that is coherently organized in a way that achieves something. [...] A system is more than the sum of its parts".[2] These two preliminary definitions of 'complexity'and 'system'open a whole world of questions for the topic at hand and relate the Arctic back to the global

[1] School of Political Studies, University of Ottawa. Asoer028@uottawa.ca
[2] Donella H. Meadows, "Thinking in Systems", Edited by Diana Wright, Sustainability Institute, (First published by Earthscan in the UK in 2009), 11-12 https://research.fit.edu/media/site-specific/ researchfitedu/coast-climate-adaptation-library/climate-communications/psychology-amp-behavior/Meadows-2008.-Thinking-in-Systems.pdf,

sphere.

This chapter is organized in three sections. The first section delves deeper in the oil and gas industry in the Arctic, between a necessity and an environmental disaster. The second section dives into not the opposite of fossil fuels but into what is framed as its opposite - renewable energies, between their promise of a sustainable future and their impacts on Indigenous governance and livelihoods. And thirdly, this last section will delve into the upcoming technologies of small modular nuclear reactors and geoengineering, outside of binary fossil fuels-renewable energies.

## The Oil and Gas Industry in The Circumpolar Arctic: Breaking A Catch-22 Situation

### Hydrocarbon and Revenue: Livelihoods and Dependency

The 2020 Norilsk oil spill in Russia left a permanent open wound in the Arctic environment. From endangering livelihood opportunities to ecological health, Nornickel's negligence caused the release of more than 21,000 tons of fuel into the environment – polluting water and land.[3] And yet, the oil and gas industry remains the economic backbone of the Russian Arctic zone. Since the Russian invasion of Ukraine in 2021 and the subsequent Western sanctions against Russia, the Russian oil and gas industry is seeing stronger economic partnership developments with its Asian neighbors. Despite the sanctions, Russia remains the world's second largest natural gas producer, behind the United States of America, with 762 bcm of natural gas produced and approximately 210 bcm exported via pipeline in 2021, mainly from Siberia. Liquified Natural Gas (LNG) exports to Europe remain high with a steady 9 million tonnes in 2022 - 318 out of 348 deliveries made in the first half of 2022 were destined for France, Belgium, and Spain – compared to the Asian market which has received 5.5 million tonnes in the last year.[4] While much attention has been given to the strengthening of the Russia-China relationship since the invasion of Ukraine, LNG exports to China have decreased by 15% seeing a two-year low. China has, however, purchased a record amount of Russian crude oil, jumping 15% from last year - preferring Russia to Saudi Arabia and compensating the reduction in LNG Russian

---

[3] "Norilsk Nickel: Mining Firm Pays Record $2bn Fine over Arctic Oil Spill," BBC News, March 10, 2021, sec. Europe, https://www.bbc.com/news/world-europe-56350953.
[4] Malte Humpert, "EU Received 300 Shipments of LNG from Russia Since Beginning of Ukraine War," High North News, June 22, 2023, https://www.highnorthnews.com/en/eu-received-300-shipments-lng-russia-beginning-ukraine-war.

exports to China in the past year.[5] Russian crude oil is now passing through Arctic waters to be delivered to China using two tankers each with a capacity of over 730,000 barrels of crude oil. While the Northern Sea Route is indeed significantly shorter than the route via the Suez Canal, an increase in Arctic shipping may mean an increase in accident risk - thereby putting at risk not only the Arctic environment but may expand beyond the Arctic through the potential of crude oil becoming encapsulated in ice, traveling beyond the perimeters of an oil spill. The Russian government and its operator of nuclear icebreakers, Rosatom, are now negotiating using non-ice class tankers, adding significant risk to the detriment of the Arctic environment and in potential non-compliance with the Polar Code[6].

The environmental risks posed by the oil and gas industry in the Arctic are significant, but as previously mentioned, the Russian Arctic oil and gas industry remains an economic backbone of the Russian government representing over 90% of its natural gas production and 10% of its oil production.[7] The EU market for Novatek's LNG produced at their Yamal plant in 2022 alone represented over $20 billion in gas revenue for Russia. While some European countries have taken effective steps to reduce the imports of Russian gas into their territories, the European market remains increasing every year since the start of the invasion of Ukraine despite the sanctions.[8] As such, in addition to Russia seeking to foster stronger ties with its Asian neighbors, the European market remains significant for the viability of the Russian Arctic oil and gas industry. Nonetheless, even though the revenues from the industry represents 45% of the federal budget, its economic significance for Indigenous communities in the Russian Arctic are disappointing with the exploitation of natural resources often resulting in land and biodiversity loss as well as human rights violations leading to loss of

---

[5] Tsvetana Paraskova, "China's Imports Of Russian Crude Oil Hit A Record High," OilPrice.Com, June 20, 2023, https://oilprice.com/Latest-Energy-News/World-News/Chinas-Imports-Of-Russian-Crude-Oil-Hit-A-Record-High.html; Malte Humpert, "Russian Oil Shipments Via Arctic Accelerate With Four More Tankers Now En Route to China," High North News, August 10, 2023, https://www.highnorthnews. com/en/russian-oil-shipments-arctic-accelerate-four-more-tankers-now-en-route-china.

[6] Malte Humpert, "Russia Drawing Up Plans to Send Arctic Crude Oil on Non-Ice Class Tankers to Asia," High North News, April 11, 2023, https://www.highnorthnews.com/en/russia-drawing-plans-send-arctic-crude-oil-non-ice-class-tankers-asia; Humpert, "Russian Oil Shipments Via Arctic Accelerate With Four More Tankers Now En Route to China"; Malte Humpert, "Russian Crude Oil Now Flowing To China Via Arctic Ocean," High North News, August 3, 2023, https://www.highnorthnews.com/en/russian-crude-oil-now-flowing-china-arctic-ocean.

[7] IEA, "Energy Fact Sheet: Why Does Russian Oil and Gas Matter? – Analysis," IEA, March 21, 2022, https://www.iea.org/articles/energy-fact-sheet-why-does-russian-oil-and-gas-matter.

[8] Humpert, "EU Received 300 Shipments of LNG from Russia Since Beginning of Ukraine War."

livelihood and community.[9]

In Europe, Western sanctions against Russia have triggered a renewed interest in Norwegian oil and gas resources. In January 2023, the Norwegian government awarded 47 new offshore oil and gas exploration permits - 29 in the North Sea, 16 in the Norwegian Sea and 2 in the Arctic Barents Sea - with the state-controlled firm Equinor winning a majority of the new licenses[10]. Severe critiques have been ushered against this decision from environmental activists, international and national organizations, and Indigenous rights defenders as not only compromising the Norwegian government's commitment to net-zero targets, but also putting at risk fragile marine ecosystems.[11] Through the new licensing, large areas of the Barents Sea would now be classified as "mature", opening the region up for yearly licensing rounds. The Barents Sea is estimated to hold around 60% of Norway's undiscovered hydrocarbon reserves, thereby potentially putting Norway as a key strategic partner as Europe's first and preferred supplier for the foreseeable future. The decision to continue forth with Arctic oil exploration comes after a legal battle in 2020 between environmental activist groups, Greenpeace, Nature and Youth Norway, and the government arguing that these planned explorations violate the right to a clean environment and a future by contributing to increasing carbon emissions. The Supreme Court of Norway ruled in favor of the state 11 to 4, thereby allowing the state to continue the expansion of the sector.[12] 2022 marked an incredible increase in revenue shares for the Norwegian government as the general revenues are estimated to be at around NOK 3,592 billion with revenues from direct

[9] "Russia's Indigenous Peoples Call for International Support to Save the Arctic," IWGIA - International Work Group for Indigenous Affairs, October 29, 2021, https://www.iwgia.org/en/news/4553-russia-indigenous-peoples-international-support-save-arctic.html; "Russian Oil Spill Exposes History of Indigenous Peoples' Rights Violations," IWGIA - International Work Group for Indigenous Affairs, June 23, 2020, https://www.iwgia.org/en/news/3790-russian-oil-spill-exposes-history-of-indigenous-peoples%E2%80%99-right-violations.html; Maria Tysiachniouk et al., "Oil and Indigenous People in Sub-Arctic Russia: Rethinking Equity and Governance in Benefit Sharing Agreements," Energy Research & Social Science 37 (March 1, 2018): 140–52, https://doi.org/10.1016/j.erss.2017.09.004.
[10] Reuters, "Norway Awards 47 Oil and Gas Exploration Permits," ArcticToday (blog), January 10, 2023, https://www.arctictoday.com/norway-awards-47-oil-and-gas-exploration-permits/.
[11] Henrik Pryser Libell and Derrick Bryson Taylor, "Norway's Supreme Court Makes Way for More Arctic Drilling," The New York Times, December 22, 2020, sec. World, https://www.nytimes.com/ 2020/ 12/22/world/europe/norway-supreme-court-oil-climate-change.html; "'The People vs Arctic Oil': Activists Target Norway at ECHR," Al Jazeera, June 15, 2021, sec. Oil and Gas, https://www.aljazeera. com/news/2021/6/15/the-people-vs-arctic-oil-activists-target-norway-at-echr; Elena F. Tracy and Wwf Arctic Programme Text Guro Lystad, "Putting a Stop to Oil and Gas Exploration Projects in Norway's Arctic Regions," High North News, November 2, 2022, sec. Op-ed, https://www.highnorthnews.com/ en/putting-stop-oil-and-gas-exploration-projects-norways-arctic-regions.
[12] "'The People vs Arctic Oil': Activists Target Norway at ECHR"; Libell and Taylor, "Norway's Supreme Court Makes Way for More Arctic Drilling"; Supreme Court of Norway, No. HR-2021-1975-S (Supreme Court of Norway October 11, 2021).

ownership being approximately NOK 530 billion. This amount, compared to NOK 1,114 billion in 2021, represents an equivalent to 26% of the Norwegian GDP and totals over 200,000 jobs[13].

This reliance on fossil fuels sounds like a running theme in the circumpolar Arctic. On the North American continent, only Greenland stands as an outlier and banned all oil exploration in 2021, except for the existing licenses which however reportedly have very limited potential.[14] According to the U.S. Geological Survey, there could be about 15.5 billion barrels of oil undiscovered and about 148 trillion cubic feet of natural gas in Greenland.[15] While weather conditions may make exploration more challenging, the prospects of resource exploration and development would have solidified Greenland's economic independence from Denmark - thereby inching closer to effective sovereignty and independence. The U.S.'and Canada's federal governments have issued a moratorium on Arctic Ocean oil and gas exploration in 2016 in a bid to protect the Arctic's fragile environment. The move, however, was criticized by Indigenous governments who noted the imperial and colonial nature of such a decision made without proper consultation and prior, free, and informed consent.[16] In Canada, the moratorium was additionally supported by the 2022 Order Prohibiting Certain Activities in Arctic Offshore Waters which prohibits oil and gas activities in the region, a move followed by the U.S. banning off-shore drilling in 1.2 million hectares of the Beaufort Sea.[17] On the U.S. side, the Willow

---

13 Frode Borgås, "Soaring Revenues Caused by High Gas Prices," Statistisk sentralbyrå - Statistics Norway, March 6, 2023, https://www.ssb.no/en/offentlig-sektor/offentlig-forvaltning/statistikk/offentlig-forvaltnings-inntekter-og-utgifter/articles-for-general-government-revenue-and-expenditure/soaring-revenues-caused-by-high-gas-prices; "Norway's Oil and Gas Tax Revenue Soars to Record $89 Bln," Reuters, January 26, 2023, sec. Energy, https://www.reuters.com/business/energy/norways-oil-gas-tax-revenue-soars-record-89-bln-2023-01-26/.

14 The Associated Press, "Greenland Suspends All Oil Exploration in Its Territory | CBC News," CBC, July 16, 2021, https://www.cbc.ca/news/business/greenland-oil-1.6105230; Morten Buttler, "Greenland Bans All Future Oil Exploration Citing Climate Concerns," Time, July 16, 2021, https://time.com/6080933/greenland-bans-oil-exploration/.

15 Jakob Kløve Keiding, "Great Potential for Critical Raw Materials in Greenland," Geological Survey of Denmark and Greenland (blog), accessed August 20, 2023, https://eng.geus.dk/about/news/news-archive/2023/june/great-potential-for-critical-raw-materials-in-greenland; "Geological Data," Mineral Resources Authority - Naalakkersuisut (blog), accessed August 20, 2023, http://https%253A%252F%252Fgovmin.gl%252Fexploration-prospecting%252Fget-an-exploration-licence%252Fgeological-data%252F.

16 Yasmina Pepa, "NWT and Nunavut Premiers React to Federal Announcement of Arctic Oil and Gas Moratorium," gouvernemental, Government of Northwest Territories, December 22, 2016, https://www.gov.nt.ca/newsroom/nwt-and-nunavut-premiers-react-federal-announcement-arctic-oil-and-gas-moratorium; John Van Dusen · CBC Van Dusen, "Nunavut, N.W.T. Premiers Slam Arctic Drilling Moratorium | CBC News," CBC, December 22, 2016, https://www.cbc.ca/news/ canada/north/nunavut-premier-slams-arctic-drilling-moratorium-1.3908037.

17 Government of Canada, "Order Prohibiting Certain Activities in Arctic Offshore Waters, 2022, Pursuant to the Canada Petroleum Resources Act," legislation and regulations, March 11, 2022, https://www.rcaanc-cirnac.gc.ca/eng/1647022447627/1647022668724?wbdisable=true.

project in Alaska by ConocoPhillips was approved in late 2023 by the Biden administration. While the project has been cut back by 40%, the area where the project is planned would still hold about 600 million barrels of oil - making it one of the largest oil and gas operations on federal public land[18]. The North Slope, where project Willow is set to take place, is already extensively developed. The Prudhoe Bay fields owned by BP Exploration, ConocoPhillips Alaska Inc., and ExxonMobil, have been active since 1977 with a capacity of 25 billion barrels of oil (of which 60% is recoverable) as well as 25 trillion cubic feet of natural gas. The Prudhoe Bay fields are the largest of North America and 20th largest worldwide.[19] In 2019, the Alaskan oil and gas industry supported 47,300 jobs (15,800 directly and 31,500 indirectly), representing over 10% of the state's total employment and contributed to $19.4 billion (35.7%) of the total GDP.[20] The pandemic, however, hit the sector hard, with a loss of over 3,000 jobs in 2020, which have since stayed down, with the year marking the lowest level of production in 40 years.[21] The Willow project stands as not only a renewal of interest in oil and gas production in Alaska, it also represents a significant economic avenue for the state. While opposition is strong, its support is equally strong with a wide range of actors both supporting and opposing the project; Indigenous nations have for instance both opposed and supported the project, citing economic avenues and ecological concerns as key arguments.[22]

On the Canadian side, while Yukon's onshore sedimentary basins contain an estimated 10 trillion cubic feet of recuperable and marketable natural gas and

---

[18] Ella Nilsen, "The Willow Project Has Been Approved. Here's What to Know about the Controversial Oil-Drilling Venture | CNN Politics," CNN, March 14, 2023, https://www.cnn.com/ 2023/ 03/14/politics/willow-project-oil-alaska-explained-climate/index.html; Mark Thiessen and Matthew Brown, "Biden's Approval of Willow Oil Project Intensifies Rift among Indigenous Alaskans," Los Angeles Times, March 17, 2023, sec. Politics, https://www.latimes.com/world-nation/story/2023-03-17/willow-oil-project-approval-intensifies-alaska-natives-rift; Noah Gordon, "The Willow Project and the Race to Pump the 'Last Barrel' of Oil," Carnegie Endowment for International Peace (blog), March 16, 2023, https://carnegieendowment.org/2023/03/16/willow-project-and-race-to-pump-last-barrel-of-oil-pub-89298.

[19] "Greater Prudhoe Bay," ConocoPhillips Alaska, accessed September 5, 2023, https://alaska.conoco phillips.com/who-we-are/alaska-operations/greater-prudhoe-bay/.

[20] Sara Teel, "June 2022 Alaska Economic Trends," Alaska Economic Trends Magazine, June 2022; "New Analysis: Alaska-Made Natural Gas and Oil Drives U.S. Economic Recovery, Strengthens All Industries," American Petroleum Institute, July 20, 2021, https://www.api.org/news-policy-and-issues/ news/ 2021/ 07/20/alaska-pwc.

[21] Hilde-Gunn Bye, "Alaska Oil and Gas Jobs Hit Hard During the Pandemic," High North News, November 17, 2020, https://www.highnorthnews.com/en/alaska-oil-and-gas-jobs-hit-hard-during-pandemic.

[22] Meera Baswan, "The Willow Project and Its Impacts on Indigenous Communities," The Indigenous Foundation (blog), 2023, https://www.theindigenousfoundation.org/articles/the-willow-project-and-its-impacts-on-indigenous-communities; Thiessen and Brown, "Biden's Approval of Willow Oil Project Intensifies Rift among Indigenous Alaskans."

up to 900 million barrels of crude oil, there is no commercial production.[23] The Northwest Territories account for just 0.1% of all Canadian crude oil and natural gas production when it is estimated that the territory could hold 37% of the country's marketable crude oil resources and 35% of marketable natural gas resources.[24] The story is similar for the Territory of Nunavut as while it does not have any crude oil or natural gas production, it is estimated that crude oil resources range from 18 to 267 billion barrels of oil and 180 to 1228 trillion cubic feet of gas according to the territorial government - the federal government estimates 18 billion barrels of oil and 181 trillion cubic feet of natural gas. The last exploration well was drilled in 1986.[25] Québec also does not have any production. Canada's Arctic oil and gas resources are therefore vastly under-explored compared to Alaska. While providing economic avenues for local inhabitants and providing revenue for territorial governments is central to the viability of both community and government, the effects of climate change as well as direct effects of fossil fuels are devastating - deeply impacting food security, housing, as well as culture and identity. The ongoing thawing of the permafrost due to rising temperatures in the Arctic regions of Canada is estimated to cost over $51 million each year as well as a yearly $25 million in lost GDP in the Northwest Territories alone.[26] The impacts for infrastructures of the thawing permafrost will result in lost communities as the land simply becomes inhabitable. Revenues are essential to continue with life in a market system by providing livelihood opportunities to individuals. Communities in the circumpolar Arctic are also over 99% dependent on fossil fuels for electricity, heating, and fuel. Fuel dependency has been shown as detrimental to the environment and human health through both direct impacts and indirect impacts through food. Arctic shipping - and subsequently black carbon pollution through the use of heavy

[23] Canada Energy Regulator Government of Canada, "CER – Provincial and Territorial Energy Profiles – Yukon," June 9, 2023, https://www.cer-rec.gc.ca/en/data-analysis/energy-markets/provincial-territorial-energy-profiles/provincial-territorial-energy-profiles-yukon.html; Yukon Government: Energy, Mines and Resources, "Yukon Oil & Gas: ANNUAL REPORT 2016" (Yukon Government: Energy, Mines and Resources, 2016), https://emrlibrary.gov.yk.ca/oilandgas/yukon-oil-and-gas-annual-report-2016.pdf.
[24] Canada Energy Regulator Government of Canada, "CER – Provincial and Territorial Energy Profiles – Northwest Territories," June 9, 2023, https://www.cer-rec.gc.ca/en/data-analysis/energy-markets/provincial-territorial-energy-profiles/provincial-territorial-energy-profiles-northwest-territories.html; Government of Northwest Territories, "Oil & Gas," Information (Government of the Northwest Territories), accessed August 14, 2023, https://www.iti.gov.nt.ca/en/oil-gas.
[25] Canada Energy Regulator Government of Canada, "CER – Provincial and Territorial Energy Profiles – Nunavut," June 9, 2023, https://www.cer-rec.gc.ca/en/data-analysis/energy-markets/provincial-territorial-energy-profiles/provincial-territorial-energy-profiles-nunavut.html; Government of Nunavut: Department of Economic Development and Transportation, "Petroleum Resources in Nunavut," 2017, https://www.gov.nu.ca/sites/default/files/2017_petroleum_brochure_eng_0.pdf.
[26] Emily Tsui, "Reducing Individual Costs of Permafrost Thaw Damage in Canada's Arctic," The Arctic Institute - Center for Circumpolar Security Studies (blog), March 4, 2021, https://www.thearcticinstitute.org/ reducing-individual-costs-permafrost-thaw-damage-canada-arctic/.

fuel oil (HFO) - has risen by 85% between 2015 and 2019, compared to 8% globally, causing drastic increase in warming through reduction of reflexivity on ice and snow.[27] Despite the introduction in 2021 of a ban on the use and carriage of heavy fuel oil in the Arctic by the International Maritime Organization, the ban contains too many loopholes to have any significant impact on effective reduction of HFO and black carbon pollution in the Arctic.[28]

On air pollution, the Willow project, Prudhoe Bay fields, and the Yamal plant are all significant sources of $CO_2$ pollution. The Yamal plant currently produces 2.6 tonnes of $CO_2$ per tonne of LNG - compared to the industry standard of 0.4 tonnes of $CO_2$.[29] If the Willow project were to match expectations in terms of oil production, the consumption of the oil produced would release approximately 277 million tons of carbon dioxide into the atmosphere during the lifetime of the project or around 9 million tons per year.[30] BP's Prudhoe Bay fields are estimated to account for 6.6 million tons of $CO_2$ pollution in 2019 - with overall activities estimated to release 8 million tons of $CO_2$.[31] In addition to $CO_2$ emissions, methane emissions from LNG pipelines from Russia to Europe have surged by 40% during the pandemic - poor infrastructure maintenance being considered as a key reason behind this increase.[32] Russia, according to the International Energy Agency, is one of

---

[27] Matteo Cimellaro, "Shipping Frenzy Threatens Indigenous Food Security," Canada's National Observer, July 13, 2023, sec. News, https://www.nationalobserver.com/2023/07/13/news/shipping-frenzy-threatens-indigenous-food-security; Julia Olsen, Natalie Ann Carter, and Jackie Dawson, "Community Perspectives on the Environmental Impacts of Arctic Shipping: Case Studies from Russia, Norway and Canada," ed. Willem Coetzee, Cogent Social Sciences 5, no. 1 (January 1, 2019): 1609189, https://doi.org/10.1080/23311886.2019.1609189; "Shipping," AMAP (blog), accessed August 14, 2023, https://eua-bca.amap.no/maritime-shipping; "LNG: The Threat to the Arctic from Liquified Natural Gas as a Shipping Fuel," Clean Arctic Alliance (blog), accessed August 14, 2023, https://cleanarctic.org/campaigns/the-arctic-climate-crisis/lng-the-threat-to-the-arctic-from-liquified-natural-gas-as-a-shipping-fuel/.

[28] "UN Adopts Ban on Heavy Fuel Oil Use by Ships in Arctic," Reuters, June 17, 2021, sec. Energy, https://www.reuters.com/business/energy/un-adopts-ban-heavy-fuel-oil-use-by-ships-arctic-2021-06-17/; "Black Carbon in the Arctic," Clean Arctic Alliance (blog), accessed August 14, 2023, https://cleanarctic.org/campaigns/the-arctic-climate-crisis/black-carbon-in-the-arctic/.

[29] Vladimir Afanasiev, 'World Needs More Gas, Not Less': Novatek Targets Sanction Date for Russia's First CCS Project, Upstream Online | Latest Oil and Gas News, March 4, 2021, sec. energy_transition, https://www.upstreamonline.com/energy-transition/world-needs-more-gas-not-less-novatek-targets-sanction-date-for-russias-first-ccs-project/2-1-974343.

[30] Gordon, "The Willow Project and the Race to Pump the 'Last Barrel' of Oil."

[31] "Selling Its Alaskan Oil Business Was a Green Win for BP—Not the Planet," Bloomberg.Com, April 15, 2021, https://www.bloomberg.com/graphics/2021-tracking-carbon-emissions-BP-hilcorp/.

[32] Isabelle Gerretsen, "Methane Emissions from Russian Pipelines Surged during the Coronavirus Pandemic," Climate Home News, March 4, 2021, https://climatechangenews.com/2021/03/04/methane-emissions-russian-pipelines-surged-coronavirus-pandemic/.

the world's largest methane emitters - 20% of worldwide emissions.[33] The need to reduce dependency on fossil fuels is thereby evident. The planet's carbon budget for staying within the 1.5 degree Celsius is set to be exhausted within 8 years if emissions remain at this constant level. For the 2 degrees threshold, this deadline is in 25 years.[34] The Arctic is estimated to be warming four times faster than the global average.[35] Climate mitigation and adaptation is thereby intertwined in a complex web of ongoing dependence and inequalities in part due to the ongoing legacy of colonialism as will be shown in the section below. Economic diversification and transitioning away from fossil fuels requires the crucial inclusion of both justice and responsibility.

## Oil and Gas Development in The Arctic and Indigenous Rights

Justice and responsibility are key for the shaping of not only a just transition away from fossil fuels, but of a sustainable future as well. Ongoing dynamics of land expropriation and rights violations underlying the continuation of colonial dynamics undermine the development of both renewable energy technologies as well as current economic opportunities within the oil and gas industry. To take a tangent, the case of Australia highlights the importance of responsibility considering global $CO_2$ pollution and land degradation as well as expropriation. The NASA visualization of global carbon sinks and emissions in 2021 shows Australia as a carbon sink, which has been previously confirmed by various studies.[36] Australia is also an oil producing country exporting to primarily Southeast and East Asia - mainly Singapore, Indonesia, South Korea, Malaysia, Brunei, Japan, and China.[37] When exported crude and refined oil is included in calculations, Australia's carbon footprint represents 3.6% of global emissions. According to Climate

---

[33]Gerretsen; "Overview – Global Methane Tracker 2022 – Analysis," IEA, 2022, https://www.iea.org/reports/global-methane-tracker-2022/overview.

[34] Axel Dalman, "Carbon Budgets: Where Are We Now?," Carbon Tracker Initiative, May 11, 2020, https://carbontracker.org/carbon-budgets-where-are-we-now/; "Remaining Carbon Budget - Mercator Research Institute on Global Commons and Climate Change (MCC)," Mercator Research Institute on Global Commons and Climate Change, accessed August 14, 2023, https://www.mcc-berlin.net/en/research/co2-budget.html.

[35] Mika Rantanen et al., "The Arctic Has Warmed Nearly Four Times Faster than the Globe since 1979," Communications Earth & Environment 3, no. 1 (August 11, 2022): 1–10, https://doi.org/10.1038/s43247-022-00498-3.

[36] Paola Yanguas Parra et al., "Evaluating the Significance of Australia's Global Fossil Fuel Carbon Footprint" (Climate Analytics for the Australian Conservation Foundation, July 2019), https://climateanalytics.org/media/australia_carbon_footprint_report_july2019.pdf; Yohanna Villalobos et al., "Was Australia a Sink or Source of $CO_2$ in 2015? Data Assimilation Using OCO-2 Satellite Measurements," Atmospheric Chemistry and Physics 21, no. 23 (December 1, 2021): 17453–94, https://doi.org/10.5194/acp-21-17453-2021.

[37] "Crude Petroleum in Australia | OEC," OEC - The Observatory of Economic Complexity, 2021, https://oec.world/en/profile/bilateral-product/crude-petroleum/reporter/aus.

Analytics, this footprint surpasses China by a factor of 9 and the U.S. by a factor of 4.[38] Therefore, while Australia is indeed a carbon sink, the exportation of the oil it produces remains instrumental in global efforts in reducing carbon dioxide emissions - highlighting the importance of responsibility in the shaping of a global just transition. Additionally, the seizure of Indigenous land in Australia to respond to this demand for resources brings forward discussions surrounding international legal frameworks.[39]

Permanent sovereignty over natural resources as well as the United Nations Declaration on the Rights of Indigenous Peoples (UNDRIP), especially Article 32 on prior, free, and informed consent, lay foundations onto which decolonial and self-determination claims are made. To come back up from down under, the resource intensive development in Arctic Russia and its subsequent land pollution has negatively impacted Indigenous communities in the region. Instead of providing economic avenues, ongoing pollution in the surroundings of the city of Norilsk has affected air, soil and water quality, greatly diminishing the capacity for the various Indigenous Peoples of the area to maintain a livelihood and ensure food security - the lifestyle of the peoples present, Dolgans, Nenets, Nganasans, Evenkis, and Enets, greatly depend on hunting, fishing, and reindeer herding.[40] The oil spill of 2020 caused by Nornickel, 21,000 tons of fuel leaked into soil and water, awarded the company a record $2 billion fine aimed at improving the environmental situation according to President Vladimir Putin. The supposed results of improved communication and interaction between Nornickel and Indigenous communities and rights groups are contentious with some listing improvements - such as direct compensations, roads, and reindeer meat processing facilities - while others point out to the dictatorial nature of the negotiations between the enterprise and the Indigenous rights groups, with some groups being dissolved and exiled after voicing critiques.[41] Russia did

[38] Yanguas Parra et al., "Evaluating the Significance of Australia's Global Fossil Fuel Carbon Footprint."

[39] Acton Peninsula, "National Museum of Australia - Aboriginal Land Rights Act," National Museum Australia (National Museum of Australia; c=AU; o=Commonwealth of Australia; ou=National Museum of Australia, December 8, 2022), https://www.nma.gov.au/defining-moments/resources/aboriginal-land-rights-act.

[40] Olesya Vikulova, "The Human Cost of Oil: How Indigenous and Ethnic Minorities Bear the Brunt of Disasters," Greenpeace International, June 26, 2020, https://www.greenpeace.org/ international/ story/43820/human-cost-oil-indigenous-ethnic-minorities-brunt-of-disasters; Alina Bykova and Pavel Sulyandziga, "A Year after Arctic Fuel Spill, Norilsk Nickel Continues to Ignore Indigenous Critics," The Barents Observer, May 29, 2021, https://thebarentsobserver.com/en/opinions/2021/05/one-year-after-massive-arctic-fuel-spill-norilsk-nickel-continues-ignore-indigenous#.YLJrHKuyEsQ.twitter.

[41] John Last, "Indigenous Groups Paying the Price for Russia's Massive Arctic Fuel Spill | CBC News," CBC News, July 13, 2020, https://www.cbc.ca/news/canada/north/norilsk-nickel-russian-fuel-spill-

not endorse UNDRIP nor ratified ILO Convention 169 citing better domestic legal frameworks, meaning that Indigenous Peoples in Russia cannot lay their land rights and self-determination claims within these international legal frameworks. Permanent sovereignty over natural resources for Indigenous nations comes in direct confrontation with the economic and strategic imperatives of the Russian federal government in Arctic resource development.

In Canada, the 2016 moratorium on Arctic Ocean oil and gas exploration and the 2022 Order Prohibiting Certain Activities in Arctic Offshore Waters may have been welcomed by environmental rights activists and groups, but its implementation proved to be highly contested among Northern governments and organizations. Former Premier of the Northwest Territories Bob McLeod issued a "red alert" in response to the 2016 moratorium, claiming irresponsibility and colonial attitudes considering the difficult and restricted economic livelihood opportunities context in the Canadian North.[42] Former Premier McLeod highlighted the impacts of pollution coming from oil and gas reserves in Alberta and British Columbia on caribou populations and permafrost, further limiting food security and damaging infrastructures. The potential economic growth from offshore oil and gas exploration investment had thereby been rendered null by the moratorium. While the moratorium was extended by the 2022 Order, the federal government signed a new accord in August 2023 with the Inuvialuit, Northwest Territories, and Yukon governments to share the decision-making process over Arctic offshore oil and gas development and ensure that Northerners are the primary beneficiaries of economic activities stemming from the development.[43] In 2013, Canadian Inuit leaders voiced their opposition to the joint statement of the Peoples Arctic conference calling for a ban on Arctic oil drilling, criticizing the involvement of Greenpeace in the process stirring the conversation.[44] Signatories include representatives from

consequences-1.5645408; Thomas Nilsen, "Nornickel Has Changed Positively, Says Taimyr Indigenous Group," The Independent Barents Observer, May 16, 2021, https://thebarentsobserver.com/en/indigenous-peoples/2021/05/taimyr-indigenous-group-says-norilsk-nickel-changing-positively; "Norilsk Nickel."

[42] The Canadian Press, "N.W.T. Premier Issues 'red Alert' on 'Colonial' Attack on Territory's Oil and Gas Future | CBC News," CBC News, November 1, 2017, https://www.cbc.ca/news/canada/north/nwt-premier-bob-mcleod-drilling-arctic-1.4381837.

[43] Ollie Williams, "Inuvialuit Sign Oil, Gas Co-Management Deal with NWT, Yukon, Ottawa," Cabin Radio, August 10, 2023, https://cabinradio.ca/140039/news/politics/inuvialuit-sign-oil-and-gas-co-management-deal-with-nwt-yukon-ottawa/.

[44] "Indigenous Statement Calls for Arctic Oil Development Moratorium," Nunatsiaq News, May 14, 2013, https://nunatsiaq.com/stories/article/65674indigenous_statement_calls_for_ban_on_all_arctic_oil_development/

Russian Indigenous groups, the Arctic Athabaskan Council, Saami organizations, Alaskan native organizations and the environmental group Avataq from Greenland. No Canadian Inuit organization signed the joint statement and instead pointed to the existing Circumpolar Inuit Declaration on Resource Development Principles. Yet, this feeling is not unanimous in Canada. Local elected officials in Nunavut have criticized the 2019 extension of the moratorium for "not going far enough", citing concerns for food security and land degradation due to climate change and the potential of a spill in addition to the existing burden of increased ship traffic in the region.[45] Similarly, across the border, Project Willow in Alaska attracted both criticism and praise from the local population, including Indigenous. Concerns have been voiced on the potential impacts of the project on caribou populations thereby endangering food security, livelihoods, and culture. While some Indigenous tribal organizations have expressed support for the project, citing livelihood opportunities and economic growth, the contenders - including the community of Nuiqsut which is the closest to the proposed project site - have argued that "any jobs and money the project brings in the short term will be negated by the environmental devastation in the long run."[46]

Oil and gas exploration and development in the Circumpolar Arctic is thereby a source of deep contestation across and within socio-economic categories responding to the present economic landscape of poor diversification and livelihood opportunities. Living in the Arctic is expensive with food prices currently soaring exponentially and housing conditions degrading.[47] While the Canadian potential oil and gas industry in the Arctic is currently at a standstill, its development could provide exceptional income to both local government, communities, and individuals. Even if actual interest in Arctic exploration and development in Canada is low with potential returns only

---

[45] Eilís Quinn, "Arctic Canadian Community Says Oil Moratorium Renewal Doesn't Go Far Enough – Eye on the Arctic," Eye On The Arctic, February 13, 2023, https://www.rcinet.ca/eye-on-the-arctic/2023/02/13/arctic-canadian-community-says-oil-moratorium-renewal-doesnt-go-far-enough/.

[46] Baswan, "The Willow Project and Its Impacts on Indigenous Communities"; "Willow Project: Could Two Lawsuits Block the Oil Project in Alaska?," Euronews, March 14, 2023, https://www.euronews.com/ green/2023/03/14/biden-administration-approves-alaskas-willow-oil-project-sparking-anger-from-environmental.

[47] Maude C. Beaumier and James D. Ford, "Food Insecurity among Inuit Women Exacerbated by Socioeconomic Stresses and Climate Change," Canadian Journal of Public Health 101, no. 3 (2010): 196–201; Cimellaro, "Shipping Frenzy Threatens Indigenous Food Security"; Anna Canny, "Juneau's Worst Glacial Outburst Flood Destroys Homes and Displaces Residents," Alaska Public Media, August 7, 2023, https://alaskapublic.org/2023/08/07/juneaus-worst-glacial-outburst-flood-destroys-homes-and-displaces-residents/; Marc Fawcett-Atkinson, "Food Prices in the North Are Astronomical, despite Subsidies. Who Benefits from Ottawa's Plan to Tackle Food Insecurity?," Canada's National Observer, March 23, 2023, sec. News, https://www.nationalobserver.com/2023/03/23/news/food-prices-north-are-astronomical-despite-subsidies.

years down the line, economic diversification remains central to development in the Canadian North. However, ongoing oil and gas development in the circumpolar Arctic has resulted and continues to result in human rights violations against Indigenous Peoples, with many groups calling for an outright ban of oil drilling in the region, who in turn see minimal economic benefit from the industry. Arctic communities are vulnerable to the effects of climate change, with adaptation and resilience strategies lacking capacity. Like Former NWT Premier McLeod specified, the ongoing environmental stress - and therefore economic stress - experienced by the territory is in part due to the oil and gas activities in the surrounding provinces. There comes a catch-22 situation: be damned if you do develop, and be damned if you don't. Providing a third pathway away from the imperative to develop oil and gas activities in the Arctic is a necessity for the environmental survival of the region and for the survival and wellbeing of peoples living there - both being indissociable from each other.

## Renewable Energies: A Promise of a Sustainable Future and Indigenous Governance

### Renewable Energy Development and Mining: More is More

The environmental and human imperatives of the just transition away from fossil fuel dependence entail the development of two sectors: renewable energy technology, and mining. According to the United Nations Climate Action, renewable energies are derived from natural sources that are replenished at a higher rate than they are consumed and generate lower emissions than burning fossil fuels.[48] Solar energy and wind energy are the most well-known and have recently captured attention in the Arctic with strong contestations from Saami reindeer herders. Geothermal energy, hydropower, ocean energy and bioenergy are also among renewable energies. Nuclear energy, as will be touched upon in more detail below, while being clean, is a controversial source of energy due to its radioactive nuclear waste and security threats as well as high operating costs. Renewable energy development requires the mining of several metals and minerals, some deemed critical. For solar panels, on average, 19 mineral products and metals are needed - among which 8 are considered critical, meaning that they are not only of particular importance for the development of the technology, but

---

[48] United Nations, "What Is Renewable Energy?," United Nations (United Nations), accessed September 6, 2023, https://www.un.org/en/climatechange/what-is-renewable-energy.

they also face supply challenges.[49] A mineral considered critical is thereby deeply linked to global geopolitical dynamics. These critical minerals for solar panels are copper, indium, selenium, tellurium, gallium, silver, germanium, and tin. These minerals are essential to the viability of the energy transition on a meaningful and global scale. All these critical minerals except for germanium and tin are found and produced in Canada. Wind turbines require concrete, steel, iron, fiberglass, polymers, aluminum, copper, zinc and rare earth elements - rare earth elements are a group of 15 elements which are essential components in everyday electrical devices and in industrial settings. In 2022, the U.S. Geological survey published a list of 50 minerals deemed critical with 15 newly added minerals such as zinc and nickel. Rare earth elements (REEs) are essential to the development of offshore wind turbines, especially used, in 43.2%, for permanent magnets.[50] While Canada has some of the largest reserves and resources of REEs worldwide, Canada is not a commercial producer with all projects still in exploratory or processing phases. The largest REEs producers in 2021 were China at 60% of world production, followed by the U.S. at 15.5%, Myanmar at 9.4%, and Australia at 7.9% of the world's production.[51]

To meet the demands of renewable energy development, significant growth in the mining industry is needed and Arctic countries such as Canada are essential to global supplies. According to the International Energy Agency and to the World Mining Data 2023 report, the world is mining less than it did before the pandemic despite needing an exponential growth in production to meet the demands for critical minerals to in turn meet either the net-zero targets scenario, the Sustainable Development scenario, or the states policies scenario by 2040.[52] In 2020, for solar PV alone, the mineral demand totaled at 0.7 Mt while the expected net-zero by 2050 scenario would

---

[49] "Mining for Clean Energy: How the Global Rise of Solar Power Will Drive Demand for Canadian Metals and Minerals" (Vancouver: Clean Energy Canada, June 2017), https://cleanenergycanada.org/wp-content/uploads/2017/06/MiningCleanEnergy2017.pdf.

[50] Jason Burton, "U.S. Geological Survey Releases 2022 List of Critical Minerals | U.S. Geological Survey," USGS: science for a changing world, February 22, 2022, https://www.usgs.gov/news/national-news-release/us-geological-survey-releases-2022-list-critical-minerals.

[51] Natural Resources Canada, "Rare Earth Elements Facts," Government of Canada - Natural Resources Canada (Natural Resources Canada, February 14, 2023), https://natural-resources.canada.ca/our-natural-resources/minerals-mining/minerals-metals-facts/rare-earth-elements-facts/20522.

[52] "Mineral Requirements for Clean Energy Transitions – The Role of Critical Minerals in Clean Energy Transitions – Analysis," IEA, accessed August 20, 2023, https://www.iea.org/reports/the-role-of-critical-minerals-in-clean-energy-transitions/mineral-requirements-for-clean-energy-transitions; "Critical Minerals – The Role of Critical Minerals in Clean Energy Transitions," IEA, accessed August 20, 2023, https://www.iea.org/topics/critical-minerals; Heather Exner-Pirot, "Overcoming Remoteness: Innovation to Support Development, Critical Minerals, and Security in the Arctic" (Macdonald Laurier Institute, 2023).

demand a total of 3.3 Mt of minerals. For wind energy, the total demand goes from 0.6 Mt to 2.9 Mt. The biggest portion of the expected rise in demand is for EVs and battery storage, going from 0.4 Mt in 2020 to 21.5 Mt in 2040 under the net-zero by 2050 scenario.[53] In Sweden, the leading producer of iron and base metals of the European Union, there are currently 12 mines in production, established from the early 1700s to 2018.[54] These mines produce gold, copper, silver, iron, zinc, and lead. In 2023, Europe's largest deposit of rare earth metals - one million tons - was found in Northern Sweden, near the city of Kiruna. The municipality of Kiruna already has two existing mines producing iron. LKAB, the mining company in charge of the site, is also planning to create a Nordic value chain by cooperating with Norwegian facilities and by establishing a circular industry park in Luleå where critical minerals will be extracted.[55] This discovery comes timely for the EU as the Commission put forward the European Critical Raw Materials Act in March 2023 which seeks to increase and diversify the EU's critical raw material supply, strengthen circularity, and support research and innovation, all boxes ticked by the potential new LKAB project near Kiruna. The EU recognizes 34 critical raw materials, including 17 strategic raw materials. The European Commission explicitly calls for diversification of supply as China provides 100% of the supply in heavy rare earth elements. The new 2023 Act calls for at least 10% the EU's consumption to be locally extracted, 20% recycled, 50% locally processed, and to cap dependency on a single country to 50% per strategic raw material. The potential for Canada to fill this diversification goal is clear.[56]

Returning to the North American continent, Greenland came under the spotlight when former U.S. President Donald Trump tried to purchase the

---

[53] "Mineral Requirements for Clean Energy Transitions – The Role of Critical Minerals in Clean Energy Transitions – Analysis."

[54] "Mines in Sweden," Mining Inspectorate of Sweden, February 23, 2021, https://www.sgu.se/en/mining-inspectorate/mines/mines-in-sweden/.

[55] Hilde-Gunn Bye, "Europe's Largest Deposit of Rare Earth Metals Found in Northern Sweden," High North News, January 13, 2023, sec. Business, https://www.highnorthnews.com/en/europes-largest-deposit-rare-earth-metals-found-northern-sweden; "Europe's Largest Deposit of Rare Earth Metals Is Located in the Kiruna Area," LKAB, February 12, 2023, https://lkab.com/en/press/europes-largest-deposit-of-rare-earth-metals-is-located-in-the-kiruna-area/.

[56] "Critical Raw Materials," European Commission, 2023, https://single-market-economy.ec.europa.eu/sectors/raw-materials/areas-specific-interest/critical-raw-materials_en; "An EU Critical Raw Materials Act for the Future of EU Supply Chains," European Council - Council of the European Union, August 18, 2023, https://www.consilium.europa.eu/en/infographics/critical-raw-materials/; M. Garside, "Critical Raw Materials: EU Supply by Mineral & Nation 2020," Statista, December 10, 2021, https://www.statista.com/statistics/1270641/critical-raw-material-supply-in-the-european-union-by-supplier-nation/; ERMA, "European Raw Materials Alliance Contributes to Europe's Industrial Resilience," European Raw Materials Alliance, February 23, 2021, https://erma.eu/european-raw-materials-alliance-contributes-to-europes-industrial-resilience/.

island in 2019; in an attempt to defend the idea, Trump's economic advisor Lawrence Kudlow made a reference to the mining potential of Greenland.[57] According to the Geological Survey of Denmark and Greenland and the Review of the critical raw material resource potential in Greenland 2023 report, the geological history of the island - four billion years - makes the island favorable for "finding and exploiting a range of mineral resources, including some of the critical and potential critical minerals."[58] South Greenland, in particular, constitutes an exceptional accumulation of critical rare minerals with known REEs deposits among which lithium and zirconium resources. East Greenland is underexplored and is thought to hold yet undiscovered significant potential, especially so for tungsten, tin, antimony, and sedimentary copper. West Greenland holds significant potential for phosphorus and REEs. North Greenland has potential for zinc and lead, from which germanium and gallium - both considered critical for solar panel production - can be produced. Finally, titanium and graphite can also be found throughout the island. Overall, production in Greenland has remained on the smaller side of the scale and there is much potential.[59] However, while a majority of Greenlanders support mining if involvement remains domestic, environmentally assessed and economically appraised according to a 2022 study, the mining of uranium has been banned by the Greenlandic parliament in 2021 - halting the development of one of the world's biggest rare earth deposits, the Kuannersuit mine, owned by an Australian company receiving funds from Chinese investors, near the town of Narsaq.[60] The ban of uranium production came after environmental concerns raised by local inhabitants. A campaign was started in 2013 called "Urani? Namiik.", meaning "Uranium? No.". The health risks, both human and for wildlife, posed by uranium and its mining are deadly, among which lung cancer, renal failure, diminished bone growth, diminished fertility, and lower viability of offspring with these effects potentially delayed for decades and generations.[61] Uranium is currently used for commercial nuclear reactors,

---

[57] Martin Pengelly, "Trump Confirms He Is Considering Attempt to Buy Greenland," The Guardian, August 18, 2019, sec. World news, https://www.theguardian.com/world/2019/aug/18/trump-considering-buying-greenland.

[58] Diogo Rosa et al., "Review of the Critical Raw Material Resource Potential in Greenland" (Copenhagen: Center for Minerals and Materials: Geological Survey of Denmark and Greenland, May 2023). 10

[59] Rosa et al.

[60] Mette Bendixen et al., "Opportunistic Climate Adaptation and Public Support for Sand Extraction in Greenland," Nature Sustainability 5, no. 11 (November 2022): 991–99, https://doi.org/10.1038/s41893-022-00922-8; Jacob Gronholt-Pedersen, "Greenland Bans Uranium Mining, Halting Rare Earths Project | Reuters," Reuters, November 10, 2021, sec. Americas, https://www.reuters.com/ world/ americas/ greenland-bans-uranium-mining-halting-rare-earths-project-2021-11-10/.

[61] Dale Dewar, Linda Harvey, and Cathy Vakil, "Uranium Mining and Health," Canadian Family Physician

and to produce isotopes for medical, industrial, and defense purposes.[62] The production of uranium is also strongly linked to ongoing human rights violations.[63]

Even though half of Kalaallit (Greenlanders) are unaware that climate change is human-caused, environmental concerns remain key for their support of mining: to repeat the adage, "Nothing about us without us" especially applies to development involving the land and its resources. Kalaallit are more likely to perceive that climate change is happening compared to their peers in Arctic oil producing countries, and twice as likely to have personally experienced its effects. This lived experience of ecological and environmental degradation structures the government and the population's opinions and policies regarding present and potential mining developments.[64]

While mining is fundamental to the viability of the global energy transition, it is not without environmental and health risks. The expansion of the mines near Kiruna directly threatens the Saami way of life, and livelihoods for the people living there - especially so for reindeer herders. In December 2020, the CERD - the UN Committee on the Elimination of Racial Discrimination - published a legal opinion which concluded that Swedish law discriminates against the Saami; and in 2022, UN advisers urged the Swedish government to not award a license to the British company Beowulf Mining to mine in the Gallok region, similarly citing threats to Saami livelihoods as the mine would generate "large amounts of dust containing heavy metals, and the deposit of toxic waste would impact the environment and water sources."[65] This battle

59, no. 5 (May 2013): 469–71; Committee on Uranium Mining in Virginia, Committee on Earth Resources, and National Research Council, "Potential Human Health Effects of Uranium Mining, Processing, and Reclamation," in Uranium Mining in Virginia: Scientific, Technical, Environmental, Human Health and Safety, and Regulatory Aspects of Uranium Mining and Processing in Virginia (Washington D.C.: National Academies Press (US), 2011), 123–77, https://www.ncbi.nlm.nih.gov/books/NBK201047/.

[62] "Nuclear Fuel Facts: Uranium," Office of Nuclear Energy U.S. Department of Energy, accessed August 20, 2023, https://www.energy.gov/ne/nuclear-fuel-facts-uranium.

[63] Susan Montoya Bryan, "Human Rights Panel to Hear Navajo Uranium Contamination Case," AP News, October 21, 2021, https://apnews.com/article/business-environment-and-nature-new-mexico-united-states-environment-4683af6491673c819814c10297a49c14; Cody Nelson, "'Ignored for 70 Years': Human Rights Group to Investigate Uranium Contamination on Navajo Nation," The Guardian, October 27, 2021, sec. Environment, https://www.theguardian.com/environment/2021/oct/27/human-rights-group-uranium-contamination-navajo-nation.

[64] Bruce C. Forbes and Florian Stammler, "Innovation Exceeds Fear of Climate Change in Greenland," Nature Climate Change 13, no. 7 (July 2023): 603–5, https://doi.org/10.1038/s41558-023-01714-4; Kelton Minor et al., "Experience Exceeds Awareness of Anthropogenic Climate Change in Greenland," Nature Climate Change 13, no. 7 (July 2023): 661–70, https://doi.org/10.1038/s41558-023-01701-9; John Last, "Mining - and Independence - at the Heart of Greenland's Election," CBC News, April 2, 2021, https://www.cbc.ca/news/canada/north/greenland-election-2021-1.5973836.

[65] "UN Advisers Urge Sweden to Stop Mine in Home of Indigenous Sami," Reuters, February 10, 2022, sec. Europe, https://www.reuters.com/world/europe/un-advisers-urge-sweden-stop-mine-home-indigenous-sami-2022-02-10/.

in Gallok has been ongoing since 2006, with some protestors comparing the site to Klondike in reference to the gold rush of 1896-99 to the Klondike river in the Yukon, Canada, where the discovery of gold suddenly attracted over 100,000 prospectors leading to the creation of boomtowns and environmental destruction severely impacting Indigenous peoples in the region in the long run.[66] The Swedish government decided in the end to award the mining license; nine out of 12 Swedish mines are in the North on Saami land – with Kiruna hosting the world's largest iron-ore mine in the world. Yet, similarly to the contentious nature of the oil and gas industry in the Arctic detailed in the first section of this chapter, the development of the mining industry in Northern Sweden is also greatly polarizing with many citing livelihood opportunities reversing or slowing down youth- and brain-drain to the South as a positive effect of the mines. Reindeer herding and reindeers themselves are essential to both the Saami way of life and to the Nordic environment and ecosystems. Mining is a threat to both.[67] Instead of falling into binary opposition between mining on one hand and reindeer herding on the other, the concept of just transition seeks to respond to the potential opposition between sustainable development goals and people's - especially Indigenous - rights. Sustainable development in the Nordic region has been described as green colonialism by Saami scholars and political leaders and activists, especially so by former Saami Parliament President Aili Keskitalo.[68]

The just transition seeks to respond to the ongoing conflicts provoked by the

[66] "'The Klondike of Ore Mining': Fighting for the Sami Way of Life | Indigenous Rights," Al Jazeera, February 20, 2019, sec. In Pictures, https://www.aljazeera.com/gallery/2019/2/20/the-klondike-of-ore-mining-fighting-for-the-sami-way-of-life.

[67] Dorothee Cambou, "Uncovering Injustices in the Green Transition: Sámi Rights in the Development of Wind Energy in Sweden," Arctic Review on Law and Politics 11 (December 9, 2020): 310–33, https://doi.org/10.23865/arctic.v11.2293; Rosie Frost, "What Sweden's Rare Earth Discovery Means for Sámi Communities," Euronews, February 11, 2023, sec. Nature, https://www.euronews.com/green/2023/02/11/mining-europes-biggest-rare-earth-deposit-could-make-life-impossible-for-sami-communities; Anne-Françoise Hivert, "Sweden Struggles to Become a 'Mining Nation,'" Le Monde.Fr, January 3, 2023, sec. International, https://www.lemonde.fr/ en/ international/article/ 2023/ 01/ 03/ sweden-rich-in-natural-resources-struggles-to-become-a-mining-nation_6010103_4.html; Karen McVeigh and Klaus Thymann, "'We Borrow Our Lands from Our Children': Sami Say They Are Paying for Sweden Going Green," The Guardian, August 10, 2022, sec. Global development, https://www.theguardian.com/global-development/2022/aug/10/indigenous-sami-reindeer-herders-sweden-green-transition; Ulf Mörkenstam, "Organised Hypocrisy? The Implementation of the International Indigenous Rights Regime in Sweden," The International Journal of Human Rights 23, no. 10 (November 26, 2019): 1718–41, https://doi.org/10.1080/ 13642987. 2019.1629907.

[68] Eva Maria Fjellheim, "Green Colonialism, Wind Energy and Climate Justice in Sápmi - IWGIA - International Work Group for Indigenous Affairs," IWGIA - DEBATES INDÍGENAS (blog), November 12, 2022, https://www.iwgia.org/en/news/4956-green-colonialism,-wind-energy-and-climate-justice-in-s%C3%A1pmi.html; Susanne Normann, "Green Colonialism in the Nordic Context: Exploring Southern Saami Representations of Wind Energy Development," Journal of Community Psychology 49, no. 1 (January 2021): 77–94, https://doi.org/10.1002/jcop.22422.

continuation of extractive and imperial logics of international intensive development continuously eroding people's voices and rights in the name of 'global'demand - especially so from the Global North to the Global South in a detrimental dynamic for the Global South.[69] The COP26 saw the adoption of the Just Transition Declaration by fourteen governments and the European Commission which pledges to: "Support workers in the transition to new jobs; Support and promote social dialogue and stakeholder engagement; Develop economic strategies that include wider economic and industrial support beyond clean energy; Promote local, inclusive, and decent work; Support for human rights in global supply chains and the importance of building climate resilience; and Report on just transition efforts in biennial transparency reports and NDCs."[70] The concept of just transition has its origin in the global trade unions of the 1980s and primarily focused on the need to promote green jobs. Since then, the term has evolved to unite climate, energy, and environmental justice - potentially even ecological justice in a bid to include the more-than-human - in promoting fairness and equity keeping into account global inequalities.[71]

## Just Transition and Technology Development: Land Rights and Green Colonialism

The development of renewable energies in the Arctic is contentious, continuously oscillating between economic opportunities for some and environmental and livelihood constraints and destruction for others. While mining, as shown above, contains its own set of environmental and social parameters, renewable energy infrastructures themselves bring their own set of social and environmental conflicts as well as opportunities. According to the Qikiqtaaluk Corporation, the for-profit branch of the Qikiqtani Inuit Association, the wind energy project in Sanikiluaq, Nunavut, aims to not only train local inhabitants and provide long-term employment, but it also aims to reduce the 100% dependency on fossil fuels in the municipality.[72] The

---

[69] Darren McCauley and Raphael Heffron, "Just Transition: Integrating Climate, Energy and Environmental Justice," Energy Policy 119 (August 2018): 1–7, https://doi.org/10.1016/j.enpol.2018.04.014; see also Corine Wood-Donnelly, "Responsibility of and for Structural (In)Justice in Arctic Governance," in Arctic Justice: Environment, Society and Governance, ed. Corine Wood-Donnelly and Johanna Ohlsson (Bristol University Press, 2023), 21–35, https://bristoluniversity pressdigital.com/display/book/9781529224832/ch002.xml.

[70] ILO, "COP26: ILO Welcomes COP26 Just Transition Declaration," International Labour Organization, November 5, 2021, https://www.ilo.org/global/about-the-ilo/newsroom/news/ WCMS_826717/lang--en/index.htm.

[71] McCauley and Heffron, "Just Transition."

[72] "Sanikiluaq Wind Energy," Qikiqtaaluk Corporation, accessed August 20, 2023, https://www.qcorp.ca/qc-services/sanikiluaq-wind-energy/.

company in charge of the project, Nunavut Nukkiksautiit Corporation, conducted a survey in 2017 to see the wind potential of the region - the results being promising, Natural Resources Canada is investing $6.5 million out of the $13 million for the wind turbine array. With the proposed 10 small scale turbines of 100kW and 800kW of battery energy storage, the project is set to displace 50% of the diesel used on an annual basis for community electricity generation. The project is shaped through a regional-community ownership model for which the mayor of Sanikiluaq, Johnnie Cookie, voiced his support.[73] However, the project is taking longer to implement, in part, due to difficult administration and communication between the involved actors - between a change in government, and additional time to review the project according to the ministerial standards. The implementation of the independent power producers program (IPPP) by Qulliq Energy Corporation will allow the diversification of energy production from renewable sources to then sell it to QEC to generate electricity for the 25 communities in Nunavut. The implementation has slowed down the development of the wind energy project in Sanikiluaq.[74] The IPPP came into effect in September 2022. This wind energy project comes after the failed turbine wind farms in Cambridge Bay, Kugluktuk and in Rankin Inlet between the late 1990s and 2000; by 2002, all operations were stopped.

Technological advances in the last two decades are now rendering renewable energy production in the Canadian Arctic a possibility - with solar panels having been installed in 2016 in Iqaluit, the capital of Nunavut. The Northwest Territories have a stronger variety of energy sources. 52.8% of the territory's electricity is generated by hydro - 253 GW.h in 2018. The territory also has four wind turbines at the Diavik Diamond Mine, although this energy is reserved for the mine itself. Diesel remains the most common source of energy for remote communities who are not connected to the hydro-based

[73] Canadian Northern Economic Development Agency, "CanNor Invests $300,000 to Expand Sanikiluaq's Multi-Purpose Community Research Centre," news releases, February 2, 2023, https://www.canada.ca/en/northern-economic-development/news/2023/02/cannor-invests-300000-to-expand-sanikiluaqs-multi-purpose-community-research-centre.html; "Sanikiluaq High Displacement Renewable Energy," Natural Resources Canada (Natural Resources Canada, April 6, 2021), https://natural-resources.canada.ca/science-and-data/funding-partnerships/funding opportunities/current-investments/sanikiluaq-high-displacement-renewable-energy/23459;Derek Neary, "$6.5 Million in Federal Funds Move Forward Sanikiluaq Wind Project," Journalistic, Nunavut News, April 13, 2021, https://www.nunavutnews.com/nunavut-news/6-5-million-in-federal-funds-move-forward-sanikiluaq-wind-project/.
[74] David Lochead, "Slow Process on QEC's Renewable Energy Program Was a Setback: Project Director," Nunatsiaq News, September 9, 2022, sec. News, https://nunatsiaq.com/stories/article/slow-process-on-qecs-renewable-energy-program-was-a-setback-project-director/; Alex Ittimangnaq et al., "Independent Power Producer Policy in Nunavut" (Pembina Institute, October 21, 2022), https://www.pembina.org/reports/public-consultation-ipp-qec.pdf.

grid of the territory - in addition, Inuvik relies on a natural gas generator as well as a diesel generator.[75] Despite strong climate constraints during the winter, close to 94% of Yukon's energy is hydro-based.[76] Out of the three Arctic territories in Canada, Nunavut relies the strongest on diesel fuel to fulfill its energy needs.[77] Keeping this in mind, the 2016 offshore oil and gas moratorium and the subsequent 2023 Act also force the continuation of importing diesel rather than producing locally, putting the territory at risk of global supply changes. Across the NWT territorial border, the development of hydroelectric project Site C dam in Northern British Columbia has resulted in ongoing tensions between on the one hand the West Moberly First Nations and the provincial government and BC Hydro on the other. The dam is expected to flood about 5.550 hectares of land and the dam's reservoir will be three times the river's average width, 83 km long.[78] Northern BC has been the site of land contestations and Treat Rights lawsuits where First Nations have sued to protect their right to prior and free informed consent according to the Treaty 8 agreement; the Supreme Court supported the claims and concluded in a landmark ruling in 2021 that the provincial government did infringe on the rights of First Nations as it allowed the development of resource exploitation industries without community consent or approval.[79] In Europe, the development of hydroelectricity, similar to Northern British Columbia, triggered ongoing land disputes between the private sector, the government, and the Saami in Northern Sweden. 80% of large-scale hydroelectric power generation is on Saami lands and its expansion, carried out in the early 20th century, did not take into account Saami interests, a development which caused major constraints on reindeer husbandry and

---

[75] "CER – Canada's Renewable Power – Northwest Territories," June 30, 2022, https://www.cer-rec.gc.ca/en/data-analysis/energy-commodities/electricity/report/canadas-renewable-power/provinces/renewable-power-canada-northwest-territories.html.

[76] "CER – Canada's Renewable Power – Yukon," Canada Energy Regulator, June 30, 2022, https://www.cer-rec.gc.ca/en/data-analysis/energy-commodities/electricity/report/canadas-renewable-power/provinces/renewable-power-canada-yukon.html.

[77] "CER – Canada's Renewable Power – Nunavut," Canada Energy Regulator, June 30, 2022, https://www.cer-rec.gc.ca/en/data-analysis/energy-commodities/electricity/report/canadas-renewable-power/provinces/renewable-power-canada-nunavut.html.

[78] Dirk Meissner, "First Nation Reaches Partial Settlement with Governments, BC Hydro over Site C Dam," CTV News, June 27, 2022, sec. Vancouver, https://bc.ctvnews.ca/first-nation-reaches-partial-settlement-with-governments-bc-hydro-over-site-c-dam-1.5965551.

[79] Giuseppe Amatulli, "What a Landmark Court Victory for B.C. First Nation Means for Indigenous Rights and Resource Development," The Conversation, August 8, 2021, http://theconversation.com/what-a-landmark-court-victory-for-b-c-first-nation-means-for-indigenous-rights-and-resource-development-164892; Matt Simmons, "Blueberry River First Nations Beat B.C. in Court. Now Everything's Changing," The Narwhal, January 25, 2023, https://thenarwhal.ca/blueberry-river-treaty-8-agreements/.

overall land use.[80] Still today, most hydroelectric projects and sites opposed by Saami reindeer herders are licensed by the Swedish state. Despite the ratification of UNDRIP by Sweden in 2007, significant gaps remain in domestic law to recognise Saami self-determination and rights regarding land use - as the case of the Kiruna mine development also shows.[81]

In Russia, the development of renewable energies is confronted by strong infrastructural challenges where decentralization of settlements and lack of existing power grids to some areas render the effective large-scale application of an energy transition impossible at this date.[82] Despite this infrastructural reality, there are currently 17 hydroelectric power plants in the Murmansk region, 2 in Yakutia, and 1 in the Arkhangelsk region; there are also 4 wind power stations in Labytnangi, in the Yamalo-Nenets Autonomous Okrug, in the Chukotka Autonomous Okrug, and in Bykov Mys; as well as solar power plants in the Yamalo-Nenets Autonomous Okrug.[83] While many settlements are located further than 100 km from large urban areas, the connection to a centralized electrical network with a power under 250kW is limited to a maximum of 10km - for higher voltage, the connection to smaller communities is not cost-efficient and is also limited to a 25-75 km range. Due to these limitations, there is currently no federal program to support renewable energy development in the North - notwithstanding the overwhelming economic importance of the gas industry in the region and nationally diminishing the appeal to renewable energy development.[84] Nonetheless, the price of electricity in the North, from 5 to 55 times higher than in the rest of Russia, could encourage the development of local infrastructures. The cost of electricity in the Far North is currently 22-237 ruble per kW.h, whereas the cost of electricity production for solar power plants is on average 9.5 ruble per kW.h and 6.3 ruble per kW.h. for wind

---

[80] Rasmus Kløcker Larsen and Katarina Inga, "Sámi Lands and Hydroelectric Power in Sweden – What's the Potential to Redress Harm and Injustice?," SEI (blog), February 20, 2020, https://www.sei.org/perspectives/sami-lands-and-hydroelectric-power-in-sweden-opportunities-to-redress-injustice/.

[81] Mörkenstam, "Organised Hypocrisy?"; Cambou, "Uncovering Injustices in the Green Transition"; Agnieszka Szpak, "Relocation of Kiruna and Construction of the Markbygden Wind Farm and the Saami Rights," Polar Science 22 (December 1, 2019): 100479, https://doi.org/10.1016/j.polar.2019.09.001.

[82] Viktoriia Brazovskaia, Svetlana Gutman, and Andrey Zaytsev, "Potential Impact of Renewable Energy on the Sustainable Development of Russian Arctic Territories," Energies 14, no. 12 (January 2021): 3691, https://doi.org/10.3390/en14123691; Valentina Ignatyeva and Sébastien Gadal, "Renewable Energy in the Russian Arctic: Energy Transition and Opportunities in the Context of Post-Pandemic Realities," in Energy of the Russian Arctic, ed. Valery I. Salygin (Singapore: Springer, 2022), 411–24; M. O. Morgunova et al., "Renewable Energy in the Russian Arctic: Environmental Challenges, Opportunities and Risks," Journal of Physics: Conference Series 1565, no. 1 (June 2020): 012086, https://doi.org/10.1088/1742-6596/1565/1/012086.

[83] Maria L. Lagutina and Valery N. Konyshev, "Rethinking Russia's Energy Policy in the Arctic," in Energy of the Russian Arctic, ed. Valery I. Salygin (Singapore: Springer, 2022), 109–24.

[84] Morgunova et al., "Renewable Energy in the Russian Arctic."

turbines.[85] While some small power plants use a combination of energies - wind-solar-diesel - these remain hyper-localized in certain villages - the first of such infrastructures was installed in 2014.[86] Industrial development on Nenets territory has, similarly to Norway and Sweden, deeply impacted reindeer migratory routes and has thereby negatively affected reindeer husbandry and overall Nenet culture.[87] Despite Nenet nomads having increased from over 13,000 in 2003 to over 16,000 in 2019 with an almost twofold increase in private reindeer farms, ongoing land pressures from industrialization as well as political pressures from the federal government - often resulting in Nenet activists and organizations to be labeled as "foreign agents" - have resulted in difficult consultation and communication channels between Indigenous representatives and local governments regarding land use and economic development and opportunities.[88]

Continuing the similar theme of strained consultation and communication channels, the ongoing lack of consultation between the private sector, the national government, and Saami representatives and communities in Norway has been described as green colonialism by Former Saami Parliament President Aili Keskitalo, where wind energy development results in the continuation of colonial policy and land and rights losses for Saami communities. Two major projects, in particular, Fosen Vind - encompassing the Storheia and Roan wind farms - and Øyfjellet Vind Park, have triggered lawsuits opposing Saami reindeer herders, the Norwegian government, and the companies Eolus Vind for the Øyfjellet Vind Park and Statkraft, TroenderEnergi, Nordic Wind Power DA, and BKW for Fosen Vind Park. In 2021, the Supreme Court of Norway ruled in favor of the herders and ordered the dismantling of the Fosen Vind Park's two wind farms. The Supreme Court ruling of October 11, 2021, HR-2021-1975-S, invalidated the licenses as "the construction violates Sámi reindeer herders'right to enjoy their own culture" which is protected under Article 27 of the UN

---

[85] Lagutina and Konyshev, "Rethinking Russia's Energy Policy in the Arctic."

[86] Lagutina and Konyshev.

[87] Anna Degteva and Christian Nellemann, "Nenets Migration in the Landscape: Impacts of Industrial Development in Yamal Peninsula, Russia," Pastoralism: Research, Policy and Practice 3, no. 1 (August 7, 2013): 15, https://doi.org/10.1186/2041-7136-3-15.

[88] Trude Pettersen, "Indigenous Peoples' Organization Declared as Foreign Agents," The Independent Barents Observer, January 28, 2016, https://thebarentsobserver.com/en/society/2016/01/indigenous-peoples-organization-fined-law-foreign-agents; Ekaterina Zmyvalova, "Human Rights of Indigenous Small-Numbered Peoples in Russia: Recent Developments," Arctic Review on Law and Politics 11 (December 9, 2020): 334–59, https://doi.org/10.23865/arctic.v11.2336; Magomedov, "'Where Is Our Land?': Challenges for Indigenous Groups in the Russian Arctic | Wilson Center," The Russia File (blog), November 14, 2019, https://www.wilsoncenter.org/blog-post/where-our-land-challenges-for-indigenous-groups-the-russian-arctic.

International Covenant on Civil and Political Rights.[89] The wind farms blocked reindeer herds from migrating and severely disrupted yearly migrations.[90] Both farms, 151 wind turbines, still have to be dismantled but the government did apologize to affected reindeer herders in 2023 in response to the Supreme Court verdict.[91] In 2020, the Saami Council addressed the UN Special Rapporteur on the Rights of Indigenous Peoples to voice concerns regarding the Øyfjellet Vind Park which, in their view, "violates the international human rights conventions and the rights of the Sámi people."[92] The Special Rapporteur José Francisco Cali Tzai replied by highlighting being "particularly disturbed" by the reports indicating "obstruction of the use of legally-protected traditional migration routes [...], the lack of good faith consultations, the failure to obtain free prior and informed consent, and over the significant and irreversible damage the Øyfjellet Wind Park poses to the Sami lands, resources, culture, language and livelihoods."[93] This letter comes after the 2019 letter from the UN High Commissioner for Human Rights which recommended among other measures the protection of Saami rights to land and resources as well preservation of culture by the Norwegian government through revisions of current administrative and legislative mechanisms. In response, the Norwegian investment bank Storebrand, which has invested 16,5 million NOK in Eolus Vind, has placed the company under observation for human

---

[89] Supreme Court of Norway.

[90] Ida Croff, "An Examination of the Norwegian State's Environmental Injustice towards the South Saami: Through the Development of Storheia and Roan Wind Farms on Fosen, in Trøndelag." (Master of Science, Lund, Lunds Universitet, 2022), https://lup.lub.lu.se/luur/ download?func= download File&recordOId=9079362&fileOId=9082480; Henrikke Sæthre Ellingsen, "Resistance to Wind Power Development in Norway: Exploring Power, Knowledge Production and Injustice at Fosen and Frøya." (MSc, Oslo, University of Oslo, 2020), https://www.duo.uio.no/ bitstream/ handle/ 10852/ 84417/5/Resistance-to-Wind-Power-Development-in-Norway---Exploring-Power--Knowledge-Production-and-Injustice-at-Fosen-and-Fr-ya--iiii-pdf.pdf; Øyvind Ravna, "The Fosen Case and the Protection of Sámi Culture in Norway Pursuant to Article 27 Iccpr," International Journal on Minority and Group Rights, 2022, 1–20, https://doi.org/10.1163/15718115-bja10085.

[91] Ministry of Petroleum and Energy, "Norwegian Government Apologises to Sámi Reindeer Herders on the Fosen Peninsula," Nyhet, Government.no (regjeringen.no, March 4, 2023), https://www.regjeringen.no/en/aktuelt/norwegian-government-apologises-to-sami-reindeer-herders-on-the-fosen-peninsula/id2965357/; Saara-Maria Salonen, "A Year after Supreme Court Verdict, Fosen Wind Farm Still Stands amid Soaring Energy Crisis," The Independent Barents Observer, October 12, 2022, https://thebarentsobserver.com/en/indigenous-peoples/2022/10/year-after-supreme-court-verdict-fosen-wind-farm-still-stands-amid.

[92] Piera Heaika Muotka, "The Saami Council Addresses UN Special Rapporteur Regarding Øyfjellet Wind AS," Saami Council, September 18, 2020, https://www.saamicouncil.net/news-archive/the-saami-council-addresses-u-special-rapporteur-regarding-the-oyfjellet-wind.

[93] José Francisco Cali Tzai, "Mandate of the Special Rapporteur on the Rights of Indigenous Peoples," December 30, 2021, https://spcommreports.ohchr.org/TMResultsBase/ DownLoadPublic CommunicationFile?gId=26929.

rights risks.[94] The Fosen Vind Park was supposed to become Europe's largest onshore wind park with a total investment of $1.26 billion – the Storheia wind farm alone, 80 turbines, was estimated to generate 288 MW.[95]

In the name of sustainable development and the energy transition - the Greater Good - Saami rights, and on a wider scale, global Indigenous rights, are to be sacrificed. Sacrificial zones and sacrificial communities go counter the UN Sustainable Development Goals which aim to "leave no one behind."[96] And yet, sustainable development and renewable energy development reproduce colonial exploitative logics of both people and land - where the unwanted noisy minority needs to yield to the demands of the majority who represent the future - anchored in existing dynamics of structural injustice and asymmetrical relations.[97] Green sacrifice zones are now replacing mined and oil and gas blackened sacrifice zones in a normative attempt by governments and other parties to provide moral justification for extensive land development in the name of the greater good. Social acceptability of renewable energy infrastructural development varies depending on use of the electricity produced, location, and where individuals live.[98] New concepts have challenged the tenets of so-called green growth within sustainable development and have called instead to espouse a degrowth or a post-development path.[99] According to these critiques, green

---

[94] Saami Council, "Saami Council Shares Norwegian Investment Bank's Concern for Human Rights Violations in Øyfjellet," August 26, 2022, https://www.saamicouncil.net/news-archive/storebrandoyfjellet.

[95] Statkraft, "Fosen Vind," accessed October 26, 2022, https://www.statkraft.com/about-statkraft/where-we-operate/norway/fosen-vind/.

[96] Anne Karam and Shayan Shokrgozar, "'We Have Been Invaded': Wind Energy Sacrifice Zones in Åfjord Municipality and Their Implications for Norway," Norsk Geografisk Tidsskrift - Norwegian Journal of Geography 77, no. 3 (May 27, 2023): 183–96, https://doi.org/10.1080/00291951.2023.2225068; Åsa Össbo, "Back to Square One. Green Sacrifice Zones in Sápmi and Swedish Policy Responses to Energy Emergencies," Arctic Review on Law and Politics 14 (2023): 112–34; Berit Skorstad, "Sacrifice Zones: A Conceptual Framework for Arctic Justice Studies?," in Arctic Justice: Environment, Society and Governance, ed. Corine Wood-Donnelly and Johanna Ohlsson (Bristol University Press, 2023), 96–108, https://bristol universitypressdigital.com/display/book/9781529224832/ch007.xml.

[97] Wood-Donnelly, "Responsibility of and for Structural (In)Justice in Arctic Governance."

[98] Sigrid Engen, "Small Hydropower, Large Obstacle? Exploring Land Use Conflict, Indigenous Opposition and Acceptance in the Norwegian Arctic," Energy Research & Social Science 95 (January 1, 2023): 102888, https://doi.org/10.1016/j.erss.2022.102888; Sunniva Petersen Jikiun, Michaël Tatham, and Velaug Myrseth Oltedal, "Saved by Hydrogen? The Public Acceptance of Onshore Wind in Norway," Journal of Cleaner Production 408 (July 1, 2023): 1–10, https://doi.org/10.1016/j.jclepro.2023.136956.

[99] Jason Hickel and Giorgos Kallis, "Is Green Growth Possible?," New Political Economy 25, no. 4 (June 6, 2020): 469–86, https://doi.org/10.1080/13563467.2019.1598964; Maria Sandberg, Kristian Klockars, and Kristoffer Wilén, "Green Growth or Degrowth? Assessing the Normative Justifications for Environmental Sustainability and Economic Growth through Critical Social Theory," Journal of Cleaner Production 206 (January 1, 2019): 133–41, https://doi.org/10.1016/j.jclepro.2018.09.175; Ashish Kothari, Federico Demaria, and Alberto Acosta, "Buen Vivir, Degrowth, and Ecological Swaraj: Alternatives to Sustainable Development and Green Economy," Development 57 (December 1, 2015): 57–3, https://doi.org/10.1057/dev.2015.24.

growth as defended by international policy makers is spearheaded by eco-modernist approaches to the climate crisis where technological advances and innovation-based responses are foundations onto which sustainability can be achieved - growth is not challenged but encouraged.[100] Without falling into a zero-sum game framework, critics are instead calling for ethical and social revisions of ways of life counter capitalist accumulation and never-ending growth. Degrowth, however, is difficult to resonate with within an Arctic context. In Northern Canada alone, livelihood opportunities,[101] housing conditions,[102] and access to healthcare and education are challenging and below national averages.[103] Forced departures due to lack of appropriate health care equipment is an ongoing issue, especially for pregnant mothers.[104] Therefore, using the tenets of these theories, a post-development or degrowth approach would call for a re-evaluation of resource exploitation worldwide for the overwhelming benefit of a select few; the oil and gas production in the Russian Arctic for instance is mainly geared towards the international market where Indigenous peoples of the area see minimal long-term benefits from the industry.

## Conclusion

Social licenses for both the renewable energy industry and the fossil fuel industry are complex and multiple, with both sides of the coin existing at the same time within and across communities. The complex web of actors involved in each project, both directly and indirectly, render the decision-making process potentially long and arduous. Additionally, ongoing legal and

---

[100] Sandberg, Klockars, and Wilén, "Green Growth or Degrowth?"; Shayan Shokrgozar, "THE CASE FOR DEGROWTH: ENERGY TECHNOLOGIES," in DEBATES IN POST-DEVELOPMENT AND DEGROWTH: VOLUME 1, ed. Alexander Dunlap, Lisa Hammelbo Søyland, and Shayan Shokrgozar, vol. 1 (Oslo: Tvergastein Journal, 2021), 94–109.

[101] Statistics Canada Government of Canada, "Inuit Participation in the Wage and Land-Based Economies in Inuit Nunangat," Statistics Canada, June 13, 2019, https://www150.statcan.gc.ca/n1/pub/89-653-x/89-653-x2019003-eng.htm.

[102] Nunavut Housing Corporation, "Nunavut Is Facing a Severe Housing Crisis: Compared to the Rest of the Country, Nunavut's Housing Statistics Are Devastating."

[103] Statistics Canada, "Health Fact Sheets: Household Food Insecurity, 2017/2018," June 24, 2020, https://www150.statcan.gc.ca/n1/pub/82-625-x/2020001/article/00001-eng.htm; Moriah Sallaffie et al., "Survey of Nunavut Post-Secondary Students: Determinants of School Completion, Post-Secondary Education, and Education Success," Canadian Journal of Education/Revue Canadienne de l'éducation 44, no. 3 (September 30, 2021): 764–87, https://doi.org/10.53967/cje-rce.v44i3.4709.

[104] Emma Tranter, "Forced to Travel during Pandemic, Nunavut Women Want Birthing Services at Home | CTV News," CTV News, January 10, 2021, https://www.ctvnews.ca/health/forced-to-travel-during-pandemic-nunavut-women-want-birthing-services-at-home-1.5260915?cache=almppngbro%3FclipId%3D89926; Lauren Eggenberger, Sheila Cruz, and Pertice Moffitt, "Dene, Métis and Inuvialuit Peoples' Voices on the Impact of Canada's Perinatal Transport and Non-Medical Escort Policy in Their Communities: An Outcome Assessment Approach and Narrative Literature Review," International Journal of Circumpolar Health 81, no. 1 (2022): 2149061, https://doi.org/10.1080/22423982.2022.2149061.

administrative frameworks can inhibit proper consultation mechanisms often leaving marginalized communities with few appeals or avenues to defend their rights - which in turn crystalizes conflictual dynamics. ESG - Environment, Social, and Governance - aims exactly to de-crystalize ongoing tensions by addressing non-financial factors and potential risks in any development plan.[105] Here, diversity and inclusion are key. Diversity and inclusion, however, have been criticized as well as it does not offer foundational change, only a seat at the table which for some doesn't go far enough to address the wrongdoings of centuries of colonial expropriation.[106] Statistics Canada released an Experimental ESG Dashboard detailing the criteria for evaluating the non-financial performance of some industries, with a particular emphasis on Indigenous rights. These criteria include GHG emission intensity, Energy consumption intensity, Water use intensity, Employment composition, Job quality, Gender wage ratio, Breaches of Privacy, Job Vacancy Rate, Governing body diversity, and Collective bargaining. These criteria and overall factors are considered as priorities for governments, businesses, and international organizations to ensure social support and economic viability of the projects and industries as a whole.[107] While some economics studies have highlighted the various issues in the implementation of the ESG from the point of view of rating disagreement and return volatility, others also criticize the ESG framework as essentially another tool within an eco-modernist, green growth development path.[108]

To highlight these tensions, small nuclear modular reactor (SMR) development and nuclear energy becomes the crux of passionate debates on its ethical and practical implications - both in terms of energy production, radioactive waste production, and its technological risk for nuclear weapon

---

[105] "Environmental Social and Governance (ESG) Investing - OECD," OECD, accessed August 20, 2023, https://www.oecd.org/finance/esg-investing.htm; "Environmental, Social and Governance (ESG) Project," Statistique Canada - Statistics Canada, March 10, 2023, https://www.statcan.gc.ca/ en/ trust/ modernization/esg.

[106] See for instance Eve Tuck and K Wayne Yang, "Decolonization Is Not a Metaphor," Decolonization:, Indigeneity,,Education,&,Society 1, no. 1 (2012): 1–40.

[107] "Environmental, Social and Governance (ESG) Project."

[108] Susanne Arvidsson and John Dumay, "Corporate ESG Reporting Quantity, Quality and Performance: Where to Now for Environmental Policy and Practice?," Business Strategy and the Environment 31, no. 3 (2022): 1091–1110, https://doi.org/10.1002/bse.2937; Doron Avramov et al., "Sustainable Investing with ESG Rating Uncertainty," Journal of Financial Economics 145, no. 2, Part B (August 1, 2022): 642–64, https://doi.org/10.1016/j.jfineco.2021.09.009; Dane M. Christensen, George Serafeim, and Anywhere Sikochi, "Why Is Corporate Virtue in the Eye of The Beholder? The Case of ESG Ratings," The Accounting Review 97, no. 1 (January 1, 2022): 147–75, https://doi.org/10.2308/TAR-2019-0506; Gerhard Halbritter and Gregor Dorfleitner, "The Wages of Social Responsibility — Where Are They? A Critical Review of ESG Investing," Review of Financial Economics 26 (September 1, 2015): 25–35, https://doi.org/10.1016/ j.rfe.2015.03.004; Exner-Pirot, "Overcoming Remoteness: Innovation to Support Development, Critical Minerals, and Security in the Arctic."

proliferation.[109] While some seek to prioritize carbon emission reduction, some highlight the environmental cost of waste storage and the potential disastrous consequences of either an incident or of the development of nuclear weapons thereby rejecting the technology as a whole. SMRs, while on a smaller scale, may offer solutions for off-grid remote communities and offer an alternative for electrical baseline in addition to solar and wind energy, due to their state of infancy, there is no evidence of them functioning in an Arctic environment.[110] However, SMRs still produce waste and while Saskatchewan has been awarded $74 million by Ottawa for SMR development in the province, Canada does not have a permanent waste solution.[111] If the goal is indeed to reduce dependence on gas and oil at all costs, nuclear energy provides an alternative.[112] The question remains of the acceptability of both waste storage - where? - and risks associated with safety in the case of an incident, as well as of the high operating costs.[113] While there is indeed no evidence of the technology functioning in an Arctic environment, so was also the case for renewable energies only a few years ago. Therefore, the technological challenges faced by nuclear energy in the Arctic are not necessarily what constitutes the main crux: the main crux is whether the risks, both security risks and economic risks, associated with nuclear energy are below the potential benefits that the technology might bring to Arctic energy resilience. In other words, what does nuclear energy bring to the table that no other energy source does, and does this unique potential outweigh the potential downsides?

Geoengineering, while a completely different technology, also sparks passionate debates where proponents argue for the development of carbon

---

[109] Martina Igini, "The Advantages and Disadvantages of Nuclear Energy," Earth.Org (blog), January 28, 2023, https://earth.org/the-advantages-and-disadvantages-of-nuclear-energy/.

[110] Heather Exner-Pirot and Jesse McCormick, "Opinion: Small Modular Reactors Represent a Significant Opportunity for First Nations," National Post, July 25, 2023, https://nationalpost.com/opinion/small-modular-reactors-represent-a-significant-opportunity-for-first-nations; Nesheiwat, "Expanding Nuclear Energy to the Arctic: The Potential of Small Modular Reactors," Atlantic Council (blog), July 22, 2021, https://www.atlanticcouncil.org/blogs/energysource/expanding-nuclear-energy-to-the-arctic-the-potential-of-small-modular-reactors/.

[111] Alexander Quon, "Ottawa Announces up to $74M for Small Modular Nuclear Reactor Development in Sask. | CBC News," CBC, August 19, 2023, https://www.cbc.ca/news/canada/saskatchewan/canada-sask-smr-development-nuclear-1.6941609; Christy Climenhaga, "This Is What Nuclear Power Could Look like on the Prairies | CBC News," CBC, May 8, 2023, https://www.cbc.ca/ news/ canada/ edmonton/what-would-nuclear-power-look-like-for-the-prairies-1.6824632.

[112] Mark Lynas, Nuclear 2.0: Why a Green Future Needs Nuclear Power (Cambridge: UIT Cambridge Ltd, 2013).

[113] Jimmy Thomson, "Is Canada Betting Big on Small Nuclear Reactors? Here's What You Need to Know," The Narwhal (blog), January 4, 2021, https://thenarwhal.ca/canada-smr-nuclear-reactors-explained/; Quon, "Ottawa Announces up to $74M for Small Modular Nuclear Reactor Development in Sask. | CBC News"; Jamie Kwong, "The Waters Could Claim Nuclear Weapons," Foreign Policy (blog), July 12, 2023, https://foreignpolicy.com/2023/07/12/nuclear-weapons-climate-change-deterrence/.

capture technology and critics argue that the lack of global understanding of the consequences of the deployment of the technology should trigger the principle of precaution.[114] Geoengineering is split into two categories: carbon geoengineering, or carbon capture technology, which seeks to remove carbon dioxide from the environment to break the link between emissions and concentration, and solar geoengineering which seeks to reflect some fraction of sunlight back into space according to the definitions offered by the Harvard Solar Geoengineering Research Program.[115] The consensus, however, does highlight the need to reduce carbon emissions and the technologies proposed by geoengineering are not final over-encompassing solutions which negate the need for concrete reductions in greenhouse gas emissions.

Thinking of energy and its related issues in the Arctic as a system calls for the better understanding of actor(s)-network(s) dynamics in conjunction with an ever-evolving environment. Energy development and its subsequent issues are thereby in between order and chaos; they are complex within an interconnected set of elements that is organized - coherence is to be seen. However, the Arctic is a dynamic system - a system that evolved in time as opposed to a static system that doesn't evolve in time. The Arctic is interconnected to the global sphere fueled by feedback loops, and it is as complex as the number of variables that composes it. The Arctic has been self-regulating for 4 billion years and recent human perturbations on its dynamics have been putting it out of its equilibrium state. While climate scientists are doing their best with the measurements and data they are collecting and while this data is already showing how temperature changes are destabilizing the Arctic as a system, since we cannot model the Arctic mathematically with accuracy, the full scale and scope of the consequences of this destabilization are unknown and unpredictable. Understanding the social dynamics behind energy issues in the Arctic through the lens of dynamical systems guides the conversation towards a questioning of the state of equilibrium. Post-development approaches to development - economic or social - in the Arctic could thereby argue for a decolonial path towards a re-establishment of equilibrium - a path already strongly advocated for decades

---

[114] Oliver Milman, "Can Geoengineering Fix the Climate? Hundreds of Scientists Say Not so Fast," The Guardian, December 25, 2022, sec. Environment, https://www.theguardian.com/ environment/ 2022/dec/25/can-controversial-geoengineering-fix-climate-crisis; TAI Bookshelf Podcast, "TAI Bookshelf Podcast - Geoengineering and Green Colonialism with Aaron Cooper (#1-2021)," balado, accessed June 9, 2022, https://soundcloud.com/arcticinstitute/tai-bookshelf-podcast-aaron-cooper.

[115] "Geoengineering | Harvard's Solar Geoengineering Research Program," Harvard's Solar Geoengineering Research Programme, 2023, https://geoengineering. environment. harvard.edu/ geoengineering.

by international Indigenous rights defense organizations, communities, and individuals. The point is not to kill with dialogue[116] - through never-ending opaque bureaucratic tools - but to foster structural change. And energy is perhaps where this existential change will play out.

## Bibliography

Acton Peninsula. "National Museum of Australia - Aboriginal Land Rights Act." National Museum Australia. National Museum of Australia; c=AU; o=Commonwealth of Australia; ou=National Museum of Australia, December 8, 2022. https://www.nma.gov.au/defining-moments/resources/aboriginal-land-rights-act.

Afanasiev Vladimir. "World Needs More Gas, Not Less": Novatek Targets Sanction Date for Russia's First CCS Project." *Upstream Online | Latest Oil and Gas News*, March 4, 2021, sec. energy_transition. https://www.upstreamonline.com/energy-transition/world-needs-more-gas-not-less-novatek-targets-sanction-date-for-russias-first-ccs-project/2-1-974343.

Agency, Canadian Northern Economic Development. "CanNor Invests $300,000 to Expand Sanikiluaq's Multi-Purpose Community Research Centre." News releases, February 2, 2023.https://www.canada.ca/en/northern-economic development/news/2023/02/cannor-invests-300000-to-expand-sanikiluaqs-multi-purpose-community-research-centre.html.

*Al Jazeera*. "The Klondike of Ore Mining': Fighting for the Sami Way of Life | Indigenous Rights." February 20, 2019, sec. In Pictures. https://www.aljazeera.com/ gallery/2019/2/20/the-klondike-of-ore-mining-fighting-for-the-sami-way-of-life.

*Al Jazeera*. "The People vs Arctic Oil': Activists Target Norway at ECHR." June 15, 2021, sec. Oil and Gas. https://www.aljazeera.com/news/2021/6/15/the-people-vs-arctic-oil-activists-target-norway-at-echr.

AMAP. "Shipping." Accessed August 14, 2023. https://eua-bca.amap.no/maritime-shipping.

Amatulli Giuseppe. "What a Landmark Court Victory for B.C. First Nation Means for Indigenous Rights and Resource Development." The Conversation, August 8, 2021. http://theconversation.com/what-a-landmark-court-victory-for-b-c-first-nation-means-for-indigenous-rights-and-resource-development-164892.

American Petroleum Institute. "New Analysis: Alaska-Made Natural Gas and Oil Drives U.S. Economic Recovery, Strengthens All Industries," July 20, 2021. https://www.api.org/news-policy-and-issues/news/2021/07/20/alaska-pwc.

Arvidsson Susanne and John Dumay. "Corporate ESG Reporting Quantity, Quality and Performance: Where to Now for Environmental Policy and Practice?" *Business Strategy and the Environment* 31, no. 3 (2022): 1091–1110. https://doi.org/10.1002/bse.2937.

Avramov Doron, Si Cheng, Abraham Lioui, and Andrea Tarelli. "Sustainable Investing with ESG Rating Uncertainty." *Journal of Financial Economics* 145, no. 2, Part B (August 1, 2022): 642–64. https://doi.org/10.1016/j.jfineco.2021.09.009.

---

[116] Eva Maria Fjellheim, "'You Can Kill Us with Dialogue:' Critical Perspectives on Wind Energy Development in a Nordic-Saami Green Colonial Context," Human Rights Review 24, no. 1 (March 2023): 25–51, https://doi.org/10.1007/s12142-023-00678-4.

Baswan Meera. "The Willow Project and Its Impacts on Indigenous Communities." *The Indigenous Foundation* (blog), 2023. https://www.theindigenous foundation.org/articles/the-willow-project-and-its-impacts-on-indigenous-communities.

BBC News. "Norilsk Nickel: Mining Firm Pays Record $2bn Fine over Arctic Oil Spill." March 10, 2021, sec. Europe. https://www.bbc.com/news/world-europe-56350953.

Beaumier Maude C., and James D. Ford. "Food Insecurity among Inuit Women Exacerbated by Socioeconomic Stresses and Climate Change." *Canadian Journal of Public Health* 101, no. 3 (2010): 196–201.

Bendixen Mette, Rasmus Leander Nielsen, Jane Lund Plesner, and Kelton Minor. "Opportunistic Climate Adaptation and Public Support for Sand Extraction in Greenland." *Nature Sustainability* 5, no. 11 (November 2022): 991–99. https://doi.org/10.1038/s41893-022-00922-8.

Bloomberg.com. "Selling Its Alaskan Oil Business Was a Green Win for BP-Not the Planet." April 15, 2021. https://www.bloomberg.com/graphics/2021-tracking-carbon-emissions-BP-hilcorp/.

Borgås Frode, "Soaring Revenues Caused by High Gas Prices." Statistisk sentralbyrå - Statistics Norway, March 6, 2023. https://www.ssb.no/en/offentlig-sektor/offentlig-forvaltning/statistikk/offentlig-forvaltnings-inntekter-og-utgifter/articles-for-general-government-revenue-and-expenditure/soaring-revenues-caused-by-high-gas-prices.

Brazovskaia Viktoriia, Svetlana Gutman, and Andrey Zaytsev. "Potential Impact of Renewable Energy on the Sustainable Development of Russian Arctic Territories." *Energies* 14, no. 12 (January 2021): 3691. https://doi.org/10.3390/en14123691.

Burton Jason. "U.S. Geological Survey Releases 2022 List of Critical Minerals | U.S. Geological Survey." USGS: science for a changing world, February 22, 2022. https://www.usgs.gov/news/national-news-release/us-geological-survey-releases-2022-list-critical-minerals.

Buttler, Morten. "Greenland Bans All Future Oil Exploration Citing Climate Concerns." Time, July 16, 2021. https://time.com/6080933/greenland-bans-oil-exploration/.

Bye Hilde-Gunn. "Alaska Oil and Gas Jobs Hit Hard During the Pandemic." *High North News*, November 17, 2020. https://www.highnorthnews.com/en/alaska-oil-and-gas-jobs-hit-hard-during-pandemic.

High North News, "Europe's Largest Deposit of Rare Earth Metals Found in Northern Sweden." *High North News*, January 13, 2023, sec. Business. https://www.highnorth news.com/en/europes-largest-deposit-rare-earth-metals-found-northern-sweden.

Bykova Alina, and Pavel Sulyandziga. "A Year after Arctic Fuel Spill, Norilsk Nickel Continues to Ignore Indigenous Critics." The Barents Observer, May 29, 2021. https://thebarentsobserver.com/en/opinions/2021/05/one-year-after-massive-arctic-fuel-spill-norilsk-nickel-continues-ignore-indigenous#.YLJrHKuyEsQ.twitter.

Cali Tzai, José Francisco. "Mandate of the Special Rapporteur on the Rights of Indigenous Peoples," December 30, 2021. https://spcommreports.ohchr.org/TMResultsBase/DownLoadPublicCommunicationFile?gId=26929.

Cambou Dorothee. "Uncovering Injustices in the Green Transition: Sámi Rights in the Development of Wind Energy in Sweden." *Arctic Review on Law and Politics* 11 (December 9, 2020): 310–33. https://doi.org/10.23865/arctic.v11.2293.

Canada Energy Regulator. "CER – Canada's Renewable Power – Nunavut," June 30,

2022. https://www.cer-rec.gc.ca/en/data-analysis/energy-commodities/ electricity/ report/canadas-renewable-power/provinces/renewable-power-canada-nunavut.html.

Canada Energy Regulator. "CER – Canada's Renewable Power – Yukon," June 30, 2022. https://www.cer-rec.gc.ca/en/data-analysis/energy-commodities/electricity/report/canadas-renewable-power/provinces/renewable-power-canada-yukon.html.

Canada, Natural Resources. "Rare Earth Elements Facts." Government of Canada - Natural Resources Canada. Natural Resources Canada, February 14, 2023. https://natural-resources.canada.ca/our-natural-resources/minerals-mining/minerals-metals-facts/rare-earth-elements-facts/20522.

Canny Anna. "Juneau's Worst Glacial Outburst Flood Destroys Homes and Displaces Residents." *Alaska Public Media*, August 7, 2023. https://alaskapublic.org/2023/08/07/juneaus-worst-glacial-outburst-flood-destroys-homes-and-displaces-residents/.

"CER – Canada's Renewable Power – Northwest Territories," June 30, 2022. https://www.cer-rec.gc.ca/en/data-analysis/energy-commodities/electricity/report/canadas-renewable-power/provinces/renewable-power-canada-northwest-territories.html.

Christensen Dane M., George Serafeim and Anywhere Sikochi. "Why Is Corporate Virtue in the Eye of The Beholder? The Case of ESG Ratings." *The Accounting Review* 97, no. 1 (January 1, 2022): 147–75. https://doi.org/10.2308/TAR-2019-0506.

Cimellaro, Matteo. "Shipping Frenzy Threatens Indigenous Food Security." *Canada's National Observer*, July 13, 2023, sec. News. https://www.nationalobserver.com/2023/07/13/news/shipping-frenzy-threatens-indigenous-food-security.

Clean Arctic Alliance. "Black Carbon in the Arctic." Accessed August 14, 2023. https://cleanarctic.org/campaigns/the-arctic-climate-crisis/black-carbon-in-the-arctic/.

Clean Arctic Alliance. "LNG: The Threat to the Arctic from Liquified Natural Gas as a Shipping Fuel." Accessed August 14, 2023. https://cleanarctic.org/campaigns/the-arctic-climate-crisis/lng-the-threat-to-the-arctic-from-liquified-natural-gas-as-a-shipping-fuel/.

Climenhaga Christy. "This Is What Nuclear Power Could Look like on the Prairies | CBC News." CBC, May 8, 2023. https://www.cbc.ca/news/canada/edmonton/what-would-nuclear-power-look-like-for-the-prairies-1.6824632.

ConocoPhillips Alaska. "Greater Prudhoe Bay." Accessed September 5, 2023. https://alaska.conocophillips.com/who-we-are/alaska-operations/greater-prudhoe-bay/.

Croff Ida. "An Examination of the Norwegian State's Environmental Injustice towards the South Saami: Through the Development of Storheia and Roan Wind Farms on Fosen, in Trøndelag." Master of Science, Lunds Universitet, 2022. https://lup.lub.lu.se/luur/download?func=downloadFile&recordOId=9079362&fileOId=9082480.

Dalman Axel. "Carbon Budgets: Where Are We Now?" Carbon Tracker Initiative, May 11, 2020. https://carbontracker.org/carbon-budgets-where-are-we-now/.

Degteva Anna, and Christian Nellemann. "Nenets Migration in the Landscape: Impacts of Industrial Development in Yamal Peninsula, Russia." *Pastoralism: Research, Policy and Practice* 3, no. 1 (August 7, 2013): 15. https://doi.org/10.1186/2041-7136-3-15.

Dewar Dale, Linda Harvey, and Cathy Vakil. "Uranium Mining and Health." *Canadian Family Physician* 59, no. 5 (May 2013): 469–71.

Donella H. Meadows, "Thinking in Systems", Edited by Diana Wright, Sustainability Institute, First published by Earthscan in the UK in 2009, https://research.fit.edu/media/site-specific/researchfitedu/coast-climate-adaptation-library/climate-communications/psychology-amp-behavior/Meadows-2008.-Thinking-in-Systems.pdf.

Eggenberger Lauren, Sheila Cruz and Pertice Moffitt. "Dene, Métis and Inuvialuit Peoples'Voices on the Impact of Canada's Perinatal Transport and Non-Medical Escort Policy in Their Communities: An Outcome Assessment Approach and Narrative Literature Review." *International Journal of Circumpolar Health* 81, no. 1 (2022): 2149061. https://doi.org/10.1080/22423982.2022.2149061.

Ellingsen Henrikke Sæthre. "Resistance to Wind Power Development in Norway: Exploring Power, Knowledge Production and Injustice at Fosen and Frøya." MSc, University of Oslo, 2020. https://www.duo.uio.no/bitstream/ handle/10852/ 84417/5/Resistance-to-Wind-Power-Development-in-Norway---Exploring-Power--Knowledge-Production-and-Injustice-at-Fosen-and-Fr-ya--iiii-pdf.pdf.

Engen Sigrid. "Small Hydropower, Large Obstacle? Exploring Land Use Conflict, Indigenous Opposition and Acceptance in the Norwegian Arctic." *Energy Research & Social Science* 95 (January 1, 2023): 102888. https://doi.org/10.1016/ j.erss. 2022. 102888.

ERMA. "European Raw Materials Alliance Contributes to Europe's Industrial Resilience." European Raw Materials Alliance, February 23, 2021. https://erma.eu/european-raw-materials-alliance-contributes-to-europes-industrial-resilience/.

*euronews.* "Willow Project: Could Two Lawsuits Block the Oil Project in Alaska?" March 14, 2023. https://www.euronews.com/green/2023/03/14/biden-administration-approves-alaskas-willow-oil-project-sparking-anger-from-environmental.

European Commission. "Critical Raw Materials," 2023. https://single-market-economy.ec.europa.eu/sectors/raw-materials/areas-specific-interest/critical-raw-materials_en.

European Council - Council of the European Union. "An EU Critical Raw Materials Act for the Future of EU Supply Chains," August 18, 2023. https://www.consilium. europa.eu/en/infographics/critical-raw-materials/.

Exner-Pirot, Heather. "Overcoming Remoteness: Innovation to Support Development, Critical Minerals, and Security in the Arctic." Macdonald Laurier Institute, 2023.

Exner-Pirot, Heather, and Jesse McCormick. "Opinion: Small Modular Reactors Represent a Significant Opportunity for First Nations." *National Post*, July 25, 2023. https://nationalpost.com/opinion/small-modular-reactors-represent-a-significant-opportunity-for-first-nations.

Fawcett-Atkinson, Marc. "Food Prices in the North Are Astronomical, despite Subsidies. Who Benefits from Ottawa's Plan to Tackle Food Insecurity?" *Canada's National Observer*, March 23, 2023, sec. News. https://www.nationalobserver.com/ 2023/ 03/ 23/news/food-prices-north-are-astronomical-despite-subsidies.

Fjellheim, Eva Maria. "Green Colonialism, Wind Energy and Climate Justice in Sápmi - IWGIA - International Work Group for Indigenous Affairs." *IWGIA - DEBATES INDÍGENAS* (blog), November 12, 2022. https://www.iwgia.org/en/news/4956-green-colonialism,-wind-energy-and-climate-justice-in-s%C3%A1pmi.html.

Eva Maria, Fjellheim, "You Can Kill Us with Dialogue: Critical Perspectives on Wind Energy Development in a Nordic-Saami Green Colonial Context." *Human Rights Review* 24, no. 1 (March 2023): 25–51. https://doi.org/10.1007/s12142-023-00678-4.

Forbes Bruce C. and Florian Stammler. "Innovation Exceeds Fear of Climate Change in Greenland." *Nature Climate Change* 13, no. 7 (July 2023): 603–5. https://doi.org/10.1038/s41558-023-01714-4.

Frost Rosie. "What Sweden's Rare Earth Discovery Means for Sámi Communities." *Euronews*, February 11, 2023, sec. Nature. https://www.euronews.com/green/2023/02/11/mining-europes-biggest-rare-earth-deposit-could-make-life-impossible-for-sami-communities.

Garside M. "Critical Raw Materials: EU Supply by Mineral & Nation 2020." Statista, December 10, 2021. https://www.statista.com/statistics/1270641/critical-raw-material-supply-in-the-european-union-by-supplier-nation/.

Gerretsen Isabelle. "Methane Emissions from Russian Pipelines Surged during the Coronavirus Pandemic." *Climate Home News*, March 4, 2021. https://climatechangenews.com/2021/03/04/methane-emissions-russian-pipelines-surged-coronavirus-pandemic/.

Gordon Noah. "The Willow Project and the Race to Pump the 'Last Barrel'of Oil." *Carnegie Endowment for International Peace* (blog), March 16, 2023. https://carnegieendowment.org/2023/03/16/willow-project-and-race-to-pump-last-barrel-of-oil-pub-89298.

Government of Canada. "Order Prohibiting Certain Activities in Arctic Offshore Waters, 2022, Pursuant to the Canada Petroleum Resources Act." Legislation and regulations, March 11, 2022. https://www.rcaanc-cirnac.gc.ca/eng/1647022447627/ 1647022 66 8724?wbdisable=true.

Government of Canada, Canada Energy Regulator. "CER – Provincial and Territorial Energy Profiles – Northwest Territories," June 9, 2023. https://www.cer-rec.gc.ca/en/data-analysis/energy-markets/provincial-territorial-energy-profiles/provincial-territorial-energy-profiles-northwest-territories.html.

———. "CER – Provincial and Territorial Energy Profiles – Nunavut," June 9, 2023. https://www.cer-rec.gc.ca/en/data-analysis/energy-markets/provincial-territorial-energy-profiles/provincial-territorial-energy-profiles-nunavut.html.

———. "CER – Provincial and Territorial Energy Profiles – Yukon," June 9, 2023. https://www.cer-rec.gc.ca/en/data-analysis/energy-markets/provincial-territorial-energy-profiles/provincial-territorial-energy-profiles-yukon.html.

Government of Canada, Statistics Canada. "Inuit Participation in the Wage and Land-Based Economies in Inuit Nunangat." Statistics Canada, June 13, 2019. https://www150.statcan.gc.ca/n1/pub/89-653-x/89-653-x2019003-eng.htm.

Government of Northwest Territories. "Oil & Gas." Information. Government of the Northwest Territories. Accessed August 14, 2023. https://www.iti.gov.nt.ca/en/oil-gas.

Government of Nunavut: Department of Economic Development and Transportation.

"Petroleum Resources in Nunavut," 2017. https://www.gov.nu.ca/ sites/ default/files/2017_petroleum_brochure_eng_0.pdf.

Gronholt-Pedersen, Jacob. "Greenland Bans Uranium Mining, Halting Rare Earths Project | Reuters." *Reuters*, November 10, 2021, sec. Americas. https://www.reuters. com/world/americas/greenland-bans-uranium-mining-halting-rare-earths-project-2021-11-10/.

Halbritter Gerhard and Gregor Dorfleitner. "The Wages of Social Responsibility — Where Are They? A Critical Review of ESG Investing." *Review of Financial Economics* 26 (September 1, 2015): 25–35. https://doi.org/10.1016/j.rfe.2015.03.004.

Harvard's Solar Geoengineering Research Programme. "Geoengineering | Harvard's Solar Geoengineering Research Program," 2023. https://geoengineering. environment.harvard.edu/geoengineering.

Heaika Muotka Piera. "The Saami Council Addresses UN Special Rapporteur Regarding Øyfjellet Wind AS." Saami Council, September 18, 2020. https://www.saamicouncil. net/news-archive/the-saami-council-addresses-u-special-rapporteur-regarding-the-oyfjellet-wind.

Hickel Jason and Giorgos Kallis. "Is Green Growth Possible?" *New Political Economy* 25, no. 4 (June 6, 2020): 469–86. https://doi.org/10.1080/13563467.2019.1598964.

Hivert Anne-Françoise. "Sweden Struggles to Become a 'Mining Nation.'" *Le Monde.Fr*, January 3, 2023, sec. International. https://www.lemonde.fr/en/international/ article/2023/01/03/sweden-rich-in-natural-resources-struggles-to-become-a-mining-nation_6010103_4.html.

Humpert Malte. "EU Received 300 Shipments of LNG from Russia Since Beginning of Ukraine War." *High North News*, June 22, 2023. https://www.highnorthnews.com/ en/eu-received-300-shipments-lng-russia-beginning-ukraine-war.

———. "Russia Drawing Up Plans to Send Arctic Crude Oil on Non-Ice Class Tankers to Asia." *High North News*, April 11, 2023. https://www.highnorthnews.com/ en/russia-drawing-plans-send-arctic-crude-oil-non-ice-class-tankers-asia.

———. "Russian Crude Oil Now Flowing To China Via Arctic Ocean." *High North News*, August 3, 2023. https://www.highnorthnews.com/en/russian-crude-oil-now-flowing-china-arctic-ocean.

———. "Russian Oil Shipments Via Arctic Accelerate With Four More Tankers Now En Route to China." *High North News*, August 10, 2023. https://www.highnorthnews.com/en/russian-oil-shipments-arctic-accelerate-four-more-tankers-now-en-route-china.

IEA. "Critical Minerals – The Role of Critical Minerals in Clean Energy Transitions." Accessed August 20, 2023. https://www.iea.org/topics/critical-minerals.

IEA. "Energy Fact Sheet: Why Does Russian Oil and Gas Matter? – Analysis." IEA, March 21, 2022. https://www.iea.org/articles/energy-fact-sheet-why-does-russian-oil-and-gas-matter.

IEA. "Mineral Requirements for Clean Energy Transitions – The Role of Critical Minerals in Clean Energy Transitions – Analysis." Accessed August 20, 2023. https://www.iea.org/reports/the-role-of-critical-minerals-in-clean-energy-transitions/mineral-requirements-for-clean-energy-transitions.

IEA. "Overview – Global Methane Tracker 2022 – Analysis," 2022. https://www.iea.org/reports/global-methane-tracker-2022/overview.

Igini Martina. "The Advantages and Disadvantages of Nuclear Energy." *Earth.Org* (blog), January 28, 2023. https://earth.org/the-advantages-and-disadvantages-of-nuclear-energy/.

Ignatyeva Valentina and Sébastien Gadal. "Renewable Energy in the Russian Arctic: Energy Transition and Opportunities in the Context of Post-Pandemic Realities." In *Energy of the Russian Arctic*, edited by Valery I. Salygin, 411–24. Singapore: Springer, 2022.

ILO. "COP26: ILO Welcomes COP26 Just Transition Declaration." International Labour Organization, November 5, 2021. https://www.ilo.org/global/about-the-ilo/newsroom/news/WCMS_826717/lang--en/index.htm.

Ittimangnaq Alex, Dave Lovekin, Katarina Savic, and Emily He. "Independent Power Producer Policy in Nunavut." Pembina Institute, October 21, 2022. https://www.pembina.org/reports/public-consultation-ipp-qec.pdf.

IWGIA - International Work Group for Indigenous Affairs. "Russian Oil Spill Exposes History of Indigenous Peoples'Rights Violations," June 23, 2020. https://www.iwgia. org/en/news/3790-russian-oil-spill-exposes-history-of-indigenous-peoples%E2%80%99-right-violations.html.

IWGIA - International Work Group for Indigenous Affairs. "Russia's Indigenous Peoples Call for International Support to Save the Arctic," October 29, 2021. https://www.iwgia.org/en/news/4553-russia-indigenous-peoples-international-support-save-arctic.html.

Jikiun Sunniva Petersen, Michaël Tatham and Velaug Myrseth Oltedal. "Saved by Hydrogen? The Public Acceptance of Onshore Wind in Norway." *Journal of Cleaner Production* 408 (July 1, 2023): 1–10. https://doi.org/10.1016/j.jclepro.2023.136956.

Karam Anne and Shayan Shokrgozar. "'We Have Been Invaded': Wind Energy Sacrifice Zones in Åfjord Municipality and Their Implications for Norway." *Norsk Geografisk Tidsskrift - Norwegian Journal of Geography* 77, no. 3 (May 27, 2023): 183–96. https://doi.org/10.1080/00291951.2023.2225068.

Kløcker Larsen Rasmus and Katarina Inga. "Sámi Lands and Hydroelectric Power in Sweden – What's the Potential to Redress Harm and Injustice?" *SEI* (blog), February 20, 2020. https://www.sei.org/perspectives/sami-lands-and-hydroelectric-power-in-sweden-opportunities-to-redress-injustice/.

Kløve Keiding Jakob. "Great Potential for Critical Raw Materials in Greenland." *Geological Survey of Denmark and Greenland* (blog). Accessed August 20, 2023. https://eng.geus.dk/about/news/news-archive/2023/june/great-potential-for-critical-raw-materials-in-greenland.

Kothari Ashish, Federico Demaria, and Alberto Acosta. "Buen Vivir, Degrowth, and Ecological Swaraj: Alternatives to Sustainable Development and Green Economy." *Development* 57 (December 1, 2015): 57–3. https://doi.org/10.1057/dev.2015.24.

Kwong Jamie. "The Waters Could Claim Nuclear Weapons." *Foreign Policy* (blog), July 12, 2023. https://foreignpolicy.com/2023/07/12/nuclear-weapons-climate-change-deterrence/.

Lagutina Maria L. and Valery N. Konyshev. "Rethinking Russia's Energy Policy in the Arctic." In *Energy of the Russian Arctic*, edited by Valery I. Salygin, 109–24. Singapore: Springer, 2022.

Last John. "Indigenous Groups Paying the Price for Russia's Massive Arctic Fuel Spill |

CBC News." *CBC News*, July 13, 2020. https://www.cbc.ca/news/ canada/north/ norilsk-nickel-russian-fuel-spill-consequences-1.5645408.

———. "Mining - and Independence - at the Heart of Greenland's Election." *CBC News*, April 2, 2021. https://www.cbc.ca/news/canada/north/greenland-election-2021-1.5973836.

Libell Henrik Pryser and Derrick Bryson Taylor. "Norway's Supreme Court Makes Way for More Arctic Drilling." *The New York Times*, December 22, 2020, sec. World. https://www.nytimes.com/2020/12/22/world/europe/norway-supreme-court-oil-climate-change.html.

LKAB. "Europe's Largest Deposit of Rare Earth Metals Is Located in the Kiruna Area," February 12, 2023. https://lkab.com/en/press/europes-largest-deposit-of-rare-earth-metals-is-located-in-the-kiruna-area/.

Lochead David. "Slow Process on QEC's Renewable Energy Program Was a Setback: Project Director." *Nunatsiaq News*, September 9, 2022, sec. News. https://nunatsiaq.com/stories/article/slow-process-on-qecs-renewable-energy-program-was-a-setback-project-director/.

Lynas Mark. *Nuclear 2.0: Why a Green Future Needs Nuclear Power.* Cambridge: UIT Cambridge Ltd, 2013.

Magomedov. "'Where Is Our Land?': Challenges for Indigenous Groups in the Russian Arctic | Wilson Center." *The Russia File* (blog), November 14, 2019. https://www.wilsoncenter.org/blog-post/where-our-land-challenges-for-indigenous-groups-the-russian-arctic.

McCauley Darren and Raphael Heffron. "Just Transition: Integrating Climate, Energy and Environmental Justice." *Energy Policy* 119 (August 2018): 1–7. https://doi.org/10.1016/j.enpol.2018.04.014.

McVeigh Karen and Klaus Thymann. "'We Borrow Our Lands from Our Children': Sami Say They Are Paying for Sweden Going Green." *The Guardian*, August 10, 2022, sec. Global development. https://www.theguardian.com/global-development/ 2022/ aug/10/indigenous-sami-reindeer-herders-sweden-green-transition.

Meissner Dirk. "First Nation Reaches Partial Settlement with Governments, BC Hydro over Site C Dam." *CTV News*, June 27, 2022, sec. Vancouver. https://bc.ctvnews.ca/first-nation-reaches-partial-settlement-with-governments-bc-hydro-over-site-c-dam-1.5965551.

Mercator Research Institute on Global Commons and Climate Change. "Remaining Carbon Budget - Mercator Research Institute on Global Commons and Climate Change (MCC)." Accessed August 14, 2023. https://www.mcc-berlin.net/en/research/co2-budget.html.

Milman Oliver. "Can Geoengineering Fix the Climate? Hundreds of Scientists Say Not so Fast." *The Guardian*, December 25, 2022, sec. Environment. https://www.theguardian.com/environment/2022/dec/25/can-controversial-geoengineering-fix-climate-crisis.

Mineral Resources Authority - Naalakkersuisut. "Geological Data." Accessed August 20, 2023. http://https%253A%252F%252Fgovmin.gl%252Fexploration-prospecting % 252Fget-an-exploration-licence%252Fgeological-data%252F.

"Mining for Clean Energy: How the Global Rise of Solar Power Will Drive Demand for Canadian Metals and Minerals." Vancouver: Clean Energy Canada, June 2017.

https://cleanenergycanada.org/wp-content/uploads/2017/06/MiningCleanEnergy2017.pdf.

Mining Inspectorate of Sweden. "Mines in Sweden," February 23, 2021. https://www.sgu.se/en/mining-inspectorate/mines/mines-in-sweden/.

Ministry of Petroleum and Energy. "Norwegian Government Apologises to Sámi Reindeer Herders on the Fosen Peninsula." Nyhet. Government.no. regjeringen.no, March 4, 2023. https://www.regjeringen.no/en/aktuelt/norwegian-government-apologises-to-sami-reindeer-herders-on-the-fosen-peninsula/id2965357/.

Minor Kelton, Manumina Lund Jensen, Lawrence Hamilton, Mette Bendixen, David Dreyer Lassen and Minik T. Rosing. "Experience Exceeds Awareness of Anthropogenic Climate Change in Greenland." *Nature Climate Change* 13, no. 7 (July 2023): 661–70. https://doi.org/10.1038/s41558-023-01701-9.

Montoya Bryan, Susan. "Human Rights Panel to Hear Navajo Uranium Contamination Case." *AP News*, October 21, 2021. https://apnews.com/article/business-environment-and-nature-new-mexico-united-states-environment-4683af6491673c819814c10297a49c14.

Morgunova, M. O., D. A. Solovyev, L. V. Nefedova, and T. S. Gabderakhmanova. "Renewable Energy in the Russian Arctic: Environmental Challenges, Opportunities and Risks." *Journal of Physics: Conference Series* 1565, no. 1 (June 2020): 012086. https://doi.org/10.1088/1742-6596/1565/1/012086.

Mörkenstam, Ulf. "Organised Hypocrisy? The Implementation of the International Indigenous Rights Regime in Sweden." *The International Journal of Human Rights* 23, no. 10 (November 26, 2019): 1718–41. https://doi.org/10.1080/ 13642987. 2019.1629907.

Natural Resources Canada. "Sanikiluaq High Displacement Renewable Energy." Natural Resources Canada, April 6, 2021. https://natural-resources.canada.ca/science-and-data/funding-partnerships/funding-opportunities/current-investments/sanikiluaq-high-displacement-renewable-energy/23459.

Neary, Derek. "$6.5 Million in Federal Funds Move Forward Sanikiluaq Wind Project." Journalistic. Nunavut News, April 13, 2021. https://www.nunavutnews.com/ nunavut-news/6-5-million-in-federal-funds-move-forward-sanikiluaq-wind-project/.

Nelson, Cody. "'Ignored for 70 Years': Human Rights Group to Investigate Uranium Contamination on Navajo Nation." *The Guardian*, October 27, 2021, sec. Environment. https://www.theguardian.com/environment/2021/oct/27/human-rights-group-uranium-contamination-navajo-nation.

Nesheiwat. "Expanding Nuclear Energy to the Arctic: The Potential of Small Modular Reactors." *Atlantic Council* (blog), July 22, 2021. https://www.atlanticcouncil.org/ blogs/energysource/expanding-nuclear-energy-to-the-arctic-the-potential-of-small-modular-reactors/.

Nilsen, Ella. "The Willow Project Has Been Approved. Here's What to Know about the Controversial Oil-Drilling Venture | CNN Politics." *CNN*, March 14, 2023. https://www.cnn.com/2023/03/14/politics/willow-project-oil-alaska-explained-climate/index.html.

Nilsen Thomas. "Nornickel Has Changed Positively, Says Taimyr Indigenous Group." *The Independent Barents Observer*, May 16, 2021. https://thebarentsobserver.com/

en/indigenous-peoples/2021/05/taimyr-indigenous-group-says-norilsk-nickel-changing-positively.

Normann Susanne. "Green Colonialism in the Nordic Context: Exploring Southern Saami Representations of Wind Energy Development." *Journal of Community Psychology* 49, no. 1 (January 2021): 77–94. https://doi.org/10.1002/jcop.22422.

Nunatsiaq News. "Indigenous Statement Calls for Arctic Oil Development Moratorium," May 14, 2013. https://nunatsiaq.com/stories/article/65674indigenous_statement_calls_for_ban_on_all_arctic_oil_development/.

Nunavut Housing Corporation. "Nunavut Is Facing a Severe Housing Crisis: Compared to the Rest of the Country, Nunavut's Housing Statistics Are Devastating." Presented at the Nunavut Housing Corporation's Appearance before the Standing Senate Committee on Aboriginal Peoples, March 23, 2016.

OEC - The Observatory of Economic Complexity. "Crude Petroleum in Australia | OEC," 2021. https://oec.world/en/profile/bilateral-product/crude-petroleum/reporter/aus.

OECD. "Environmental Social and Governance (ESG) Investing - OECD." Accessed August 20, 2023. https://www.oecd.org/finance/esg-investing.htm.

Office of Nuclear Energy U.S. Department of Energy. "Nuclear Fuel Facts: Uranium." Accessed August 20, 2023. https://www.energy.gov/ne/nuclear-fuel-facts-uranium.

Olsen, Julia, Natalie Ann Carter, and Jackie Dawson. "Community Perspectives on the Environmental Impacts of Arctic Shipping: Case Studies from Russia, Norway and Canada." Edited by Willem Coetzee. *Cogent Social Sciences* 5, no. 1 (January 1, 2019): 1609189. https://doi.org/10.1080/23311886.2019.1609189.

Össbo, Åsa. "Back to Square One. Green Sacrifice Zones in Sápmi and Swedish Policy Responses to Energy Emergencies." *Arctic Review on Law and Politics* 14 (2023): 112–34.

Paraskova, Tsvetana. "China's Imports Of Russian Crude Oil Hit A Record High." *OilPrice.Com*, June 20, 2023. https://oilprice.com/Latest-Energy-News/World-News/Chinas-Imports-Of-Russian-Crude-Oil-Hit-A-Record-High.html.

Pengelly, Martin. "Trump Confirms He Is Considering Attempt to Buy Greenland." *The Guardian*, August 18, 2019, sec. World news. https://www.theguardian.com/world/2019/aug/18/trump-considering-buying-greenland.

Pepa, Yasmina. "NWT and Nunavut Premiers React to Federal Announcement of Arctic Oil and Gas Moratorium." Gouvernemental. Government of Northwest Territories, December 22, 2016. https://www.gov.nt.ca/newsroom/nwt-and-nunavut-premiers-react-federal-announcement-arctic-oil-and-gas-moratorium.

Pettersen, Trude. "Indigenous Peoples'Organization Declared as Foreign Agents." *The Independent Barents Observer*, January 28, 2016. https://thebarentsobserver.com/ en/society/2016/01/indigenous-peoples-organization-fined-law-foreign-agents.

Qikiqtaaluk Corporation. "Sanikiluaq Wind Energy." Accessed August 20, 2023. https://www.qcorp.ca/qc-services/sanikiluaq-wind-energy/.

Quinn, Eilís. "Arctic Canadian Community Says Oil Moratorium Renewal Doesn't Go Far Enough – Eye on the Arctic." *Eye On The Arctic*, February 13, 2023. https://www.rcinet.ca/eye-on-the-arctic/2023/02/13/arctic-canadian-community-says-oil-moratorium-renewal-doesnt-go-far-enough/.

Quon, Alexander. "Ottawa Announces up to $74M for Small Modular Nuclear Reactor Development in Sask. | CBC News." *CBC*, August 19, 2023. https://www.cbc.ca/news/canada/saskatchewan/canada-sask-smr-development-nuclear-1.6941609.

Rantanen, Mika, Alexey Yu Karpechko, Antti Lipponen, Kalle Nordling, Otto Hyvärinen, Kimmo Ruosteenoja, Timo Vihma, and Ari Laaksonen. "The Arctic Has Warmed Nearly Four Times Faster than the Globe since 1979." *Communications Earth & Environment* 3, no. 1 (August 11, 2022): 1–10. https://doi.org/10.1038/s43247-022-00498-3.

Ravna, Øyvind. "The Fosen Case and the Protection of Sámi Culture in Norway Pursuant to Article 27 Iccpr." *International Journal on Minority and Group Rights*, 2022, 1–20. https://doi.org/10.1163/15718115-bja10085.

Reuters. "Norway Awards 47 Oil and Gas Exploration Permits." *ArcticToday* (blog), January 10, 2023. https://www.arctictoday.com/norway-awards-47-oil-and-gas-exploration-permits/.

*Reuters.* "Norway's Oil and Gas Tax Revenue Soars to Record $89 Bln." January 26, 2023, sec. Energy. https://www.reuters.com/business/energy/norways-oil-gas-tax-revenue-soars-record-89-bln-2023-01-26/.

*Reuters.* "UN Adopts Ban on Heavy Fuel Oil Use by Ships in Arctic." June 17, 2021, sec. Energy. https://www.reuters.com/business/energy/un-adopts-ban-heavy-fuel-oil-use-by-ships-arctic-2021-06-17/.

*Reuters.* "UN Advisers Urge Sweden to Stop Mine in Home of Indigenous Sami." February 10, 2022, sec. Europe. https://www.reuters.com/world/europe/un-advisers-urge-sweden-stop-mine-home-indigenous-sami-2022-02-10/.

Rosa, Diogo, Per Kalvig, Henrik Stendal, and Jakob Kløve Keiding. "Review of the Critical Raw Material Resource Potential in Greenland." Copenhagen: Center for Minerals and Materials: Geological Survey of Denmark and Greenland, May 2023.

Saami Council. "Saami Council Shares Norwegian Investment Bank's Concern for Human Rights Violations in Øyfjellet," August 26, 2022. https://www.saamicouncil.net/news-archive/storebrandoyfjellet.

Sallaffie, Moriah, Maria Cherba, Gwen K. Healey Akearok, and Jessica Penney. "Survey of Nunavut Post-Secondary Students: Determinants of School Completion, Post-Secondary Education, and Education Success." *Canadian Journal of Education/Revue Canadienne de l'éducation* 44, no. 3 (September 30, 2021): 764–87. https://doi.org/10.53967/cje-rce.v44i3.4709.

Salonen, Saara-Maria. "A Year after Supreme Court Verdict, Fosen Wind Farm Still Stands amid Soaring Energy Crisis." *The Independent Barents Observer*, October 12, 2022. https://thebarentsobserver.com/en/indigenous-peoples/2022/10/year-after-supreme-court-verdict-fosen-wind-farm-still-stands-amid.

Sandberg, Maria, Kristian Klockars, and Kristoffer Wilén. "Green Growth or Degrowth? Assessing the Normative Justifications for Environmental Sustainability and Economic Growth through Critical Social Theory." *Journal of Cleaner Production* 206 (January 1, 2019): 133–41. https://doi.org/10.1016/j.jclepro.2018.09.175.

Shokrgozar, Shayan. "THE CASE FOR DEGROWTH: ENERGY TECHNOLOGIES." In *DEBATES IN POST-DEVELOPMENT AND DEGROWTH: VOLUME 1*, edited by Alexander Dunlap, Lisa Hammelbo Søyland,

and Shayan Shokrgozar, 1:94–109. Oslo: Tvergastein Journal, 2021.

Simmons, Matt. "Blueberry River First Nations Beat B.C. in Court. Now Everything's Changing." *The Narwhal*, January 25, 2023. https://thenarwhal.ca/blueberry-river-treaty-8-agreements/.

Skorstad, Berit. "Sacrifice Zones: A Conceptual Framework for Arctic Justice Studies?" In *Arctic Justice: Environment, Society and Governance*, edited by Corine Wood-Donnelly and Johanna Ohlsson, 96–108. Bristol University Press, 2023. https://bristoluniversitypressdigital.com/display/book/9781529224832/ch007.xml.

Statistics Canada. "Health Fact Sheets: Household Food Insecurity, 2017/2018," June 24, 2020. https://www150.statcan.gc.ca/n1/pub/82-625-x/2020001/article/00001-eng.htm.

Statistique Canada - Statistics Canada. "Environmental, Social and Governance (ESG) Project," March 10, 2023. https://www.statcan.gc.ca/en/trust/modernization/esg.

Statkraft. "Fosen Vind." Accessed October 26, 2022. https://www.statkraft.com/about-statkraft/where-we-operate/norway/fosen-vind/.

Supreme Court of Norway, No. HR-2021-1975-S (Supreme Court of Norway October 11, 2021).

Szpak, Agnieszka. "Relocation of Kiruna and Construction of the Markbygden Wind Farm and the Saami Rights." *Polar Science* 22 (December 1, 2019): 100479. https://doi.org/10.1016/j.polar.2019.09.001.

TAI Bookshelf Podcast. "TAI Bookshelf Podcast - Geoengineering and Green Colonialism with Aaron Cooper (#1-2021)." Balado. Accessed June 9, 2022. https://soundcloud.com/arcticinstitute/tai-bookshelf-podcast-aaron-cooper.

Teel, Sara. "June 2022 Alaska Economic Trends." *Alaska Economic Trends Magazine*, June 2022.

The Associated Press. "Greenland Suspends All Oil Exploration in Its Territory | CBC News." *CBC*, July 16, 2021. https://www.cbc.ca/news/business/greenland-oil-1.6105230.

The Canadian Press. "N.W.T. Premier Issues 'red Alert'on 'Colonial'Attack on Territory's Oil and Gas Future | CBC News." CBC News, November 1, 2017. https://www.cbc.ca/news/canada/north/nwt-premier-bob-mcleod-drilling-arctic-1.4381837.

Thiessen, Mark, and Matthew Brown. "Biden's Approval of Willow Oil Project Intensifies Rift among Indigenous Alaskans." *Los Angeles Times*, March 17, 2023, sec. Politics. https://www.latimes.com/world-nation/story/2023-03-17/willow-oil-project-approval-intensifies-alaska-natives-rift.

Thomson, Jimmy. "Is Canada Betting Big on Small Nuclear Reactors? Here's What You Need to Know." *The Narwhal* (blog), January 4, 2021. https://thenarwhal.ca/canada-smr-nuclear-reactors-explained/.

Tracy, Elena F., and Wwf Arctic Programme Text Guro Lystad. "Putting a Stop to Oil and Gas Exploration Projects in Norway's Arctic Regions." *High North News*, November 2, 2022, sec. Op-ed. https://www.highnorthnews.com/en/putting-stop-oil-and-gas-exploration-projects-norways-arctic-regions.

Tranter, Emma. "Forced to Travel during Pandemic, Nunavut Women Want Birthing Services at Home | CTV News." *CTV News*, January 10, 2021. https://www.ctvnews.ca/health/forced-to-travel-during-pandemic-nunavut-

women-want-birthing-services-at-home-
1.5260915?cache=almppngbro%3FclipId%3D89926.

Tsui, Emily. "Reducing Individual Costs of Permafrost Thaw Damage in Canada's Arctic." *The Arctic Institute - Center for Circumpolar Security Studies* (blog), March 4, 2021. https://www.thearcticinstitute.org/reducing-individual-costs-permafrost-thaw-damage-canada-arctic/.

Tuck, Eve, and K Wayne Yang. "Decolonization Is Not a Metaphor." *Decolonization:,Indigeneity,,Education,&,Society* 1, no. 1 (2012): 1–40.

Tysiachniouk, Maria, Laura A. Henry, Machiel Lamers, and Jan P. M. van Tatenhove. "Oil and Indigenous People in Sub-Arctic Russia: Rethinking Equity and Governance in Benefit Sharing Agreements." *Energy Research & Social Science* 37 (March 1, 2018): 140–52. https://doi.org/10.1016/j.erss.2017.09.004.

United Nations. "What Is Renewable Energy?" United Nations. United Nations. Accessed September 6, 2023. https://www.un.org/en/climatechange/what-is-renewable-energy.

Van Dusen, John Van Dusen · CBC. "Nunavut, N.W.T. Premiers Slam Arctic Drilling Moratorium | CBC News." *CBC*, December 22, 2016. https://www.cbc.ca/ news/ canada/north/nunavut-premier-slams-arctic-drilling-moratorium-1.3908037.

Vikulova, Olesya. "The Human Cost of Oil: How Indigenous and Ethnic Minorities Bear the Brunt of Disasters." Greenpeace International, June 26, 2020. https://www.greenpeace.org/international/story/43820/human-cost-oil-indigenous-ethnic-minorities-brunt-of-disasters.

Villalobos, Yohanna, Peter J. Rayner, Jeremy D. Silver, Steven Thomas, Vanessa Haverd, Jürgen Knauer, Zoë M. Loh, Nicholas M. Deutscher, David W. T. Griffith, and David F. Pollard. "Was Australia a Sink or Source of $CO_2$ in 2015? Data Assimilation Using OCO-2 Satellite Measurements." *Atmospheric Chemistry and Physics* 21, no. 23 (December 1, 2021): 17453–94. https://doi.org/10.5194/acp-21-17453-2021.

Virginia, Committee on Uranium Mining in, Committee on Earth Resources, and National Research Council. "Potential Human Health Effects of Uranium Mining, Processing, and Reclamation." In *Uranium Mining in Virginia: Scientific, Technical, Environmental, Human Health and Safety, and Regulatory Aspects of Uranium Mining and Processing in Virginia*, 123–77. Washington D.C.: National Academies Press (US), 2011. https://www.ncbi.nlm.nih.gov/books/NBK201047/.

Williams, Ollie. "Inuvialuit Sign Oil, Gas Co-Management Deal with NWT, Yukon, Ottawa." *Cabin Radio*, August 10, 2023. https://cabinradio.ca/140039/news/ politics/inuvialuit-sign-oil-and-gas-co-management-deal-with-nwt-yukon-ottawa/.

Wood-Donnelly, Corine. "Responsibility of and for Structural (In)Justice in Arctic Governance." In *Arctic Justice: Environment, Society and Governance*, edited by Corine Wood-Donnelly and Johanna Ohlsson, 21–35. Bristol University Press, 2023. https://bristoluniversitypressdigital.com/display/book/9781529224832/ch002.xml.

Yanguas Parra, Paola, Bill Hare, Ursula Fuentes Hutfilter, and Niklas Roming. "Evaluating the Significance of Australia's Global Fossil Fuel Carbon Footprint." Climate Analytics for the Australian Conservation Foundation, July 2019. https://climateanalytics.org/media/australia_carbon_footprint_report_july2019.pdf

Yukon Government: Energy, Mines and Resources. "Yukon Oil & Gas: ANNUAL

REPORT 2016." Yukon Government: Energy, Mines and Resources, 2016. https://emrlibrary.gov.yk.ca/oilandgas/yukon-oil-and-gas-annual-report-2016.pdf.

Zmyvalova, Ekaterina. "Human Rights of Indigenous Small-Numbered Peoples in Russia: Recent Developments." *Arctic Review on Law and Politics* 11 (December 9, 2020): 334–59. https://doi.org/10.23865/arctic.v11.2336.

# CHAPTER 4

# IMPACT OF CLIMATE CHANGE ON THE ARCTIC

## Rabia Kalfaoğlu[1]

The Arctic region covers approximately 6% of the Earth's surface. Geographically, about 33% of the region consists of landmass, with the remaining half divided between the Arctic Ocean, including continental shelves shallower than 500 meters (1,640 feet), and the other half comprising oceanic waters deeper than 500 meters.[2] The Arctic region is experiencing one of the most significant impacts of global climate change. According to the Intergovernmental Panel on Climate Change (IPCC),[3] this polar region, located above the Earth's northernmost latitude 66°33'N, is considered an area where climate change is primarily looming.[4]

The Arctic tends to feel the effects of global warming in the early stages and more intensely. By the initial quarter of the 21st century, the global mean temperature has exhibited an elevation of approximately 1.1°C in relation to the 18th century, marked by the onset of the Industrial Revolution. The Arctic has warmed at about at four times the rate of the rest of the world and average temperatures have increased by approximately 2°C, though recent research indicates a doubling of this rate. Warmer temperatures are affecting both the Arctic Ocean and Arctic land areas. Satellite observations show significant sea ice losses in the Arctic over the last 40 years.[5] In the absence

[1] Assistant Professor, Recep Tayyip Erdogan University, Türkiye. ORCID: 0000-0003-3514-3784, E-mail: Rabia.kalfaoglu@erdogan.edu.tr.

[2] Bird et al., Circum-Arctic Resource Appraisal: Estimates of Undiscovered Oil and Gas North of the Arctic Circle, United States Geological Survey, 2008. https://doi.org/10.3133/fs20083049.

[3] The expert body dealing with climate matters is the Intergovernmental Panel on Climate Change (IPCC), which operates under the auspices of the World Meteorological Organization (WMO) and the United Nations Environment Programme (UNEP). The IPCC is responsible for assessing the latest scientific information on climate change, its impacts, and potential adaptation and mitigation strategies. Despite differing viewpoints, the IPCC serves as a critical source of consensus-based information for policymakers and the global community in understanding the complex dynamics of climate change.

[4] IPCC, 2023: Summary for Policymakers. In: Climate Change 2023: Synthesis Report. Contribution of Working Groups I, II and III to the Sixth Assessment Report of the Intergovernmental Panel on Climate Change [Core Writing Team, H. Lee and J. Romero (eds.)]. IPCC, Geneva, Switzerland, pp. 1-34, doi: 10.59327/IPCC/AR6-9789291691647.001

[5] Goodman et al., "Climate Change and Security in the Arctic." A product of The Center for Climate and Security (CCS), an institute of the Council on Strategic Risks (CSR), and The Norwegian Institute of

of substantial mitigation measures against global warming, projections indicate the potential onset of ice-free summer months in the Arctic in the near future.

The Arctic climate is characterized by long, harsh winters and short, cool summers, with some central areas maintaining year-round ice cover. January temperatures range from -40 to 0 °C, occasionally dropping below -50 °C in many Arctic regions, while July sees averages between -10 and +10 °C, occasionally rising to +30 °C in specific land areas. This climate experiences minimal radiation flux in winter and intense radiation in summer, with the polar night bringing constant darkness and the polar day ensuring the sun never dips below the horizon. The annual energy balance is usually positive, except on the Greenlandic plateau, but summer temperatures approach almost zero due to significant snow and ice melting.[6]

Characteristics of the Arctic climate include a significant contribution of warm air convection from the temperate and low latitudes to the poles. The Arctic climate is affected by the retreat of sea ice, which responds sensitively to climate changes. It is observed that reduced sea ice in the Arctic leads to fewer snow-covered days each year. Less snow and ice cover have the effect of exposing darker land surfaces and ocean waters, allowing for more absorption of solar radiation.

In the Arctic, sea ice cover grows during the winter and reaches its maximum extent in March. As the Sun returns in March and strengthens throughout spring and summer, the sea ice begins to melt and reaches its minimum extent in September. The decline in Arctic Sea ice volume is even more pronounced, with a 35% reduction by the end of the winter season and a 75% reduction by the end of the summer season. Record reductions in sea ice extent in the Arctic were recorded in September 2012 and 2020 – 3.39 million square kilometers and 3.81 million square kilometers respectively.[7] In the period from 1979 to 2022, the sea ice extent in the Arctic, measured during the winter months in March, decreased by 32,000 km2 per year, and during the summer months measured in September, it decreased by 74,000 km2 per year. More specifically, the summer Arctic Sea ice extent has decreased by

International Affairs (NUPI). Edited by Francesco Femia and Erin Sikorsky (CCS). January 2021. https://climateandsecurity.org/wp-content/uploads/2021/01/Climate-Change-and-Security-in-the-Arctic_CCS_NUPI_January-2021-1.pdf.

[6] Арктическая энциклопедия: в 2-х томах – дополненное и переработанное издание «Северной энциклопедии». М.: Издательство «Паулсен», 2017 – Т. 1. с. 172

[7] NSIDC, "Charctic Interactive Sea Ice Graph | Arctic Sea Ice News and Analysis," 2023, https://nsidc.org/arcticseaicenews/charctic-interactive-sea-ice-graph/.

approximately 40% since 1979, which is equivalent to around 2.5 million square kilometers and accounts for one-fifth of the average North Hemisphere Sea ice extent.[8] During the summer months, an almost ice-free Arctic Ocean is considered a rare event for a 1.5°C global warming scenario, but it is anticipated to become the norm for a 2.5°C warming scenario.[9]

**Figure 1.** Arctic Sea Ice Extent[10]

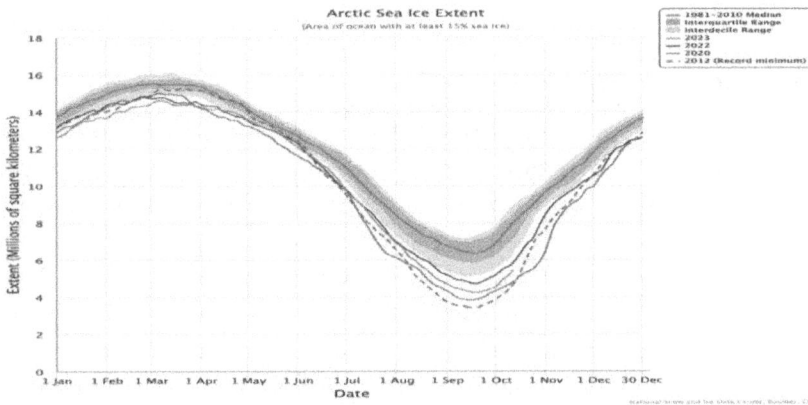

*Source: National Snow & Ice Data Center*

Monitoring temperature changes in the Arctic reveals that in 2021, the positive anomaly in the annual average temperature was 2.9°C above normal. Despite these findings being lower than in 2020 and a general slowdown in the rate of temperature increase, the warming in the North Pole has already led to significant reductions in the ice cover. The rate of ice retreat is increasing during the summer months, and the time for recovery in the winter is decreasing.[11] Based on observed trends and model predictions, the IPCC anticipates that the minimum annual Arctic Sea ice extent will fall below 1 million km² at least once before the middle of the 21st century.[12]

---

[8] "Arctic and Baltic Sea ice," last modified May 09, 2023, https://www.eea.europa.eu/ims/arctic-and-baltic-sea-ice.

[9] Ibid.

[10] For detailed information see https://nsidc.org/arcticseaicenews/charctic-interactive-sea-ice-graph/.

[11] Арктический и антарктический научно-исследовательский институт опубликовал Обзор гидрометеорологических процессов в Северной полярной области Земли за 2021 год. Росгидромет. 2022. https://www.meteorf.gov.ru/press/news/27834/

[12] IPCC, "2021: Summary for Policymakers." In: Climate Change 2021: The Physical Science Basis. Contribution of Working Group I to the Sixth Assessment Report of the Intergovernmental Panel on Climate Change [Masson-Delmotte, V., P. Zhai, A. Pirani, S.L. Connors, C. Péan, S. Berger, N. Caud, Y. Chen, L. Goldfarb, M.I. Gomis, M. Huang, K. Leitzell, E. Lonnoy, J.B.R. Matthews, T.K. Maycock, T. Waterfield, O. Yelekçi, R. Yu, and B. Zhou (eds.)]. Cambridge University Press, Cambridge, United Kingdom and New York, NY, USA, 2021, pp. 3–32, doi:10.1017/9781009157896.001.

**Figure 2.** Observed and projected decline in Arctic sea-ice area[1]

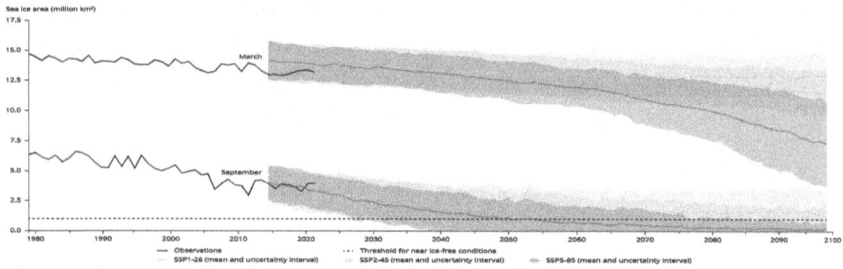

*Source: European Environment Agency*

All these processes present significant challenges in the Arctic region, posing threats not only to the Arctic ecosystem but also to the global climate system. These processes are irreversible, but successful adaptation to ongoing changes and mitigation of their adverse consequences largely depend on the effective implementation of international environmental cooperation. Global efforts are being undertaken to combat the adverse effects of global warming and greenhouse gas-induced phenomena such as ocean warming and the melting of sea ice, which result in rising sea levels. In this regard, the Paris Agreement plays a pivotal role. The agreement's provisions compel all nations to significantly reduce global greenhouse gas emissions to limit the global temperature increase of this century to 2°C, while also aiming to further restrict it to 1.5°C to continue efforts to prevent or reduce adverse impacts and related losses and damages, an important effort as the IPCC indicates that climate-related risks for natural and human systems are higher with the increased level[2]. This underscores the urgency of adopting measures to limit temperature increases, as the consequences become more severe with higher temperature thresholds.[3]

Another perspective on climate change is its significant impact on regional economic pursuits due to glacier melt in the Arctic region. The melting of sea ice has led to the anticipation of a more accessible Northern Sea Route (NSR), which could potentially reduce transit times between Europe and Asia by up to 40%. This development is likely to be accompanied by easier access

---

[1] For detailed information see https://www.eea.europa.eu/ims/arctic-and-baltic-sea-ice

[2] Susanne, Baur, Alexander, Nauels and Carl-Friedrich, Schleussner, 1.5°C to survive: evidence from the IPCC Special Reports, https://climateanalytics.org/publications/15c-to-survive-evidence-from-the-ipcc-special-reports#:~:text=The%20IPCC%20Special%20Reports%20SR,%C2%B0C%20colder%20on%20average.

[3] "Global Temperatures Set to Reach New Records in next Five Years," World Meteorological Organization, May 15, 2023, https://public.wmo.int/en/media/press-release/global-temperatures-set-reach-new-records-next-five-years.

to energy resources in the region.[4] According to the estimates of the US Geological Survey, approximately 13% of the world's undiscovered oil reserves and about 30% of natural gas reserves are estimated to be in the Arctic region (Bird et al. 2008). Under these conditions, there is an observed tendency among Arctic states to ensure sustainable development and environmental protection in the region. At the same time, the European Union (EU) and many Asian countries, including China, India, Japan, and South Korea, are showing interest in Arctic development. Their commitment to solving Arctic issues stems from a combination of ecological, economic, and commercial factors. In this context, the Arctic region can be seen as an emerging market where key contemporary issues such as climate change, geopolitical competition, access to natural resources, international governance, and more intersect.

For the past year, international environmental cooperation in the Arctic has been suspended. Projects developed and implemented within the framework of the Barents/European Arctic Council and the Arctic Council have been indefinitely put on hold due to the changing political situation, particularly considering the Ukraine conflict. Meanwhile, the region's environmental issues are far from being fully resolved. Addressing these challenges requires the coordination and combined efforts of regional states, presenting new challenges and tasks. The cessation of cooperation between Western countries and Russia could impact not only the overall environmental situation in the region but also the quality of life for indigenous populations, who are particularly vulnerable to environmental conditions. As a result, the restoration of international environmental cooperation, which would be beneficial for both Russia and the Western countries participating in the Barents/European Arctic Council and the Arctic Council, should become a priority for the governments of all relevant parties.

## The Ecological Effects of Arctic Warming

The warming of the Arctic region has given rise to complex ecological consequences that resonate on both regional and global scales. One of the most pronounced effects is the rapid melting of ice sheets and glaciers, significantly contributing to the alarming rise in global sea levels. This

---

[4] Goodman et al., "Climate Change and Security in the Arctic." A product of The Center for Climate and Security (CCS), an institute of the Council on Strategic Risks (CSR), and The Norwegian Institute of International Affairs (NUPI). Edited by Francesco Femia and Erin Sikorsky (CCS). January 2021. https://climateandsecurity.org/wp-content/uploads/2021/01/Climate-Change-and-Security-in-the-Arctic_CCS_NUPI_January-2021-1.pdf

phenomenon not only poses a global threat to coastal regions but also disrupts the intricate fabric of the Arctic's unique ecosystems. Indigenous communities in the Arctic are another segment profoundly affected by Arctic warming. Their traditional means of sustenance are becoming increasingly precarious due to shifting ice patterns and variations in wildlife populations, jeopardizing food security and cultural heritage. As we confront the extensive consequences of Arctic warming, it is crucial to recognize the urgency of safeguarding this vital ecosystem for the well-being of both local communities and the broader global environment.[5]

The diminishing sea ice in the Arctic results in increased absorption of sunlight by the ocean, influencing ocean circulation and weather patterns, and contributing to rising global sea levels. The global average sea level has risen approximately 21-24 cm since 1880. The rising sea level is primarily due to a combination of melting ice from glaciers and ice sheets and the thermal expansion of seawater as it warms. Since the beginning of satellite observations in the early 1990s, sea levels have risen by 1.06 cm solely due to the melting of the Greenlandic ice sheet. In a worst-case scenario, the melting of the Arctic and Antarctic ice sheets by the year 2100 could result in an additional 17.9 cm increase in the average sea level. However, a 15 cm rise could potentially double the frequency of storm surges on the western coasts of North America and Europe, posing a significant threat to the lives of millions of people, particularly in the world's largest coastal cities.[6]

Climate change is driving a concerning trend in the Arctic region, with more frequent and severe extreme weather events, such as storms and heavy rainfall. These changes are particularly noticeable in the taiga and tundra zones, historically untouched by large-scale disturbances for centuries. The warming and drying conditions have resulted in a rising incidence of intense wildfires, which, in turn, trigger a chain reaction of environmental consequences. These wildfires not only alter the composition of vegetation, shifting from grassy and sedge plants to more easily ignitable shrubs and woody species, but they also expedite the degradation of permafrost. To compound matters, these fires release additional greenhouse gases into the atmosphere, exacerbating the global climate crisis. Furthermore, the rising

---

[5] Adam J. P. Smith, Doug M. Smith, Judah Cohen, and Matthew W. Jones, Arctic warming amplifies climate change and its impacts, https://sciencebrief.org/uploads/ reviews/ScienceBrief_ Review_ ARCTIC_Oct2021.pdf October 2021.

[6] Slater Thomas, Anna E. Hogg, and Ruth Mottram, "Ice-sheet losses track high-end sea-level rise projections," Nature Climate Change." Nature Climate Change 10 (August 2020): 879–881, https://doi.org/10.1038/s41558-020-0893-y

temperatures associated with climate change facilitate the proliferation of insects that harm vegetation, further straining the delicate Arctic ecosystem.

Climate change and its associated impacts disrupt the habitats of existing plant species and living organisms in the Arctic region, leading to a decrease or extinction of these species and/or their migration. The warming climate leads to changes in temperature and precipitation patterns, resulting in the loss of critical habitats and resources for Arctic flora and fauna. Many species, especially those highly specialized for the extreme conditions of the Arctic, are facing an unstable situation. Some may struggle to adapt, leading to a decline in their populations, while others may face the risk of extinction. For example, the reduction in ice cover periods is closely linked to the presence of specific phytoplankton species, including krill, which are a primary food source for virtually all Arctic organisms. This reduction in ice-related organisms can lead to a decrease in population for marine birds and mammals, jeopardizing their well-being and even survival. Additionally, as their natural habitats change or disappear, some species are forced to migrate in search of suitable conditions, potentially disrupting other ecosystems and competing with resident species. In recent years, due to the rapid decline in ice cover, thousands of walruses have migrated to the coasts of both Russia and the United States.[7]

Finally, it is undoubtedly of utmost importance to assess the condition of the indigenous populations living in the region. Currently, more than 4 million people are living in the Arctic and sub-Arctic regions, and as a result, climate change is impacting the local inhabitants in the region. The Arctic region is grappling with an array of new challenges that have a profound impact on the health and way of life of its indigenous communities, including shifts in lifestyle, dietary patterns, and employment structures.[8] Indigenous peoples living in the Arctic are making efforts to maintain their traditional way of life, but climate change is disrupting this way of life and leading to a transformation in adapting to the new environment. One of the foremost concerns revolves around public health, with new and emergent health threats causing considerable apprehension. These threats are manifested through changes in lifestyle, dietary habits, and employment opportunities, all of which significantly affect the overall well-being of Arctic inhabitants. Moreover, food security has emerged as a critical issue for indigenous

---

[7] Камцов В.М., Порфирьев Б.Н. Климатические изменения в Арктике: последствия для окружающей среды и экономики.Арктика: экология и экономика. 2, no. 6 (2012): 66-79.
[8] IPCC. "The ocean and cryosphere in a changing climate", 2019, https:// report.ipcc.ch/srocc/pdf/ SROCC_FinalDraft_FullReport.pdf.

communities in the region. Alterations in their natural habitat and a decline in the populations of wild animals, birds, and fish pose a substantial threat to the food and water security of these communities.[9] These multifaceted challenges underscore the pressing need for concerted efforts to address the impact of climate change on the Arctic's indigenous populations and ensure the preservation of their unique way of life.[10]

## The Geoeconomic Effects of Arctic Warming

The Arctic region is experiencing the effects of climate change that extend beyond the realm of ecology and have the potential to create new economic opportunities for Arctic nations. With the melting of sea ice, access to underground resources in the region has become increasingly accessible. The seabed beneath the Arctic Ocean holds many valuable underground resources that have remained largely unexplored until today. In addition to global warming, particularly in the last decade, the interest in the region has grown, especially among Arctic countries, as deep-sea drilling technologies have advanced.[11]

The depths of the Arctic region are rich in various resources, including but not limited to petroleum, coal, natural gas, platinum metals, copper-nickel ores, iron, phosphorus, polymetals, gold, diamonds, titanium, tantalum, niobium, fluorite, chromium, manganese, mica, molybdenum, tungsten, and vanadium.[12] The Arctic mainland is believed to host unique reserves of copper-nickel ores, tin, platinum group metals, agricultural chemical ores, rare metals and rare earth elements, gold, diamonds, tungsten, mercury, ferrous metals, and gemstones. In the Arctic shelf, there are estimated reserves of placer tin, gold, diamonds, manganese, silver, fluorite, gemstones, and various precious stones. The lands and water areas of the Arctic also contain significant resources of iron, manganese, chromium, and titanium. Furthermore, the waters and islands of the Arctic have substantial tin-carrying potential. The tin-carrying potential of the Russian Arctic shelf, for

---

[9] Post, Eric, Richard B. Alley, Torben R. Christensen, Marc Macias-Fauria, Bruce C. Forbes, Michael N. Gooseff, Amy Iler et al. "The polar regions in a 2 C warmer world." Science advances 5, no. 12 (2019): eaaw9883.

[10] Камцов В.М., Порфирьев Б.Н. Климатические изменения в Арктике: последствия для окружающей среды и экономики// Арктика: экология и экономика. No 2(6), 2012, 66-79.

[11] "Evolution of Arctic Energy Development: A Timeline (1962-Present)," Stimson, September 15, 2013, https://www.stimson.org/2013/evolution-arctic-energy-development-timeline-1962-present/.

[12] "Арктика: как разбудить «спящий» регион," Национальный Отраслевой Журнал 12, 456 (2019): 69-80, https://ngv.ru/upload/iblock/8bd/8bd3cce6338529d05a0ca03367ee81c9.pdf

example, can be compared to some of the world's largest regions.[13]

Exploration for oil and natural gas in the Arctic region has primarily taken place in the onshore areas, as conducting exploration activities in the offshore areas with ocean depths exceeding 500 meters poses significant geographical challenges. The first comprehensive study on oil and gas exploration in the Arctic was conducted by the United States Geological Survey (USGS) in 2008. According to the findings of the report, it is estimated that the Arctic region holds approximately 90 billion barrels of undiscovered conventional oil (which accounts for around 13-16% of the global total), 1,669 trillion cubic meters of natural gas (approximately 25-30% of the global total), and 44 billion barrels of natural gas liquids (NGLs), which constitute about 38% of the global total. On average, more than 70% of the undiscovered oil resources are believed to be in the Arctic Alaska, Amerasia Basin, East Greenland Rift Basin, East Barents Basin, and West Greenland - East Canada regions. Additionally, more than 70% of the undiscovered natural gas is thought to be in the West Siberian Basin, East Barents Basin, and Arctic Alaska regions. It is estimated that approximately 84% of the undiscovered oil and natural gas is in offshore areas.[14] Research indicates that the Arctic region covers the largest geographical area in terms of undiscovered energy resources, accounting for about 22% of the world's total undiscovered resources. This is one of the significant reasons for the increased interest in the region in recent years.

Due to the challenging weather conditions and geographical factors, much of the Arctic region is covered by ice for a significant portion of the year. This has posed numerous difficulties for oil and natural gas exploration in the region, and these challenges continue to persist. Consequently, countries have primarily focused on developing large oil and gas fields to reduce the cost of development. The opening of the Tazovskoye gas field in Russia's distant north in 1962 marked the beginning of a series of hydrocarbon reserve discoveries in the region. Subsequently, in 1967, a gas and oil field were discovered in Prudhoe Bay, Alaska. As of 2009, there were 61 major oil and gas fields discovered in the Arctic, with 43 located in Russia, 11 in Canada, 6

---

[13] Энергия Арктики. М.О. Моргунова, А.Я. Цуневский, под научн. ред. В.В. Бушуева, М.: ИЦ «Энергия», 2012, С. 38-41.

[14] Bird Kenneth J., Ronald R. Charpentier, Donald L. Gautier, David W. Houseknecht, Timothy R. Klett, Janet K. Pitman, Thomas E. Moore, Christopher J. Schenk, Marilyn E. Tennyson, and Craig R. Wandrey. 2008. "Circum-Arctic Resource Appraisal: Estimates of Undiscovered Oil and Gas North of the Arctic Circle.", United States Geological Survey, Fact Sheet. https://doi.org/10.3133/fs20083049.

in Alaska, and 1 in Norway.[15]

Another economic benefit of increased Arctic accessibility is the potential for new trade routes. Maritime transportation plays a highly significant role in the Arctic region, being crucial for both the residents and the workforce in the area. It serves as a primary means for delivering essential supplies like food and fuel to the population, transporting equipment to industrial facilities, and shipping various products. As the extent of sea ice continues to diminish, and navigation seasons extend from two and a half to three months, and sometimes up to five months, the region is becoming more accessible, sparking increased interest in the development of commercial maritime operations in the Arctic. Consequently, research on new trade routes in the region has started. Undoubtedly, the most important of these routes is the Northern Sea Route (NSR). In addition to the NSR, there are three other international trade routes in the Arctic. Since 2007, the Northwest Passage (NWP), which is believed to be navigable for shipping, connects the Atlantic and Pacific Oceans through the Canadian Arctic Archipelago. Despite increasing activities in the NWP, such as fishing, servicing local communities, and serving mining and oil and gas facilities, the unpredictability of ice conditions and other natural factors will continue to make this route challenging for navigation.

The Northern Sea Route is considered one of the advantages for Russia resulting from climate change, as it is expected that the melting of Arctic ice will create a passage between the Pacific and Atlantic Oceans. The NSR has the potential to reduce the distance between Europe and Asia by up to 40 per cent, compared to the contemporary Suez Canal Route.[16] For instance, on August 23, 2018, one of the world's largest and technologically advanced cargo ships, the Venta, owned by the Danish logistics giant AP Moller-Maersk Group, departed from Vladivostok. It successfully traversed the Northern Sea Route and delivered its cargo to St. Petersburg on September 27. The entire route was completed by the ship in 34 days. For comparison, the route through the Suez Canal typically takes 48 days. This marked the first container ship in the world to travel from Asia to Europe via the

---

[15] Philip Budzik, "Arctic Oil and Natural Gas Potential," U.S. Department of Energy, Energy Information Administration, Accessed October 2009, https://www.arlis.org/docs/vol1/ AlaskaGas/ Paper/ Paper_ _2009_ArcticOilGasPotential.pdf.

[16] "Николай Корчунов: военная активность России в Арктике никому не угрожает." RIA Novosti 2021, https://ria.ru/20210601/aktivnost-1734886866.html.

Northern Sea Route.[17] Given that the navigational route has been historically open only from July to November, the expansion of this timeframe due to global warming could make the route accessible year-round until 2050.

The importance of the NSR has increased markedly after the speech of the President of Russia during the annual address to the Federal Assembly in 2018, when V.V. Putin announced that by 2024 it is planned to increase the volume of NSR cargo turnover to 80 million tons per year. In August 2023, the Russian Ministry of Transport published the passport of the federal project "Development of the Northern Sea Route," which focuses on the development of the country's northernmost sea route. This document, spanning 133 pages, outlined changes aimed at improving key indicators for the expansion of the northern sea route network. According to this document, the total capacity of the seaports along the Northern Sea Route will be increased to 83 million tons annually by 2025, with a transportation volume of 80 million tons per year. The year-round navigation period for the Northern Sea Route has been slightly shifted. Initially planned to open in the winter of 2023/24, it has now been postponed to the winter season of 2024/25. Furthermore, according to the document, the transportation volume should reach 80 million tons in 2024 and increase to 150 million tons by 2030.[18]

However, many experts view the significant expansion of international transit through the NSR with skepticism due to the influence of various weather-related factors. These include the high unpredictability of ice distribution from year to year, the substantial risk to navigation due to the variability of ice cover and potential ship freezing, and the inability to adhere to preset schedules for container and automobile transportation sectors due to rapidly changing weather conditions. Additionally, there are economic concerns, such as substantial insurance premiums due to high risks and the costs of icebreaker and pilotage services. The large distances between NSR ports and underdeveloped port infrastructure also negatively impact the expansion of international transit. However, according to experts working in the Arctic Council, the NSR, which already has a certain level of infrastructure, is considered more feasible compared to other Arctic routes.

---

[17] "Первый контейнеровоз прошел по Северному морскому пути." Vedomosti 2018, https://www.vedomosti.ru/business/articles/2018/09/26/782107-konteinerovoz-severnomu-morskomu.

[18] "Паспорт федерального проекта 'Развитие Северного морского пути.'" The Ministry of Transport of the Russian Federation. 2023, https://mintrans.gov.ru/documents/8/12714.

## The Risks Posed by Geopolitical Activities to Arctic Ecology

The preservation of the pristine state of the Arctic is threatened by both ongoing natural processes like climate change and anthropogenic activities primarily related to the extraction of mineral resources present in this region. Indeed, climate change is rapidly increasing ecological risks in the Arctic. It poses significant threats to infrastructure, raises the risk of technological disasters, contributes to coastal erosion, increases the frequency of flooding, leads to intense forest fires, and poses threats to the livelihoods of indigenous communities. These changes in the Arctic ecosystem have wide-ranging and interconnected consequences that affect both the local environment and global climate systems.

The primary anthropogenic environmental issue in the Arctic region is associated with the accumulation of environmental pollution in concentrated areas of industrial, transportation, energy, and social activities in the Arctic where the development of mineral resources, raw material processing, and transportation take place. Among the primary sources of pollution in Arctic waters are river and maritime fleet ships, continental drainage, offshore mining, transportation of pollutants over long distances through ocean currents and atmospheric flows, and disposal of radioactive waste and nuclear reactors.

The most significant accumulations of pollutants and disturbances in Arctic natural landscapes occurred from the 1930s to the 1980s, when the northern regions (especially in Russia) experienced intense industrialization and extensive extraction of natural resources. During those years, the proportion of enterprises involved in the extraction and processing of natural resources, accompanied by the generation of significant amounts of solid, liquid, and gaseous waste, accounted for approximately 70% of the total number of facilities. The environmental and social consequences of focal industrial development during that period were not adequately assessed, leading to the formation of impact zones with severe anthropogenic disruptions to the natural environment. This not only affected the prospects for preserving the natural resource potential but also had implications for the health and well-being of the population, including the indigenous people of the Arctic.

The potential devastating consequences of any oil spill in the Arctic Ocean are another significant concern. The marine ecosystems in the Arctic region are particularly sensitive and vulnerable to oil spills resulting from explosions, pipeline leaks, or transportation accidents. The lack of infrastructure and the remoteness of the region mean that responding to a spill could take days or weeks. The short summers, low temperatures, and limited sunlight in the Arctic make it possible for the Arctic Ocean ecosystems to recover from such damage to take many years.

The grounding of the Exxon Valdez oil tanker off the coast of Alaska in 1989 and the subsequent oil spill demonstrated the potential harm that such spills can cause to the environment and highlighted the challenges of cleaning up polar waters. Following this incident, as well as the Deepwater Horizon oil spill in 2010, environmentalists called for Arctic countries, including the United States, to halt oil and gas activities in the region. Cleaning up an oil spill in the Arctic is extremely difficult, and the Arctic nations lack the infrastructure to support safe drilling and cleanup efforts. As a result, there have been numerous oil spills, both large and small, in the region over the years.

In May 2020, a subsidiary of the Russian nickel mining company Norilsk Nickel suffered damage to a diesel fuel tank, resulting in a spill of over 20,000 tons of diesel fuel into the Ambarnaya River near the industrial city of Norilsk. Following this incident, Russian President Vladimir Putin declared a state of emergency to address the disaster, and Norilsk Nickel's teams worked diligently to localize the spill and collect the leaked diesel fuel. According to Norilsk-Taymir Energy Company, the total damage to the environment amounted to approximately \$291 million USD (21.4 billion rubles).[19] As long as there is an increase in shipping activities involving the transportation of oil and other chemicals in the region, the risk of accidental oil and pollutant releases is expected to persist.

Various measures need to be implemented to strike a balance between anthropogenic impact and environmental protection. Undoubtedly, one of the most important measures is to develop and implement projects aimed at reducing and remediating environmental damage related to climate change and other environmental issues. An important step is the analysis of the ecological impact of underground resource use in the region. This is crucial for understanding the environmental effects of activities such as mining and energy production and can aid in the development of sustainable resource management policies. Finally, there is a need to carefully examine the environmental impacts of oil and gas production and transportation in the Arctic region. Developing and implementing transition strategies towards

---

[19] "Норникель' оценивает ущерб от разлива топлива в 21,4 млрд рублей." Норникель. October 2020. https://www.nornickel.ru/news-and-media/press-releases-and-news/nornikel-otsenivaet-ushcherb-ot-razliva-topliva-v-21-4-mlrd-rubley/?sphrase_id=3392885.

sustainable energy sources can help reduce environmental risks in the region. These measures can contribute to the protection of the Arctic and the preservation of the global environment.

## Arctic Cooperation: The Relevance Amidst Climate Change

Arctic countries participate in international platforms to collectively address climate change issues. Certainly, the Arctic Council, established in 1996, stands out as one of the intergovernmental forums among these platforms dedicated to addressing matters concerning the Arctic region. It consists of eight Arctic states (Canada, Denmark, Finland, Iceland, Norway, Russia, Sweden, and the United States) and six Indigenous Permanent Participant organizations. The council addresses various topics, including climate change, through scientific cooperation, policy coordination, and collaboration among member states. The main activities in the field of international cooperation, including environmental cooperation, are carried out within the framework of six working groups (Arctic Contaminants Action Program; Arctic Monitoring and Assessment Programme Working Group; Conservation of Arctic Flora and Fauna; Emergency Prevention, Preparedness and Response; Protection of the Arctic Marine Environment Working Group; Sustainable Development Working Group).

The Arctic Council is a critical platform for sustainable development and cooperation in the Arctic region. This council operates by transferring its presidency among the eight Arctic countries every two years. At the core of its meetings lies a significant emphasis on climate change and environmental issues. At the Ministerial Meeting of the Arctic Council held in Reykjavik in 2021, where the presidency was set to be handed over to Russian Federation, participating countries emphasized the importance of climate and cooperation. However, following this meeting, all these collaborations came to a silent pause with the outbreak of the Ukraine War. On March 3, 2022, just one week after the start of the Ukraine War, seven out of the eight members of the Arctic Council (Denmark, Iceland, Canada, Norway, the United States, Finland, Sweden) announced the temporary suspension of the activities of the Council's working bodies.[20] Additionally, these seven countries suspended their participation in all Arctic Council events under Russia's chairmanship from 2021 to 2023. Furthermore, collaboration with Russian scientists, institutes, and researchers was also halted. The suspension

---

[20] Комментарий официального представителя МИД России М.В.Захаровой в связи с заявлением западных стран-членов Арктического совета, 2022 https://mid.ru/ru/foreign_ policy/ news/ 1802852/.

of international cooperation within the Arctic Council, which serves as the primary platform for coordinating the efforts of Arctic states, including in the field of ecology, was condemned by the Russian Ministry of Foreign Affairs. Russia's Ambassador at Large, the senior Russian official in the Arctic Council, Nikolay Korchunov, stated that such a decision by Western countries would negatively impact efforts to address the risks and challenges of "soft" security in the Arctic. He also emphasized Russia's interest in preserving the Council's project activities, which should continue once the situation allows.[21] A pause in the activities of the Arctic Council could have devastating consequences for the fragile Arctic ecosystem.[22]

Russian and Western scientists have become increasingly interdependent in their efforts to study climate change and its consequences. They have recognized that attempting to address these issues independently of Russia would be quite challenging. In this context, some Western experts and politicians criticize the idea of severing interactions with Russian experts. The interactions and mutual dependencies among Russian and Western scientists, as well as the local populations in the region, can be difficult to terminate abruptly or wait for these connections to cease. For example, the United States Ambassador to the Kingdom of Denmark, L.D. Weisberg, emphasized that the decision was made hastily but now calls for strategic patience. Similarly, the United States Ambassador to the Kingdom of Norway, Anniken Krutnes, stated her views following the Ukraine conflict: "The paradox is that Russia is the largest country in the region both in terms of population and continental shelf, and without Russia, no problem, such as the climate crisis, methane, and greenhouse gas emissions, can be resolved (…) Hopefully, we can continue collaboration through research projects, conferences, but right now, we have to do it without Russia, and I hope that at some point, we can come together again.".[23]

After a prolonged period of silence, limited yet significant communication took place at the 13th Arctic Council meeting held in Salekhard, Russia. Representatives from the eight Arctic States and six Permanent Participants convened both in person and online to mark the conclusion of Russia's two-

---

[21] В МИД РФ заявили о возможном выходе России из Арктического совета при нарушении ее прав, 2023 https://tass.ru/politika/17742861.
[22] Aryn Baker, "Ukraine's Conflict Has Rippled All the Way to the Arctic," Time, March 9, 2022, https://time.com/6156189/russia-ukraine-conflict-risks-arctic-climate/.
[23] "Nordic Security Perspectives in the Arctic," Wilson Center, May 5, 2022, https://www.wilson center.org/event/nordic-security-perspectives-arctic?utm_source=event&utm_medium=email&utm_campaign=pi&emci=e027eb35-6dc5-ec11-997e-281878b83d8a&emdi=d2efd33f-88cc-ec11-997e-281878b83d8a&ceid=257448.

year Chairmanship and the beginning of Norway's Chairmanship for the years 2023-2025. The Council's 130-plus transformative projects, covering a range of topics from science to maritime affairs, have created fractures along regional boundaries for over a year, making a return to the status quo seem impossible. Nonetheless, this interaction holds promise for future collaborations.

While the Ukraine crisis may cast a shadow over the regional peace, it is argued that "completely shutting the doors" is not feasible. Isolating Russia from Arctic dialogue and central forums like the Arctic Council is likely to have long-term consequences. Countries bordering the Arctic Ocean have inherent responsibilities towards each other due to their geographical positions, and ending these relationships entirely is not possible. Both scientists working in the region and the local populations have interactions with one another. In this context, it is anticipated that Arctic countries will eventually realize this and return to conducting joint research with Russia.

## Conclusion

The Arctic region is an undeniable and critical indicator of the consequences of climate change. Rapid warming leading to the melting of glaciers and sea ice not only affects the region itself but also triggers a chain reaction worldwide by altering climate systems and raising sea levels. Its environmental impacts run deep, affecting coastal areas and biodiversity, especially the fragile Arctic ecosystems and the unique species they harbor. This, in turn, generates climate concerns pushing the world toward an undesirable fate. Therefore, countries in the Arctic region need to seriously consider building and maintaining confidence in addressing climate change. This issue should be given top priority in international policymaking processes and collaborative initiatives.

Moreover, warming in the Arctic also has serious consequences for indigenous communities, who face the disruption of their traditional ways of life due to changing ice patterns and difficulties accessing resources. The need for sustainable and inclusive approaches to address these issues is crucial.

On a broader scale, the geo-economic consequences of the Arctic's changing landscape cannot be overstated. The warming processes in the Arctic open new economic prospects, improve conditions for further development of hydrocarbon and other raw material resources, and significantly facilitate navigation. However, they pose a threat not only to the Arctic ecosystem but also to the Earth's climate system as a whole. These processes are irreversible, but successful adaptation to the ongoing changes and mitigating their negative consequences largely depend on effective international environmental cooperation. It is worth noting that given the scale of potential negative consequences, such cooperation cannot be limited to the Arctic region alone; it should represent the united efforts of the entire global community, considering regional specifics.

The Arctic Council is an important tool for countries in the Arctic region to cooperate on a common platform on regional issues. However, the emergence of conflicts within this union due to the consequences of the Ukrainian war will undoubtedly negatively affect climate change initiatives in the region. These potential impacts have the potential to influence environmental, political and strategic dynamics at both regional and international levels. Disruptions after the Ukrainian war may weaken the regional cooperation capacity of the Arctic Council countries. This may make it difficult to take joint and effective steps against a significant global threat such as climate change. The necessity of international cooperation and coordination is clear when addressing issues such as climate change movements, sea ice melting, ecosystem imbalances and environmental sustainability in the region. Potential differences between countries in the Arctic region may further complicate addressing these issues and finding sustainable solutions.

Finally, overcoming challenges in the Arctic requires collaborative efforts on many fronts, including environmental protection, indigenous rights, sustainable resource management, and international diplomacy. Protecting this vital region is not only a regional concern but also a global imperative for a sustainable future. In this context, further exploration and understanding of the Arctic, environmental protection, addressing climate change, responsible use of Arctic resources, including natural reserves, as well as active participation in Arctic cooperation and governance to promote peace and stability in the region, will continue to be important topics on the agenda. These issues will persistently hold a significant place on the global agenda.

## Bibliography

Adam J. P. Smith, Doug M. Smith, Judah Cohen, and Matthew W. Jones, Arctic warming amplifies climate change and its impacts, October 2021, https://sciencebrief.org/uploads/reviews/ScienceBrief_Review_ARCTIC_Oct2021.pdf

"Arctic and Baltic Sea Ice". Last modified May 09, 2023. https://www.eea.europa.eu/ims/arctic-and-baltic-sea-ice

Baker, Aryn. "Ukraine's Conflict Has Rippled All the Way to the Arctic." *Time,* March 9,

2022. https://time.com/6156189/russia-ukraine-conflict-risks-arctic-climate/.

Bird, Kenneth J., Ronald R. Charpentier, Donald L. Gautier, David W. Houseknecht, Timothy R. Klett, Janet K. Pitman, Thomas E. Moore, Christopher J. Schenk, Marilyn E. Tennyson, and Craig R. Wandrey. *Circum-Arctic Resource Appraisal: Estimates of Undiscovered Oil and Gas North of the Arctic Circle.* United States Geological Survey, 2008. https://doi.org/10.3133/fs20083049.

Budzik, Philip. "Arctic Oil and Natural Gas Potential." U.S. Department of Energy, Energy Information Administration October, 2009. https://www.arlis.org/ docs/ vol1/AlaskaGas/Paper/Paper_EIA_2009_ArcticOilGasPotential.pdf.

Goodman, Sherri, Kate Guy, Marisol Maddox (CCS); Vegard Valther Hansen, Ole Jacob Sending, Iselin Németh Winther (NUPI). "Climate Change and Security in the Arctic." Edited by Francesco Femia and Erin Sikorsky (CCS). A product of the Center for Climate and Security (CCS), an institute of the Council on Strategic Risks (CSR), and The Norwegian Institute of International Affairs (NUPI). January, 2021. https://climateandsecurity.org/wp-content/uploads/2021/01/Climate-Change-and-Security-in-the-Arctic_CCS_NUPI_January-2021-1.pdf

Stimson. "Evolution of Arctic Energy Development: A Timeline (1962-Present)." September 15, 2013. https://www.stimson.org/2013/evolution-arctic-energy-development-timeline-1962-present/

IPCC. "The ocean and cryosphere in a changing climate." 2019. https:// report.ipcc.ch/srocc/pdf/SROCC_FinalDraft_FullReport.pdf

IPCC, "2021: Summary for Policymakers." In: Climate Change 2021: The Physical Science Basis. Contribution of Working Group I to the Sixth Assessment Report of the Intergovernmental Panel on Climate Change [Masson-Delmotte, V., P. Zhai, A. Pirani, S.L. Connors, C. Péan, S. Berger, N. Caud, Y. Chen, L. Goldfarb, M.I. Gomis, M. Huang, K. Leitzell, E. Lonnoy, J.B.R. Matthews, T.K. Maycock, T. Waterfield, O. Yelekçi, R. Yu, and B. Zhou (eds.)]. Cambridge University Press, Cambridge, United Kingdom and New York, NY, USA, 2021, pp. 3−32, doi:10.1017/ 9781009 15 78 96. 001.

IPCC, "2023: Summary for Policymakers." In: Climate Change 2023: Synthesis Report. Contribution of Working Groups I, II and III to the Sixth Assessment Report of the Intergovernmental Panel on Climate Change [Core Writing Team, H. Lee and J. Romero (eds.)]. IPCC, Geneva, Switzerland, 2023, pp. 1-34, doi: 10.59327/IPCC/AR6-9789291691647.001

NSIDC. "Charctic Interactive Sea Ice Graph | Arctic Sea Ice News and Analysis." 2023. https://nsidc.org/arcticseaicenews/charctic-interactive-sea-ice-graph/.

Post, Eric, Richard B. Alley, Torben R. Christensen, Marc Macias-Fauria, Bruce C. Forbes, Michael N. Gooseff, Amy Iler, Jeffy T. Kerby, Cristine L. Laidre, Michael E. Mann, Johan Olofsson, Julienne C. Stroeve, Fran Ulmer, Ross A. Virginia and Muyin Wang. "The Polar Regions in a 2°c Warmer World." *Science Advances* 5, No. 12 (Dec 2019): 1-12. https://doi.org/10.1126/sciadv.aaw9883.

Slater, Thomas, Anna E. Hogg, and Ruth Mottram. "Ice-sheet losses track high-end sea-level rise projections." Nature Climate Change." *Nature Climate Change* 10 (August 2020): 879−881. https://doi.org/10.1038/s41558-020-0893-y

Susanne, Baur, Alexander, Nauels and Carl-Friedrich, Schleussner, 1.5°C to survive:

evidence from the IPCC Special Reports, https://climateanalytics.org/ publications/ 15c-to-survive-evidence-from-the-ipcc-special reports#:~:text=The%20IPCC%20Special%20Reports%20SR,%C2%B0C%20colder%20on%20average.

Wilson Center. "Nordic Security Perspectives in the Arctic." May 5, 2022. https://www.wilsoncenter.org/event/nordic-security-perspectives-arctic?utm_source=event&utm_medium=email&utm_campaign=pi&emci=e027eb 35-6dc5-ec11-997e-281878b83d8a&emdi=d2efd33f-88cc-ec11-997e-281878b83d8a&ceid=257448

World Meteorological Organization. "Global Temperatures Set to Reach New Records in next Five Years." May 15, 2023. https://public.wmo.int/en/media/press-release/global-temperatures-set-reach-new-records-next-five-years.

"Арктика: как разбудить «спящий» регион." *Национальный Отраслевой Журнал* 12, 456 (2019): 69-80. https://ngv.ru/upload/ iblock/ 8bd/8bd3 cce63385 29 d05 a 0ca 03367ee81c9.pdf

"Арктическая энциклопедия: в 2-х томах – дополненное и переработанное издание «Северной энциклопедии». М.: Издательство «Паулсен», Т. 1. (2017): 688 с.

Арктический и антарктический научно-исследовательский институт опубликовал Обзор гидрометеорологических процессов в Северной полярной области Земли за 2021 год. Росгидромет. 2022. https://www.meteorf.gov.ru/ press/ news/27834/

В МИД РФ заявили о возможном выходе России из Арктического совета при нарушении ее прав. 2023. https://tass.ru/politika/17742861

"Николай Корчунов: военная активность России в Арктике никому не угрожает." *RIA Novosti* 2021. https://ria.ru/20210601/aktivnost-1734886866.html

Камцов В.М., Порфирьев Б.Н. Климатические изменения в Арктике: последствия для окружающей среды и экономики// Арктика: экология и экономика. 2,6 (2012): 66-79.

Комментарий официального представителя МИД России М.В.Захаровой в связи с заявлением западных стран-членов Арктического совета, 2022 https://mid.ru/ ru/foreign_policy/news/1802852/

"'Норникель'оценивает ущерб от разлива топлива в 21,4 млрд рублей." *Норникель*. October, 2020, https://www.nornickel.ru/news-and-media/press-releases-and-news/nornikel-otsenivaet-ushcherb-ot-razliva-topliva-v-21-4-mlrd-rubley/?sphrase_id=3392885.

"Паспорт федерального проекта 'Развитие Северного морского пути.'" The Ministry of Transport of the Russian Federation. 2023. https://mintrans.gov.ru/ documents/8/12714.

"Первый контейнеровоз прошел по Северному морскому пути." Vedomosti 2018, https://www.vedomosti.ru/business/articles/2018/09/26/782107-konteinerovoz-severnomu-morskomu

Энергия Арктики. М.О. Моргунова, А.Я. Цуневский, под научн. ред. В.В. Бушуева, М.: ИЦ «Энергия», (2012): 38-41.

# SECTION II

## COUNTRY-LEVEL ANALYSES

# CHAPTER 1

## UNITED STATES ARCTIC POLICY FROM WHITE HILLS TO BLUE WATERS

Aslıhan Genç[1]

The Arctic region is changing as global warming and melting glaciers facilitate access to valuable resources. In addition to energy reserves, valuable minerals and fishing activities, new routes will change the geopolitics of this region with the ease of transit through transport hubs. This situation is causing states to shift their attention to this geography, both commercially and politically, revealing the power struggle in the region. As an Arctic state, the United States, while analysing its policy and security in the region, determines its strategy by considering the changes in this region.

The United States became an Arctic nation in 1867 when it bought Alaska from the Russian Empire. Although this policy was criticised at the time, the realisation of Alaska's riches changed this situation.[2] This region is America's largest state and most sparsely populated. America's Arctic indigenous peoples make a living from animal husbandry and fishing. In addition, about two million people visit this region every year for its unique winter landscape and natural beauty. For the United States, the Arctic is also important to the dynamics of national and homeland security and serves a variety of purposes, including environmental protection, sustainable development, promoting the inclusion of indigenous rights in decisions that affect their future, and supporting scientific research. America's main goal in the Arctic is to protect national interests and the homeland, to solve common problems in cooperation with other Arctic states, and to be a safe, stable, and conflict-free region.

This chapter analyses the Arctic policy of the United States. In this context, the military, economic and political interests of the United States in the region will be examined. In the study, the Arctic policy of the United States in the historical process will be evaluated and then its relations with the states in the

[1] Trakya University, Edirne, Türkiye, Ph.D. Candidate, ORCID: https://orcid.org/0000-0002-5592-4513, aslihanngenc@gmail.com.
[2] "Purchase of Alaska, 1867", USA Office of the Historian, last modified May 12, 2023, https://history.state.gov/milestones/1866-1898/alaska-purchase.

region will be revealed.

## The Geography of the Country and Its Geopolitical Importance

With a surface area of 9.147 million square kilometres, Alaska is the largest of the 50 US states. The area referred to as "the American Arctic'extends from roughly 15 to 170° west longitude.[3] Although sparsely populated, the region became increasingly important for both defence and resource exploitation. Today, the Arctic is rich in oil, natural gas, and valuable minerals. Unlike Antarctica, it has also long been an energy corridor for supra-ice bombing routes and sub-ice nuclear submarine voyages. With the development of aviation technologies, the location of the region has become an area to be evaluated. Alaska has access to the Beaufort Sea, the Chukchi Sea, the Bering Sea and has a maritime border with Russia through the Bering Strait and the Chukchi Sea. The Arctic provides the shortest transit route between the two nuclear powers, the Russia and the USA. Less than 4,500 miles from the Russian Arctic settlements are the American cities of Seattle, Chicago, Washington, and New York, key hubs for social, cultural, and political entities.

The geopolitical importance of the Arctic was recognised by US Secretary of State William Seward at the time of the purchase of Alaska. The United States became an Arctic country after the purchase of Alaska from the Russian Empire in 1867.[4] The purchase of these lands was criticised by then Secretary of State William H Seward as "buying a handful of snow and ice", and opponents of the Alaska purchase insisted on calling it "Seward's Folly" or "Seward's Icebox" until 1896, when they were convinced that Alaska was a valuable addition to American soil.[5] At that time, Iceland and Greenland were also to be secured. Although explorers such as Robert Peary and Vilhjalmur Stefansson tried to make America aware of the geopolitical importance of the region, interest in the Arctic was not sufficient.

Alaska is the largest and most sparsely populated state in the United States. The state has a population of about 737,400, with more than half living in the two major cities of Anchorage and Fairbanks. Approximately 18 percent of

---

[3] Joseph S. Roucek, "The Geopolitics of the Arctic", The American Journal of Economics and Sociology, 42, no. 4, (1983): 463.
[4] "Purchase of Alaska, 1867", USA Office of the Historian, last modified May 12, 2023, https://history.state.gov/milestones/1866-1898/alaska-purchase
[5] "Check fort he Purchase of Alaska (1868)", modified May 12, 2023, National Archives, https://www.archives.gov/milestone-documents/check-for-the-purchase-of-alaska#transcript

Alaska's population is indigenous.[6] Indigenous peoples include the Aleut, Alutiiq, Yup'ik, Iñupiaq (Northwest Alaska Inuit), Athabaskan, Tlingit and Haida. The Yup'ik, Athabaskans and Iñupiaq live above the Arctic Circle and depend on hunting and fishing for their subsistence. Oil and mining are important industries in Alaska. Fishing and tourism are also important. Nearly two million people travel to Alaska each year to see the glaciers and wildlife.

**Historical Interaction in the Arctic Region**

Over the past decade, various cultural and intellectual studies of the US Arctic past have been undertaken by think tanks, media, and academics, contributing to the development of the country's Arctic interests. In its 19th century vision, America's interest in the Arctic remained more passive. Although Alaska was purchased from the Russian tsar in 1967, the region remained outside of America's expansion plans for economic gain and settlement.[7] For more than 40 years, the US government has presented its core interests in the Arctic through a series of government documents, including:

- President Richard Nixon's 1971 National Security Decision Memorandum (NSDM-144)[8],
- President Ronald Reagan's 1983 National Security Decision Directive (NSDD-90)[9]
- President W. Clinton's Arctic direction of foreign policy under (1993–2001), formulated in Presidential Directive No. 26 (NSC-26)
- President George W. Bush's National Security Presidential Directive 66 and Homeland Security Presidential Directive 25[10], signed in 2009[11]
- President Barack Obama's National Strategy for the Arctic Region[12]

[6] "The United States", modified May 15, 2023, https://arctic-council.org/about/states/the-united-states/
[7] Dorothy Ross, The Origins of American Social Science. (Baltimore: Johns Hopkins University Press, 1992)
[8]"National Security Decision Memoranda, National Archives, last modified May 18, 2023, https://www.nixonlibrary.gov/national-security-decision-memorandNational Security Decision Memoranda, Richard Nixon, National Archives, a-nsdm
[9] "National Security Decision Directives Reagan Administration, Intelligence Resource Program, modified May 20, 2023, https://irp.fas.org/offdocs/nsdd/index.html
[10] "National Security Presidential Directives George W. Bush Administration", lastmodified May 20, 2023, https://irp.fas.org/offdocs/nspd/index.html
[11] "National Security Presidential Directive and Homeland Security Presidental Directive", modified May 20, 2023, https://irp.fas.org/offdocs/nspd/nspd-66.htm#:~:text=Project%20a%20sovereign%20United%20States,disputes%20in%20the%20Arctic%20region.
[12] "Natiinal Strategy For The Arctic Region", The Wite House, last modified May 20, 2023, https://web.archive.org/web/20210215024218/https://obamawhitehouse.archives.gov/sites/default/files/docs/nat_arctic_strategy.pdf

- The 2016 Report to Congress from the Department of Defense on Strategy to Protect United States National Security Interests in the Arctic Region[13].
- President Trump's 2020 new national security and defence strategy for the polar regions in 2020. [14]
- The Biden-era National Strategy for the Arctic was released in 2022.[15] What should be understood from all these documents is that they were made for the United States to establish guidelines compatible with geostrategic realities in the region.

**Relations with other Arctic Countries**

Arctic states generally emphasise cooperation and peaceful resolution of disputes in the region. In this context, the Arctic Council plays an important role in maintaining dialogue and cooperation among states. The Arctic states are concerned with maintaining stability in the region and acting together to address common challenges. The Arctic states work together in many areas, including indigenous peoples, sustainable economies, natural resource extraction, environmental protection, scientific research and search and rescue in the region. However, evolving geopolitical changes sometimes complicate competition and relations between states in the region. America has various disputes with regional states. These are situations that sometimes pose a problem for the full functioning of the US regional policy.

Bilateral relations between the Russian Federation and the United States, which have the longest Arctic coastline, are complex. They cooperate on issues such as search and rescue and scientific research. However, tensions sometimes arise over issues such as military activities and resource development. The strategic location of the Bering Strait, which forms the border between the two states, raises some issues. As a result of the climate crisis and melting glaciers in the region, it is important for the littoral states along the Bering Strait, which lies between the Northwest Passage and the Northeast Passage, to establish dominance in this area. Supporting maritime safety and fisheries law enforcement in the Bering Strait along the US-Russia

---

[13] "Report to Congress on Strategy to Protect United States National Security Interest in the Arctic Region" Department of Defense, https://dod.defense.gov/Portals/1/Documents/pubs/2016-Arctic-Strategy-UNCLAS-cleared-for-release.pdf.

[14] "Memorandum on Safeguarding U.S. National Interests in the Arctic and Antartic Regions", The White House, last modified May 23, 2023, https://trumpwhitehouse.archives.gov/presidential-actions/memorandum-safeguarding-u-s-national-interests-arctic-antarctic-regions/.

[15] National Strategy For The Arctic Region, The White House, last modified May 23, 2023, https://www.whitehouse.gov/wp-content/uploads/2022/10/National-Strategy-for-the-Arctic-Region.pdf

Maritime Boundary Line (MBL) in the Bering Sea responds to distress calls at sea.[16] There are also disputes between the Russian Federation and the United States over the status of the Northeast Passage. This is also a route that Russia and China are considering as an alternative to the Strait of Malacca and the Suez Canal. It is also on the transit route of the Polar Silk Road project. While Russia considers this area to be its internal waters, the United States has responded by arguing that the route falls within international waters under Article 136 of UNCLOS.[17] In addition, the two states signed a joint fisheries agreement on this border in 1988. In 2013, because of melting glaciers and changing geography, a Joint Declaration on Enhanced Fisheries Cooperation was signed to ensure continued cooperation on this issue. The United States also argues that the Lomonosov and Mendeleyev Ridges are oceanic ridges and are not connected to the continental territory of any state, contradicting Russia's claims of sovereignty.[18]

Russia's assertion of sovereignty by planting a titanium flag on the Lomonosov Ridge in 2007 on the grounds that it is an extension of Siberia was seen as polar imperialism by the US and Canada.[19] In addition, military initiatives create problems between the two states. The uncertain actions of these states, which have security concerns about each other, are leading to the rapid militarisation of the Arctic. Especially in the aftermath of the Ukraine crisis, states have increased their defence spending, which is reflected in the trade, energy, and security sectors.

Among the regional states, Denmark's Arctic policy is in line with the US security perspective. Like Sweden and Finland, which viewed NATO's presence in the region with suspicion because it increased the Russian threat, Denmark shed its doubts and began to support the organisation's activities in the region after the Russia-Ukraine war. Russia's increasing military activity in the region is recognised as a geopolitical challenge. In addition, China's growing political presence in the Arctic and its desire to undertake major projects in Greenland sometimes cause disagreements between the Greenlandic and Danish governments. At this point, the US and Danish governments made joint appeals to the Nuuk Home Rule Government with

---

[16] Heather A. Conley, Matthew Melino, and Andreas Østhagen, Maritime Futures: The Arctic and the Bering Strait Region (Lanham, MD: Rowman & Littlefield, 2017), 25.

[17] Michael Byers, "International Law and the Arctic", Cambridge Studies in International and Comparative Law, (Cambridge University Press, United Kingdom, 2013), 144.

[18] Rebecca Pincus, "The History of USA-Russia Relations in the Bering Strait", The Palgrave Handbook of Arctic Policy and Politics, Ed. Ken S Coates and Carin Holroyd, (Palgrave Macmillan), 341.

[19] Tom Parfitt, "Russia Plants Flag on North Pole Seabes" The Guardian, Aug 2, 2007, last modified August 2, 2023, https://www.theguardian.com/world/2007/aug/02/russia.arctic

economic offers to counter China's interests in an airport project and mining potential in Greenland.[20] At the same time, a Defence Cooperation Agreement (DCA) was negotiated in 2022 and signed on 14 February 2023, allowing the US to station its troops in Denmark. The two countries conduct joint military exercises.[21] The US is Denmark's closest security ally and has had a military presence in Greenland for decades. The US has reconsidered its investment in the Thule base in Greenland following Russia's war in Ukraine.[22] This base is important for US early warning and missile defence. It was also renamed Pituffik Spaceport in April 2023.[23] Given the changing geopolitical environment in the region, the two countries will continue to strengthen their cooperation in the fields of security and scientific research.

Map 1. Arctic Sea Routes[24]

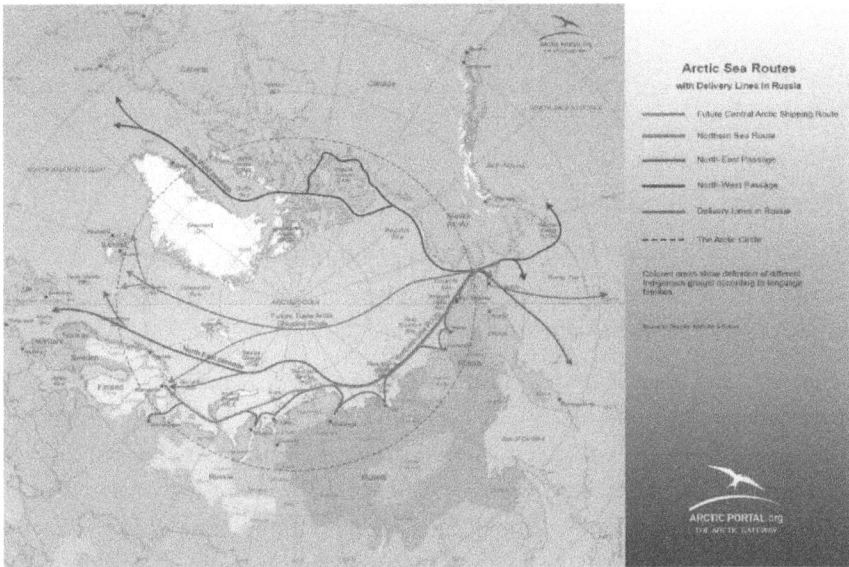

*Source: Arctic Portal*

[20] Martin Breum, "How a Dispute over China and Greenland's Airports Worked Its Way Toward a Solution", Arctic Today, 30 June 2018, last modified August 2, 2023, https://www.arctictoday.com/dispute-china-greenlands-airports-worked-way-toward-solution/

[21] "U. S. Security Cooperation with Denmark", U. S. Department of State, last modified August 4, 2023, https://www.state.gov/u-s-security-cooperation-with-denmark/

[22] "United States Plans to Invest Greenland Military Base", The Local, last modified August 4, 2023, https://www.thelocal.dk/20220523/united-states-plans-to-invest-in-greenland-military-base

[23] "New Name for Thule Air Base in Greenland", High North News, last modified August 4, 2023 https://www.highnorthnews.com/en/new-name-thule-air-base-greenland

[24] Arctic Portal, Development in the Russian Arctic , https://arcticportal.org/ap-library/news/3332-development-in-the-russian-arctic.

**Map 2.** Pituffik Space Base with Previous Name Thule

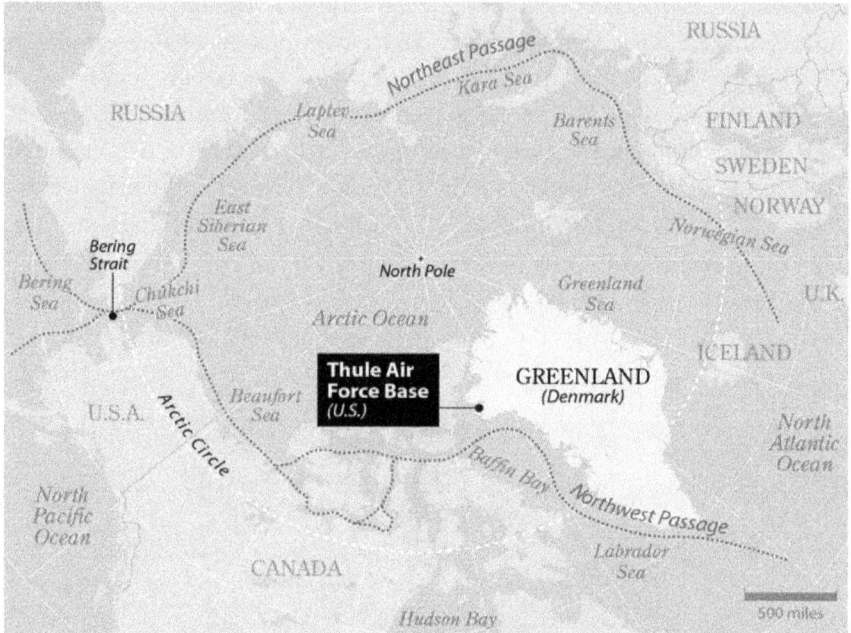

*Source: Inside Climate News, for Bibliography (Inside Climate News , last modified 02.03.2024 https://insideclimatenews.org/news/26022023/thule-air-base-greenland-russia-climate-change/)*

The US and Canada have historically strong ties and well-established mechanisms for cooperation. They work bilaterally and in partnership through the Arctic Council to combat climate change, build sustainable economies, and address common challenges. President Biden and Prime Minister Trudeau agreed to launch the Roadmap for a Renewed U.S.-Canada Partnership and an expanded U.S.-Canada Arctic Dialogue. In addition, the leaders are working to preserve the cultures of the Gwich'in and Inuvialuit peoples who migrate across shared borders, and to protect the calving grounds of the Porcupine caribou herd. They have also agreed to accelerate and secure private and public investment in strategic mining, processing and fabrication by June 2022.[25] The two countries also share common approaches to China and seek to harmonise their policies. They share a common stance against coercive and unfair economic practices with China. In the region,

---

[25] Adam Lajeunesse, "Arctic Geopolitics and Security from the Canadian Perspective, Handbook on Geopolitics and Security in the Arctic, Ed: Joachim Weber, https://www.state.gov/u-s-relations-with-canada/ , 43-44.

there is a dispute between Canada and the United States over the Beaufort Sea. The disputed area is rich in oil and natural gas. According to studies conducted in the area, there are enough reserves to meet Canada's natural gas needs for 20 years.[26][27] Although the resource potential in the disputed area is high, technological challenges and the high cost of accessing these resources suggest that access to the region's resources will be limited in the long term.

Norway and the United States have a long tradition of friendship based on democratic values and mutual respect. Partnerships exist in security, environmental protection, and scientific research. Norway is a co-founder of NATO and a committed strategic ally. Within the security paradigm, it acts with NATO, of which it is a member, which positions it as an actor close to the United States. It organises joint exercises with NATO and hosts many operations. At the same time, US military personnel train in Norway for cold-weather exercises. As partners in the fight against climate change and the green transition, the two countries are co-leading the Green Shipping Challenge.[28] It will continue its political partnership with Norway (2023-2025), which chairs the Arctic Council. The US and Norway also have strong ties, with around 5 million Americans claiming the same ancestry.[29] In this context, Norway and the US have friendly and cooperative relations. Both countries act together in this geography within the framework of their national interests.

Sweden and Finland have similar foreign policy behaviours, and in the region, Washington has become an important partner for both states. The Russia-Ukraine war and Finland's membership in NATO, and possibly soon Sweden's, will continue to maintain compatible security paradigms. This will strengthen both countries'alliance with the United States. In addition, the two countries have common interests in sustainable energy, climate change prevention, and economic and security cooperation with the United States. The bilateral relationship between Iceland and the United States is based on cooperation and mutual support. As one of the first countries to recognise Iceland's independence, the US and Iceland work together in many areas, including peaceful cooperation in the Arctic and the use of renewable energy.

---

[26] Clive Schofield and Andreas Østhagen, "A Divided Arctic:Maritime Boundary Agreements and Disputes in the Arctic Ocean, Handbook on Geopolitics and Security in the Arctic, Ed:Joachim Weber, 176-177.

[27] "Beaufort Sea Boundar", Michael Byers, International Law and the Arctic, 62.

[28] U.S. Announcements Under the Green Shipping Challenge at COP27, U. S. Department of State, last modified May 12, 2023 https://www.state.gov/u-s-announcements-under-the-green-shipping-challenge-at-cop27/

[29] "U.S. Relations With Norway", U. S. Department of State, last modified August 4, 2023, https://www.state.gov/u-s-relations-with-norway/.

At the same time, they share a common security policy within NATO and continue to strengthen their economic ties.

## Its Military, Economic and Political Importance

Today, there are three main drivers of US policy in the Arctic. The first is the growing Russian and Chinese threat in the region. The second is the environmental and climatic factors that have transformed the Arctic marine and terrestrial space. Finally, there are global economic reasons.[30] In addition, US Arctic Policy includes the economic function provided by factors such as Alaska's energy resources, mining and fishing. But economic activity in Alaska is under threat from low global energy prices and the depletion of some oil wells. In addition, the region's indigenous people are becoming climate refugees as they leave their homes, which are subject to coastal erosion due to freshwater scarcity and permafrost melting, which is significantly altering their traditional livelihoods. These are all risk factors in the US Arctic region of Alaska. Although the US Arctic policy has basically been stagnant for the last decade, the Russia-Ukraine war in 2019 and China's increasing presence in the region have led to action for change in Arctic policy.

One of the key events influencing geopolitical developments in the region was the announcement of the Polar Silk Road project in 2013, and China's accession to the Arctic Council as a permanent observer in 2018. All this made China visible in the Arctic economically, diplomatically, and scientifically, and coincided with the US chairmanship of the Arctic Council (2015-2017). Since 2009, the Obama administration has viewed climate change in the Arctic as a national security issue that requires special attention.[31] During the Arctic chairmanship, the US administration created new regional leadership positions, such as a US Special Representative for the Arctic and Executive Director of the Arctic Executive Committee, to increase public visibility on Arctic issues. He was the first president to visit Alaska, in part to chair the GLACIER (Global Leadership in the Arctic Cooperation, Innovation, Engagement, and Resilience) conference, which brought together 20 foreign ministers from the Obama administration. The Arctic Council, including observer members, called for national action plans

---

[30] Heather A. Conley and Matthew Melino, "The Implications of U.S. Policy Stagnation toward the Arctic Region", May 2019, CSIS, 2. https://www.csis.org/analysis/implications-us-policy-stagnation-toward-arctic-region

[31] Ibid.

to combat climate change. Russia and China have not signed GLACIER.[32] President Obama's three-day visit to Alaska during his chairmanship of the Arctic Council was intended to send a strong message about his policy in the region. These include improving the economic and living conditions of Arctic indigenous peoples, the safety, security and governance of the Arctic Ocean, and the effects of climate change.[33] Another notable event during Obama's visit to Alaska was the Sino-Russian naval exercise involving five Chinese naval vessels off the coast of Vladivostok, Russia, off Alaska's Aleutian Islands.[34]

There has been no effective change in the leadership of the Arctic Council during Trump's presidency. However, at the national level, the Trump administration has begun to dismantle the Arctic governance structures put in place during the Obama administration, emphasising economic development while ignoring the impacts of the climate crisis. While the US budget for Arctic science and research remained flat, both Republicans and Democrats continued to attend the Arctic Council Ministerial. One of the most significant developments during this period was the resumption of oil and gas drilling, with expedited environmental reviews in onshore and offshore areas of the Arctic National Wildlife Refuge (ANWR).[35] New areas in the Chukchi Sea have been reserved for drilling leases and oil exploration has been encouraged along the Beaufort Sea coast in ANWR, estimated to be America's largest undiscovered onshore oil field. In 2017, the Governor of Alaska signed a Joint Development Agreement with China worth an average of $43 billion to develop liquefied natural gas (LNG) for export to China.[36] Although there was a desire for economic development of the Arctic region in the US during this period, the limited US infrastructure in the region affected economic development. Although Dutch Harbor in the southern Bering Sea, 800 miles from the US Bering Strait, is a strategic area, the lack of an adequate icebreaker fleet also limits access to these resources. In recent years, as the number of passages through the Bering Strait has increased,

---

[32] "Conference on GLACIER", IISD, last modified June 12, 2023, http://sdg.iisd.org/ events/ conference-on-global-leadership-in-the-arctic-cooperation-innovation-engagement-and-resilience-glacier/

[33]"President Obama's Trip to Alaska", The White House, last modified June 20, 2023, https://obamawhitehouse.archives.gov/2015-alaska-trip.

[34] Jeremy Page, "Chinese Navy Ships Came Within 12 Nautical Miles of U. S. Coast", The Wall Street Journal, last modified June 20, 2023, https://www.wsj.com/articles/chinese-navy-ships-off-alaska-passed-through-u-s-territorial-waters-1441350488

[35] Changes in the Arctic: Background and Issues for Congress, Congressional Research Service, 3-4, last modified June 20, 2023, https://sgp.fas.org/crs/misc/R41153.pdf

[36] Josephine Mason, "We're Engaged:Alaska Gets China Backing for Natural Gas Project", last modified June 21, 2023, https://www.reuters.com/article/us-trump-asia-china-gas-idUKKBN1D90C1

there has been an urgent need for talent to navigate this narrow passage, as well as for communications and awareness of the sea area.

Under former President Trump, Arctic state policy was primarily concerned with security and oil and gas extraction and development. The United States has not appointed a special ambassador to the region for years, and at the 2019 Arctic Council Ministerial Meeting, the Trump administration also refused to cooperate on a joint statement that mentioned climate change or the Paris Agreement. It was also the first meeting of the eight Arctic states since 1996 without a formal joint statement.[37] The budget for a new fleet of icebreakers was used to build a wall on the border with Mexico. The US Coast Guard said it urgently needed to strengthen its icebreaker fleet, but House Republicans instead used the 2019 House appropriations bill for the proposed US-Mexico border wall to build the wall. Democrats accused Republicans of "wasting a staggering $4.9 billion on a border wall" and said the "misallocation of resources" in a region of heightened tensions with Russia should be reassessed.[38] The US icebreaker fleet has only two operational ships. These ships are responsible for collecting scientific data, assisting ships stuck in the ice, and responding to oil spills. They also protect US interests in the polar regions, where climate change is melting sea ice. One of the two icebreakers is the Polar Star and the other is the Healy. Polar Star was commissioned more than 40 years ago and is still in service, although it is nearing the end of its service life. It organises an annual expedition to Antarctica to resupply McMurdo Station. The other icebreaker, the Healy, visited the North Pole for the first time in 2001. It is a medium-sized Coast Guard icebreaker.[39] Healy suffered an engine fire in the Arctic in August 2020, which took almost a year to repair before completing the expedition through the Northwest Passage in 2021.[40] Healy's last sailing was on 30 September 2022. The ship is still in service.[41] The US Coast Guard says it needs six new icebreakers, one of which must be delivered immediately.

[37] Victoria Herrmann, In The Arctic, America is its Own Worst Enemy", CNN, May 10, 2019, last modified June 22, 2023, https://edition.cnn.com/2019/05/10/opinions/victoria-herrmann-arctic-america-is-its-own-worst-enemy

[38] Mariam Khan, "Republicans Propose Reallocating Coast Guard Ship Funding to Trump's Border Wall", ABC News, August 9, 2018, last modified June 28, 2023, https://abcnews.go.com/Politics/republicans-propose-reallocating-coast-guard-ship-funding-trumps/story?id=57109998 .

[39] CGC Healy, United States Coast Guard, last modified June 28, 2023, https://www.pacificarea.uscg.mil/Our-Organization/Cutters/cgcHealy/

[40] Emily Hofstaedter, "Icebreaker USCGC Healy to Navigate Northwest Passage This Summer", Knom, last modified June 28, 2023, https://knom.org/2021/03/25/icebreaker-uscg-healy-to-navigate-northwest-passage-this-summer/.

[41] USCGC Healy Reaches North Pole, UNOLS, last modified June 28, 2023, https://www.unols.org/news/ships-news/uscgc-healy-reaches-north-pole

Designing and building new icebreakers takes many years and costs billions of dollars. The US needs a new fleet of icebreakers to balance Russian and Chinese forces in the region and to ensure the Coast Guard's access to its strategic and economic interests in the region. In addition, since the US does not have an icebreaker to patrol the North Pole, it must rely on Russia and other states to do so. Adding new ships to the Coast Guard will also reduce the cost of funding repairs to aging vessels. President Joe Biden acknowledged the critical existence of the Arctic Ocean in his speech at the Coast Guard Academy[42] graduation in 2021.[43] The Polar Security Cutter programme was established to begin construction of the new Polar Class icebreaker, with a start date of 2021 and a completion date of the first half of 2024. However, as construction has not yet started and the actual date is uncertain, it has been pushed back to 2027.[44] The Coast Guard wants to buy a $150 million icebreaker to fill the gap. The best candidate is the Aiviq, which is used by Shell for Arctic oil exploration in the Beaufort and Chukchi seas. Among the states in the region, the Russian Federation currently has the largest icebreaker fleet, with over 40 ships, and this number is expected to increase.[45]

Similarly, the People's Republic of China, which defines itself as a "near-regional state", has two icebreakers and is building its first nuclear-powered icebreaker. The presence of these fleets is important for China to strengthen its emergency response capacity along the Polar Silk Road[46] and its coordination in the region.[47]

One of the most recent Arctic-related documents released by the US is the

---

[42] President Biden Commencement Address at U. S. Coast Guard Academy, C-Span, https://www.c-span.org/video/?511881-1/president-biden-commencement-address-us-coast-guard-academy

[43] Arctic Strategic Outlook, U. S. Department of Homeland Security, last modified June 29, 2023, https://www.uscg.mil/Arctic/.

[44] James Di Pane, U. S. Needs Icebreakers to Keep Up With China and Russia in Arctic, The Heritage Foundation, Jun 18, 2021, last modified July 1, 2023, https://www.heritage.org/global-politics/commentary/us-needs-icebreakers-keep-china-and-russia-arctic

[45] Sen. Roger Wicker and Sen. Dan Sullivan, "Polar Icebreakers Are Key To America's National Interest", Defense News, Oct 19, 2020, last modified July 20, 2023, https://www.defensenews.com/opinion/commentary/2020/10/19/polar-icebreakers-are-key-to-americas-national-interest/#:~:text=Russia%20has%20the%20world's%20largest,planned%20in%20the%20next%20decade.

[46] China's 2018 strategy document, known as the White Paper, includes the Silk Road Initiative as well as infrastructure investment, commercial voyages and scientific research along the Arctic and Arctic transport. See also: https://english.www.gov.cn/archive/whitepaper/

[47] Malte Humpert, "China to Build New Heavy Icebreaker and Lift Vessel for Arctic", High North News, Nov 16, 2021, last modified July 20, 2023, https://www.highnorthnews.com/en/china-build-new-heavy-icebreaker-and-lift-vessel-arctic#:~:text=Currently%20China%20operates%20two%20conventionally,was%20subsequently%20modified%20and%20refurbished.

Department of the Navy's Blueprint for a Blue Arctic, dated 5 October 2021. This document sets out a draft plan for the next twenty years for the Arctic that will emerge with more accessible resources and navigable sea lanes. This forward-looking document highlights the transition from white to blue waters and emphasises the impact of climate change in the region. It discusses the projection of US naval power in the region, joint forces and interagency cooperation, and a unified approach with allies. It also focuses on developing and expanding the integrated capabilities of the US Navy, Marine Corps, and Coast Guard teams to achieve enduring national interests in the region. It provides guidance on how to ensure the Navy's continued presence in Arctic waters to meet the challenging demands of the Blue Arctic in an era of great power competition and emphasises America's readiness to compete effectively and efficiently to maintain the appropriate balance of power. It is important to establish cooperative partnerships to ensure coordination with key allies and partners in this region.

The Biden administration released its Arctic National Strategy on 7 October 2022, with an ambitious vision for domestic and international leadership in the region.[48] The new US Arctic strategy is based on four mutually reinforcing pillars. These are security, climate change and environmental protection, sustainable economic development, and international cooperation and governance. While acknowledging that the climate crisis is one of the region's greatest challenges, the new strategy document emphasises that the US seeks a peaceful, stable, prosperous and cooperative Arctic region. It also has multiple goals, including protecting the Arctic's nearly four million indigenous peoples from the adverse effects of climate change, sustaining economic prosperity, and investing in new development opportunities in a world affected by the climate crisis.

**Security Relationship with the Arctic Region**

With the new security document, the US has clearly stated its Arctic policy, emphasising that it is committed to ensuring security with its allies in the region, and by appointing an ambassador to the region, it has also emphasised that it takes the indigenous peoples of the region into account. The latest policy documents are also a stern warning to Russia over the war in Ukraine. Especially in the last decade, Russia and China's cooperation, investment and leadership claims in the Arctic have increased. The strategy document, which

---

[48] Department of the Navy Releases Strategic Blueprint for a Blue Arctic, Jan 5, 2021, last modified July 20, 2023, https://www.navy.mil/Press-Office/Press-Releases/display-pressreleases/Article/2463000/department-of-the-navy-releases-strategic-blueprint-for-a-blue-arctic/

acknowledges the growing economic and military presence of these states, portrays Russia and China as rivals and potential challengers to peace and stability in the Arctic. As a result, the United States is seeking to expand its military presence in the Arctic. Chief among these commitments is increased cold-weather exercises with NATO allies and the expansion of the US Coast Guard's icebreaker fleet with three new Polar Security Cutter Programs, the first icebreakers to be built in American shipyards in 45 years. At the same time, the Biden administration is nominating Alaskan and head of the US Arctic Study Commission Mike Sfraga to be the nation's first Arctic ambassador on 13 February 2023.[49][50] The United States has more than 22,000 active-duty troops in Alaska and also maintains a base in Greenland. Last month, the Pentagon created an Office of Arctic Strategy and Global Resilience for the Arctic, headed by Iris Ferguson as assistant secretary of defence. As such, it will oversee various elements of the White House's Arctic strategy, such as coordination with US security partners and.[51] As can be seen from all this, US Arctic policy has changed in line with the international conjuncture and has become a geography that has increasingly become a priority in the last 10 years. With the Russia-Ukraine war in 2019, the US, which wants to act by evaluating the analysis of the opportunities and risks that the effects of the global climate crisis will have in this region, will pursue a more active policy in the region. One criticism of US policy in the region is that it has been slow to understand the strategic implications of great power competition in the Arctic. The US assumed that the strategic value of the Arctic would remain limited and that its current minimalist policy stance would be sufficient and failed to analyse the activities of its two rivals, Russia and China, in the region in the short and medium term. As a result of the debate on the adequacy of the current posture, the process of change finally took place in the aftermath of Russia's war in Ukraine.

## Added Values in The Arctic and Their Prospects in The Region

Energy-related activities in the region are important to the US. America is

---

[49] "Arctic Caucus Co-Chairs Introduce Legislation to Make the Arctic Ambassador", Angus King, March 20, 2023, last modified August 2, 2023, https://www.king.senate.gov/newsroom/press-releases/arctic-caucus-co-chairs-introduce-legislation-to-make-the-arctic-ambassador-at-large-a-permanent-position#:~:text=On%20February%2016%2C%202023%2C%20President,the%20nation's%20first%20Arctic%20Ambassador.

[50] "Murkowski Welcomes Nomination of Dr. Mike Sfraga to be Ambassador", Murkowski, last modified August 2, 2023, https://www.murkowski.senate.gov/press/release/murkowski-welcomes-nomination-of-dr-mike-sfraga-to-be_-ambassador-at-large-for-the-arctic-region

[51] Jim Garamone, "DOD Establishes Arctic Strategy and Global Resilience Office", U.S. Department of Defense, last modified August 2, 2023, https://www.defense.gov/News/News-Stories/ Article/Article/3171173/dod-establishes-arctic-strategy-and-global-resilience-office/

interested in exploring and developing these resources in the Arctic region to increase its energy security and reduce its dependence on foreign energy sources. The US Geological Survey estimates that up to 30% of the world's untapped natural gas reserves and 13% of its oil reserves lie beneath the Arctic tundra and sea ice. The 2016 Arctic document also states that the fisheries value of Alaska, where the US has 1,609,344 square kilometres of continental shelf and EEZ in the Arctic region, is about $3 billion, and that the oil and natural gas reserves, as well as valuable minerals such as copper, nickel and iron, are about $1 trillion.[52] In a report on the energy potential of the Arctic coast, the US National Petroleum Council estimated that US oil production in 2040 will be one million barrels per day. The report also recognised that much of the conventional oil and gas potential of the US Arctic coast could be developed using existing technologies.[53] Prudhoe Bay in Alaska, the largest oil field ever discovered, is one of the largest oil reserves in the region and has alternative sea routes. In addition, the increase in Arctic maritime traffic and its growth as a result of global warming, hydrocarbon resources, scientific studies and tourism activities represents an opportunity for the U.S.[54] The melting of sea ice in the Arctic has opened up new maritime trade routes, such as the Northern Sea Route. It is important to use these routes safely and securely, which has led to a decline in transport between the Americas, Europe and Asia. The US is committed to freedom of navigation on these routes.[55] America attaches importance to environmental management in this region. It is committed to protecting the environment of indigenous Arctic peoples in its own country and in this region and to addressing climate change. In addition, the US has worked with Arctic nations to launch the International Environmental Surveillance (8ICS), a region-wide disease surveillance system managed by the Centres for Disease Control and Prevention. Initiated the first comprehensive scientific assessment of the impacts of climate change, the Arctic Climate Impact Assessment (ACIA), completed in 2004.[56] Signed the "Agreement on Cooperation in Preparing for and Combating Arctic Marine Oil

---

[52] Department of Defense, "Report to Congress on Strategy to Protect United States National Security Interest in the Arctic Region" 2016, https://dod.defense.gov/Portals/1/Documents/pubs/2016-Arctic-Strategy-UNCLAS-cleared-for-release.pdf

[53]Stanislav Pritchin, "Russia's Untapped Arctic Potential", Chatham House, https://www.chathamhouse.org/expert/comment/russia-s-untapped-arctic-potential.

[54] Nihat Yılmaz, Ali Çiftçi. 'Arktika Bölgesi'nin Siyasal Önemi ve Siyasal ve Hukuksal Statüsü'nün Karşılaştırmalı Değerlendirmesi', Muğla Sıtkı Koçman University, Journal of Social Sciences Institute, (2013): 31.

[55] Arild Moe, Øystein Jensen "Opening of New Arctic Shipping Routes", Directorate-General for External Policies, Policy Department, (2010): 12.

[56] Arctic Climate Impact Assesment (ACIA) Scientific Report, https://www.caff.is/assessment-series/37-arctic-climate-impact-assessment-acia-scientific-report

Pollution"[57] in 2013 and chaired the Expert Groups on Marine Environmental Response and Search and Rescue in the implementation of the "Agreement on Cooperation in Aviation and Maritime Matters".[58] In this context, it is involved in efforts to reduce greenhouse gas emissions and support climate research. The Arctic Council, one of the most important international organisations in the Arctic region, held its first chairmanship in 1998-2000 and its second in 2015-2017. The first chairmanship focused on improving human health, climate change in the Arctic and sustainable development of Arctic tourism.[59] During the last chairmanship, it addressed cooperation in search and rescue, preparedness for and response to oil spills, security in the Arctic Ocean, including maritime transport, addressing the effects of climate change, pursuing innovative technologies, advancing health research, improving telecommunications infrastructure, and improving economic and living conditions in the Arctic. America's next Arctic chairmanship is 2031-2033.[60]

## Conclusion

The new US Arctic strategy document places a strong emphasis on economic development as well as security. US investment in the Arctic is expected to increase over the next 10 years. The main impact of the new document is to update US policy in the region. It calls for the US to reassess the importance and challenges of the region and place it on the federal agenda. For the first time since the acquisition of Russian Alaska in 1867, the US is taking steps to conspicuously assert its status as an Arctic nation. Unpredictable and uncertain programmes, such as the postponement of the delivery of icebreakers from 2024 to 2027, as foreseen in the Polar Security Cutter Programme, are situations that should be questioned for the US. Then there is the uncertainty of the spill over effects of the war in Ukraine on the poles, and the uncertainties that may arise in a world that continues to warm. The US should analyse all this. It should focus on realistic policies to implement its short, medium and long-term plans according to the dynamics in the region, and it is important that they are sustainable. By following the indigenous peoples in the region and their life cycles, it should show the

[57] Agrement on Cooperation on Marine Oil Pollution Preparedness and Response in the Arctic https://disasterlaw.ifrc.org/sites/default/files/media/disaster_law/2021-03/EDOCS-2068-v1-ACMMSE08_KIRUNA_2013_agreement_on_oil_pollution_preparedness_and_response_signedAppen dices_Original_130510.pdf
[58] Agrement on Cooperation on Aeronautical and Maritime Search and Rescue in the Arctic, https://oaarchive.arctic-council.org/items/9c343a3f-cc4b-4e75-bfd3-4b318137f8a2
[59] "Establishment of the Arctic Council", last modified May 12, 2023, https://2009-2017. state.gov/e/oes/ocns/opa/arc/ac/establishmentarcticcouncil/
[60] "Arctic Region", U. S. Department of State, last modified May 18, 2023, https://www.state.gov/key-topics-office-of-ocean-and-polar-affairs/arctic/

public that it exists as an Arctic regional state in its domestic policies. Again, it has strengthened its relations with the states in the region after the war in Ukraine. At this point, with NATO increasing its activities in the region, Finland becoming a member of this organisation and possibly Sweden's NATO membership, the security axis in the region will change for Russia and China, which the US clearly sees as a threat. There will be not only global warming but also economic and political warming in the Arctic. What Washington needs to do is to implement the Arctic National Strategy through clearer actions rather than inspiring words.

## Bibliography

Agreement to Prevent Unregulated High Seas Fisheries in the Central Arctic Ocean, https://www.aalco.int/userfiles/File/Agreement%20to%20Prevent%20Unregulated%20High%20Seas%20Fisheries%20in%20the%20Central%20Arctic%20Ocean.pdf

Agrement on Cooperation on Aeronautical and Maritime Search and Rescue in the Arctic, https://oaarchive.arctic-council.org/items/9c343a3f-cc4b-4e75-bfd3-4b318137f8a2

Agrement on Cooperation on Marine Oil Pollution Preparedness and Response in the Arctic   https://disasterlaw.ifrc.org/sites/default/files/media/disaster_law/2021-03/EDOCS-2068-v1-ACMMSE08_KIRUNA_2013_agreement_on_oil_   pollution_ preparedness_and _response_signedAppendices_Original_130510.pdf

Angus King, "Arctic Caucus Co-Chairs Introduce Legislation to Maket he Arctic Ambassador", Angus King, March 20, 2023, last modified August 2, 2023, https://www.king.senate.gov/newsroom/press-releases/arctic-caucus-co-chairs-introduce-legislation-to-make-the-arctic-ambassador-at-large-a-permanent-position#:~:text=On%20February%2016%2C%202023%2C%20President,the%20nation's%20first%20Arctic%20Ambassador.

Arctic Climate Impact Assesment (ACIA) Scientific Report, https://www.caff.is/assessment-series/37-arctic-climate-impact-assessment-acia-scientific-report

Arctic Council. "The United States". last modified May 15, 2023. https://arctic-council.org/about/states/the-united-states/

Arctic Strategic Outlook. U. S. Department of Homeland Security. last modified June 29, 2023, https://www.uscg.mil/Arctic/

Breum, Martin. "How a Dispute over China and Greenland's Airports Worked Its Way Toward a Solution", Arctic Today, 30 June 2018. last modified August 2, 2023. https://www.arctictoday.com/dispute-china-greenlands-airports-worked-way-toward-solution/

Byers, Michael, "International Law and the Arctic". *Cambridge Studies in International and Comparative Law,* Cambridge University Press. United Kingdom. 2013.

Congressional Research Servic. "Changes in the Arctic:Background and Issues for Congress". last modified June 20, 2023, https://sgp.fas.org/crs/misc/R41153.pdf

Conley, Heather A., Matthew Melino, and Andreas Østhagen, *Maritime Futures: The Arctic and the Bering Strait Region.* Lanham, MD: Rowman & Littlefield, 2017.

Department of Defense, "Report to Congress on Strategy to Protect United States

National Security Interest in the Arctic Region" 2016, https://dod.defense.gov/Portals/1/Documents/pubs/2016-Arctic-Strategy-UNCLAS-cleared-for-release.pdf

Department of Defense. "Report to Congress on Strategy to Protect United States National Security Interest in the Arctic Region". last modified May 15, 2023. https://dod.defense.gov/Portals/1/Documents/pubs/2016-Arctic-Strategy-UNCLAS-cleared-for-release.pdf

Department of the Navy Releases Strategic Blueprint for a Blue Arctic. Jan 5, 2021, last modified July 20, 2023. https://www.navy.mil/Press-Office/Press-Releases/display-pressreleases/Article/2463000/department-of-the-navy-releases-strategic-blueprint-for-a-blue-arctic/

Di Pane, James, "U. S. Needs Icebreakers to Keep Up With China and Russia in Arctic". The Heritage Foundation, Jun 18, 2021, last modified July 1, 2023. https://www.heritage.org/global-politics/commentary/us-needs-icebreakers-keep-china-and-russia-arctic

Fletcher, Sierra. "Bering Sea Vessel Trafic Risck Analysis". December 2016, last modified June 22, 2023. https://oceanconservancy.org/wp-content/uploads/2017/01/bering-sea-vessel-traffic-1.pdf

Garamone, Jim. "DOD Establishes Arctic Strategy and Global Resilience Office". U.S. Department of Defense, last modified August 2, 2023. https://www.defense.gov/News/News-Stories/Article/Article/3171173/dod-establishes-arctic-strategy-and-global-resilience-office/

Heather A. Conley and Matthew Melino. "The Implications of U.S. Policy Stagnation toward the Arctic Region" May 2019, CSIS. https://www.csis.org/analysis/implications-us-policy-stagnation-toward-arctic-region

Herrmann, Victoria. In The Arctic, America is its Own Worst Enemy". CNN. May 10, 2019. last modified June 22, 2023. https://edition.cnn.com/ 2019/05/10/opinions/victoria-herrmann-arctic-america-is-its-own-worst-enemy

High North News."New Name for Thule Air Base in Greenland", last modified August 4, 2023 https://www.highnorthnews.com/en/new-name-thule-air-base-greenland

Hofstaedter, Emily. "Icebreaker USCGC Healy to Navigate Northwest Passage This Summer". Knom, last modified June 28, 2023. https://knom.org/2021/ 03/25/icebreaker-uscg-healy-to-navigate-northwest-passage-this-summer/

Humpert, Malt. "China to Build New Heavy Icebreaker and Lift Vessel for Arctic", High North News. Nov 16, 2021. last modified July 20, 2023. https://www.highnorth news.com/en/china-build-new-heavy-icebreaker-and-lift-vessel-arctic#:~:text=Currently%20China%20operates%20two%20conventionally,was%20subsequently%20modified%20and%20refurbished.

IISD, "Conference on GLACIER", modified June 12, 2023, http://sdg.iisd.org/events/conference-on-global-leadership-in-the-arctic-cooperation-innovation-engagement-and-resilience-glacier/

Jeremy, Page. "Chinese Navy Ships Came Within 12 Nautical Miles of U. S. Coast". The Wall Street Journal, last modified June 20, 2023. https://www.wsj.com/articles/chinese-navy-ships-off-alaska-passed-through-u-s-territorial-waters-1441350488

Khan, Mariam, "Republicans Propose Reallocating Coast Guard Ship Funding to

Trump's Border Wall". ABC News August 9, 2018, last modified June 28, 2023, https://abcnews.go.com/Politics/republicans-propose-reallocating-coast-guard-ship-funding-trumps/story?id=57109998

Lajeunesse, Adam "Arctic Geopolitics and Security from the Canadian Perspective. In: *Handbook on Geopolitics and Security in the Arctic*, Ed: Joachim Weber, 2020. https://www.state.gov/u-s-relations-with-canada/

Mason, Josephine. "We're Engaged: Alaska Gets China Backing for Natural Gas Project", last modified June 21, 2023. https://www.reuters.com/article/us-trump-asia-china-gas-idUKKBN1D90C1

Moe, Arild. Jensen, Øystein "Opening of New Arctic Shipping Routes", Directorate-General for External Policies, Policy Department, 2010.

Murkowski Welcomes Nomination of Dr. Mike Sfraga to be Ambassador", last modified August 2, 2023, https://www.murkowski.senate.gov/press/release/murkowski-welcomes-nomination-of-dr-mike-sfraga-to-be_-ambassador-at-large-for-the-arctic-region

National Archives, "Check for the Purchase of Alaska (1868)", modified May 12, 2023, https://www.archives.gov/milestone-documents/check-for-the-purchase-of-alaska#transcript

National Security Decision Memoranda. National Archives, modified May 18, 2023. https://www.nixonlibrary.gov/national-security-decision-memorandNational Security Decision Memoranda, Richard Nixon, National Archives, a-nsdm

National Security Decision Directives Reagan Administration, Intelligence Resource Program, last modified May 20, 2023. https://irp.fas.org/offdocs/nsdd/index.html

National Security Presidential Directive and Homeland Security Presidental Directive", last modified May 20, 2023. https://irp.fas.org/offdocs/nspd/nspd-66.htm#:~:text=Project%20a%20sovereign%20United%20States,disputes%20in%20the%20Arctic%20region.

"National Security Presidential Directives George W. Bush Administration", last modified May 20, 2023. https://irp.fas.org/offdocs/nspd/index.html

Parfitt, Tom. "Russia Plants Flag on North Pole Seabes". The Guardian. Aug 2, 2007. last modified August 2, 2023. https://www.theguardian.com/ world/2007/ aug/ 02/russia.arctic

Pincus, Rebecca. "The History of USA-Russia Relations in the Bering Strait". In: *The Palgrave Handbook of Arctic Policy and Politics*. Ed. Ken S. Coates and Carin Holroyd. Palgrave Macmillan. 2020.

Roucek, Joseph S. "The Geopolitics of the Arctic", *The American Journal of Economics and Sociology*, Vol. 42, No: 4, 1983.

Schofield, Clive and Østhagen, Andreas. "A Divided Arctic: Maritime Boundary Agreements and Disputes in the Arctic Ocean". In: *Handbook on Geopolitics and Security in the Arctic*, Ed:Joachim Weber, 2020.

Stanislav Pritchin, "Russia's Untapped Arctic Potential", Chatham House, 29 Ocak 2018, https://www.chathamhouse.org/expert/comment/russia-s-untapped-arctic-potential. (6 Haziran 2018)

The White House. last modified May 23, 2023. https://www.whitehouse.gov/wp-content/uploads/2022/10/National-Strategy-for-the-Arctic-Region.pdf President Biden Commencement Address at U. S. Coast Guard Academy. C-Span.

https://www.c-span.org/video/?511881-1/president-biden-commencement-address-us-coast-guard-academy.

The White House, "National Strategy For The Arctic Region", last modified May 20, 2023,
https://web.archive.org/web/20210215024218/https://obamawhitehouse.archives.gov/sites/default/files/docs/nat_arctic_strategy.pdf

The White House. "Memorandum on Safeguarding U.S. National Interests in the Arctic and Antartic Regions", modified May 23, 2023. https://trumpwhitehouse.archives.gov/presidential-actions/memorandum-safeguarding-u-s-national-interests-arctic-antarctic-regions/

"United States Plans to Invest Greenland Military Base". The Local. last modified August 4, 2023, https://www.thelocal.dk/20220523/united-states-plans-to-invest-in-greenland-military-base

U.S. Department of State "Arctic Region", last modified May 18, 2023, https://www.state.gov/key-topics-office-of-ocean-and-polar-affairs/arctic/

U. S. Department of State. "U. S. Security Cooperation with Denmark". last modified August 4, 2023. https://www.state.gov/u-s-security-cooperation-with-denmark/

U. S. Department of State. "U.S. Relations With Norway". last modified August 4, 2023. https://www.state.gov/u-s-relations-with-norway/

U.S. Announcements Under the Green Shipping Challenge at COP27. U. S. Department of State, last modified May 12, 2023. https://www.state.gov/u-s-announcements-under-the-green-shipping-challenge-at-cop27/

U.S. Department of State. "Establishment of the Arctic Council", last modified May 12, 2023. https://2009-2017.state.gov/e/oes/ocns/opa/ arc/ac/ establishmentarctic council/

United States Coast Guard. CGC Healy. last modified June 28, 2023, https://www.pacificarea.uscg.mil/Our-Organization/Cutters/cgcHealy/

USA Office of the Historian. "Purchase of Alaska, 1867". last modified May 12, 2023. https://history.state.gov/milestones/1866-1898/alaska-purchase

USCGC Healy Reaches North Pole, UNOLS. last modified June 28, 2023. https://www.unols.org/news/ships-news/uscgc-healy-reaches-north-pole

White House, "President Obama's Trip to Alaska", last modified June 20, 2023, https://obamawhitehouse.archives.gov/2015-alaska-trip

Wicker, Sen. Roger and Sullivan, Sen. Dan. "Polar Icebreakers Are Key to America's National Interest". Defense News, Oct 19, 2020, last modified July 20, 2023. https://www.defensenews.com/opinion/commentary/2020/10/19/polar-icebreakers-are-key-to-americas-national-interest/#:~:text=Russia%20has%20the%20world's%20largest,planned%20in%20t he%20next%20decade.

Yılmaz, Nihat, Çiftçi, Ali, "Arktika Bölgesi'nin Siyasal Önemi ve Siyasal ve Hukuksal Statüsü'nün Karşılaştırmalı Değerlendirmesi", *Muğla Sıtkı Koçman Üniversitesi, Sosyal Bilimler Enstitüsü Dergisi*, Sayı 31, 2013.

# CHAPTER 2

# THE CANADIAN PERSPECTIVE ON INTERNATIONAL RELATIONS INSIDE THE CIRCUMPOLAR NORTH

## Jackson Walling[1]

International relations surrounding the Arctic have evolved as time has progressed, intersecting on a liberal-realist axis. In which the international relations surrounding the Arctic have diverged between a liberalist international zone of peace, and a realist zone of competition and possible conflict.[2] This metamorphosis is reflected within the history surrounding the geopolitical environment of the Arctic.[3] During the Cold War, the Soviet Union and United States imposed a theoretical 'ice curtain' across the Arctic's geopolitical landscape, because of the ideological and geo-strategic contest taking place between both states.[4] Nevertheless, after the culmination of the Cold War, Mikael Gorbachev's 1987 Murmansk speech conceptualized the Arctic as a 'zone of peace'. Leading to the materialization of Arctic exceptionalism as a narrative that represents the Arctic geopolitical landscape. Asserting that the Arctic is insulated from regular geo-political dynamics; geo-political competition and embodies its own geo-political region.[5] The conclusion of Cold War antagonism, introduced a rapidly transformative time in Arctic politics, converting from militarization and a space of conflict, to one that idealized cooperation amongst states, for the greater good of the environmentally sensitive area. The strategic significance of the Arctic faded, and the possibility of confrontation subsided, with the inauguration of the Arctic Council, which instituted the notion of civility within the region as a whole. Arguably, this affability was ingrained into the Arctic geo-political landscape, but good things don't last forever. This reputation of being sheltered from broader international relations ended since the Russian

---

[1] Trent University, Doctoral Candidate in Canadian Studies.
[2] Gricius Gabriella. "Conceptualising the Arctic as a Zone of Conflict." Central European Journal of International and Security Studies 15, no. 4 (December 22, 2021): 4–30. https://doi.org/10. 51870/ CEJISS.A150401.
[3] Walker, R. B. J. "Security, Sovereignty, and the Challenge of World Politics." Alternatives 15, no. 1 (January 1, 1990): 3–27. https://doi.org/10.1177/030437549001500102.
[4] Iseman, Peter A. "Lifting the Ice Curtain." The New York Times, October 23, 1988, sec. Magazine. https://www.nytimes.com/1988/10/23/magazine/lifting-the-ice-curtain.html.
[5] Åtland Kristian. "Mikhail Gorbachev, the Murmansk Initiative, and the Desecuritization of Interstate: Relations in the Arctic." Cooperation and Conflict 43, no. 3 (2008): 289–311.

invasion of Ukraine in winter of 2022.[6] The Arctic in the contemporary world is now reverting to an area where conflict and competition trumps cooperative and collective gains. The drastic effects of climate change and states seeing the Arctic as an area of self-interest has re-emerged in the contemporary landscape, due to the proposition of economic opportunities.

## The Geopolitical Dynamic of the Arctic

From World War II through the Cold War to present day, the geopolitical dynamics of the Arctic have experienced metamorphosis as time has progressed, due to pressurizing factors. Symptomatically, states have had to navigate the Arctic geopolitical dynamics with these changing tides. However, this introduces a pertinent question, when navigating this change, did states ever shed their own interests within the Arctic? Interest concerning the Arctic amongst sovereign states are embedded in Arctic exceptionalism, as Lackenbauer and Dean point out.[7] Arctic exceptionalism and the romanization of the Arctic is explicitly linked to Arctic states and their identity politics, "constructing narratives that incorporate visions of the region."[8] These visions are constructed with a country's self-interest front of mind. Thus, though Arctic politics have experienced a transfiguration over time, flipping back and forth between an arena of conflict and cooperation, have states ever left their own self-interests at the door, and put the collective international community first within the Arctic? Countries continuously postulate this notion, but history reflects a differing narrative, specifically that countries have never left their self-interest outside of the political dynamic in the Arctic region. Any notion that states leave their self-interests outside of the Arctic political dynamic can be perceived as disingenuous. Although the geo-political dynamic has changed its orientation, the Arctic is not as unique to international relations as some may think. As noted by Murray, the Arctic is not idiosyncratic in the game of international politics.[9] Arctic states have proven time and again, national self-interests are not restricted within Arctic boundaries. As a result, in pursuit of these self-interests within the Arctic,

---

[6] Devyatkin Pavel. "Arctic Exceptionalism: A Narrative of Cooperation and Conflict from Gorbachev to Medvedev and Putin." The Polar Journal, (2023): 1–22. https://doi.org/10.1080/2154896X.2023.2258658.

[7] Ryan Dean and P. Whitney Lackenbauer. "Chapter 14: Arctic Exceptionalisms." In The Arctic and the World Order. School of Advanced International Studies, 2021. https://rideauinstitute.ca/wp-content/uploads/2021/01/Chapter-14-Lackenbauer.pdf.

[8] Ryan Dean and P. Whitney Lackenbauer. "Chapter 14: Arctic Exceptionalisms." In The Arctic and the World Order, pg. 328. School of Advanced International Studies, 2021. https://rideauinstitute.ca/wp-content/uploads/2021/01/Chapter-14-Lackenbauer.pdf.

[9] Murray, Robert W. "(Mis)Understanding the Arctic." E-International Relations (blog), April 3, 2014. https://www.e-ir.info/2014/04/03/misunderstanding-the-arctic/.

Arctic nations have had to adapt to the changing circumstances surrounding international relations within the Arctic region. A specific country that comes to mind is Canada.

## The Arctic and the Geography of Canada

The Arctic region accounts for 40% of Canada's landmass, but accounts for less than one percent of Canada's population in the present day.[10] Yet, throughout history, Canada has consistently strived for sovereignty over its Arctic region, based upon the country's own self-interest in the region. Because the Arctic is ingrained into the Canadian National identity and is an area that reflects a history and future for Canada, that must be controlled to ensure Canada's self-interest. As Carolyn James and Patrick James point to, sovereignty has been "the fundamental Canadian sleigh dog in the Arctic fight."[11] There are three elements of sovereignty, they include a defined area, a system of governance and people within the defined territory. Correspondingly, sovereignty is strongly associated with security,[12] because postulating and preserving sovereignty installs an ability to control "what happens and respond to threats in the Arctic."[13] Sovereignty and security are intertwined with the Canadian state, whose sovereignty, at times throughout history, has been contested and under threat. For that reason, Canada has continually had to navigate the international relations within the Arctic region to ensure, secure and assert sovereignty over its own circumpolar geographical landscape, with self-interest top of mind.

Thus, as the natural environment and global politics surrounding the Arctic has evolved, so has the Canadian states'pursuit for sovereignty. Throughout history, and within the contemporary environment, Canada has navigated an international environment that has constantly evolved, in a harmonious and chameleon like fashion, in its quest to assert sovereignty over its exterior Arctic territories based on self-interest. As a result of the evolutionary nature of international relations pertaining to the Arctic, Canada has utilized a contingent realist framework; based on structural realism, which has allowed

---

[10] Arctic Council. "Canada." Arctic Council. Accessed November 6, 2023. https://arctic-council.org/about/states/canada/.

[11] Carolyn James and Patrick James. "Canada, the United States and Arctic Sovereignty: Architecture without Building?" American Review of Canadian Studies 44, no. 2 (2014): 187–204.

[12] Ron Huebert. "Canadian Arctic Sovereignty and Security in a Transforming Circumpolar World." Foreign Policy for Canada's Tomorrow. Canadian International Council, 2009. https://royaldutchshellplc.com/wp-content/uploads/1947/04/ArcticSovereigntySecurity-831.pdf.

[13] Gricius Gabriella. "A Decolonial Approach to Arctic Security and Sovereignty." Arctic Year Book, 2021. https://arcticyearbook.com/arctic-yearbook/2021/2021-scholarly-papers/377-a-decolonial-approach-to-arctic-security-and-sovereignty.

the state to evolve in its pursuit of asserting sovereignty over its Arctic territories. Although scholars have argued that the political dynamic of the Arctic has followed a liberal-realist axis, contingent realism as an analytical framework articulates Canada's continuous positioning within the Arctic political dynamic. Thus, it is more fruitful to base Canada's continuous manoeuvring within the Arctic political environment through a contingent realist lens. Utilizing a contingent realist analytical framework from international relations, we can appraise the evolution of Canadian Arctic International Relations up to present day, to explain actions taken by Canada, in its ambition of asserting sovereignty over its exterior Arctic territories by any means necessary.

Therefore, the purpose of this chapter is to appraise the evolution of Canadian international relations within the Arctic, through the scope of historical context, utilizing a contingent realist frame of mind and analytical framework from international relations.[14] This presents the best opportunity to explain Canada's historical and contemporary actions, in regard to navigating the political dynamic in the Arctic, with the goal of asserting sovereignty. Scholarship in relation to the Arctic's differentiating political dynamic and the way in which Arctic nations have navigated this evolving situation is lacking in some regards. More particularly, how Canada has navigated this overwhelming political situation. This is arguably the first time that the evolution of the Arctic political dynamic has ever been investigated through a Canadian perspective, and how the Canadian state trans versed its pursuit of sovereignty overtime. Because of this, the study you are about to read focuses on the most salient events pertaining to Canadian Arctic international relations through a contingent realist state of mind. However, it should be noted that this chapter is largely dependent on generalizations, rather than a completely refined framework of analysis. Doing so, institutes greater opportunity for further research to enhance and expand our understanding of Canadian international relations pertaining to the Arctic's international political landscape. It is pertinent to understand that the contingent realist framework displayed and articulated in this chapter denotes that Canada has modified its approaches to asserting sovereignty, while aligned with the geopolitical dynamic surrounding the Arctic at the time of each salient event. This investigation of the Canadian government's evolving perspective in relation to Arctic international relations, and Canadian Arctic

---

[14] Glaser Charles L. "Realists as Optimists: Cooperation as Self-Help." International Security 19, no. 3 (1994): 50–90. https://doi.org/10.2307/2539079; Glaser Charles L. "Structural Realism in a More Complex World." Review of International Studies 29, no. 3 (2003): 403–14.

sovereignty proceeds as follows.

First, this chapter discusses structural realism, contingent realism and security policy outlooks derived from international relations that will be utilized to explain Canada's progression and evolution of safeguarding sovereignty over its Arctic region. Combining these insights will provide greater overall understanding regarding Canada's pursuit of asserting sovereignty through international relations. From here, the chapter examines certain salient events, from World War II to present day. By appraising these events, through an international relations perspective, the harmonious nature in which the Canadian government has manoeuvred through the international political dynamic surrounding the Arctic overtime will become apparent. All of which is constructed on the overarching goal of asserting sovereignty over its Arctic region, in the name of self-interest. Although international relations have reverted and forth between competition and cooperation within the Arctic, contingent realism reflects Canada's foreign policy outlook pertaining to the Arctic, and to some degree can explain Canada's pervasive actions in the Arctic. Thus, the point of this section is to articulate what structural realism actually is, and how Canada has utilized this framework harmoniously, modifying its approaches overtime, with the political dynamic of the Arctic always in mind. Along with their own self interests in mind when it comes to asserting sovereignty.

## Contingent Realism's Advantages over Structural Realism

Structural realism, also known as neorealism, examines "the world as it actually is rather than how it ought to be."[15] The primary difference between realists and structural realists is that classical realists articulate that the roots of global conflict arise from the inferiority of human nature. While structural realists believe that global conflict is entrenched by an anarchic international system. Thus, structural realists view the international system as a structure that is based predominantly on anarchy, because there is no credible power above individual states, to enforce agreements or a power that regulates their actions taken by states.[16] Building off this, Kenneth Waltz's *Theory of International Politics* furthered our overall understanding of international relations, specifically structural realism.[17] Arguing that the inherent anarchic

---

[15] Arash Heydarian Pashakhanlou. Realism in Practice: An Appraisal. E-IR Edited Collection. E-International Relations, 2018. https://www.e-ir.info/2018/01/15/the-past-present-and-future-of-realism/.

[16] Kenneth Waltz, Hertbert Buutterfield, and Hedley Bull. Theory of International Politics. 1st ed. (Waveland Press, 1979).

[17] Ibid.

nature of the international system, institutes the capabilities of a sovereign state in relation to international politics, guides a sovereign state's actions on the international stage. This establishes that states are always looking to acquire relative power in relation to their status in the international system through competition, ultimately ensuring their survival. Therefore, relative power is what ensures a state's survival; thus, states continuously compete for proportional power in the international system. As a result, the structure of the international system varies, based upon a state's relative power, and their overall capabilities. Symptomatically, sovereign states are inherently principled actors in the international system. However, they are also unitary actors, prioritizing their own security, meaning that each state always keeps their own interests in mind.[18] Because of this, states are unaware of other states'intentions, therefore causing states to be inherently pessimistic regarding international relations. Thus, structural realism does not foreclose the prospect that states have additional motives, other than security. These assumptions preclude that states ultimately must look out for themselves, because they are the only ones that are concerned for themselves.[19] As a result, many realist thinkers stress that cooperation amongst states is unrealistic, because "any cooperation that emerges under anarchy will be tenuous, unstable and limited to issues of peripheral importance."[20] Building off this notion of cooperation, through a structural realist lens, cooperation through global institutions is rather optimistic, considering its definition. A realist analysis prognosticates that states will work through international institutions, seeing institutions as an entity that can achieve their goals. If the opportunity to utilize an institution in the pursuit of a goal or self-interests presents itself, states will not hesitate to use them. Notwithstanding, this should not suggest that realists perceive institutions to matter, but if it is in the interests of the state to utilize them, they will.[21]

Although structural realism is a predominant feature in international relations, Charles Glaser's *"Realists as Optimists: Cooperation as Self-Help"* articulates that it is inherently flawed, suggesting that his theory of contingent realism is a more fruitful interpretation of international relations that is based on a refurbished version of structural realism. Glaser's line of argumentation

---

18 Tripp Emily. "Realism: The Domination of Security Studies." E-International Relations (blog), June 14, 2013. http://www.e-ir.info/2013/06/14/realism-the-domination-of-security-studies/.
19 Glaser Charles L. "Realists as Optimists: Cooperation as Self-Help." International Security 19, no. 3 (1994): 50–90. https://doi.org/10.2307/2539079.
20 Ibid.
21 Glaser, Charles L. "Structural Realism in a More Complex World." Review of International Studies 29, no. 3 (2003): 403–14.

surrounding contingent realism involves eliminating the prejudice toward competition. Structural realist arguments oftentimes praise the notion of competition, propagating that a country's self-help is reliant on competition. However, this overlooks the risks that are an intrinsic part of competition. As well as, ignoring the reality that cooperation and cooperative policies also play an important role in a country's self-help. In addition, rather than focusing on the structural realist notion of power, contingent realism focuses primarily on military capabilities. Glaser denotes that structural realists are too focused on power and suggests that this line of argumentation should be converted towards military capabilities, specifically a "states ability to perform military operations."[22] This requires incorporating contrasting variables into this analytical framework, particularly offense-defence balance and offense-defence distinguishability. Offense-defence balance expresses that a country's military-mission capabilities are determined by its overt power. Correspondingly, offense-defence distinguishability permits us to consider if a state can translate their power into military capabilities.[23] The reasoning for integrating these variables is by doing so, the structural realist assertion that power wins all fights, is corrected. Articulating that states need to be cognizant of when to be offensively minded through power, and when to be defensively minded and yearn for cooperation. Finally, the last correction Glaser asserts is that the rudimentary structural realist argument evokes that states acting within the international structure are unable to communicate their motives. But in contrast, should be focused on illustrating that their countries motives on the international stage pertaining to security are considerate. Thus, allowing countries to peer into the motives of their adversaries and allies, permitting countries to pursue cooperative military policies, that can theoretically lead to collective gains and possibly revitalize their 'opponents'view of their own country.[24] Moreover, regarding international institutions, contingent realism doesn't not rule out the possibility that institutions can play a part in ensuring a state's self-interest. Contingent realism see's institutions parallel to structural realism, conveying that institutions are inherently based upon state self-interest and the composition of the international system but can lead to cooperation amongst states, because they display a state's interests up front for all states to see. Contingent realism does not believe that institutions are the only way states can cooperate, this line of argumentation sees it as a tool that can lead to self-

---

[22] Glaser, Charles L. "Realists as Optimists: Cooperation as Self-Help." International Security 19, no. 3 (1994): 50–90. https://doi.org/10.2307/2539079.

[23] Ibid.

[24] Ibid.

interests.[25]

Contingent realism branches off from conventional structural realism, rectifying many of its shortcomings. Contingent realism illustrates that states are not as immersed in a competitive state of mind within international relations as many may think, this form of realism perpetuates that the selection of competition and cooperation are distinctly conditional, "with no general preference for competition."[26] Thus, moving on from structural realism, contingent realism corrects several shortcomings. Specifically, by moving away from the assumption that all states look for competition, integrate offensive and defensive variables, and policy signalling to display a state's motives. In addition, this form of realism does not rely on institutions for cooperation, as it sees international institutions as an apparatus that can solidify self-interest, and lead to cooperation amongst other states.

From here, building off the generalizations pertaining to contingent realism and its overall analytical framework, we can appraise the evolution of Canadian government actions in relation to asserting sovereignty over Canada's geographical region, in ever changing Arctic political environment, through a frame of mind based primarily on self-interest. This appraisal is within the context of contingency realist framework and pertains to some of the most salient events in Canada's history pertaining to Arctic international relations, they include Canada/US Arctic relations during World War II and the Cold War, the Northwest Passage, and the Arctic Council.

## Canada's Arctic Security Relationships and Contingent Realists Outlooks

During the early 19th century, the Canadian Arctic was left in a "state of nature", until the onset of the Second World War, when Canada's security and sovereignty were brought to the forefront. Through initiatives established by Prime Minister Mackenzie King. Specifically instituting the US-Canada Permanent Joint Board on Defense (PJBD). This triggered the construction of infrastructure projects, such as a series of airfields designated the Northwest Staging Route; between Edmonton and Fairbanks, Alaska, the Alaska Highway, and almost the Canol Project (a 1000 km oil pipeline from Norman Wells oil fields to Whitehorse).[27] At this moment in time, the

---

[25] Ibid.

[26] Glaser, Charles L. "Realists as Optimists: Cooperation as Self-Help." International Security 19, no. 3 (1994): 50–90. https://doi.org/10.2307/2539079.

[27] P. Whitney Lackenbauer and Daniel Heidt. "The Advisory Committee on Northern Development:

amplitude of these projects masked any previous investments made in the region by Canada. But thanks to financing by the United States government, most of these projects were completed. But with that, this instilled a sense of fear that the United States was operating independently within its geographical borders.[28] This established a sense of uneasiness amongst government officials and the Prime Minister himself. But with the conclusion of World War 2, the United States withdrew from Canadian Arctic territories. Extending permanent proprietorship over northern facilities in the Arctic to Canada, at the request of Prime Minister Mackenzie King.

At face value, the history surrounding the institutionalization of the PBJD may display aspects that are reflective of a liberal institutionalist framework,[29] nullifying structural realism. For instance, Scholarship pertaining to liberalism in international relations often fails to acknowledge that the realities of state v. state relations during World War II were conditional. Because, the global political landscape was under the guise of anarchy, modifying states to all care about their own self-interests. However, this overlooks the risks that are an intrinsic part of competition, and this optimistic perspective does not consider the reality, nor the possibility, that states may use other states for their own self-interest. Though structural realism may not be strongly reflected in the context of this specific history, contingent realism is. Leading up to, and during World War II, continental defence was top of mind for Canada but did not have the financial resources to develop the interior and exterior of Canada's geographical area northwest of Baffin's Island, as well as the Northwest territories, and what is now Nunavut. Though Canada was a predominant middle power at the time, its military capabilities and financial resources were nothing in comparison to the US war machine.[30] North American continental defence was equally as important to the US, as it was to Canada, but the US had the capability and the resources to develop such a vast landscape. As a result, there was no reason to compete with the US, in an arms race, to protect the same area, or fear that the US was going to invade Canada to protect the continent. Contingent realism suggests that states are not always striving for competition and are aware of the inherent risks that

---

Context and Meeting Minutes, 1948-71." Documents on Canadian Arctic Sovereignty and Security DCASS. University of Calgary Centre for Military and Strategic Studies, revised 2019. https://live-arts.ucalgary.ca/sites/default/files/teams/25/dcass4-acnd-rev-ed.pdf.

[28] Ibid.

[29] Carolyn James and Patrick James. "Canada, the United States and Arctic Sovereignty: Architecture Without Building?" American Review of Canadian Studies 44, no. 2 (2014): 187–204.

[30] Sean M. Maloney. "Who Has Seen The Wind? An Historical Overview of Canadian Special Operations." Canadian Military Journal. Government of Canada, National Defence, Canadian Defence Academy. Accessed November 6, 2023. http://www.journal.forces.gc.ca/vo5/no3/special-03-eng.asp.

come with competition, as well as cooperation, specifically cooperative military policies. The offense-defence balance variable suggests that Canada was aware of its own limited capabilities when it came to developing the Arctic region. Offense-defence balance variables, articulate the "ratio of the cost of the offensive forces to the cost of the defensive forces."[31] Because of this, defence often trumps offensive actions. Through this analytical mindset, it's easier to identify Canada's actions, as one that reflects a contingent realist frame of mind. For instance, Canada discerned that they were not capable of developing its Arctic region faster than the US, thus instituting a cooperation for self-help approach. Because it made more sense to employ the financial prowess of the United States, rather than invest in more offensive military capabilities. Correspondingly, the second variable, offense-defence distinguishability permits us to consider if a state can translate their power into military capabilities. Canada, being a middle power at the time and an active participant in World War II, was essentially too busy to develop its Arctic region at a suitable pace. Hence, employing the United States to develop its region at a rapid pace, because the security of the continent took precedent. The PJBD displayed and signalled its intentions during its inauguration, specifically tightening continental defence.[32] Once the development projects were completed and World War II culminated, the United States gave proprietorship of the projects to Canada and disbanded its forces willingly, at the request of Prime Minister Mackenzie King. If the United States had not left voluntarily, contingent realism wouldn't be relevant. However, unlike structural realism, which primarily focuses on absolute gains and zero-sum competition, contingent realism see's this type of bilateral policy and institution, as one that reflects self-help. Countries are open to cooperation in the security realm, as long as it benefits them. If cooperation results in decreasing its own military capabilities, and lessens their military capability and security, states will not cooperate.[33] The Canadian states were aware of their military shortcomings and recognized that the US capabilities were far greater than their own when it came to developing the Arctic region. Thus, Canada instituted a self-help approach, utilizing cooperation to its own benefit with regards to developing its northern region

---

[31] Glaser Charles L. "Realists as Optimists: Cooperation as Self-Help." International Security 19, no. 3 (1994): 50–90. https://doi.org/10.2307/2539079.

[32] P. Whitney Lackenbauer and Daniel Heidt. "The Advisory Committee on Northern Development: Context and Meeting Minutes, 1948-71." Documents on Canadian Arctic Sovereignty and Security DCASS. University of Calgary Centre for Military and Strategic Studies, revised 2019. https://live-arts.ucalgary.ca/sites/default/files/teams/25/dcass4-acnd-rev-ed.pdf.

[33] Glaser Charles L. "Structural Realism in a More Complex World." Review of International Studies 29, no. 3 (2003): 403–14.

in its pursuit of asserting sovereignty, with the direct assistance of the US.[34] From here, Canada's Arctic sovereignty began to advance, and accelerated further during the Cold War.

From the beginning of the Cold War until the fall of the USSR, nuclear conflict was always at risk, and Canada's Arctic region was the possible epicentre for this hostility to boil over; a direct route from Moscow to Washington were over the Arctic Ocean and Canadian territory. Because of this, territory within Canada's Arctic borders became militarily strategic for the United States, who at times scrutinized the region as unguarded and underprepared,[35] pushing Canada into a contrasting circumstance between continental security concerns and the affirmation of sovereignty over such a vast geographical area. Though the materialization of this discussion at face value might appear as if the US was pressuring Canada to take continental defence and their security cooperation seriously,[36] this actually formalized a Canadian self-help perspective when it comes to its continental security, almost in parallel to Canada and the US's relationship in World War II. During this time, the US financed and developed the creation of the Distant Early Warning (DEW) Line, a homogeneous line of 63 radar and communication centre's that crosses the Canadian Arctic starting in Western Alaska and stretching to Greenland. The project itself was the largest Arctic security investment of its time, but it was not without controversy.[37] Again, supported primarily by US financing, representatives in Ottawa were anxious of this perception and its relation to Canada's Arctic sovereignty and the possibility of the US asserting de facto sovereignty.[38] This prompted Canada to continuously control the overall narrative surrounding the project through signalling, stressing that the depiction of control needed to be maintained throughout its inception, while preserving its relationship with Washington. This strategy benefitted Canada in the long run, as a deal between the US and

[34] P. Whitney Lackenbauer and Daniel Heidt. "The Advisory Committee on Northern Development: Context and Meeting Minutes, 1948-71." Documents on Canadian Arctic Sovereignty and Security DCASS. University of Calgary Centre for Military and Strategic Studies, revised 2019. https://live-arts.ucalgary.ca/sites/default/files/teams/25/dcass4-acnd-rev-ed.pdf.

[35] P. Whitney Lackenbauer, Matthew J. Farish, and Jennifer Arthur-Lackenbauer. "The Distant Early Warning (DEW) Line: A Bibliography and Documentary Resource List." Prepared for the Arctic Institute of North America, October 2005. https://pubs.aina.ucalgary.ca/aina/dewlinebib.pdf.

[36] P. Whitney Lackenbauer and Daniel Heidt. "The Advisory Committee on Northern Development: Context and Meeting Minutes, 1948-71." Documents on Canadian Arctic Sovereignty and Security DCASS. University of Calgary Centre for Military and Strategic Studies, revised 2019. https://live-arts.ucalgary.ca/sites/default/files/teams/25/dcass4-acnd-rev-ed.pdf.

[37] P. Whitney Lackenbauer, Matthew J. Farish, and Jennifer Arthur-Lackenbauer. "The Distant Early Warning (DEW) Line: A Bibliography and Documentary Resource List." Prepared for the Arctic Institute of North America, October 2005. https://pubs.aina.ucalgary.ca/aina/dewlinebib.pdf.

[38] Ibid.

Canada was brokered, that supported the colonization of the north, Canada's Arctic sovereignty, and Canadian companies like Western Electric.[39] This period of collaboration and parallel objectives inspired the creation of the North American Aerospace Command (NORAD) in 1958, a bilateral agreement, establishing that Canada and the US collectively take responsibility and command of continental defence. The agreement centralized and integrated continental air defence force, with a specific focus on detection, validation, and warnings in the Arctic region. The prospect of Soviet bombers traveling over the Arctic, with the purpose of attacking America, frightened Washington. Thus, cooperating with Canada, the two countries established the only ever binational defence structure, operating through a unifying effort. Like the DEW line, the NORAD agreement strengthened Canada's defence infrastructure in the Arctic, but also bolstered the notion of Canadian sovereignty, because "the lack of a viable threat tipped the equation in favour of sovereignty."[40] This notion was solidified after the US State department announced in 1953, that they saw no reason to challenge Canada's control over the Arctic islands.

From this historical perspective, scholars like Patrick et al. denote that constructivism contributed to these investments,[41] specifically which the Canadian state yielded to public discourse. Although it is true that the Canadian public were apprehensive of excessive US integration regarding Arctic military development and sovereignty overall. It's not disjointed to postulate that the Canadian populace did not have access to the full reality of the situation. Speculatively speaking it's fair to say that access to information and understanding on international relations at the time was poor, inspiring Canadians to think their borders were being disrespected.[42] However, the reality of the Canadian state's Arctic military and financial capabilities in 1950-1960 were insufficient in comparison to the US, who were competing and conflicting with the USSR.[43] Thus, similar to World War II, Canada's international relations perspective of the time reflects contingent realism

---

[39] Ibid.

[40] P. Whitney Lackenbauer and Daniel Heidt. "The Advisory Committee on Northern Development: Context and Meeting Minutes, 1948-71." Documents on Canadian Arctic Sovereignty and Security DCASS. University of Calgary Centre for Military and Strategic Studies, revised 2019. https://live-arts.ucalgary.ca/sites/default/files/teams/25/dcass4-acnd-rev-ed.pdf.

[41] Carolyn James and Patrick James. "Canada, the United States and Arctic Sovereignty: Architecture Without Building?" American Review of Canadian Studies 44, no. 2 (2014): 187–204.

42 Ole R. Holsti. "Public Opinion and Foreign Policy: Challenges to the Almond-Lippmann Consensus." International Studies Quarterly 36, no. 4 (December 1992): 439–66.

[43] P. Whitney Lackenbauer, Matthew J. Farish, and Jennifer Arthur-Lackenbauer. "The Distant Early Warning (DEW) Line: A Bibliography and Documentary Resource List." Prepared for the Arctic Institute of North America, October 2005. https://pubs.aina.ucalgary.ca/aina/dewlinebib.pdf.

arguably. For instance, just because the US was in conflict with the USSR, did not mean Canada had to follow. As referenced in Glaser's framework surrounding contingent realism, countries don't always lean to conflict, because the costs can be great. Although Canada had to take the US's intentions at face value, they were not deceitful. A contingent realist framework suggests that states lean to cooperation, specifically taking into account the offensive-defensive balance and offense-defence distinguishability in relation to Canada's Arctic military capabilities. The DEW line approximates 3000 miles, Canadian military infrastructure, and financial resources, did not have the capacity to establish such a project. This exact same notion applies to Canada's bilateral agreement that established NORAD. Consequently, Canada's military capabilities were not capable of protecting its Arctic geography; thus, it could not convert its power into military capabilities. Influencing the Canadian state to look for cooperation amongst its US neighbours. Signalling intentions surrounding continental defence, encouraged Canada that the US intentions were righteous, as a result the "lack of a viable threat tipped the equation in favour of sovereignty."[44] Thus, permitting Canada to establish stronger continental defence capabilities through agreements and institutions. When it comes to Canada and US collaborating pertaining to continental defence, the Canadian state was not apprehensive, it knew its rank in the world structure, and were aware that it would be paradoxical to 'try'and compete in an arms race to secure the same area.[45] As a result, the DEW line and the projects that followed, as well the NORAD agreement, strengthened Canada's defence infrastructure in the Arctic, but also bolstered the notion of Canadian sovereignty. Especially after the US State department announced in 1953, that they saw no reason to challenge Canada's control over the Arctic islands.[46] Through this framework, it becomes apparent that Canada harmoniously navigated the international structure, in pursuit of asserting sovereignty over its Arctic region. Canada took into account the contradiction in regard to competing with the US in continental defence and saw the self-interest that could arise if the state cooperated with the US, taking into account offensive-defensive balance/distinguishability and discerning through signalling that the US

[44] Michael T. Fawcett. "The Politics of Sovereignty - Continental Defence and the Creation of NORAD." Canadian Military Journal 10, no. 2 (2010): 33–40.
[45] Glaser, Charles L. "Realists as Optimists: Cooperation as Self-Help." International Security 19, no. 3 (1994): 50–90. https://doi.org/10.2307/2539079.
[46] P. Whitney Lackenbauer and Daniel Heidt. "The Advisory Committee on Northern Development: Context and Meeting Minutes, 1948-71." Documents on Canadian Arctic Sovereignty and Security DCASS. University of Calgary Centre for Military and Strategic Studies, revised 2019. https://live-arts.ucalgary.ca/sites/default/files/teams/25/dcass4-acnd-rev-ed.pdf.

would not take up a greedy stance, such as claiming de facto sovereignty over the area. Thus, as the argument stands, contingent realism can account for these events within the cold war period. This framework of analysis pertaining to the navigation of international relations follows Canada further into the later part of the 20th century, specifically regarding Canada's claim of sovereignty over the Northwest Passage.

Canada's history surrounding the Northwest Passage is extensive but followed a pattern of neglect during the early 20th century. The passage itself is a narrow body of water that encompasses 10,000 kilometres, connecting the Atlantic and Pacific Ocean. Internationally, the passage is highly regarded as a future backbone of ensuring the globalization of international trade, while opening the region up and making it easier to transport Arctic minerals and natural resources. Maritime sovereignty is a complex endeavour in international relations scholarship.[47] During the 20th century, maritime sovereignty was constricted to three nautical miles, unless there were unprecedented circumstances, specifically historic waters. Historic waters are defined as those "closely tied to land, such as bays or inlets."[48] This is the case in which Canada has built its legal claim to authority of the passage, and overall sovereignty over the Arctic Archipelago waters.[49] The passage being within Canada's territorial waters, bestows that if opposing ships from other sovereign nations transverse the passage is subjected to Canadian oversight, specifically via the Canadian Coast Guard and Navy. Whereas, if the passage was under the entitlement of being an international strait, sovereign nations would be accredited unrestrained passage. During this period, specifically the late 20th century, Canada believed it met the criteria to assert sovereignty over the area. The Canadian Department of External Affairs in late 1950 maintained that historic waters were when a state had jurisdiction over a certain area of water over a period of years and had the general acceptance of the international community.[50] Although Canada did meet some of the criteria, the general acceptance of this claim was disputed by the US and the European Union, who see the passage as an international strait. One of the

---

[47] Adam Lajeunesse. "Documents on Canadian Arctic Maritime Sovereignty 1950-1988." Documents on Canadian Arctic Sovereignty and Security DCASS. University of Calgary Centre for Military and Strategic Studies, September 2018. http://cmss.ucalgary.ca/research/arctic-document-series.

[48] Ibid.

[49] Donat Pharand. "Canada's Sovereignty Over the Northwest Passage." Michigan Journal of International Law 10, no. 2 (1989): 653–78.

[50] P. Whitney Lackenbauer and Daniel Heidt. "The Advisory Committee on Northern Development: Context and Meeting Minutes, 1948-71." Documents on Canadian Arctic Sovereignty and Security DCASS. University of Calgary Centre for Military and Strategic Studies, revised 2019. https://live-arts.ucalgary.ca/sites/default/files/teams/25/dcass4-acnd-rev-ed.pdf.

major reasons for this was Canada had a limited presence in the Arctic, due to financial constraints. Correspondingly, as noted by Lackenbauer and Kikkert, the US government was uncertain how Canada was instituting the claim of sovereignty over the passage, and some parts of its exterior Arctic Isles.[51] However, during the 1950s and 1960s, Canada secured some established level of recognition, as American activity was managed by the Canadian state. This does not suggest that the US fully acknowledged Canada's sovereignty over the passage, but rather it did not challenge the Canadian state, implying some status of ownership. Lackenbauer and Kikkert suggest that this was all a part of Canada's policy strategy, as noted by Arctic sovereignty advisor Ivan Head, who suggested that time was the greatest ally of Canada, because as time passed, it continued to strengthen Canada's claim of the passage pertaining to historical waters.[52] However, the policy itself was not verbalized until the SS Manhattan's contended expedition in 1969. The supertanker, affiliated with Humble Oil Company coordinated a transit through the Northwest Passage, to gauge the practicality of transporting crude oil through northern waters. Considering the passage an international strait, the company nor the American government notified Canada of this voyage, nor sought permission to transverse this body of water within Canadian territory.[53] Correspondingly, a similar situation transpired in the mid-1980s after the US Coast guard vessel Polar Sea transcended from Greenland to Alaska. Although the US government informed Canadian officials that the Polar Sea would be traversing the passage, they did ask for permission to do so, still considering the passage an international strait. Overall, during the Pierre Trudeau and Brian Mulroney years of government, this instigated a feeling of uneasiness amongst the Canadian government, as it was perceived that ultimately America was attempting to embezzle Canadian resources, thus requiring firm action by the Canadian state.[54]

This period in Canada's history was arguably the first time that Canada and the US had to address the certainty surrounding the sovereignty over the Northwest Passage. Many scholars reflect that this time in Canada history

---

[51] P. Whitney Lackenbauer. "Canada's Northern Strategies: From Trudeau to Trudeau, 1970-2020." Documents on Canadian Arctic Sovereignty and Security (DCASS). Documents on Canadian Arctic Sovereignty and Security. University of Calgary Centre for Military and Strategic Studies, 2020. http://cmss.ucalgary.ca/research/arctic-document-series.

[52] Ibid.

[53] Adam Lajeunesse. "Documents on Canadian Arctic Maritime Sovereignty 1950-1988." Documents on Canadian Arctic Sovereignty and Security DCASS. University of Calgary Centre for Military and Strategic Studies, September 2018. http://cmss.ucalgary.ca/research/arctic-document-series.

[54] Rob Huebert. "Canadian Arctic Security Issues: Transformation in the Post-Cold War Era." International Journal 54, no. 2 (Spring 1999): 203–29.

reflects a liberal institutionalist approach,[55] yet many discredit the possibility that the Canadian state was a rational actor during this period globally, which transcended between competition and cooperation. Contingent realism points to the notion that states are rational actors, picking and choosing approaches that always keep self-interests in mind.[56] The offense-defence balance and distinguishability play's an integral role at explaining these contextual generalizations. At the time, Canada's overt power did not translate into Arctic military capabilities. All-encompassing, Canada did not have the capacity to defend its Arctic region, thus its defensive variables were not sufficient to counteract US actions in the Northwest Passage. As a result, the Canadian government deciphered that it needed to invest in its offensive capabilities, igniting stronger defensive positions overall. The Pierre Trudeau government implemented significant change, specifically assigning year-round arctic training for Canada armed forces members, and establishing a new northern headquarters in Yellowknife.[57] Furthermore, this inspired the 1971 White Paper, which emphasized the Canadian Armed forces primary commitment was to affirm and protect sovereignty in the Arctic, resulting in the relocation of half of the Canadian Armed forces from Europe who were assisting NATO at the time. Although discourse surrounding these initiatives were discounted, the Canadian government acknowledged that their defensive capabilities in the Arctic were lacking, thus instituting an offensive-minded approach.[58] Canada was unable to convert its power into Arctic security capabilities at the time of the Manhattan dilemma; thus, it invested in offensive capabilities, to bolster its claims of sovereignty and ultimately better secure its Arctic region. After these investments and strategic actions were made, discourse surrounding the Manhattan incident dissipated. However, fast-forwarding to the Mulroney era, the Polar Sea dilemma reinvigorated the conversation that the US was challenging Canada's claim over the Northwest Passage yet again. This resulted in the Mulroney government constructing and implementing the 1987 White paper, which built off the Trudeau years, but greatly increased the security of the north. Investing in five northern airfields, fabricating eight polar icebreakers, and a

[55] Carolyn James and Patrick James. "Canada, the United States and Arctic Sovereignty: Architecture Without Building?" American Review of Canadian Studies 44, no. 2 (2014): 187–204.

[56] Shadunts, Alen. "The Rational Actor Assumption in Structural Realism." E-International Relations (blog), October 28, 2016. https://www.e-ir.info/2016/10/28/the-rational-actor-assumption-in-structural-realism/.

[57] P. Whitney Lackenbauer. "Canada's Northern Strategies: From Trudeau to Trudeau, 1970-2020." Documents on Canadian Arctic Sovereignty and Security (DCASS). Documents on Canadian Arctic Sovereignty and Security. University of Calgary Centre for Military and Strategic Studies, 2020. http://cmss.ucalgary.ca/research/arctic-document-series.

[58] Ibid.

new fleet of nuclear-powered submarines. These investments convey the impression that they were funded based on security, however they were acquired for the assertion of northern sovereignty.[59] Both governments knew their defensive capabilities were not cutting it, especially when it came to protecting the Arctic, thus it invested in offensive variables to better bolster its claim of northern sovereignty over the Northwest Passage. In accordance with this contingent realist framework,[60] the Mulroney Government also turned to a bilateral agreement, specifically the Canada-US agreement on Arctic cooperation.[61] Analytically, contingent realism suggests that rational states turn to agreements when they are aware of another state's motives. Although these agreements oftentimes focus on arms control, they can translate elsewhere. The Arctic cooperation agreement articulated that the US committed to notifying Canada when ships travelled through the Northwest Passage. As a result of this, the US signified to Canada that they respected its claim of sovereignty even without formally acknowledging it, highlighting Canada's de facto sovereignty over the Northwest Passage. All-encompassing, all three contextual situations and the remedies that followed, all correspond with a contingent realist framework.

The turn of the 21st century, introduced a factor to Arctic sovereignty that was alluded to in the past, but was scientifically verified, explicitly climate change. Over the past thirty years the Arctic's ice coverage has shrunk, by 12.5% per decade.[62] Indicatively, the Canadian Arctic interior waters are beginning to open at a significant pace. It is one of the broadly recognized factors that influenced the rise of Prime Minister Stephen Harper's concerns pertaining to Arctic sovereignty and security.[63] Sovereignty being a principal feature on his 2005 campaign trail, Harper articulated to Canadians that security and sovereignty of Canada's arctic region "was the single most

[59] Adam Lajeunesse and Rob Huebert. "From Polar Sea to Straight Baselines: Arctic Policy in the Mulroney Era." Documents on Canadian Arctic Sovereignty and Security (DCASS). Documents on Canadian Arctic Sovereignty and Security. University of Calgary Centre for Military and Strategic Studies, 2017. http://cmss.ucalgary.ca/research/arctic-document-series.

[60] Glaser, Charles L. "Realists as Optimists: Cooperation as Self-Help." International Security 19, no. 3 (1994): 50–90. https://doi.org/10.2307/2539079.

[61] "Canada—United States: Agreement on Arctic Cooperation and Exchange of Notes Concerning Transit of Northwest Passage." International Legal Materials 28, no. 1 (1989): 141–45.

[62] MIT Climate Portal. "How Much Has Arctic Ice Declined, and How Does That Compare to Past Periods in the Earth's History?" Accessed November 6, 2023. https://climate.mit.edu/ask-mit/how-much-has-arctic-ice-declined-and-how-does-compare-past-periods-earths-history.

[63] Dolata Petra. "A New Canada in the Arctic? Arctic Policies under Harper." Études Canadiennes / Canadian Studies. Revue Interdisciplinaire Des Études Canadiennes En France, no. 78 (June 1, 2015): 131–54. https://doi.org/10.4000/eccs.521.

important duty of the federal government."[64] In correlation with this, Harper asserted that his conservative party would invest in defending Canadian sovereignty through military investments, instead of flag planting and discounted rhetoric. In 2008/2009, the Harper government released its Canada First Defense Strategy, again emphasizing security and sovereignty, and articulating the need to increase defence spending.[65] The Harper conservative instituted a hard security approach to defending the Canadian Arctic. Expanding the Canadian Rangers; a primarily indigenous reservist group responsible for military monitoring and presence in the Arctic. Legislating the procurement of Arctic/Offshore Patrol ships, establishing a deep-water Arctic mooring station and refuelling facility in Nanisivik.[66] As well as launching the RadarSat-2, a Canadian designed, constructed and engineered satellite; possessing the capability to see through clouds and darkness.[67] In addition, Harper established a military training facility in Resolute Bay, a new reservist unit in Yellowknife, and ultimately stressed the importance of Arctic training.[68] These investments represented a 'use it or lose'approach to Canadian Arctic sovereignty. This attitude, brandished by the Prime Minister, followed him throughout his mandate. In Harper's 2010 Arctic strategy, he asserted that Canada needed to reaffirm its status as an Arctic power, however the government focus was not primarily security policy and investment. Categorically, the Harper government diverted from a primarily hard security approach to one that referenced the need for the global community to follow a rules-based approach in the Arctic, while at the same time encouraging economic and social development, and stewardship. At a rudimentary level, this approach seemed well intended, but mirrored a colonial minded white saviour strategy that inhibited indigenous Arctic communities from self-determination.[69] Nevertheless, moving forward, Arctic security and sovereignty continued to be a top foreign policy priority

[64] P. Whitney Lackenbauer. "Canada's Northern Strategies: From Trudeau to Trudeau, 1970-2020." Documents on Canadian Arctic Sovereignty and Security (DCASS). Documents on Canadian Arctic Sovereignty and Security. University of Calgary Centre for Military and Strategic Studies, 2020. http://cmss.ucalgary.ca/research/arctic-document-series.
[65] P. Whitney Lackenbauer. "Canada's Northern Strategies: From Trudeau to Trudeau, 1970-2020." Documents on Canadian Arctic Sovereignty and Security (DCASS). Documents on Canadian Arctic Sovereignty and Security. University of Calgary Centre for Military and Strategic Studies, 2020. http://cmss.ucalgary.ca/research/arctic-document-series.
[66] Ibid.
[67] Rob Huebert. "Renaissannce in Canadian Arctic Security?" Canadian Military Journal, Winter -2006 2005. http://www.journal.forces.gc.ca/vo6/no4/doc/north-nord-eng.pdf.
[68] Ibid.
[69] P. Whitney Lackenbauer. "Canada's Northern Strategies: From Trudeau to Trudeau, 1970-2020." Documents on Canadian Arctic Sovereignty and Security (DCASS). Documents on Canadian Arctic Sovereignty and Security. University of Calgary Centre for Military and Strategic Studies, 2020. http://cmss.ucalgary.ca/research/arctic-document-series.

for the conservative government until 2015.

The emergence of Stephen Harper in 2005, until 2015, sovereignty and security of the Canadian Arctic was a key staple of his government. Instituting and legislating significant security investments based on asserting sovereignty, through a use it or lose it mindset. Scholarship pertaining to Harper's Arctic policy renaissance often subscribes to constructivism and hyper nationalism, for establishing this approach. However, a contingent realist framework concerning security, submits that this is mildly short sighted. Firstly, contingent realism suggests that government leaders are rational actors, continuously calculating the "costs of alternative action and seeking to maximize their expected utility."[70] From his role as a member of parliament to his time as Prime Minister, Harper continuously stressed the importance of ensuring sovereignty over Canada's Arctic territory, underlining the importance the region played for Canada's future, specifically natural resources, newly emerging shipping lanes, such as the northwest passage, and increasingly tense global security situation. Through the lens of contingent realism, Harper's history concerning the Canadian Arctic, institutes a rational actor strategy when it comes to security and sovereignty, taking all factors into account.[71] This is reflected in his ability to decipher Canada's offense-defence balance and distinguishability. Prior to Harper, security and sovereignty was neglected by the Paul Martin government, resulting in lacking defensive capabilities and investment's in offense, such as through military investments.[72] Thus, when Harper entered office, there was an understanding that offensive-defensive balance and distinguishability needed to be considered. Canada, at this stage of Arctic international relations power, did not convert to the capabilities needed, regarding security and asserting sovereignty over the Arctic. Due to the vastness of the Canadian Arctic region, more military investments were needed, because ultimately Canadian forces were unequipped and unable to protect and secure Canada's northern sovereign borders. Offense-defence balance represents the financing in military forces needed to support offensive missions, to offset adversaries

---

[70] Robert Keohane, ed. "Theory of World Politics: Strucutral Realims and Beyond." In International Institutions and State Power, 1st ed., 39. Routledge, 1989. https://www.taylorfrancis.com/ chapters/ mono/10.4324/9780429032967-3/theory-world-politics-structural-realism-beyond-robert-keohane.

[71] Schmidt, Brian C, and Colin Wight. "Rationalism and the 'Rational Actor Assumption' in Realist International Relations Theory." Journal of International Political Theory 19, no. 2 (June 1, 2023): 158–82. https://doi.org/10.1177/17550882221144643.

[72] P. Whitney Lackenbauer. "Canada's Northern Strategies: From Trudeau to Trudeau, 1970-2020." Documents on Canadian Arctic Sovereignty and Security (DCASS). Documents on Canadian Arctic Sovereignty and Security. University of Calgary Centre for Military and Strategic Studies, 2020. http://cmss.ucalgary.ca/research/arctic-document-series.

and in some cases allies, defensive military investments. Through this lens, it becomes obvious that Canada needed to institute these investments and break free of the status quo that ravaged prior governments. In parallel to this, offense-defence distinguishability also played a role in these investments. Canadian security and military forces, during the Harper years, did not have the capacity to convert its power into separate distinguishable capabilities. The Canadian armed forces did not have the capability to secure sovereignty over the Arctic, as a result the Canadian state was unable to maintain offensive capabilities as well as defensive ones. The primary factor regulating this is the geography surrounding the Canadian Arctic, and the drastic effects of climate change. Contingent realist's frameworks also note that states rationally choose between competition and cooperation, by navigating the geopolitical environment with self-interest in mind.[73] Throughout Canada's history, as illustrated by our historical generalization of salient events in Canada's pursuit of security and sovereignty of the Arctic, Canada rationally decided when it needed to be competitive or cooperative, oftentimes leaning towards cooperation and self-help. However, in contrast to these other historical situations, Harper turned to more of a competitive approach. What is meant by this is, Canada was not competing with its allies, specifically the United States, but rather was competing with the international community in Arctic security. As the Arctic continued to open, the Canadian Arctic region was becoming more susceptible to foreign incursion, and the Canadian state was hardly equipped to deal with these possibilities. Thus, it instituted significant measures to rectify their lacking security situation. Through this landscape of thought, it becomes apparent that a contingent realist framework was top of mind for Harper and his conservative government. By instituting such drastic measures, that results in the procurement, acquisition and instituting policies. This strengthened Canadian Arctic security, while posturing a sovereignty mindset, for all the international community to see, in a time where international cooperation in the Arctic was beginning to subside. Therefore, through this train of thought, it is not out of line to state that contingent realism played a significant role in Harper's decision making.

## Conclusion

Overall, looking back on Canada's history, from World War II until 2015, the Canadian state has had to navigate the geopolitics and continental politics surrounding the security and sovereignty of the Canadian Arctic region.

---

[73] Glaser, Charles L. "Realists as Optimists: Cooperation as Self-Help." International Security 19, no. 3 (1994): 50–90. https://doi.org/10.2307/2539079.

Security and sovereignty being mutually inclusive terms, ultimately reflects the position of the Canadian state for the past 80 years. Congruently, the Canadian states actions pertaining to security and bolstering sovereignty, reflect a contingent realism foundation, that has for the most part, been sustained. The Canadian states being rational actors, reflects this notion, specifically through its harmonious navigation of an international system of anarchy, with a self-help/self-interest approach in mind, utilizing agreements, signalling and institutions for its own benefit. This is also true when considering the state of its own offense-defence balance, and offense-defence distinguishability, whether it be piggy backing off of the US during World War II, until the culmination of the Cold War when it came to Arctic security development, Canada always kept its interests in mind. Likewise, the Canadian state considered the increasingly competitive attitudes of the US when it came to the Arctic and translated their focus to military investment that bolster Canadian offensive and defence capabilities within the Arctic region. All-encompassing, in contrast to popular belief, Canada from World War II until the 21st century, harmoniously asserted a contingent realist framework, to ensure their own self-interests.

Moving forward, several aspects pertaining to Canada's Arctic sovereignty were not addressed. Specifically, whether contingent realism corresponds with the current Trudeau government security agenda; the reasoning for not addressing this aspect of Canadian Arctic sovereignty and security is because the government has yet to complete its mandate. This is a starting point for other academics, particularly identifying whether the Trudeau governments actions in relation to Arctic security reflect a contingent realist's approach. Furthermore, this chapter only reflects on salient national security policies and historical context, there are a lot of other aspects pertaining to Canadian Arctic sovereignty, such as environmental policy, diplomacy, indigenous relations, northern development, and social issues, that all need to be investigated. Innovative and contemporary research concerning the Canadian Arctic and sovereignty is needed in academic scholarship, particularly from scholars who are not Canadian. Doing so, will introduce a modernistic approach to the study of Canada and the Arctic, which will benefit the body of research at large. Correspondingly, contingent realism is the not the only framework that is applicable to Canadian Arctic sovereignty, liberalism, constructivism and colonialism are all routes of study that need to be taken, to ensure that scholarship pertaining to Canadian sovereignty is well rounded. Scholarship in connection with the Canadian Arctic will only become more relevant as time goes on, thus there is plenty of room in this realm of study, and I hope after reading this you feel inspired to direct your focus to this continuously developing avenue of study.

## Bibliography

Adam Lajeunesse. "Documents on Canadian Arctic Maritime Sovereignty 1950-1988." Documents on Canadian Arctic Sovereignty and Security DCASS. University of Calgary Centre for Military and Strategic Studies, September 2018. http://cmss.ucalgary.ca/research/arctic-document-series.

———. "The Distant Early Warning Line and the Canadian Battle for Public Perception - Canadian Military Journal." Canadian National Defence. Canadian Military Journal, June 20, 2007. http://www.journal.forces.gc.ca/vo8/no2/lajeunes-eng.asp.

Adam Lajeunesse and Rob Huebert. "From Polar Sea to Straight Baselines: Arctic Policy in the Mulroney Era." Documents on Canadian Arctic Sovereignty and Security (DCASS). Documents on Canadian Arctic Sovereignty and Security. University of Calgary Centre for Military and Strategic Studies, 2017. http://cmss.ucalgary.ca/research/arctic-document-series.

Arash Heydarian Pashakhanlou. *Realism in Practice: An Appraisal.* E-IR Edited Collection. E-International Relations, 2018. https://www.e-ir.info/2018/01/15/the-past-present-and-future-of-realism/.

Arctic Council. "Canada." Arctic Council. Accessed November 6, 2023. https://arctic-council.org/about/states/canada/.

Åtland, Kristian. "Mikhail Gorbachev, the Murmansk Initiative, and the Desecuritization of Interstate: Relations in the Arctic." *Cooperation and Conflict* 43, no. 3 (2008): 289–311.

"Canada—United States: Agreement on Arctic Cooperation and Exchange of Notes Concerning Transit of Northwest Passage." *International Legal Materials* 28, no. 1 (1989): 141–45.

Carolyn James and Patrick James. "Canada, the United States and Arctic Sovereignty: Architecture Without Building?" *American Review of Canadian Studies* 44, no. 2 (2014): 187–204.

Devyatkin, Pavel. "Arctic Exceptionalism: A Narrative of Cooperation and Conflict from Gorbachev to Medvedev and Putin." *The Polar Journal* 0, no. 0 (2023): 1–22. https://doi.org/10.1080/2154896X.2023.2258658.

Dolata, Petra. "A New Canada in the Arctic? Arctic Policies under Harper." *Études Canadiennes / Canadian Studies. Revue Interdisciplinaire Des Études Canadiennes En France*, no. 78 (June 1, 2015): 131–54. https://doi.org/10.4000/eccs.521.

Donat Pharand. "Canada's Sovereignty Over the Northwest Passage." *Michigan Journal of International Law* 10, no. 2 (1989): 653–78.

Glaser, Charles L. "Realists as Optimists: Cooperation as Self-Help." *International Security* 19, no. 3 (1994): 50–90. https://doi.org/10.2307/2539079.

———. "Structural Realism in a More Complex World." *Review of International Studies* 29, no. 3 (2003): 403–14.

Gricius, Gabriella. "A Decolonial Approach to Arctic Security and Sovereignty." Arctic Year Book, 2021. https://arcticyearbook.com/arctic-yearbook/2021/2021-scholarly-papers/377-a-decolonial-approach-to-arctic-security-and-sovereignty.

———. "Conceptualising the Arctic as a Zone of Conflict." *Central European Journal of International and Security Studies* 15, no. 4 (December 22, 2021): 4–30. https://doi.org/10.51870/CEJISS.A150401.

Iseman, Peter A. "Lifting the Ice Curtain." *The New York Times*, October 23, 1988, sec. Magazine. https://www.nytimes.com/1988/10/23/magazine/lifting-the-ice-curtain.html.

Kenneth Waltz, Hertbert Buutterfield, and Hedley Bull. *Theory of International Politics*. 1st ed. Waveland Press, 1979.

Michael T. Fawcett. "The Politics of Sovereignty - Continental Defence and the Creation of NORAD." *Canadian Military Journal* 10, no. 2 (2010): 33–40.

MIT Climate Portal. "How Much Has Arctic Ice Declined, and How Does That Compare to Past Periods in the Earth's History?" Accessed November 6, 2023. https://climate.mit.edu/ask-mit/how-much-has-arctic-ice-declined-and-how-does-compare-past-periods-earths-history.

Murray, Robert W. "(Mis)Understanding the Arctic." *E-International Relations* (blog), April 3, 2014. https://www.e-ir.info/2014/04/03/misunderstanding-the-arctic/.

Ole R. Holsti. "Public Opinion and Foreign Policy: Challenges to the Almond-Lippmann Consensus." *International Studies Quarterly* 36, no. 4 (December 1992): 439–66.

P. Whitney Lackenbauer. "Canada's Northern Strategies: From Trudeau to Trudeau, 1970-2020." Documents on Canadian Arctic Sovereignty and Security (DCASS). Documents on Canadian Arctic Sovereignty and Security. University of Calgary Centre for Military and Strategic Studies, 2020. http://cmss.ucalgary.ca/ research/ arctic-document-series.

P. Whitney Lackenbauer and Daniel Heidt. "The Advisory Committee on Northern Development: Context and Meeting Minutes, 1948-71." Documents on Canadian Arctic Sovereignty and Security DCASS. University of Calgary Centre fro Military and Strategic Studies, revised 2019. https://live-arts.ucalgary.ca/sites/ default/files/ teams/25/dcass4-acnd-rev-ed.pdf.

P. Whitney Lackenbauer, Matthew J. Farish, and Jennifer Arthur-Lackenbauer. "The Distant Early Warning (DEW) Line: A Bibliography and Documentary Resource List." Prepared for the Arctic Institute of North America, October 2005. https://pubs.aina.ucalgary.ca/aina/dewlinebib.pdf.

P. Whitney Lackenbauer and Peter Kikkert. "Legal Appraisals of Canada's Arctic Sovereignty: Key Documents, 1905-56." Documents on Canadian Arctic Sovereignty and Security (DCASS). University of Calgary Centre fro Military and Strategic Studies. Accessed August 15, 2023. https://cmss.ucalgary.ca/sites/cmss.ucalgary.ca/ files/ dcassv2.pdf.

Rob Huebert. "Canadian Arctic Security Issues: Transformation in the Post-Cold War Era." *International Journal* 54, no. 2 (Spring 1999): 203–29.

———. "Renaissannce in Canadian Arctic Security?" *Canadian Military Journal*, Winter - 2006 2005. http://www.journal.forces.gc.ca/vo6/no4/doc/north-nord-eng.pdf.

Robert Keohane, ed. "Theory of World Politics: Strucutral Realims and Beyond." In *International Institutions and State Power*, 1st ed., 39. Routledge, 1989. https://www.taylorfrancis.com/chapters/mono/10.4324/9780429032967-3/theory-world-politics-structural-realism-beyond-robert-keohane.

Ron Huebert. "Canadian Arctic Sovereignty and Security in a Transforming Circumpolar

World." *Foreign Policy for Canada's Tomorrow.* Canadian International Council, 2009. https://royaldutchshellplc.com/wp-content/uploads/1947/04/ Arctic SovereigntySecurity-831.pdf.

Ryan Dean and P. Whitney Lackenbauer. "Chapter 14: Arctic Exceptionalisms." In *The Arctic and the World Order*, pg. 328. School of Advanced International Studies, 2021. https://rideauinstitute.ca/wp-content/uploads/2021/01/Chapter-14-Lackenbauer.pdf.

———. "Chapter 14: Arctic Exceptionalisms." In *The Arctic and the World Order*. School of Advanced International Studies, 2021. https://rideauinstitute.ca/wp-content/uploads/2021/01/Chapter-14-Lackenbauer.pdf.

Schmidt, Brian C, and Colin Wight. "Rationalism and the 'Rational Actor Assumption'in Realist International Relations Theory." *Journal of International Political Theory* 19, no. 2 (June 1, 2023): 158–82. https://doi.org/10.1177/17550882221144643.

Sean M. Maloney. "Who Has Seen The Wind? An Historical Overview of Canadian Special Operations." *Canadian Military Journal.* Government of Canada, National Defence, Canadian Defence Academy. Accessed November 6, 2023. http://www.journal.forces.gc.ca/vo5/no3/special-03-eng.asp.

Shadunts, Alen. "The Rational Actor Assumption in Structural Realism." *E-International Relations* (blog), October 28, 2016. https://www.e-ir.info/2016/10/28/the-rational-actor-assumption-in-structural-realism/.

Tripp, Emily. "Realism: The Domination of Security Studies." *E-International Relations* (blog), June 14, 2013. http://www.e-ir.info/2013/06/14/realism-the-domination-of-security-studies/.

Walker, R. B. J. "Security, Sovereignty, and the Challenge of World Politics." *Alternatives* 15, no. 1 (January 1, 1990): 3–27. https://doi.org/10.1177/030437549001500102.

# CHAPTER 3

## THE POLICIES OF THE RUSSIAN FEDERATION TOWARDS THE ARCTIC REGION

Ebru Caymaz[1]

The Arctic region has been on the Russian government's agenda since the early 2000s, with the economic and commercial potential provided by its rich underground resources and alternative maritime trade routes serving as a key interest. As stated by Vladimir Putin during the Arctic Forum in 2011, the shortest route between the Asia-Pacific region and Europe's largest markets lies along the Arctic. This route is calculated as almost a third shorter than the traditional southern route.[2]

Being the largest Arctic state, there are quite different views in the literature regarding the Arctic policies of the Russian Federation (RF) ranging from aggressive and expansionist to defensive, and collaborative. Albeit the existence of different views in the literature regarding the Russian Federation's (RF) Arctic policies, these policies have three main goals: utilizing the Arctic's natural resources, promoting the NSR as an international maritime route, and protect its ecosystem. According to some scholars, the RF's decision to proceed its strategic bomber patrol flights in the Arctic region, its placement of a titanium Russian flag made on the ocean floor at the North Pole in August 2007, and the scope of the Arctic Strategy published in 2008 indicate that its Arctic policies are aggressive, expansionist, and based on 'power diplomacy'.[3,4] While its invasion of Ukraine in 2022 has provoked several harsh criticisms and multiple sanctions against the RF, the protests against its Chairmanship of the Arctic Council between 2021-2023 have also heavily affected the sustainable development process in the region. On the other hand, the most recent Foreign Policy Concept published in March 2023 indicates a significant political shift to the development of the

---

[1] Assoc. Prof. Dr., Canakkale Onsekiz Mart University, ebru.caymaz@comu.edu.tr
[2] Bryanski, B., "Russia's Putin Says Arctic Trade Route to Rival Suez", Reuters, 22 Eylül 2011, http://ca.reuters.com/article/topNews/idCATRE78L5TC20110922?pageNumber=1&virtualBrandChannel=0.
[3] Schepp M. ve Traufetter, G., "Riches at the North Pole: Russia Unveils Aggressive Arctic Plans," Spiegel Online International, 2009, January 29.
[4] Willett L., The Navy in Russia's "Resurgence", RUSI Journal, 154: 1, 2009, ss. 50–55.

Russian Arctic.

On the other hand, according to some views, the RF's current Arctic doctrine can be explained with Moscow's pragmatic interests, such as competition for natural resources and/or control of the NSR. That's why, there are studies examining the RF's intentions toward the Arctic region as essentially defensive for the protection of its legitimate interests, or at least as acceptable as the demands of other Arctic states in terms of international Arctic cooperation.[5,6,7] These studies emphasize that the RF's fundamental interest is the development of the Russian Arctic which has rich natural resources while remains underdeveloped in terms of infrastructure, local economy, social institutions, and communication systems. According to this view, the RF does not pursue a revisionist Arctic policy, on the contrary, it strives to resolve all disputes it encounters in the region through peaceful means provided by international law. Therefore, this chapter aims to outline the political shifts while examining the policies of the RF towards the Arctic region.

## The Geography of the Country and Its Geopolitical Importance

Upon the establishment of the Principality of Kyiv in the 10th century, Russians maintained their political existence respectively as the Principality of Moscow (1340-1547), Tsardom of Russia (1547-1721), Russian Empire (1721-1917), Soviet Union (1922-1991), and Russian Federation. While the RF's historical development stems from the geographical conditions of the country, Russian political and security thought was also determined by foreign occupations.[8]

After the collapse of the Soviet Union, the RF confronted with three difficult tasks: defining national identity, national interests, and security policies. The post-Soviet geography was defined as an area of strategic interest under the name "Near Abroad". That's why, geopolitics and Eurasian-ism were embodied in policies as the two main elements of Russian security thought.[9]

The geopolitical thought system includes the sum of military, strategic, political, and economic interests of a state. In this context, the geopolitical

---

[5] Oreshenkov A., "Arctic Diplomacy," Russia in Global Affairs, (4), October-December 2009.

[6] Belov P., "Demographic Aspects of Russia's Arctic Geopolitics", in Geopolitics: Theory, History, Practice, Moscow: Prostranstvo I Vremya, 2012.

[7] Heininen L., Arctic Strategies and Policies – Inventory and Comparative Study, The Northern Research Forum &The University of Lapland. Akureyri, Iceland, August 2011.

[8] Service, R., A History of Modern Russia, From Nicholas II to Putin, London: Penguin Books, 2003.

[9] Huasheng, Z., "Russia and Its Near Abroad: Challenges and Prospects", Valdai Discussion Club, March 2021.

behaviour of each state offers a perspective that takes historical and current dynamics into account. It is possible to define geopolitics as "the use of geography as an element of power and the thoughts that political leaders and academics have on this subject".[10] In line with this view, the RF has historically transformed its naval power and its elements into a widespread foreign policy tool through the gains brought by strategic continuity. Strategic continuity paved the way for the development and preservation of Russian geopolitical memory as well.

## Historical Interaction in the Arctic Region

The RF's interest in the Arctic region began with the voyages of the Soviet Union navy to explore the NSR for commercial purposes between 1910 and 1915, and the first successful cruise on this route took place around this time.[11] In 1926, the Soviet Union determined its borders in the North and claimed rights over the region between the Kola Peninsula, the Arctic Point, and the Bering Strait; further repeated these claims in 1928 and 1950.[12] The Soviet Union, which began to show military interest in the region in the 1930s, also implemented a rapid industrialization policy. Several military bases were established and rapidly armed in the Arctic region, which turned into a geopolitical and geostrategic competition area between the USSR and the USA during the Cold War.[13]

After signing the United Nations Convention on the Law of the Sea (UNCLOS) in 1997, RF was the first state to apply to the UN in 2001 and seek the right to expand its continental shelf in the Arctic region while being one of the first states among the Arctic countries to develop the official Arctic strategy and shape the Arctic doctrine. The RF's Arctic doctrine can be examined in three periods: 1991-2007; 2008-2013; and 2014-Present. From a wider angle, the RF's Arctic policies prioritize security and economic concerns associated with other issues which entail readiness to secure and exploit its interests.

---

[10] Goldstein, J. S.; Pevehouse, J. C., International Relations, Pearson, 2011.

[11] The Stimson Center, "Evolution of Arctic Territorial Claims and Agreements: A Timeline (1903-Present), 15 Eylül 2013, https://www.stimson.org/2013/evolution-arctic-territorial-claims-and-agreements-timeline-1903-present/.

[12] Astrasheuskaya N.; Foy, H., "Polar Powers: Russia's Bid For Supremacy in the Arctic Ocean", 28 Nisan 2019, https://www.ft.com/content/2fa82760-5c4a-11e9-939a-341f5ada9d40.

[13] Huebert, R. "A New Cold War in the Arctic?! The Old One Never Ended!", Arctic Yearbook, 2019.

## The RF's Military, Economic and Political Importance for the Arctic Region

After the Cold War, the RF pursued an initially pragmatic foreign policy which was reflected in its approach towards the region. Considerable investments have been made in arms procurement and military infrastructure that evoke the concern of dual use. While the Ministry of Arctic Development continues to fund infrastructure projects, the RF has prioritized opening up oil and gas pipelines, developing tourism, and building icebreakers.[14]

To overcome the hindrance caused by more than 5000 sanctions of the Western states, the RF has started to cooperate with Türkiye and Italy (ie. Arctic LNG-2 Project). Apart from shipping lanes, the RF has successfully maintained to development of its railway networks in the High North. Hydrocarbon resources from the western Siberia can be transported thanks to the Northern Siberian Main Line. Developing Obskaya station holds the potential to draw 23 million tons of cargo. Besides, 220 tons of cargo are projected to arrive at the ports of Murmansk, St.Petersburg, Arkhangelsk and Ust-Luga by 2025.[15]

In terms of Russian mega projects in the High North, the Northern Latitudinal Passage (NLP) stands out as one of the most significant ones due to its great potential for boosting cargo flows while enhancing connectivity at the same time. The NLP involves the construction of railways that will connect the Arctic Ocean with the High North's industrial settlements. Therefore, it is projected to become an essential driver in terms of logistical development. In addition to the length of the passage, the planned routes would stimulate the Yamal peninsula's industrial and economic development.[16]

## Security Relationship with the Arctic Region

The RF's ambitious Arctic vision involving defence and security dimensions has renewed the Arctic interest of NATO since the early 2000s. This process has also led to a new strategic approach based on NATO's enlargement in

---

[14] Jordan, J., "Russia's Coercive Diplomacy in the Arctic", The Arctic Institute, 2021, https://www.thearctic institute.org/russia-coercive-diplomacy-arctic/.

[15] Pokrovskaya O. D, Fedorenko; Kamaletdinov, V. D., Northern Latitudinal Railway Project: Priorities and Drivers                                                                    . In: Ashmarina S.I., Horák J., Vrbka J., Šuleř P. (eds) Economic Systems in the New Era: Stable Systems in an Unstable World. IES 2020. Lecture Notes in Networks and Systems, Vol 160. Springer, Cham.

[16] Caymaz, E., "Enhancing Industrial Development in the Russian Arctic: The Northern Latitudinal Passage, the Arctic Institute, April 2022.

the region.[17] In addition to increasing military exercises of the Northern Flank, the establishment of the Joint Force Command (JFC) for High North and North Atlantic operations, as well as Swedish-Finnish NATO accession have stimulated the RF in return. Sweden's and Finland's membership aspirations have deeply affected and even reshaped the entire security landscape. While the recent activities of the US, RF, and China in and around the Arctic have placed novel pressures, NATO also reshaped its security approach towards the region. The massive Trident Juncture NATO Exercise in 2019 with more than 50,000 participants from NATO and other partner countries and the establishment of JFC Norfolk to increase readiness in the High North signal a significant shift in terms of NATO's posture.[18]

**Figure 1.** A Comparison of Icebreakers[19]

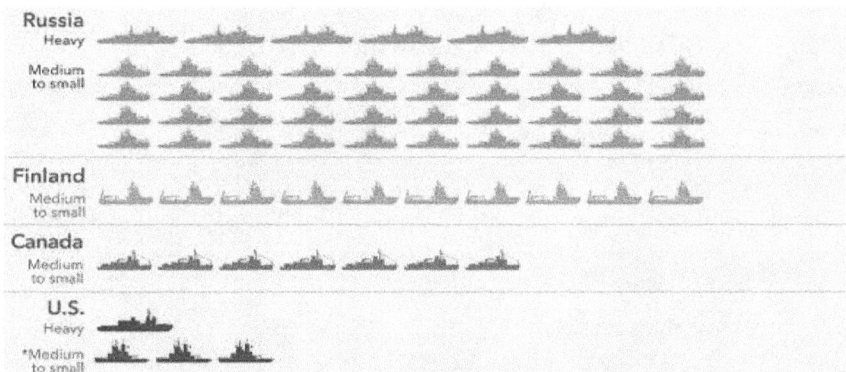

*Source: US Coast Guard*

Since 2014, the deterioration of relations between the West and the RF has manifested itself in several ways in the Arctic. The RF's strategic security goal for the region is defined as "ensuring a favourable operational regime in the Arctic zone of the Russian Federation, including maintenance of the necessary combat capabilities of general-purpose troops (forces) of the Armed Forces of the Russian Federation and other troops, military formations, and military agencies in this region."[20] This goal includes strengthening the Coastal Defense Corps of the RF Federal Security Service,

---

[17] Depledge, D., "NATO and the Arctic the Need for a New Approach", The Rusi Journal, Vol. 165, No.5/6, 2020.

[18] Tamnes, R. "The Significance of the North Atlantic and the Norwegian Contribution', in John Andreas Olsen (ed.), NATO and the North Atlantic: Revitalising Collective Defence, RUSI Whitehall Paper, 87, London: Taylor and Francis, 2017, pp. 8–31.

[19] US Coast Guard, https://blog.usni.org/wp-content/uploads/2021/11/620x-1.jpg.

[20] Heininen, L.; Sergunin, A.; Yarovoy, G., "Russian Strategies in the Arctic: Avoiding a New Cold War", Valdai Discussion Club Grantees Report, 2014.

strengthening border controls in the Russian Arctic, and establishing technical control in the straits and estuaries along the entire NSR. The created Arctic Group Forces are not only tasked with defending the region but also with protecting the RF's economic interests in the region[21]. Accordingly, the RF has started to present its deterrence by conducting larger military exercises in the Arctic. Not surprisingly, the RF conducted its largest exercise called 'Ocean Shield'in 2023 with the attendance of more than 6,000 military personnel assisted by 30 military vessels and boats. According to the Russian Defense Ministry "during the exercise, measures for the protection of maritime communications, transportation of armies and military cargo, as well as for the defence of the sea coast [sic] will be worked out. In total, it is planned to perform more than 200 combat training, including the practical use of weapons."[22]

**Map 1.** The RF's Military Bases in the Arctic[23]

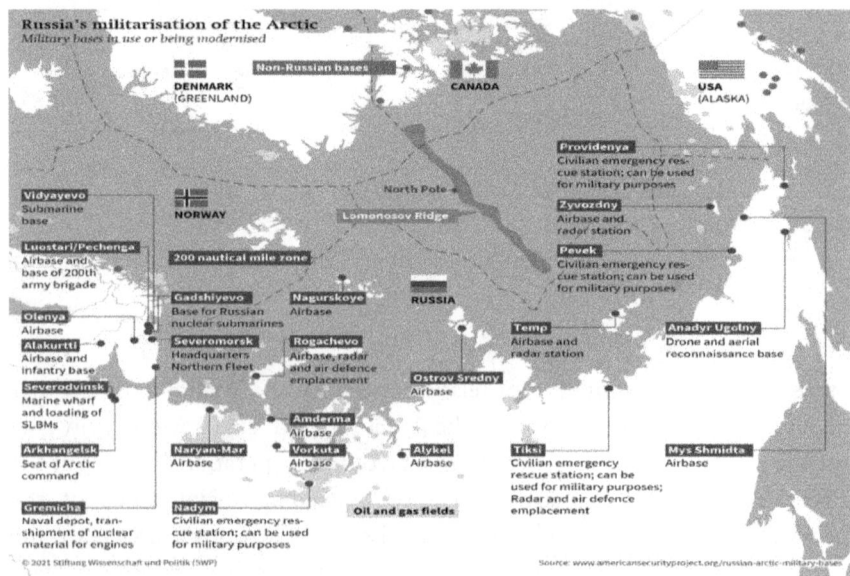

*Source: American Security Project (ASP)*

**Values Added to the Arctic**

According to the multifaceted development plans for the northern regions of

---

[21] Ibid.

[22] Teslova, E., "Russia Starts Ocean Shield 2023 Naval Exercises in Baltic Sea", AA News Agency Europe, 2 August 2023.

[23] Franiok, N., Russian Arctic Military Bases (American Security Project, 22 April 2020), https://www.americansecurityproject.org/russian-arctic-military-bases.

the RF, the Arctic region is asserted as the most important strategic resource area of the RF between 2016 and 2020. In addition to military modernization, and assertiveness, advancing the development of the NSR stands out prominent issue in Russian policy. Since infrastructure facilitates access, inhabitation, connection, and productivity, the RF has accelerated its mega projects throughout the Arctic region.

Some studies perceive the recent developments as the return of great power competition and the end of the "Arctic exceptionalism."[24,25,26] The RF's latest foreign policy concept in 2023 signals further changes in the dynamics within the region. First, the previous statement of 'constructive international cooperation'is removed in the latest policy. Instead, new domestic objectives are set: ensuring socio-economic development in the Russian Arctic, and increasing environmental sustainability while reducing threats.

Besides, the indigenous groups are also mentioned in the policy paper for the first time. They are outlined as an integral part of socio-economic development. The development of the NSR still occupies the core of the Concept and the role of the Arctic Council as a high-level forum is still being recognized. However, all multilateral formats of international cooperation with the Western states such as the Barents Euro-Arctic Council and the Arctic Five are excluded. Instead, 'mutually beneficial cooperation with non-Arctic states that pursue a constructive policy towards Russia and are interested in international activities in the Arctic, including infrastructure development of the Northern Sea Route"is emphasized.[27] Accordingly, there is the expression of 'foreign'instead of 'Arctic'states in the State Policy Framework. Therefore, in addition to Polar Silk Road partnerships with China, new bilateral agreements with non-Arctic states such as Türkiye and India are expected in the near future.

## The RF's Expectations from the Arctic (energy, political, security, military, economic etc.)

The Russian Government approved the draft document titled 'Foundations of the State Policy of the Russian Federation in the Arctic', which outlines the RF's national interests and basic strategies in the Arctic region and its

[24] Saxena, A, "The Return of Great Power Competition to the Arctic", The Arctic Institute, 2020, https://www.thearcticinstitute.org/return-great-power-competition-arctic/.
[25] Olesen, M. R., "The end of Arctic Exceptionalism?". Danish Foreign Policy Review, Vol. 103, 2020.
[26] Shvets, D.; Hossain, K., "The Future of Arctic Governance: Broken Hopes for Arctic Exceptionalism?", Current Developments in Arctic Law, Vol. 10, 2022, pp.49-63.
[27] Lipunov, N.; Devyatkin, P., "The Arctic in the 2023 Russian Foreign Policy Concept, The Arctic Institute, May 2023.

final version was published in 2008. In this 6-page document, approved under the name 'State Policy of the Russian Federation in the Arctic to 2020 and Beyond', the national interests of the RF in the Arctic region are listed as follows:

- Development of resources in the Arctic region,
- Transforming the NSR into a national transportation corridor and communication line,
- Preservation of the region as an international cooperation zone.[28]

The 2008 Document draws road maps such as strengthening the Arctic Council and cooperating with the EU, using trade routes efficiently, and assisting ships that will use the route, as well as ensuring the continuation of RF's rights in the Svalbard Treaty, developing technology in the Arctic region and creating a more modern environment while developing the infrastructure. Therefore, the first stage of the RF's Arctic policy was completed on time while both the second and third stages have been running behind schedule. Specifically, there is a disconnection between domestic efforts to modernize the infrastructure as the international conditions involving economic sanctions are less favourable to enable such modernization. Table 1 given below summarizes the evolution process of Russian national interests in the Arctic.

**Table 1.** Evolution of Russian National Interests in the Arctic as Outlined in Basic Principles 2020 and Basic Principles 2035[29]

| Basic Principles of RF State Policy in the Arctic to 2020 (Adopted in 2008) | Basic Principles of RF State Policy in the Arctic to 2025 (Adopted in 2020) |
|---|---|
| - Highlighting the Russian Arctic region as a strategic resource base to offer solutions for the issues of both economic and social development of the country. <br> - Maintaining the Arctic as a peaceful region supported by cooperation. <br> - Preserving the Arctic's unique ecological systems. <br> -Highlighting the NSR as a national transport route in the region. | - Ensuring the RF's sovereignty and territorial integrity. <br> - Preserving peace in the Arctic through stable and mutually beneficial partnerships. <br> - Ensuring high living standards and prosperity for the Russian Arctic. <br> - Developing the Russian Arctic as a strategic resource base while employing resources to advance economic growth. <br> - Developing the NSR as a competitive national transport corridor on a global scale. |

---

[28] Medvedev, D., Foundations of the State Policy of the Russian Federation in the Arctic up to and Beyond 2020", 2008, [Osnovy Gosudarstvennoi Politiki Rossiiskoi Federatsii v Arktike na Period do 2020 Goda I Dal'neishuiu Perspektivu] http://www.rg.ru/2009/03/30/arktika-osnovy-dok.html.

[29] Klimenko, E., "Russia's New Arctic Policy Document Signals Continuity Rather Than Change", SIPRI Commentary, 6 April 2020.

- Protecting the Arctic environment, as
well as homeland and indigenous
minorities residing in the Arctic.

## Relations with Other Arctic Countries

The socio-economic crises faced by the USSR in the 1980s encouraged the leader of the period, Mikhail Gorbachev, to pursue a more conciliatory foreign policy. Herein, the 'peace zone'discourse used by Gorbachev for the Arctic region in his remarkable speech in Murmansk on October 1, 1987, is quite striking. He emphasized that the Arctic region geographically brings together the Asian, European, and American continents and called for the problems in the region to be solved through bilateral and multilateral cooperation.[30] Following Gorbachev's moderate approach, the military elements in the region were significantly reduced; bilateral and multilateral dialogues have been initiated among the Arctic states to ensure successful environmental management and sustainability of resources.

The RF stands out as a key participant in the creation of a new institutional landscape within the Arctic both in the 1990s and early 2000s. Albeit its increasingly anti-Western foreign policy, Putin's speech during the Security Conference in Munich (2007) highlighted RF's intention to act cooperatively in Arctic matters. That cooperative approach even survived after the invasion of Georgia in 2008 and Ukraine in 2014; significant deals, such as between ExxonMobil and Rosneft (2011), were signed between Russian and Western firms. On the other hand, the RF's Arctic policies confront ongoing problems since balancing priorities can be highly challenging at a time of economic stagnation.[31]

In line with the recent developments, much political discussion revolved around the issues of international stability and the possibility of conflict in the region. Upon Ukraine's invasion in 2014, a sharp deterioration in relations between the West and the RF was experienced. In August 2014, Putin highlighted the fact that the RF will "pay more attention to issues of development of the Arctic and the strengthening of our position."[32] Putin's

---

[30] Mikhail Gorbachev's Speech in Murmansk at the Ceremonial Meeting On the Occasion of the Presentation Of the Order of Lenin and the Gold Star to the City of Murmansk, 1 Ekim 1987, https://www.barentsinfo.fi/docs/Gorbachev_speech.pdf.
[31] Foxall, A., "Russia's Policies towards a Changing Arctic: Implications for UK Security", The Henry Jackson Society Russia Studies Centre, June, 2017.
[32] Walker, S., Ragozin, L., Weaver, M., 'Putin Likens Ukraine's forces to Nazis and threatens standoff in the Arctic', The Guardian, 29 August 2014, https://www.theguardian.com/world/2014/aug/29/putin-ukraine-forces-nazis-arctic.

speech was endorsed by the adoption of Russia's updated Military Doctrine that states "the main tasks of the Armed Forces, other troops and bodies in peacetime to protect national interests of the Russian Federation in the Arctic region."[33] Soon after the adoption of the updated doctrine, the RF's Minister of Defense declared that "a broad spectrum of potential challenges and threats to our national security is now being formed in the Arctic."[34] The RF's withdrawal from the Barents Euro-Arctic Council implies further structural changes in the multilateral cooperative bodies in the Arctic.

## Conclusion and Discussion

The Arctic region is no longer isolated from global geopolitical shifts. While the duality of the activities of both parties in the region escalates the tension, there is an urgent need for constructive relations based on the soft power of diplomacy. Although there are predictions in the current literature that global warming, globalization, urbanization, and demographic changes are rapidly transforming the cultures, economies, and socio-political structures in the Arctic region, and that current developments based on emerging economic opportunities will cause conflicts, the RF's security, especially regarding Arctic maritime transportation has two ignored positive trends. The first one is a clear shift towards discussing soft security issues rather than continuing to include hard security threats in its published official documents. Secondly, the RF states that it aims to solve NSR-related problems based on negotiation with other regional actors and cooperation with the Arctic Council, International Maritime Organization, and relevant United Nations institutions/structures. Therefore, having open access to three oceans and holding the highest capacity for strategic nuclear submarines and icebreakers, the RF's main goals in the Russian Arctic are expected to remain the same: utilizing the Arctic's natural resources, promoting the NSR as an international maritime route, and protect its ecosystem.

On the other hand, despite the official statement about ensuring peace and cooperation within the Arctic, the Northern Fleet is expected to increase its military capabilities in response to NATO's enlargement initiatives in the region. When the new Policy Concept is examined from a wider angle, it can be asserted that the RF emphasizes its self-sufficiency against all kinds of

---

[33] Voennaya doktrina Rossiyskoy Federatsii' [Military Doctrine of the Russian Federation], 25 December 2014, http://www.scrf.gov.ru/security/military/document129/

[34] Bender, J., 'Russian Defense Minister Explains Why the Kremlin is Militarizing the Arctic', Business Insider UK, 26 February 2015, http://uk.businessinsider.com/why-the-kremlin-is-militarizing-the-arctic-2015-2?r=US&IR=T.

sanctions, but the RF is also open to cooperation with the parties who are eager to respect its national interests. That's why the expression of 'Arctic'is replaced with 'foreign'states. Therefore, it is concluded that in addition to previous partnerships with China, by employing new agreements with newly emerging actors, such as Türkiye and India, the RF will continue to enhance its infrastructure in the Arctic. Accordingly, there is a need for comprehensive studies that include multidisciplinary dimensions in the analysis which can promote a more in-depth understanding of the region, and therefore the resolution of disputes between actors, as well as cooperation, and sharing of expertise.

## References

Astrasheuskaya N.; Foy, H., "Polar Powers: Russia's Bid For Supremacy in the Arctic Ocean", 28 Nisan 2019, https://www.ft.com/content/2fa82760-5c4a-11e9-939a-341f5ada9d40.

Belov P., "Demographic Aspects of Russia's Arctic Geopolitics", *in Geopolitics: Theory, History, Practice,* Moscow: Prostranstvo I Vremya, 2012.

Bender, J., 'Russian Defense Minister Explains Why the Kremlin is Militarizing the Arctic', *Business Insider UK, 26* February 2015, http://uk.businessinsider.com/why-the-kremlin-is-militarizing-the-arctic-2015-2?r=US&IR=T.

Bryanski, B., "Russia's Putin Says Arctic Trade Route to Rival Suez", *Reuters,* 22 Eylül 2011,
http://ca.reuters.com/article/topNews/idCATRE78L5TC20110922?pageNumber =1&virtualBrandChannel=0.

Caymaz, E., "Enhancing Industrial Development in the Russian Arctic: The Northern Latitudinal Passage*, the Arctic Institute,* April, 2022.

Depledge, D., "NATO and the Arctic the Need for a New Approach", *The Rusi Journal,* Vol. 165, No.5/6, 2020.

Foxall, A., "Russia's Policies towards a Changing Arctic: Implications for UK Security", The Henry Jackson Society Russia Studies Centre, June, 2017.

Franiok, N., *Russian Arctic Military Bases* (American Security Project, 22 April 2020), https://www.americansecurityproject.org/russian-arctic-military-bases.

Jordan, J., "Russia's Coercive Diplomacy in the Arctic", *The Arctic Institute,* 2021, https://www.thearcticinstitute.org/russia-coercive-diplomacy-arctic/.

Goldstein, J. S.; Pevehouse, J. C., *International Relations,* Pearson, 2011.

Heininen L., *Arctic Strategies and Policies – Inventory and Comparative Study,* The Northern Research Forum &The University of Lapland. Akureyri, Iceland, August, 2011.

Heininen, L.; Sergunin, A.; Yarovoy, G., "Russian Strategies in the Arctic: Avoiding a New Cold War", *Valdai Discussion Club Grantees Report,* 2014.

Huasheng, Z., "Russia and Its Near Abroad: Challenges and Prospects", Valdai Discussion Club, March 2021.

Huebert, R. "A New Cold War in the Arctic?! The Old One Never Ended!", *Arctic Yearbook,* 2019.

Klimenko, E., "Russia's New Arctic Policy Document Signals Continuity Rather Than Change", *SIPRI Commentary*, 6 April 2020.

Lipunov, N.; Devyatkin, P., "The Arctic in the 2023 Russian Foreign Policy Concept, The Arctic Institute, May 2023.

Medvedev, D., Foundations of the State Policy of the Russian Federation in the Arctic up to and Beyond 2020", 2008, [Osnovy Gosudarstvennoi Politiki Rossiiskoi Federatsii v Arktike na Period do 2020 Goda I Dal'neishuiu Perspektivu] http://www.rg.ru/2009/03/30/arktika-osnovy-dok.html.

Mikhail Gorbachev's Speech in Murmansk at the Ceremonial Meeting On the Occasion of the Presentation Of the Order of Lenin and the Gold Star to the City of Murmansk, 1 Ekim 1987, https://www.barentsinfo.fi/docs/Gorbachev_speech.pdf.

Olesen, M. R., "The end of Arctic Exceptionalism?". *Danish Foreign Policy Review*, Vol. 103, 2020.

Oreshenkov A., "Arctic Diplomacy," *Russia in Global Affairs*, (4), October-December, 2009.

Pokrovskaya O. D, Fedorenko ve Kamaletdinov, V. D.,   Northern Latitudinal Railway Project: Priorities and Drivers. In: Ashmarina S.I., Horák J., Vrbka J., Šuleř P. (eds) *Economic Systems in the New Era: Stable Systems in an Unstable World*. IES 2020. Lecture Notes in Networks and Systems, Vol 160. Springer, Cham.

Saxena, A, "The Return of Great Power Competition to the Arctic", The Arctic Institute, 2020, https://www.thearcticinstitute.org/return-great-power-competition-arctic/.

Schepp M.; Traufetter, G., "Riches at the North Pole: Russia Unveils Aggressive Arctic Plans," *Spiegel Online International*, 2009, January 29.

Service, R., A History Of Modern Russia, From Nicholas II To Putin, London: Penguin Books, 2003.

Shvets, D.; Hossain, K., "The Future of Arctic Governance: Broken Hopes for Arctic Exceptionalism?", *Current Developments in Arctic Law*, Vol. 10, 2022, pp.49-63.

Tamnes, R. "The Significance of the North Atlantic and the Norwegian Contribution', in John Andreas Olsen (ed.), NATO and the North Atlantic: Revitalising Collective Defence, RUSI Whitehall Paper, 87, London: Taylor and Francis, 2017, pp. 8–31.

Teslova, E., "Russia Starts Ocean Shield 2023 Naval Exercises in Baltic Sea", AA News Agency Europe, 2 August 2023.

The Stimson Center, "Evolution of Arctic Territorial Claims and Agreements: A Timeline (1903-Present), 15 Eylül 2013, https://www.stimson.org/2013/evolution-arctic-territorial-claims-and-agreements-timeline-1903-present/.

US Coast Guard, https://blog.usni.org/wp-content/uploads/2021/11/620x-1.jpg.

Voennaya doktrina Rossiyskoy Federatsii'[Military Doctrine of the Russian Federation], 25 December 2014, http://www.scrf.gov.ru/security/military/document129/.

Walker, S., Ragozin, L., Weaver, M., 'Putin Likens Ukraine's forces to Nazis and threatens standoff in the Arctic', *The Guardian,* 29 August 2014, https://www.theguardian.com/world/2014/aug/29/putin-ukraine-forces-nazis-arctic.

Willett L., The Navy in Russia's "Resurgence", *RUSI Journal*, 154: 1, 2009, ss. 50–55.

# CHAPTER 4

# POLICIES OF FINLAND TOWARDS THE ARCTIC REGION

Yeliz Albayrak[1]

The Arctic region holds great significance for Finland throughout its history. Finland is an active Polar actor. Finland is a part of the Arctic Council's eight permanent members and among the 29 consultative parties involved in decision-making regarding Antarctica as stated by the Ministry for the Foreign Affairs of Finland.[2] Finland's Arctic strategy is a comprehensive effort to establish its strategic goals and policies in the Arctic region. The strategy aims to ensure active participation of Finland in the Arctic geography, seize potential opportunities in the region and promote sustainable development. Additionally, it also encompasses promoting sustainable utilization of natural resources in the Arctic region and strengthening environmental protection measures. Finland seeks to boost the stability and prosperity of the Arctic region by enhancing international collaboration in the area.

Finland is widely seen as a major player in the Arctic region. The Rovaniemi Declaration,[3] signed in 1991 by the United States of America, the Union of Soviet Socialist Republics, Denmark, Canada, Norway, Sweden, Iceland, and other countries, acknowledged Finland as an Arctic nation for the first time and led to the implementation of the Arctic Environmental Protection Strategy. Subsequently, Finland became an Arctic state by joining the Arctic Council, created through the Ottawa Declaration[4] of 1996. With its strategic geopolitical location positioned between Russia and other European countries, Finland is a significant stakeholder. This strategic position highlights Finland's vital role in the Arctic region, especially concerning neighbouring countries, including areas like culture, environment, economy, politics and security. Finland actively upholds and safeguards mutual interests

---

[1] Lecturer, İstanbul Aydın Üniversitesi, yelizalbayrak@aydin.edu.tr
[2] Ministry for Foreign Affairs of Finland., https://um.fi/arctic-cooperation
[3] Arctic Council, Arctic Environmental Protection Strategy. Declaration on the Protection of Arctic Environment. Rovaniemi, June 1991, http://library.arcticportal.org/id/eprint/1542
[4] Ottawa Declaration, Declaration on the Establishment of the Arctic Council, Joint Communique of the Governments of the Arctic Countries on the Establishment of the Arctic Council. Ottawa, September 19, 1996. https://oaarchive.arctic-council.org/handle/11374/85

within the region as well.

The Finnish Government has issued three distinct Arctic Region Strategies, specifically in the years 2010, 2013, and 2021, in response to the persistent alterations in political dynamics and climate change within the region. Each of these strategy documents has undergone revisions due to the fluctuating conditions, thereby presenting varying vantage points concerning Finland's Arctic approach. The successive publication of the Arctic Region Strategies by the Finnish Government highlights their proactive approach to adapting and navigating the complex interplay of geopolitical shifts and environmental transformations in the Arctic. These strategies are dynamic frameworks that ensure Finland remains aware of evolving circumstances while formulating robust and responsive policy initiatives to address the distinct challenges and opportunities presented by the Arctic region. Commencing with the assertion 'As an Arctic country, Finland is a natural actor in the Arctic,'the initial strategy document was released in July 2010[5] during the tenure of the Mari Kiviniemi government.

Addressing a wide array of dimensions including Arctic security, environment, economy, infrastructure, transport, and indigenous peoples, it emphasizes the endorsement of regional and international organizations, while also focusing on enhancing the influence of the European Union and the Arctic Council in the region. The foundational articulation of Finland as an inherent participant in Arctic affairs within the 2010 strategy document reflects the nation's strategic intent to assert its role as an active stakeholder in the region. The comprehensive appraisal of various factors, including security, sustainability, socio-economic concerns, and collaboration with native populations, highlights the all-encompassing methodology ingrained in Finland's Arctic strategy. In addition, the document carefully addresses the imperative of strengthening the influence of the European Union and the Arctic Council in the region, demonstrating Finland's commitment to advancing multilateral cooperation and governance in the Arctic. This strategic focus underlines the importance of promoting international cooperation and coordination in addressing the multifaceted challenges of the Arctic.[6] Finland began positioning itself as an Arctic state, encompassing its entire region, including the Helsinki metropolitan area from the early 2000s. This move was part of the country's efforts to establish its Arctic

---

[5] Finland PMO, Finland's Strategy for the Arctic Region. Prime Minister's Office (PMO), Helsinki, 2010. https://arcticportal.org/images/stories/pdf/J0810_ Finlands.pdf
[6] Finland PMO, (2010)

identity.[7]

The document deliberately focused on the increasing importance of the Arctic region after the Cold War and highlighted Finland's strategic position between NATO and Russia. There was also an exploration of the region's natural resources and their potential future benefits. This emphasized the potential transformation of the Arctic into a new channel for transporting energy to Europe. The 2010 strategy document emphasized foreign relations as a key focus within its Arctic policy framework.

The 2013 strategy document,[8] based on the 2010 predecessor, shows a careful and knowledgeable approach to the changing dynamics of the Arctic realm. It demonstrates Finland's dedication to actively participating in the region's increasing importance and fostering a strategic roadmap that not only prioritises the country's national interests but also aligns with the broader goals of sustainable development and international cooperation in the Arctic. Furthermore, this strategic update highlights Finland's commitment to utilising its extensive experience in Arctic affairs, with the objective of managing the complex interplay of geopolitical interests whilst also fostering cooperative relationships and mutual prosperity in the Arctic region. The new strategy is based on four essential policies defined by the government: Arctic nationhood, emphasizing Finland's identity as an Arctic nation; Arctic expertise, highlighting the nation's extensive knowledge of Arctic matters; sustainable development and environmental concerns, underlining the responsible and eco-friendly approach towards development; and international cooperation, focusing on collaborative efforts within the global community.[9]

These policies encompass Finland's comprehensive and multifaceted approach towards the Arctic, demonstrating its commitment to responsible participation, ecological conservation, and collaborative ventures in the global arena. By prioritising these principles, Finland proactively addresses the intricate challenges and possibilities presented by the Arctic region, while nurturing mutually beneficial associations with a diverse array of stakeholders.

---

[7] Lähteenmäki M., "Footprints in the snow: The long history of Arctic Finland. Helsinki," Finland: Prime Minister's Office Publication, https://urn.fi/URN:ISBN:978-952-287-429-0.,2017.

[8] Finland PMO, Finland's Strategy for the Arctic Region 2013. Government resolution on 23 August 2013. https://arcticparl.org/wp-content/uploads/2021/12/3.1-The-Arctic-strategy-Finland.pdf

[9] Finland PMO, 2013, s.7

Finland's 2021 Arctic strategy[10] prioritises the respect of Arctic nature, the protection of the climate, and the promotion of sustainable development in all Finnish activities within the region. Its values embody the principles of conservation, environmentalism, and equitable development. The strategy entails prioritising climate change mitigation and adaptation, as well as enhancing the well-being and rights of all inhabitants, with a special emphasis on the Sami people as an indigenous community. Furthermore, the strategy emphasises Arctic expertise, which includes promoting sustainable livelihoods, conducting cutting-edge research, and improving infrastructure and logistics. Central to Finland's strategic approach is its recognition of the Arctic Council as the primary platform for discussing Arctic matters.[11] Finland actively promotes enhancing the institutional capacity of the Arctic Council, thereby reinforcing its commitment to effective multilateral cooperation in shaping Arctic agendas and initiatives. The 2021 strategy exhibits divergences from prior strategies regarding its content. Owing to the evolving political conditions within the region during recent years, concerns of security and prospects for the future of the area have surged in significance and hence been incorporated into the strategy. Given the changing political milieu, Finland has stimulated international collaboration and dialogue, all while highlighting the looming threats within the region.

The importance of institutions like the European Union, NATO, and the Arctic Council is evident regarding regional security, peacebuilding, and political balance within the geographical context. This holds especially true amidst changing security concerns and political balances arising due to new prospective sea trade routes caused by climate change and altered geographical conditions. Since Russia holds significant power in the Arctic, the conflict between Russia and Ukraine has impacted the security and politics of the region. This has prompted the Arctic nations to act on the matter. The NATO military exercises have resulted in the development of fresh agendas on Arctic security concerning the extension of the US military presence in the area. Additional military exercises are currently being planned for the region. An additional 2022 report[12] has been produced to assess the scenario created by the Russia-Ukraine conflict. Focusing on the Arctic

---

[10] Finland PMO, working group of public servants responsible for Arctic issues Steering group for the Strategy for Arctic Policy https://julkaisut.valtioneuvosto.fi/bitstream/ handle/10024/163247/ VN_2021_55.pdf?sequence=1&isAllowed=y

[11] Finland PMO, 2021 s.11

[12] Arctic Centre at the University of Lapland, Arctic cooperation in a new situation: Analysis on the impacts of the Russian war of aggression. 2022. https://julkaisut.valtioneuvosto.fi/ bitstream/ handle/ 10024/164521/VN_Selvitys_2022_3.pdf?sequence=1&isAllowed=y

situation in the wake of the Russian war, the report intends to highlight how potential effects from this conflict can harm international cooperation within the Arctic region and the accomplishment of sustainable development objectives. Focusing on the Arctic situation in the wake of the Russian war, the report intends to highlight how potential effects from this conflict can harm international cooperation within the Arctic region and the accomplishment of sustainable development objectives. The report examines current international and national Arctic policies in this changed situation.

## The Geography of the Country and Its Geopolitical Importance

Finland lies between the East and West. As an Arctic nation, Finland shares borders with three other Arctic nations, namely Sweden, Norway and Russia. Further, Finland is the northernmost country in the European Union. Within the geographical context of Finland's Arctic region, it is worth noting that the Lapland province possesses significant importance.[13] Numerous Finnish companies possess the necessary expertise and are well-positioned to utilise their Arctic proficiency, expanding their capabilities not just in the Baltic region but also in the wider market of offshore wind energy construction.[14] Finland's strategic location along the Baltic Sea not only serves as a lifeline for its economy but also underscores the nation's strong maritime heritage and commitment to sustainable marine transportation practices.[15]

According to Arctic Council data, Finland's current population is 5,500,000 and Lapland, which holds strategic importance, has a population of 180,000 residents. The indigenous people of Finland are of the Sami race. Finland's Arctic Strategy from 2013 designates the whole country as being situated in the Arctic, with almost one-third of its landmass located in the Lapland province above the Arctic Circle[16] Finland's geographical features include a wealth of natural resources, including extensive forests, an intricate network of lakes and valuable mineral deposits. These resources, which form an important part of the national economy, underpin Finland's economic sustainability. In addition to its natural endowments, Finland occupies a central position within the Arctic security framework. Finnish Lapland, sandwiched between the Kola Peninsula, home to Russia's nuclear-capable Northern Fleet, and the Norwegian coastal regions critical to the protection

---

[13] Finland PMO, 2021, p.12.

[14] Finland PMO, 2021, p.54

[15] Helsinki Security Forum, "The Decisive Role of Geography in Finland's (Future) NATO Policy"., 10.02.2023., https://helsinkisecurityforum.fi/news/the-decisive-role-of-geography-in-finlands-future-nato-policy/

[16] Arctic Council., https://arctic-council.org/about/states/finland/

of the North Atlantic Sealines, plays a pivotal role in the broader regional security landscape. Moreover, Finland's proximity to Russia and its strategic access to the Baltic Sea make it an important transit corridor between Russia[17] and Europe. This unique geographical position gives Finland the status of a central crossroads, facilitating the flow of goods, services and ideas between these two expansive regions.

In addition, the intricate intertwining of geography and history has given rise to indigenous populations within Finland. In particular, the northern regions of the country are home to the Sami people, who have inhabited these Arctic landscapes for centuries. Their presence underscores the profound influence of geography on the cultural and social fabric of the nation and reflects the harmonious coexistence of diverse communities within the geographical confines of Finland.

## Historical Interaction in the Arctic Region

The war between Sweden and Russia resulted in Finland becoming a Grand Duchy, coming under Russian Empire rule as an independent entity in 1808-1809. After enduring more than a century of Russian Empire rule, Finland declared independence in 1917 and later became a separate entity from the Russian Federation.[18] In 1944, Finland's surrender of the Petsamo region to the Soviet Union cut off the country's access to the Arctic Ocean and was the catalyst for a pause in Finnish economic progress in the Arctic region. Research facilities founded in Utsjoki Kevo in 1954 and Kilpisjärvi in 1964 have gained global recognition as distinguished centres dedicated to Arctic and sub-Arctic research. These initiatives have conducted comprehensive analyses of the climate and environmental circumstances within the Fell Mountain regions, whilst simultaneously investigating the borders that separate wooded and forested areas.[19] The extensive studies reveal that the northern regions of Finland possess clear characteristics of both Arctic and sub-Arctic regions. In 1991, Finland was officially declared as an Arctic country with the Rovaniemi Declaration. Later in 1996, it gained the status of an Arctic state as it became a part of the Arctic Council established under the Ottawa Declaration.[20]

---

[17] Helsinki Security Forum.
[18] Finnish Government., https://valtioneuvosto.fi/en/government/history
[19] Kotilainen, J., Colpaert, A., "Repositioning Finland as an Arctic country"., Nordia Geographical Publications 43: 1, 11–18., p.13.,2015.
[20] Arctic Finland, "Timeline from the Cold War to the founding of the Arctic Council" https://www.arcticfinland.fi/EN/Stories/Arctic-Era

The Finnish Government has issued three Arctic Region Strategies in response to the changing political dynamics and climate conditions in the region. Technical abbreviations are explained upon first use. The document follows conventional academic structure and employs objective, value-neutral language with clear causal connections between statements. The language is formal with precise subject-specific vocabulary, free of grammatical and spelling errors. Quotes are clearly marked with consistent citation style and formatting. These strategies, released in 2010, 2013, and 2021, have undergone revisions due to fluctuating conditions, resulting in diverse perspectives on Finland's Arctic approach. The 2021 Arctic strategy of Finland highlights the utmost importance of all Finnish operations in the region to prioritise a deep-seated reverence for the Arctic's natural surroundings, the conservation of its climate, and the unwavering promotion of principles that facilitate sustainable growth.[21]

Finland, which is geographically classified as a subregion of the Arctic, has recently demonstrated an increase in political and commercial efforts to bolster its position in the Arctic. Finland's border proximity with Russia prompts a re-evaluation of the country's internal and external policies from a broader perspective. This is particularly important considering the current stagnation in Arctic collaboration at the Arctic Council level. To strengthen its position in this area, Finland could adopt a proactive approach in envisioning potential action scenarios that encompass future relations with its neighbour, Russia.

**Finland's Military, Economic and Political Importance for the Arctic Region**

In the geopolitical landscape, the Arctic region stands as a critical arena, commanding profound global attention due to its potential to serve as a bellwether for international cooperation. The region's escalating importance necessitates strategic foresight, fostering a collaborative environment that upholds fairness, inclusivity, and stability while proactively averting any potential conflicts. Finland, by signing the international agreements has been accepted as an Arctic country and playing a significant role for the region in terms of political practices and determining some key concepts as well. "Finland's Arctic interests and Arctic expertise are relevant to the whole country and, on the other hand, the Arctic character of Finland supports and

---

[21] Finland PMO, (2021) Working group of public servants responsible for Arctic issues Steering group for the Strategy for Arctic Policy Bknz; https://julkaisut.valtioneuvosto.fi/ bitstream/handle/ 10024/ 163247/VN_2021_55.pdf?sequence=1&isAllowed=y .

enhances Finland's international image as an Arctic country in international contexts".[22]

As stated by Väätänen, throughout Finland's history, its geopolitical position has been shaped by its location between Sweden and Russia. Following centuries of Swedish rule, Finland gained autonomy as a part of the Russian empire in the year 1809. Finland later declared independence in the year 1917.[23] Following the Swedish domination ended in up early 19th century, Finland had struggles with Russia during its history several times. The security concerns towards the Russia created the term "Finlandisation".[24] The term refers to Finland's policy of maintaining strict neutrality between Moscow and the West during the Cold War decades during the Cold War. As Kotilainen and Colpaert stated, Finland, with the introduction of the EU's New Neighborhood Policy, countries were potentially subject to its extraterritorial ambitions. At the same time, due to the crisis in Ukraine, the political climate became more tense, and the Russian Federation, along with neighbouring regions adjacent to the EU, demonstrated an avid desire to position themselves strategically regarding the EU's evolving economic and natural resource policies.[25] During the summer of 2022, plans were unveiled by Finland to construct a 200 km border barrier fence along its extensive border with Russia in an effort to deter and manage large-scale instrumentalized migration, consequently enhancing the efficiency of territorial surveillance. This decision reflects the nation's commitment to fortifying its borders and ensuring a structured approach to migration control.[26] Due to its geopolitical importance, Finland has gained a remarkable key role following the developments sourced from Russia and the EU.

Finland has gained a reputation for its unwavering dedication to safeguarding and sustaining the natural environment in the Arctic. The country prioritizes maintaining ecosystem and natural resource management in the region to promote the long-term well-being of the Arctic. In addition, the Arctic presents an array of economic prospects, including energy, mining, maritime transport, and tourism. Finland is actively developing various projects and

---

[22] Finland PMO, 2021

[23] Väätänen V., Securing Anticipatory Geographies: Finland's Arctic Strategy and the Geopolitics of International Competitiveness, Geopolitics, 26:2, 615-638, 2021.

[24] Drishti, News Analysis, 22 November 2022, https://www.drishtiias.com/daily-news-analysis/finlandization

[25] Kotilainen, J., Colpaert, A., p, 15.

[26] Middleton, A., "Navigating Uncertainties: Finland's Evolving Arctic Policy and the Role of a Regionally Adaptive EU Arctic Policy"., The Arctic Institute EU-Arctic Series., 22.08.2023., https://www.thearctic institute.org/navigating-uncertainties-finland-evolving-arctic-policy-role-regionally-adaptive-eu-arctic-policy/

partnerships to benefit from opportunities and support the Arctic economy. As an important political and geographical actor in the Arctic, Finland promotes sustainability, economic development, and regional security. Due to these efforts, Finland's expertise in the Arctic is essential.

**Table 1.** Areas of Finnish Arctic Expertise[27]

**Areas of Finnish Arctic expertise**

- Offshore industry
- Maritime industry
- Shipping
- Carriage by sea
- Weather and ice information services
- Forestry
- Mining and minerals
- Metals
- Tourism
- Traditional livelihoods
- Low-temperature expertise
- Winter testing
- Metrology
- Generation and distribution of electricity and thermal energy
- Energy saving and energy efficiency
- Wind power technology
- Construction and infrastructure
- Environmental technology
- Management of environmental impacts
- Sustainable social concepts
- Arctic environmental expertise
- Health and well-being in the Arctic
- Waste management technology
- Information technology
- Public e-services
- Innovation-driven development
- Cold climate research
- Bio- and nano-sciences
- Risk analyses
- Oil spill prevention technologies
- Materials technology
- Water management

## Security Relationship with the Arctic Region

As stated in the 2021 strategy report "The security policy-related developments in the Arctic region impact Finland's national security. From Finland's perspective, the security of the Arctic region is closely linked to the security situation in the Baltic Sea area and the rest of Europe, which has been marked by increasing tensions in the 2010s"[28] According to the Finnish government's published strategies, it is apparent that its security policy is evolving over the years and cannot be evaluated separately from the impact of Russia. Finland's military forces are highly experienced in surviving the Arctic, thanks to the country's climate and geographical location hence, Finland can extend cold climate training and exercises to its international partners, ultimately contributing to increased interoperability of its armed forces. Notably, the Finnish Armed Forces play a crucial role in assisting civil safety and rescue agencies, encompassing search and rescue missions as well as the mitigation of potential ecological harm and natural disasters.[29]

---

[27] Finland PMO, 2013.
[28] Finland PMO, 2021.
[29] Finland PMO, 2013, pp 40-41.

Therefore, following the latest developments, the role of Finland in terms of Arctic security has updated inevitably. In the context of increasing military mobility and potential actions in the region, after years of a security concept that considered Russia's cooperation and interests during the Cold War, Finland turned its face towards Europe through its participation in the European Union and many post-Cold War collaborations. Finally, by joining NATO, Finland has changed its security role in the region, cooperating with the European Union, NATO and the United States against growing Russian aggression.

**Table 2.** Military Data of Finland and Sweden[30]

|  | Finland | Sweden |
| --- | --- | --- |
| Active duty personnel | 22,000 | 23,600 |
| Reserve personnel | 900,000 | 31,300 |
| Military expenditures as % of GDP (2021) | 2 | 1.3 |
| Main battle tanks | 239 | 121 |
| Self-propelled artillery | 72 | 48 |
| Multiple rocket launchers | 100 | 0 |
| Fighter aircraft | 62(+64) | 94 |
| Submarines | 0 | 5 |
| Combat ships | 8 | 7 |
| Mine sweepers | 10 | 9 |

The Arctic region is, of course, important to us, and we share the same challenges and concerns with our Allies and partners," said Finnish Defence Forces deputy chief of staff for strategy, Army Maj. Gen. Janne Jaakkola"[31] during the meeting upheld in Finland by the Arctic Security Forces Roundtable (ASFR) in 2023. "The Finnish Defence Forces participates in Arctic research cooperation and conducts military exercises in the north, both nationally and together with its international partners. Finland's strength lies in capable Defence Forces, developed to operate in Arctic conditions, and possessing Arctic expertise of a high international level."[32] As stated by Pasternak, "Since its independence, Finland has largely remained on the path of national defence, with the whole society involved in safeguarding the security of the country. The military focuses on this objective, with the biggest post-Cold War change being the deepened cooperation with

[30] Katsman,M., Vark,A., A safer Europe: 'Finland and Sweden join NATO as contributors., 2022. https://militairespectator.nl/artikelen/safer-europe-finland-and-sweden-join-nato-contributors Mr. drs. A. van Vark
[31] U.S. Europian Command Public Affairs., Apr 27, 2023., https://www.eucom.mil/pressrelease/ 42356/international-military-leaders-in-finland-for-arctic-security
[32] Finland PMO, 2021., pp 19.

NATO…"[33,34]

NATO participation issue has brought a new dimension to Finnish security perception in terms of armed forces capacity and coordination. New strategies and military collaborations are on the agenda of Finland for the future as well as updating the Air fleets as stated by the Finnish Air forces; "The current Hornet fleet will be phased out as planned from the year 2025. The first Finnish F-35 fighters will begin service with the Finnish Air Force in 2025 as part of the training of Finnish personnel in the United States."[35]

In addition to the 2021 strategy document, Finland has diligently crafted a comprehensive evaluation report in 2022 to assess the repercussions of the Russia-Ukraine conflict. This report thoroughly explores the prevailing landscape of international and domestic Arctic policies, offering valuable insights into Finland's ambitions to integrate with NATO, potential region-specific challenges stemming from Russia, collaborative efforts, and the current status of global agreements.[36] This demonstrates Finland's proactive approach in understanding and navigating the complex dynamics of the Arctic region and international relations in terms of security of Arctic region.

## Values Added to the Arctic

According to The Strategy for Arctic Policy 2021, the Finnish Arctic policy identifies four areas:

- Climate change, mitigation and adaptation.

- Inhabitants, promotion of well-being and the rights of the Sámi as an indigenous people.

- Expertise, livelihoods and leading-edge research.

- Infrastructure and logistics.[37]

The issues addressed in this strategy are directly related to the well-being of the Arctic region and its inhabitants. The strategy's main goals are to promote peace, support the economy, and protect the region's natural environment.

[33] Pasternak.,S.C., "The defence of Finland and Sweden: Continuity and variance in strategy and public opinion"., FIIA BRIEFING PAPER 240., 07.06.2018., https://www.fiia.fi/sv/publikation/the-defence-of-finland-and-sweden?read#viite3

[34] Zoom Maps., https://mapsontheweb.zoom-maps.com/post/713866717788618752/finland-became-the-31st-nation-to-join-nato

[35] History of the Finnish Air Force., https://ilmavoimat.fi/en/history

[36] Arctic Centre at the University of Lapland,.pp 3.,2022

[37] Finland PMO, pp.11,.2021.

Finland plays a crucial role in sustaining and preserving the Arctic's core values. It achieves this by defining the significant challenges and potential solutions, offering cooperation to resolve them while holding an essential position in Arctic-Euro organizations. Barents Region Euro-Arctic Council which was Established in 1993 by Finland, Norway, Sweden, and Russia, the Barents region. This Council functions as an intergovernmental regional cooperation forum and as a common point for Arctic corporation.[38] Plus, the "The Northern Dimension" as being a common forum and a joint policy between EU, Russia, Norway and Iceland" as a strong emphasis on cross-border cooperation in Arctic area with Russia. Also, Finland as being a crossway between the Europe and Russia holds a significant role for preserving and functioning of The Northern Dimension in terms of connecting the mutual benefits of the Arctic Region." The Northern Dimension is a joint policy between EU, Russia, Norway and Iceland. The ND Policy was initiated in 1999 and renewed in 2006. The policy aims to provide a framework to:

- promote dialogue and concrete cooperation;

- strengthen stability, well-being and intensified economic cooperation;

- promote economic integration, competitiveness and sustainable development in Northern Europe.

In addition to the four ND Partners namely EU, Russia, Norway and Iceland, also participating are:

- EU Members States in their national capacity

- Regional Councils, the Arctic Council (AC), the Barents Euro-arctic Council (BEAC), the Council of the Baltic Sea States (CBSS) and the Nordic Council of Ministers (NCM)[39]

By being a part of the international and regional organizations directly or indirectly, Finland is promoting the core Arctic values. As stated in the 2013's strategy report, "Finland is committed to multilateral cooperation at both global and regional levels to achieve its Arctic goals and address global threats. One of its key objectives is to bolster its position as an Arctic nation

---

[38] Barents Euro-Arctic Council., https://web.archive.org/web/20150317011317/ http://www.beac.st/in-English/Barents-Euro-Arctic-Council

[39] Northern Dimension., European External Action Service., https://web.archive.org/web/ 2015031100 2936/http://eeas.europa.eu/north_dim/index_en.htm

and advance international Arctic collaboration."[40] Furthermore, all strategic reports that have been published have tackled concerns pertaining to the welfare and portrayal of native communities dwelling within the area. This demonstrates Finland's dedication to promoting impartial and fair advancement whilst safeguarding the liberties of its indigenous people. Furthermore, prioritizing the well-being and rights of indigenous peoples highlights Finland's commitment to a comprehensive and lasting strategy in its regional enterprises.

The investments of Finland for the Arctic region in terms of the well-being of the region such as infrastructural, cultural and economic potential, are promoting the values of the Arctic as well. According to the pronouncement made by the former Prime Minister of Finland, Mr. Paavo Lipponen, "the nation has undertaken the task of formulating a well-defined strategy with the aim of advancing critical infrastructure projects of domestic significance within the European Union. This strategic endeavour encompasses the imperative enhancement of accessibility to the northern regions of Finland, catering to the multifaceted requirements of both industrial and tourism sectors. Furthermore, Finland aspires to emerge as a preeminent global center for the domains of logistics, telecommunications, and substantial data management, thereby underscoring its commitment to fostering international prominence in these pivotal spheres."[41] Some of the recommendations stated by Lipponen "regarding the Arctic and northern politics during Finland's parliamentary term 2015–2019 to promote the values of Arctic are as follows:

- Under the leadership of the state authorities, cooperation between the Nordic countries will be in-tensified in the field of energy. The Nordic countries must strengthen their competitive position and actively influence the development of EU energy markets.

- Deterioration of the Finns'language skills will be arrested. In particular, learning Swedish will be restructured so that Nordic labour markets can be effectively availed of.

- A joint programme will be drafted on the prime ministerial level to remove frontier barriers between the Nordic countries.

- Northern universities will be strengthened and cooperation between

[40] Finland PMO, pp. 43,2013.
[41] Lipponen, P., "Finland's Prospects in Arctic Economic Growth". The Confederation of Finnish Industries.30.03.2015.  https://ek.fi/en/current/news/study-by-paavo-lipponen-finlands-prospects-in-arctic-economic-growth/

179

them developed. One Arctic University, capable of competing internationally, will be set as a goal."[42]

## Finland's Expectations from the Arctic (energy, political, security, military, economic etc.)

As stated in the Strategy of 2021 PMO, "In the shared interest of all Arctic nations, the preservation of stability and peace in the Arctic region holds paramount importance. Finland is resolutely committed to making substantive contributions toward the realization of this collective objective. Notably, since the formulation of the preceding Arctic strategy, the Arctic region has undergone notable transformations in its security policy landscape. These shifts necessitate careful recognition and scrutiny, and it is incumbent upon Finland to wield its influence judiciously, thereby contributing to the preservation of regional stability. One observable consequence of these changes is the escalating military activities and presence within the Arctic, coupled with an intensification of tensions. These developments are, in part, attributed to the intricate interplay of challenges and opportunities arising from climate change, notably the exploitation of the region's natural resources. The implications of these dynamics underscore the imperative for nuanced strategic considerations and proactive diplomatic efforts within the Arctic context."[43]

The 2023 report delves into the imperative for Finland to reevaluate its regional expectations and policies, a requirement arising from the repercussions of the Russia-Ukraine conflict. This reassessment is prompted by the shifting dynamics within the region, primarily attributable to heightened Russian aggression. Furthermore, the report scrutinizes the evolving landscape of Finnish-Russian relations and the development of a security understanding aligned with the European Union and NATO. The reports states that "The Arctic collaboration has undergone a significant transformation since Russia's invasion of Ukraine, resulting in an unparalleled situation and this shift demands a complete reassessment of Arctic cooperation as well for the future. The geopolitical changes caused by global warming have captured significant attention in the Arctic region and caused new international logistic or security matters or opportunities. Besides, Finland's assumptions in Arctic policy have been weakened and affected by the Russian conflict that occurred only a year or two ago. There is a pressing need for prompt climate action, specifically the implementation of measures

---

[42] Lipponen, P.,2015.
[43] Finland PMO, pp. 17,2021.

to strengthen the region's resilience. In this context, it is important to acknowledge that although the shift towards more sustainable energy practices in the West could be accelerated by utilizing Russian energy resources, it may also exacerbate the strain on resources within the Arctic."[44] As mentioned in the report, due to recent developments, Finland's trade volume with Russia has decreased and ongoing collaborations and partnerships have been suspended. This has prompted Finland to reassess its interests in the Arctic region, including military, economic, and political aspects. The support provided to Ukraine, encompassing both military and humanitarian aid, the developments regarding NATO membership, and the position of the European Union towards Russia, prompted Finland to reassess its Arctic aspirations.

**Figure 1.** Finland Export to Russia[45]

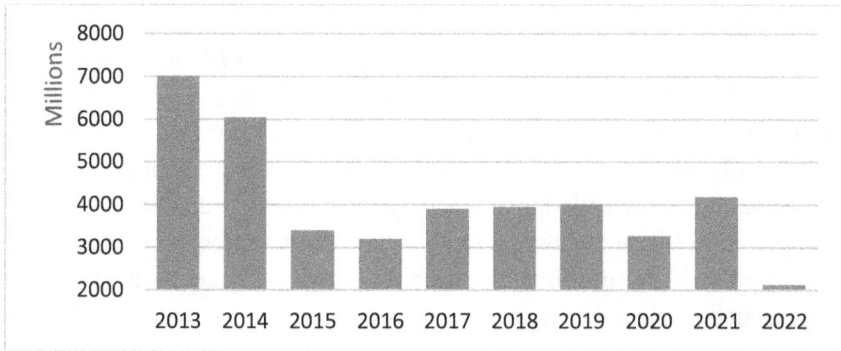

*Source: Tradingeconomics.com*

According to an article published on the Arctic Institute website by Raspotnik, Stepien and Koivurova, "the economic consequences are set to significantly affect the European Union's climate goals, encompassing energy resources and minerals,"[46] and its situation may have serious and unclear consequences in the future. One of the important economic conclusions of the Russia – Ukraine war, is the icebreaker's trade between Finland and Russia. As the biggest supplier of icebreakers worldwide, Finnish companies has been living difficulties in terms of working with Russia as being the most significant customer of icebreakers. "Finland bans export of icebreaker to Russia and according to a Finnish broadcaster reports the Finnish Ministry

---

[44] Arctic Centre at the University of Lapland, pp.3.2022

[45] https://tradingeconomics.com/finland/exports/russia

[46] Raspotnik, A., Stępień, A. Koivurova, T., The European Union's Arctic Policy in the Light of Russia's War against Ukraine. April 26.2022. https://www.thearcticinstitute.org/european-union-arctic-policy-light-russia-war-against-ukraine/

for Foreign Affairs has denied Helsinki Shipyard an export license for an icebreaker on order for Russian mining firm Norilsk Nickel."[47]

As for the defence and military issue, "Finland, which shares a massive 1,340-kilometre (800-mile) border with Russia in the Arctic, is investing in future security and military measures. The country consistently allocates 2% of its gross domestic product towards defence spending. As part of its partnership with the United States over the past few decades, Finland has acquired superior American defence products, including JASSM missiles, Stingers and GLRMS systems. Most recently, Helsinki has purchased 18 F-18 fighter jets to replace its F-64 Hornets fleet."[48] Furthermore as a NATO ally and EU participant, Finland is in a key position for future military and defence agendas.

Finland's arctic railway investments and projects are enhancing the future well-being and safeguarding of the arctic environment and habitat of indigenous people. The *Sustainable Growth Programme for Finland - Recovery and Resilience Plan* prepared by the Finnish government in 2021 hints that for "sustainable transportation, '*Digirail project*', this initiative will reduce emissions by developing distribution networks for electric vehicle charging, implementing low-emission fuel systems, and digitising railway transportation sustainability by adopting naturalistic strategies and the aim of this program is to substitute the train management system with one that delivers environmental advantages."[49]

According to a report in the Railway Gazette, "the Ministry of Transport and Communications in Finland has recently published an assessment that identifies the optimal rail link for connecting Finnish Lapland to the Arctic Ocean. The report suggests a 465 km route that begins in Rovaniemi, passes through Sodankylä, and ends in Kirkenes, Norway, as the most suitable and effective alternative."[50] Possible infrastructure investments preserving the region's stability and well-being of Finland with the Arctic seem to be getting ready to act for future.

---

[47] Blenkey, N.,Finland bans export of icebreaker to Russia, October 05, 2022., https://www.marinelog.com/news/finland-bans-export-of-icebreaker-to-russia/

[48] "Analiz: Arktik rekabeti artıyor! ABD'nin Arktik planı İsveç ve Finlandiya'nın önemi." 31 August 2022. https://m5dergi.com/one-cikan/analiz-arktik-rekabeti-artiyor-abdnin-arktik-plani-isvec-ve-finlandiyanin-onemi/

[49] "Sustainable Growth Programme for Finland Recovery and Resilience Plan"., Publications of The Finnish Government 2021., pp.104. 2021. https://julkaisut.valtioneuvosto.fi/ bitstream/handle/ 10024/ 163363/VN_2021_69.pdf?sequence=1&isAllowed=y

[50] Railway Gazette International, 2021.

**Figure 2.** Finland–Arctic Ocean Rail Route Proposed[51]

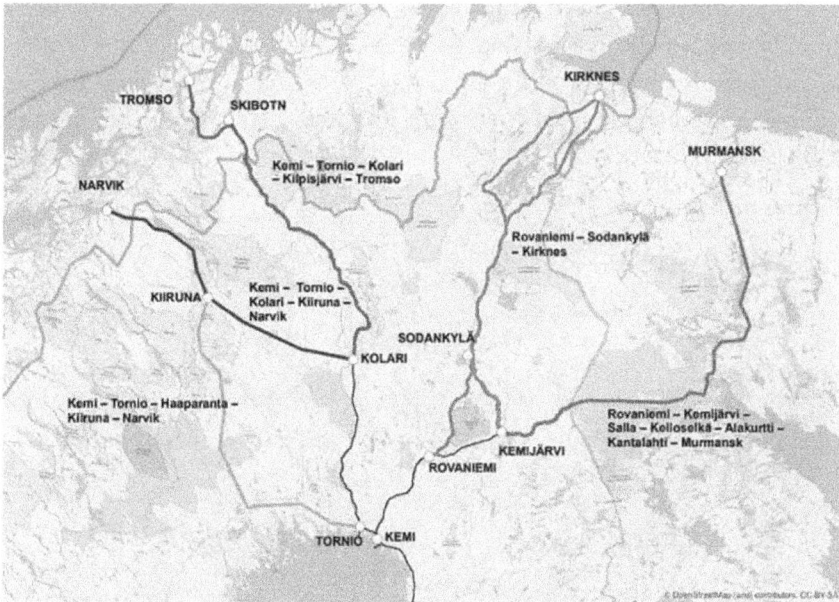

*Source: Railway Gazette International*

## Relations with Other Arctic Countries

Finland maintains cordial and collaborative relations with other Arctic countries. Its foreign policy aims at upholding stability and encouraging international cooperation. Finland participates actively in several international organizations associated with the Arctic, such as the Barents Euro-Arctic Council, the European Union, the Arctic Council and NATO. Mainly through scientific and expert networks. Finland also maintains bilateral relations with relevant partners. Notably, the country prioritizes the Arctic Council as the primary platform for dealing with Arctic region issues.

According to the latest report by the Arctic Center, "Finland in the late 1980s, took the lead in promoting Arctic cooperation among states amidst the Cold War era. Central to this initiative was Finland's proposal for collaborative efforts among eight Arctic states, the Nordic countries, the United States, Canada and Russia with the primary objective of safeguarding the Arctic region and led to the signing of the Arctic Environmental Protection Strategy in Rovaniemi. Following this, the Arctic Council, which was created through

---

[51] Railway Gazette International, 21 March 2018., https://www.railwaygazette.com/infrastructure/finland-arctic-ocean-rail-route-proposed/46158.article

the Ottawa Declaration in 1996 and Finland is relying on the Arctic Council to play an important role in the governance of the Arctic region and for future coordination of the relationship between Arctic countries.[52] The report's foundation also rests upon the unfolding events set in motion by Russian aggression in February 2022, covering the initial six months up to mid-September.[53]

**Figure 3.** Arctic Zone[54]

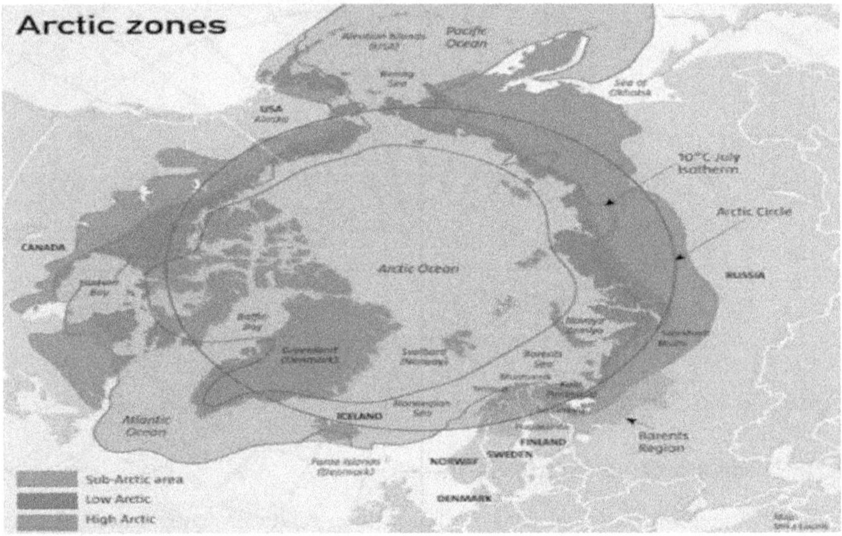

*Source: Finland PMO*

Although the Relationships with Russia has been deteriorating, Finland maintains positive relationships with other Arctic countries and cooperates harmoniously with them through various organizations. However, the aggressive actions of Russia have complicated the situation, requiring new strategies to manage relationships with other Arctic nations. Finland's important connections for maintaining and stabilizing future relationships will be with NATO, the EU, the Arctic Council, and the Barents Euro-Arctic Council.

**Conclusion and Discussion**

It is evident that the Arctic region, traditionally regarded as a distant and frigid locale, has assumed greater significance considering climate change and

---

[52] Arctic Centre at the University of Lapland., pp.33. 2022
[53] Arctic Centre at the University of Lapland., pp.6.
[54] Finland PMO, 2013.

evolving political landscapes. Thanks to its abundance of valuable resources, distinctive ecosystem and indigenous communities. The Arctic represents a promising arena for collaboration and mutually beneficial partnerships besides the region, which has gained commercial and military significance through the new sea routes in the Arctic Ocean, presents a unique and compelling environment that requires unfaltering international cooperation. Finland's stance in the Arctic has been significantly altered due to Russia's presence in the area throughout the years. Finland has developed three strategies and formulated situation reports at regular intervals to ascertain its Arctic strategy. The strategies underlined the significance of international harmony within the region and discussed concerns regarding the environment, economy and security of the Arctic area annually. Russia's annexation of Crimea before the unfolding Russian-Ukrainian conflict prompted Finland to reassess its Arctic strategy, underlining Europe's increased responsibility to maintain security and stability in the area. Despite these developments, it was noted to Finland, a member of NATO along with Sweden, that collaboration with international organisations was more crucial than ever before for the implementation of the Arctic strategy. Although Finland's potential long-term strategies and its contribution to regional prosperity cannot be entirely separated from regional politics, it will always be recognised as a country that embraces collaboration within the region.

Finland's commitment to cooperating in the Arctic region not only attests to its dedication to stability and shared prosperity but also reflects its role as a responsible actor on the global stage. By actively collaborating with international organisations and cultivating partnerships, Finland plays a key role in addressing the intricate challenges and opportunities offered by the Arctic, thereby strengthening its standing as a nation devoted to advancing peace and sustainable growth in the area.

## Bibliography

"Analiz: Arktik rekabeti artıyor! ABD'nin Arktik planı İsveç ve Finlandiya'nın önemi." 31 August 2022. https://m5dergi.com/one-cikan/analiz-arktik-rekabeti-artiyor-abdnin-arktik-plani-isvec-ve-finlandiyanin-onemi/

Arctic Centre at the University of Lapland, Arctic cooperation in a new situation: Analysis on the impacts of the Russian war of aggression. Pp,3,6,33.,2022. https://julkaisut.valtioneuvosto.fi/bitstream/handle/10024/164521/VN_Selvitys_2022_3.pdf?sequence=1&isAllowed=y &isAllowed=y

Arctic Environmental Protection Strategy. "Declaration on the Protection of Arctic Environment. Rovaniemi, June 1991. http://library.arcticportal.org/id/eprint/1542

Arctic Finland, "Timeline from the Cold War to the founding of the Arctic Council" https://www.arcticfinland.fi/EN/Stories/Arctic-Era

Barents Euro-Arctic Council., https://web.archive.org/web/ 20150317011317/ http://www.beac.st/in-English/Barents-Euro-Arctic-Council

Blenkey, N., "Finland bans export of icebreaker to Russia"., October 05,2022. https://www.marinelog.com/news/finland-bans-export-of-icebreaker-to-russia/

Declaration on the Establishment of the Arctic Council,Joint Communique of the Governments of the Arctic Countries on the Establishment of the Arctic Council. Ottawa, September 19, 1996. https://oaarchive.arctic-council.org/handle/11374/85

Finland's Arctic and Antarctic cooperation, Ministry for Foreign Affairs of Finland., https://um.fi/arctic-cooperation

Finland's Strategy for Arctic Policy., Working group of public servants responsible for Arctic issues Steering group for the Strategy for Arctic Policy" Finnish Government Helsinki.pp, 11, 19, 2021. https://julkaisut.valtioneuvosto.fi/bitstream/handle /10024/163247/VN_2021_55.pdf?sequence=1

Finland's Strategy for the Arctic Region 2013. Government resolution on 23 August 2013. pp.7,40,41,43. 2013. https://arcticparl.org/wp-content/uploads/2021/ 12/ 3.1-The-Arctic-strategy-Finland.pdf

Finland's Strategy for the Arctic Region. Prime Minister's Office (PMO), Helsinki, 2010. https://arcticportal.org/images/stories/pdf/J0810_ Finlands.pdf

Helsinki Security Forum, "The Decisive Role of Geography in Finland's (Future) NATO Policy"., 10.02.2023., https://helsinki security forum.fi/news/the-decisive-role-of-geography-in-finlands-future-nato-policy/

Finnish Government., https://valtioneuvosto.fi/en/government/history

History of the Finnish Air Force., https://ilmavoimat.fi/en/history

Katsman, M., Vark, A., A safer Europe: 'Finland and Sweden join NATO as contributors, 2022. https://militairespectator.nl/artikelen/safer-europe-finland-and-sweden-join-nato-contributors

Kotilainen, J., Colpaert, A., "Repositioning Finland as an Arctic country", *Nordia Geographical Publications* 43: 1, 11–18., p.15.,2015.

Lähteenmäki, M., *Footprints in the snow: The long history of Arctic Finland. Helsinki.* Finland: Prime Minister's Office Publication, 2017. https://urn.fi/URN:ISBN:978-952-287-429-0.,2017.

Middleton, A., "Navigating Uncertainties: Finland's Evolving Arctic Policy and the Role of a Regionally Adaptive EU Arctic Policy"., The Arctic Institute EU-Arctic Series., 22.08.2023., https://www.thearcticinstitute.org/navigating-uncertainties-finland-evolving-arctic-policy-role-regionally-adaptive-eu-arctic-policy

Northern Dimension., European External Action Service., https://web.archive.org/ web/20150311002936/http://eeas.europa.eu/north_dim/index_en.htm

Pasternak., S.C., "The defence of Finland and Sweden: Continuity and variance in strategy and public opinion"., FIIA BRIEFING PAPER 240., 07.06.2018., https://www.fiia.fi/sv/publikation/the-defence-of-finland-and-sweden?read#viite3

Railway Gazette International"Finland – Arctic Ocean rail route proposed"., ,21 March 2018., https://www.railwaygazette.com/infrastructure/finland-arctic-ocean-rail-route-proposed/46158.article

Raspotnik, A., Stępień, A. Koivurova, T., The European Union's Arctic Policy in the Light of Russia's War against Ukraine. April 26.2022. https://www.thearctic

institute.org/european-union-arctic-policy-light-russia-war-against-ukraine/

"Sustainable Growth Programme for Finland Recovery and Resilience Plan"., Publications of The Finnish Government 2021., pp.104. 2021. https://julkaisut. valtioneuvosto.fi/bitstream/handle/10024/163363/VN_2021_69.pdf?sequence=1 &isAllowed=y

Trading economics., https://tradingeconomics.com/finland/exports/russia

U.S. Europian Command Public Affairs., Apr 27, 2023., https://www.eucom.mil/ pressrelease/42356/international-military-leaders-in-finland-for-arctic-security

Väätänen V., Securing Anticipatory Geographies: Finland's Arctic Strategy and the Geopolitics of International Competitiveness, Geopolitics, 26:2, 615-638, 2021.

Zoom Maps., https://mapsontheweb.zoom-maps.com/post/7138667 177886 18 7 52/ finland-became-the-31st-nation-to-join-nato

# CHAPTER 5

# THINKING THE ARCTIC IN SWEDISH GEOPOLITICS: POLICIES AND PRACTICES

## Emre Sipahioğlu[1]

## Introduction

We are in an era in which the influence of geography is reflected in national and global policies and the international order is connected with strategic location. In the 21st century, the fact that the countries of Northern Europe are far from the irregular zones that we define as the geography of war does not mean that they ignore their security policies. At this point, there is a need for a geopolitical security order in a world of anarchic order. Sweden has been seeking 'status'through regional cooperation after the Cold War but has returned to a defensive security approach with Russia's aggressive realist policies. In globalisation studies, the seeking of status may change according to the influence of the political order. In this sense, the regional anarchic structure of geography leads to changes in the understanding of "status". In international relations, there is an understanding of status based on three theories: social identity, rationalist instrumentalism and constructionism. What position does Sweden hold in terms of status? We can read the policies of a country with an ongoing war in its "neighbourhood" from the perspective of the search for a new identity within the scope of ontological security. The possession of extensive military technology and advanced war equipment is important for a country's international status. Individual security equipment and economies may be insufficient to ensure peace and security in the Northern European region, so a shift towards "collective security" policies is essential. In this context, NATO, the world's largest security co-operation, comes into play.

This chapter uses a larger perspective to understand the changes and transformations of Sweden's regional as well as global co-operation process. With the idea that the discipline of international relations is stuck in a narrow field, not only security but also historical transformations will be examined.

---

[1] International Security and Strategic Studies Master Student at MEF University, İstanbul

Sweden's new security identity is explained in the context of cooperation, starting from the pre-Cold War period. In this way, both the status and the global policy change are better explained. Accordingly, Sweden's security policy within the framework of 'cooperation'in Arctic Geopolitics is first analysed, followed by an examination of Arctic policies between the post-Cold War period and 2011, and an analysis of this process under different headings until today. Finally, the developments and differences in this process are reviewed. The goal of this chapter is to analyse how Sweden has reacted to the developments in the Arctic region over the years and how its behaviour has changed according to the developments in its environment.

## The Geography of the Country and Its Geopolitical Importance

Geographically, Sweden is one of the few countries "included" in the Arctic geography, but not completely within the Arctic Region. The northernmost point in Sweden is Treriksröset at 69° 03'21" North latitude and 20° 50'14" East longitude. This point is north of the Arctic Circle and is therefore recognised as part of the Arctic geography.

The northern parts of Sweden are under the influence of the Arctic climate. The northern parts of Sweden experience polar day (day without night) and polar night (night without day) during certain periods of the year. Sweden's Arctic coast can be covered by sea ice during the winter months. This is a typical feature of Arctic Seas. Arctic foxes, Arctic hares, reindeer and other cold-climate animals are found in these regions.

Sweden is located on the east coast of the Scandinavian Peninsula and borders Russia, Norway and Finland. It also borders the Baltic Sea. Sweden has an area of 450,295 square kilometres and is the fifth-largest country in Europe and the third-largest country in the European Union. In the west of Sweden are the Scandinavian Mountains, which extend into the Norrland Region. These mountains have the highest peaks in Sweden. In the east of the country, there are large forests and plains. Sweden has large plains and lakes, the largest of which is Vänern. Sweden is strategically located in the north-east of the Baltic Sea. The Baltic Sea is important as a transit route from Eastern Europe to Western Europe and is at the centre of trade, energy transport and maritime security. Sweden is located at a critical transit point in this region and is important for regional balance and security. The Baltic Sea is part of the trade routes from the United Kingdom to Russia and is an important European maritime transport route. Sweden's position in this region can be instrumental in ensuring maritime trade and maritime security.

**Map 2.** Countries Within the Arctic Circle, Arctic Region Countries, Political Map.[2]

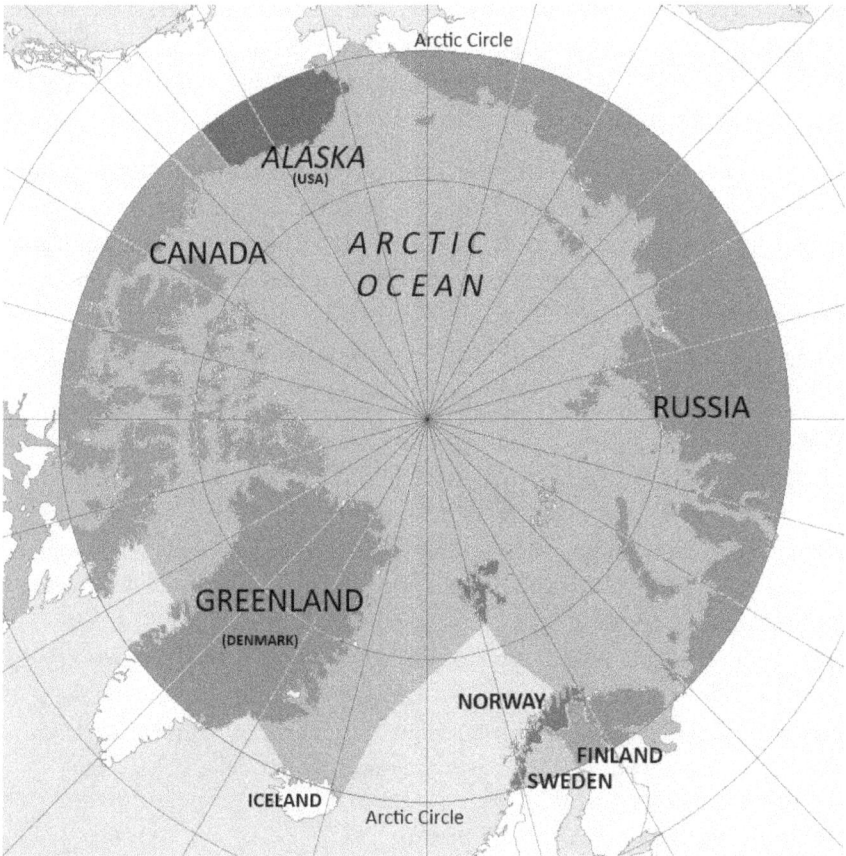

Geopolitically, Sweden is an important country economically, security, transit routes and politically. More recently, after the collapse of the Soviet Union, it has almost the same geostrategic importance as Estonia, Lithuania and Latvia. Although Sweden and Russia do not have a border in direct contact, Sweden is seen as an important actor for the protection of the region. This important strategic position gives Sweden new missions. Because of Russia's regional threats, Sweden feels obliged to be a strong state both economically and militarily.

The concept of geopolitics should not be seen only as geography. Geopolitics is the totality of a country's capabilities with its location. A country can

---

[2] Dreamstime, Countries Within The Arctic Circle, Arctic Region Countries, Political Map, https://www.dreamstime.com/countries-arctic-circle-political-map-image277328555.

integrate its geographical position with economic, political, energy and security in the global field. From this perspective, the science of history also provides important clues for geopolitics. The past of countries, the concepts of friend and enemy, their bilateral relations with neighbouring countries and their integration with the world are all associated with history. History enables us to predict what happened in the past for the future.

Europe needs to establish a balance of power against Russia in the geopolitics of the region. Along with the Baltic Sea, Sweden has an important position in North Baltic security. Ships sailing from St. Petersburg must sail parallel to Sweden, which has the longest coastline on the Baltic Sea. The geopolitical importance of Sweden is almost the same as the geopolitical importance of the Gulf of Finland or Estonia. Therefore, Sweden has an important position in the European balance of power in the continental shelf issue.

With global warming, the opening of the Northern passes and the opening of alternative routes in the Arctic have also directly affected the Baltic Sea. The Arctic, which has lost 40% of its ice sheet since 1979, has become an alternative to global transport with the new sea routes opened. While logistic tankers need to reach Europe via the Suez Canal or by travelling around Africa, Arctic connections can be established with new routes. The container ship Venta Maersk, owned by the Danish company Maersk, crossed the Arctic Ocean and reached the Port of St. Petersburg via the Baltic Sea[3] without using the Suez Canal route, where 90 per cent of maritime trade takes place. This is an event that increases the importance of the Baltic Sea.

## Relations with Other Arctic Countries

Although Sweden has no direct coastal connection to the Arctic, it has a strategic position for the Arctic countries and the region. Sweden, which was a glacier area 14,000 years ago, has a role in glaciers again today. Founded in 1397, the Kalmar Union was an important period for Sweden. The reason we mention this union is that Denmark, Norway, Sweden, Iceland, Finland, Greenland, Iceland, Sweden, Iceland, Finland and Greenland, as well as many other countries, lived in the area of the common country. Sweden's relations with neighbouring countries continued until 1523. Sweden, which became stronger during the Thirty Years'War between 1618 and 1648, was perceived as dangerous by Denmark, Norway, Prussia and Russia. These countries started the Northern Wars against Sweden (between 1700 and 1721) and

---

[3] IILSS, Navigational Regimes of Particular Straits, Northeast Passage (Barents Sea and the Chukchi Sea) case study, https://iilss.net/tag/northern-sea-route/

Russia dominated the Baltic coast. King Charles of Sweden was defeated in 1709 and took refuge in the Ottoman Empire. He started to control Sweden from the Ottoman lands. Then the Ottoman Empire defeated Russia in 1711. In this way, Sweden regained its former power. In 1814, the Norway - Sweden union was established, and this union continued until 1905. The Finnish War and the Napoleonic Wars were important for Sweden. Sweden lost Finland at the end of the Finnish War. Later, together with Britain, Sweden participated in the Napoleonic Wars against France. Sweden, which continued its independence policy after the Napoleonic Wars, did not enter into any war with neighbouring countries. Sweden joined the United Nations in 1946 and the European Union in 1995 and has maintained common tasks with both European and neighbouring countries. Sweden is a member of the Arctic Council, which was established in 1996. This membership is important for European hegemony in the Arctic region. This council, established by the states in the Arctic region, is Sweden's ticket to the Arctic Ocean. Sweden, which has a say in the decisions taken in the Arctic, is indirectly a member of the policies of the other seven countries. It has a say in many issues such as energy studies, global warming research, and transit routes in the Arctic region. Sweden, which has the longest coastline in the Baltic Sea, also has a strategic position in the passage of ships passing through the Arctic to the port of Petersburg.

## Sweden's Security Policy Framework

There has not been a hot conflict in Scandinavia since World War II. However, this does not mean that the region is free from conflict. In particular, the development of war technology at the strategic level has led to the battlefield becoming unmanned. However, I must say that the enemy dictates how you should fight and use what weapons.

A report published in 1971 used two concepts to summarise Sweden's understanding of Cold War defence:[4] Periphery "Defence" and "Deep Defence". "Periphery Defence" aims to defend the frontier, while "Deep Defence" adopts the People Defence perspective and is similar to the Total Defence Concept. The aim of Deep Defence is to extend the war as long as possible.

With the post-Cold War atmosphere of cooperation and peace, the debate on "Arctic exceptionalism" has also come to the front. The "Arctic Environmental Protection Strategy" (1991) and the Arctic Council (1996),

---

[4] Gunnar Åselius, "Swedish Strategic Culture after 1945," pp. 28

which was officialised with the "Ottawa Declaration", have been important actors to concretise cooperation. However, looking at the Arctic region as an "exceptional" region may be misleading. This is because many security issues in the region are intertwined with each other, complicating the basis of conflict. Despite this, the regional actors wanted to adopt the "High North, Low Tension" approach.[5]

The civilian presence in post-Cold War conflict environments has intensified. On the other hand, military forces are increasingly involved in "military operations other than war" (peacekeeping, humanitarian assistance, peace monitoring).[6]

### Security Relationship with the Arctic Region

#### Neutrality in the Cold War

Since the 19th century, Sweden has adopted a policy of neutrality. Therefore, it is said that the policy of neutrality is a traditional Swedish policy. In the early years of the Cold War, this neutrality was sought to be concretised, especially through discussions on a regional Nordic Security Alliance independent of the two powers. However, the failure to establish the Nordic Alliance and Norway and Denmark's preference for the Western alliance as NATO founding members pushed Sweden to take a different position. In this case, Sweden adopted the traditional policy of neutrality.

During the Cold War, the mechanisms that Sweden attached importance to and maintained interaction with were the United Nations (UN), Nordic Cooperation and national neutrality in the event of conflict. On the other hand, it also worked to develop its security policies within the framework of the European Commission.[7] For Sweden, neutrality is not only a security policy. According to Malmborg, this policy is an element of Swedish identity.[8] In Mannerström's words "to go their way in quiet and calm"[9]. Neutrality as an element of identity, however, does not mean that it reflects Sweden's entire political and military culture.

One of the important issues to be emphasised when talking about Sweden's

[5] Gjørv & Hodgson" Comprehensive Security in the Arctic: Beyond "Arctic Exceptionalism" in On Thin Ice? Perspectives on Arctic Security, Ed. Duncan Depledge and P. Whitney Lackenbauer (Ontario, NAADSN) 2020, pp. 2

[6] Yalçınkaya, "Savaşın Değişimi ve Savaş Çalışmalarında Farklı Disiplinler", March, 2010, pp.15

[7] F.Fulya Tepe, "Swedish Neurality and Its Abandonment" İstanbul Ticaret Üniversitesi Sosyal Bilimler Dergisi 6/11 (Spring 2007/2) p.183-201

[8] David Nagy,"Swedish Neutrality: How long can it last? Danube Institute. (March 2022).

[9] Nagy,"Swedish Neutrality," 2022

neutrality is Sweden's secret relations with NATO during the Cold War. These relations were revealed in later research.[10] Thus, Sweden, which emphasised neutrality rhetorically, behaved as a member of the NATO alliance throughout the Cold War.[11] According to Nagy, Sweden's Cold War policy can be defined as neutrality. It was adopted as a policy that minimised the tension between the two poles without being involved in any pole. On the other hand, Sweden's historical experiences and geopolitics show that neutrality is dysfunctional in times of war.[12] Therefore, continued neutrality is referred to as "ethical ambiguity" or "paradox".[13] It has also been theorised that this Swedish paradox was the reason behind the assassination of Olof Palme.[14]

After 1960, the Olaf Palma influence steered Sweden towards a higher-profile security policy. In 1963, Sweden announced a policy of "active neutrality". According to Malmborg, active neutrality was defined as playing a role in conflict resolution.[15]

**Neutrality after the Cold War**

The absence of the Soviet threat meant a transformation in Sweden's foreign policy. From this period onwards, Sweden reduced its military budget and adopted an "international" agenda through both the EU and the UN.[16] Due to increasing intra-state tensions, a change in the policy of neutrality was inevitable. It can be said that there are two important indicators of the changing understanding of neutrality for Sweden. One of them is Sweden's EU membership and the other is its involvement in the NATO Partnership for Peace Initiative. The 1995 EU membership and its contribution to the EU Foreign and Security Policy meant the end of Sweden's neutrality. As a matter of fact, according to Edström & Gyllensporre, 1991-1994 is the "death of neutrality" and 1994-2002 is the period of adaptive and operative

---

[11] F. Fulya Tepe, "Swedish Neurality and Its Abandonment" 183-201
[12] Robert Dalsjö (2014) The hidden rationality of Sweden's policy of neutrality during the Cold War, Cold War History, 14:2, 175-194, DOI: 10.1080/14682745.2013.765865
[13] Sussanne Berger," the great paradox of swedish neutrality in the cold war and today" (December 2015). https://warontherocks.com/2015/12/the-great-paradox-of-swedish-neutrality-in-the-cold-war-and-today/
[14] Sussanne Berger, "Great paradox of Swedish Neutrality" in the cold war and today" (December 2015).
[15] F.Fulya Tepe, "Swedish Neurality and Its Abandonment" 183-201
[16] Nima Khorrami, "Small and Non-Aligned: Sweden's Strategic Posture in the Arctic" Arctic Institute, (September 1, 2020) (https://www.thearcticinstitute.org/small-non-aligned-sweden-strategic-posture-arctic-part-i/).

doctrine building.[17]

## Arctic Policy in the Cold War Period

We have already discussed Sweden's neutrality and non-alignment policies. How did this political approach materialise in the Arctic region? Although Sweden was not a NATO ally during the Cold War, the geopolitics of the country was not ignored. Because, considering the situation before the dissolution of the Warsaw Pact, the Baltic was an important Soviet sea. From this point of view, the Baltic Sea was as important as the Arctic for Sweden.

Sweden has acted in the Arctic as part of its general policy of neutrality. Although the north of Sweden is surrounded by Norway and Finland, the region has always been important for Sweden. Therefore, the military structure is based on the idea of defending both the Arctic and the Baltic at the same time. Moreover, bilateral and multilateral relations with Norway and Finland are also important to cooperate against potential threats in the Arctic. To understand Sweden's defence, it is useful to look at the Soviet offensive plans at the time. Although Sweden was not the first target due to its geopolitics, it was an important route for air, land and cruise missiles.[18] According to one plan, there is a planned route of operations through Finland to the city of Boden. According to this plan, the Arctic coast of Norway is to be surrounded, Finland is to be occupied and Sweden is to be surrounded.[19] On the other hand, according to Soviet thought,[20] If the United States moves to strike at the heart of the Soviet Union, it will have to do so with warplanes from Sweden.

As a borderless country in the Arctic Ocean, Sweden's Norttbotten Region is also strategically important in terms of threats from the Arctic. Traditionally, Sweden has planned for an invasion from the sea, but it has also considered the possibility of armies coming from the North. There are several reasons why the Norrbotten Region is important. These are the area's proximity to the Soviets, the area's coastline to the Baltic Sea, the location of the military zone in this area, and the availability of immediate reaction capacity in terms of air defence capabilities.

The Boden and Lulea military facilities in the Norrbotten region were actively

[17] Lassenius, Oscar," Swedish strategic culture in the Post-Cold War era : a case study of Swedish military strategic doctrine", January 1, 2020, Finnish National Defence University,pp.57, https://core.ac.uk/works/95325177.

[18] Keys, "Sweden: NATO's Silent Partner", p.9

[19] Gustafsson," The Soviet Threat to Sweden during the Cold War".

[20] Gustafsson," The Soviet Threat to Sweden during the Cold War".

used until the end of the Cold War. They are still in use today and have been handed over to the Swedish Air Force and Land Forces.[21] Sweden has strengthened its forces in the Norrbotten region to protect itself from possible conflicts in the Arctic. Sweden is in a defensive position in the Norrbotten area. It can be said that the defence position in the region is also compatible with Sweden's neutrality policy.

## Arctic Policy after the Cold War

The issues that Sweden has emphasised after the Cold War are the protection of the Arctic ecosystem and biodiversity, and the reduction of carbon emissions. For such issues, scientific research has been emphasised. Sweden is also aware of the economic potential of the region, but for Sweden, economic activities should be carried out with environmental sensitivities. Issues such as the protection of the cultural values and rights of local peoples living in the Arctic region have been a part of the Arctic policy.

With the end of the Cold War, Russia's strategic-military sensitivities towards the Arctic region have changed. In this period, the Arctic region was perceived as a burden for Russia rather than a source of gain.[22] In the absence of the Soviet threat, Sweden projected the priority of national defence into the international arena, and the whole of Sweden became the subject of defence. This meant that Sweden did not separate between the Baltic Sea and the Arctic and aimed for a high level of preparedness in each region.[23]

The post-Cold War peaceful atmosphere has been disrupted by several events. In 2008, Russia's war in Georgia served as a warning to Europe and Western countries. This warning was combined with another perception in Swedish society: "If Sweden is attacked, the EU and Western countries will come to Sweden's aid."

Although Russia's intervention in Georgia did not raise serious concerns, the events of 2014 have been an "alarm" situation for Western countries. In 2014, the annexation of Crimea and the Ukraine crisis were important in showing the limits of the EU-Eastern Partnership Project and the EU Common Foreign and Security Policy. The subsequent economic crises and the 2015 refugee crisis have weakened the prospects for a Common Foreign and Security Policy. Sweden started to lose faith in the coherence and

[21] Barrie et al. "Northern Europe, The Arctic and the Baltic: The ISR Gap" (December, 2022)
[22] Alexander Sergunin," Arctic Security Perspectives from Russia" in Routledge Handbook of Arctic Security, ed. Gunhild Hoogensen Gjorv, Marc Lanteigne & Horatio Sam-Aggrey (New York, Routledge) 2020, pp.130.
[23] Lassenius, "Swedish strategic culture in the Post-Cold War era," p. 64.

functionality of the EU. Especially after BREXIT, Sweden lost an important partner in the EU in terms of security policies. Since 2015, it has returned to the "Total Defence Concept" adopted during the Cold War. In this context, it has allocated more resources to regional and civil defence elements.

## Arctic Policy in 2011

It can be said that the most important part of the strategy document announced in 2011 is the issue of climate change.[24] Climate change will affect the sea routes, sociology and cultural structure of the region. Being aware of this situation, Sweden took over the chairmanship of the Arctic Council in 2011 and showed what kind of policy it would follow. When we evaluate both the Cold War period and its aftermath, we can say that this document is unique in several issues. One of these points is the will to improve the humanitarian situation in the region. Another issue is the handling of economic development with environmental sensitivities.

When Sweden took over the chairmanship of the Arctic Council, there were some doubts. These doubts stemmed from the perception of Sweden as a "reluctant/undecisive" Arctic country. Indeed, Sweden published its official Arctic strategy later than other states. According to Marchenkov, this was a response to the strategies of other states.[25] Sweden is perceived as an "undecided" Arctic country because of its low contribution to the Arctic region and its low contribution to Arctic-specific organisations.[26]

The sea routes envisaged to be opened with the melting glaciers in the region are considered important by Sweden for the economy of the region. The most important and shortest route connecting Europe and Asia is the Suez Canal. However, the Suez Canal harbours many threats and disadvantages. Therefore, an alternative route to the Suez Canal is attractive. The change in the world logistics network in favour of the Arctic region is of course a great advantage for the countries close to the Arctic and the Arctic coastal countries. On the other hand, the development of new routes also raises the issue of route security. The most important issue for Sweden is the potential negative impact on the environment of maritime traffic that will increase with the new routes.[27]

While Sweden wants to keep its relations with the five Arctic coastal states

---

[24] Government Offices of Sweden, "Sweden's Strategy for the Arctic Region" (2011).
[25] Marchenkov, "Consistency and Adaptability:New Aspects of the Arctic Policy of Sweden"
[26] Eklund, "The Swedish Chairmanship: Foresight and Hindsight in Arctic Activism" 2019
[27] GOS, 2011

strong, the Arctic Five (Canada, Denmark, Norway, Russia and the USA) have established decision-making mechanisms among themselves. Within this mechanism, Finland, Sweden and Iceland are excluded. However, according to Sweden, the claims of the littoral states in the Arctic Ocean should essentially be resolved according to the Convention of the Law of the Sea. For states, international law is an important political force. If great power competition intensifies, countries like Sweden will be in a position to choose sides. However, this is a constraint for Sweden's non-alignment policy.[28]

The Arctic region has become important for Sweden not because of its executive role, but because of the changing economic, political, social and environmental conditions in the Arctic. Since 2009, the importance of the Arctic region has been increasing. In addition to the effects of climate change, one of the important reasons for the region to gain importance is that Russia has started to increase its military capabilities in the region again. The uncertain effects of climate change and the rising great power rivalry create uncertainties for the stability of the region.

**Arctic Policy in 2020**

Significant changes are observed in the document published in 2020. As emphasised in the previous document and in this document, Sweden has declared that it will take the lead in sustainable development and environmental protection. Again, in parallel with the previous document, it can be said that the Arctic Council stands out as the main co-operation institution. The actors that Sweden considers suitable for partnership are the EU, Nordic and Barents Cooperation Initiatives. Within the scope of cooperation, Sweden would like other EU member states to contribute to the work in the Arctic region. Among these countries, Germany is particularly emphasised and said to be an important partner. The "human dimension" policy, one of Sweden's priorities in 2011, also emphasised policies to develop, empower and build resilience among the people of the region.

According to Sweden, the Arctic is becoming increasingly militarised.[29] What is meant by militarisation is the proliferation of military elements in the region and the increase in military capacity. On the other hand, there is an ongoing problem of mistrust with Russia since 2014. The basis of this mistrust is Russia's aggressive foreign policies. Therefore, the most important emphasis in this document is on security policy.

---

[28] Khorrami, "Small and Non-Aligned: Sweden's Strategic Posture in the Arctic"
[29] GOS, 2020

Russia's military build-up in the Arctic region has significant implications for neighbouring small states.[30] In addition to capacity increases, Russia has violated the air and sea borders of Sweden and Finland several times.[31] However, Russia's position necessitates a relationship with Russia. Sweden therefore emphasises points of common interest in its relations with Russia.[32]

Sweden's primary aim is to preserve the "cooperation, peace" image of the Arctic region. In this regard, Sweden is moving forward in two ways. One is confidence-building co-operation and the second is to develop its national military capacity. The reason why he sees cooperation as a method is that he foresees that in the event of a conflict Swedish territory could be made available to neighbouring and allied countries. Therefore, Sweden needs to gain joint readiness and operational capability. On the other hand, Sweden does not see security only in terms of military capacity building. As emphasised in the previous document, Sweden approaches security from a holistic perspective.

Since the Cold War, Sweden has been saying that it will increase its security and defence capacity through various mechanisms. The basis of Russia's Cold War-era Arctic strategy is modernisation within the scope of "second strike capability". On the other hand, the annexation of Crimea and the US sanctions against Russia since 2014 have been instrumental in the development of Russian Chinese cooperation.[33]

## What a Change Between 2011 and 2020

Since 2011, the agenda of international politics and the Arctic region has undergone significant changes. After the 2014 Crimean annexation and the Ukraine crisis, Europe-Russia relations have become increasingly strained. The migrant crisis started in Europe; European integration was eroded by the Brexit process. Finally, the Ukraine-Russia War has been the culmination of tensions in West-Russia relations. In Sweden's view, the Arctic is a region of escalating tensions. Although the underlying reason behind the tension is the possibility of military conflict, the phenomenon that triggers strategic rivalry

---

[30] Aiswarya Lakshmi, "Is Russia Militarizing the Arctic?" (August 20, 2015). https://www.marine link.com/news/militarizing-russia396525)

[31] Rob Huebert," The Evolving Arctic Security Environment" in On Thin Ice? Perspectives on Arctic Security, ed. Duncan Depledge & P.Whitney Lackenbauer (Ontario, NAADSN), 2021 pp.52

[32] GOS, 2020

[33] Demirci, "How will Sweden's and Finland's Membership in NATO Impact Arctic Geopolitics?" (June 09, 2022) https://www.orionpolicy.org/orionforum/106/how-will-sweden%E2%80%99s-and-finland %E2%80%99s-membership-in-nato-impact-arctic-geopolitics

is climate change.[34]

Sweden has practically focussed on the following issues in its chairmanship of the Arctic Council, which it took over in 2011: Environment and climate, Arctic indigenous peoples and developing the Arctic Council. In many respects, Swedish Arctic policy has been continuous. The most important change, however, has been about military security issues. Whereas in 2011 several issues were seen as opportunities for co-operation, in 2020 they were perceived as sources of conflict. Marchenkov used the concepts of "consistency and compatibility" for this situation.[35] The most important reason for these significant changes is the changing security environment. When Sweden took over the Chairmanship of the Arctic Council in 2011, it thought that it could develop areas of cooperation with Russia.

In 2016, Sweden published its environmental policy for the Arctic. According to this document, taking new measures to struggle against climate change is emphasised.[36] Therefore, protecting the Arctic region and its environmental features requires a global policy. On the other hand, the Arctic region contains important natural resources. As access to the region and its resources becomes easier, maritime activities and interest in the region will increase.[37] According to Sweden, the role of each actor in the international security structure is realised in a specific area. According to this distinction, the UN is involved in peacekeeping operations, the EU in civilian and military training missions and NATO in the collective security of the European continent. This functional distinction is important because it prevents "mission repetition."[38]

## Conclusion

Following the Russo-Ukraine War, Sweden formally applied for NATO membership and abandoned its traditional policy of neutrality. Such a choice is not surprising given Sweden's continued interactions with its NATO allies since the Cold War years. Sweden is pleased that the European Union is giving more attention to the Arctic region but has limited faith in the European Union on security and foreign policy issues. Therefore, it prefers close cooperation with NATO. With the end of the Cold War, the

---

[34] Oscar Lassenius, "SWEDISH STRATEGIC CULTURE IN THE POST-COLD WAR ERA: A CASE STUDY OF SWEDISH MILITARY STRATEGIC DOCTRINE", Diploma Thesis, August 2020, Finnish National Defence University, pp.77
[35] Marchenkov, "Consistency and Adaptability: New Aspects of the Arctic Policy of Sweden" (2022)
[36] MEE, "Environmental Policy for the Arctic", pp.2
[37] MEE, "Environmental Policy for the Arctic", pp.4
[38] SOU, 2016:57

geostrategic importance of the Arctic region declined, but today great power rivalry has returned to the region and the Arctic region is part of a geopolitical competition.[39] However, it should be noted that, unlike the Cold War, there is a multi-actor tension in the region.

In other words, the course of great power competition has always been decisive for countries like Sweden. Actors seeking political influence in great power competition have also pursued alternative policies. What is the situation today? Today, the United States has appointed its first specially authorised ambassador.[40] During his visit to Canada, NATO Secretary General Stoltenberg stated that Russia is a strategic threat to NATO in the region. Russia is perceived by Sweden as an unpredictable actor. China is also becoming an important actor in the region. As mentioned in the 2020 document, China has not shown any military activity in the region so far but has defined itself as a "Near-Arctic State", developed the "Polar Silk Road" project and started to build nuclear icebreaker ships.[41]

The territorial border claims mentioned in both documents are an important issue. Because the serious loss of ice cover in the long term will increase the confusion in border claims. Although the Arctic region is a region where "like-minded" countries are in the majority, there are significant differences in the areas of interest and threat.[42] The USA, on the other hand, has not yet become a party to UNCLOS, although it frequently emphasises international law.[43] In the intensifying great power competition, UNCLOS, to which Russia and China are parties but the US is not, is an important question mark.[44]

The 2022 Ukraine War affected all areas. Even in the Arctic Council, where security issues are not a priority, the securitising effect of the war came to the fore and cooperation mechanisms established with Russia were frozen.[45] Without cooperation in the region, the survival of the region is at risk.

---

[39] Harri Mikkola, "The Geostrategic Arctic", Finnish Institute of International Affairs (April 2019) No:259. https://www.fiia.fi/wp-content/uploads/2019/04/bp259_geostrategic_arctic.pdf ).

[40] Astri Edvardsen, "US Wants Mike Sfraga as US' First Arctic Ambassador" (Feb 17, 2023) https://www.highnorthnews.com/en/us-wants-mike-sfraga-us-first-arctic-ambassador).

[41] (GOS, 2020; Barrie et. al,"Northern Europe, The Arctic and The Baltic: The ISR Gap " 2022: 6)

[42] Khorrami, "Small and Non-Aligned: Sweden's Strategic Posture in the Arctic"

[43] The White House, "National Strategy for the Arctic Region", October 2022, Washington

[44] Trine Jonassen, "Security Issues Have Taken Over the Arctic Agenda, says Swedish and Danish Arctic Ambassadors" (Apr 19, 2023) Accessed 03.04.2023. https://www.highnorthnews.com/en/security-issues-has-taken-over-arctic-agenda-says-swedish-and-danish-arctic-ambassadors)

[45] Trine Jonassen, "Security Issues Have Taken Over the Arctic Agenda, says Swedish and Danish Arctic Ambassadors" Apr 19, 2023, (Accessed, 18.04.2023) https://www.highnorthnews.com/en/security-issues-has-taken-over-arctic-agenda-says-swedish-and-danish-arctic-ambassadors).

Maritime dominance has played an important role in the strategic thinking of countries throughout world history. When we look at recent history, it is seen that aircraft carriers have played a major role in this dominance. However, the developing war technology and the specific characteristics of the Arctic call into question the need for aircraft carriers. Today, it can be said that important conflicts have started in the Arctic Sea, but these conflicts are at the beginning stage for now. As in other parts of the world, a multi-actor system has started to emerge in the Arctic. The bipolar system of the Cold War era has been left behind, but the post-Cold War peace climate has also been damaged.

## Bibliography

Åselius, Gunnar. "Swedish Strategic Culture after 1945." *Cooperation and Conflict* 40, no. 1 (2005): 25–44. http://www.jstor.org/stable/45084413.

Dalsjö, Robert, "The hidden rationality of Sweden's policy of neutrality during the Cold War, Cold War History," (2014) 14:2, 175-194, DOI: 10.1080/14682745. 2013. 765865

Demirci, Cem, "How will Sweden's and Finland's membership in NATO impact Arctic Geopolitics?" June 09, 2022(Accessed: 28.05.2023)

https://www.orionpolicy.org/orionforum/106/how-will-sweden's-and-finland's-membership-in-nato-impact-arctic-geopolitics

Douglas Barrie, Childs, N., Yohann, M., Sabatino, E. & Schreer, B. "Northern Europe, The Arctic and The Baltic: The ISR Gap", December 2022, The International Institute for Strategic Studies

Edvardsen, Astri "US Wants Mike Sfraga as US'First Arctic Ambassador" (Feb 17, 2023) (Accessed: 12.05.2023) https://www.highnorthnews.com/en/us-wants-mike-sfraga-us-first-arctic-ambassador

Eklund, Niklas. "The Swedish Chairmanship: Foresight and Hindsight in Arctic Activism." Springer Polar Sciences (2019): n. pag.

Government Offices of Sweden (2020). Sweden's strategy for the Arctic region. Retrieved from www.government.se/contentassets/85de9103bbbe4373 b55eddd7f71608da/swedens-strategy-for-the-arctic-region-2020.pdf

Government Offices of Sweden(2011) Sweden's strategy for the Arctic region (Article no: UD11.041). Stockholm, Sweden: Ministry of Foreign Affairs. Retrieved from https://www.government.se/contentassets/85de9103bbbe4373b55eddd7f71608da /swedens-strategy-for-the-arctic-region

Gustafsson, Bengt, "The Soviet Threat to Sweden during the Cold War " (Accessed:19.05.2023)

https://phpisn.ethz.ch/lory1.ethz.ch/collections/coll_sovthreat/Introduction2f3a.html?navinfo=46465

Gjørv, Gunhild Hoogensen & Hodgson, Kara K. " Comprehensive Security in the Arctic: Beyond "Arctic Exceptionalism" in On Thin Ice? Perspectives on Arctic Security, Edited by Duncan Depledge and P. Whitney Lackenbauer, 2-11, Ontario: NAADSN,

2020

Huebert, Rob " The Evolving Arctic Security Environment" in On Thin Ice? Perspectives on Arctic Security, edited by Duncan Depledge & P.Whitney Lackenbauer, 48-54, Ontario: NAADSN, 2021

Keys, J. E., Jr, "Sweden: Nato's Silent Partner?, " Master's thesis, NAVAL POSTGRADUATE SCHOOL MONTEREY CA, 1984

Khorrami, Nima, "Small and Non-Aligned: Sweden's Strategic Posture in the Arctic" September 1, 2020, (Accessed: 18/04/2023)https://www.thearctic institute.org/small-non-aligned-sweden-strategic-posture-arctic-part-i/

Lakshmi, Aiswarya "Is Russia Militarizing the Arctic ?" (August 20, 2015). (Accessed: 12.05.2023) https://www.marinelink.com/news/militarizing-russia396525

Lassenius, Oscar "SWEDISH STRATEGIC CULTURE IN THE POST-COLD WAR ERA: A CASE STUDY OF SWEDISH MILITARY STRATEGIC DOCTRINE", Diploma Thesis, August 2020, Finnish National Defence University,

Marchenkov M.L. Consistency and Adaptability: New Aspects of the Arctic Policy of Sweden. Arktika i Sev- er [Arctic and North], 2022, no. 47, pp. 126–141. DOI: 10.37482/issn2221-2698.2022.47.126

Mikkola, Harri "The Geostrategic Arctic", Finnish Institute of International Affairs (April 2019) No:259. https://www.fiia.fi/wp-content/uploads/2019/04/ bp259_geostrategic_arctic.pdf ).

Ministry for Foreign Affairs (2016). Summary of Security in a new era - Report by the Inquiry on Sweden's International Defence and Security Cooperation. Retrieved from www.government.se/statements/2016/09/statement-from-the-minister-for-foreign-affairs-regarding-the-report-on-swedens-international-defence-and-security-policy-cooperation/

Ministry of the Environment and Energy,"New Swedish environmental policy for the Arctic". 25 January 2016, (Memorandum)

Nagy, David, "Swedish Neutrality: How long can it last?" Danube Institute (March 2022). https://danubeinstitute.hu/en/research/swedish-neutrality-how-long-can-it-last

"Russia a strategic challenge for NATO in Arctic, Stoltenberg says" (August 26, 2022) (Accessed: 10.05.2023) https://www.arctictoday.com/russia-a-strategic-challenge-for-nato-in-arctic-stoltenberg-says/?wallit_nosession=1

Sergunin, Alexander "Arctic Security Perspectives from Russia" in Routledge Handbook of Arctic Security, edited by Gunhild Hoogensen Gjorv, Marc Lanteigne & Horatio Sam-Aggrey ,129-139, New York: Routledge, 2020

Sussanne Berger," the great paradox of swedish neutrality in the cold war and today" (December 2015). https://warontherocks.com/2015/12/the-great-paradox-of-swedish-neutrality-in-the-cold-war-and-today/

Tepe, F. Fulya, "Swedish Neutrality and Its Abandonment" İstanbul Ticaret Üniversitesi Sosyal Bilimler Dergisi 6, Number:11(Spring, 2007/2): 183-201 https://www.ticaret.edu.tr/uploads/kutuphane/dergi/s11/M00167.pdf

The White House, "National Strategy for the Arctic Region", October 2022, Washington

Yalçınkaya, Haldun, "Savaşın Değişimi ve Savaş Çalışmalarında Farklı Disiplinlerden," in Savaş: Farklı Disiplinlerde Yeni Yaklaşımlar, edited by Haldun Yalçınkaya, 13-30. Ankara, Siyasal Kitabevi, 2010

# CHAPTER 6

## NORWAY'S ARCTIC POLICIES

Allison G. Kondrat[1]

Norway has one of the smallest populations in Europe and is known for its liberal, autonomous system of government. Norway employs a multiparty political system and operates under a democratic parliament and a constitutional monarchy. Internal operations and ministries in Norway function in decentralized, local arenas (with some external federal oversight).[2] Under this socio-political system, the Norwegian public has consistently reported some of the highest levels of trust internationally in their government, institutions, and society.[3] This impressive domestic feat complements Norway's international strategic stronghold.[4] This chapter will examine Norway's geopolitics, historical, and modern interactions with the Arctic. Specifically, Norway's geographic location as a foothold for international security operations is discussed. The interactions of Norway, with other countries in the Arctic, throughout history are explored. Additionally, the modern importance of Norway in the military, economic, and political contexts of the Arctic region is discussed, as is Norway's expectations of its Arctic neighbours. In doing so, the importance of Norway

---

[1] Allison G. Kondrat, MA, is a second-year doctoral student in the Department of Criminal Justice and Criminology at Sam Houston State University. Her research interests include racial and ethnic disparities in public policy, violent extremism, national security, and substance use disorders. Her recent work has appeared in Crime & Delinquency.
[2] Christensen, Fimreite, and Lægreid, "Crisis Management–The Case of Internal Security in Norway"; Katrine Fangen and Yngve Carlsson, "Right-wing extremism in Norway: Prevention and intervention," in Right-wing extremism in Europe: country analyses, counter-strategies and labor-market oriented exit strategies, ed. Ralf Melzer, Sebastian Serafin, and Friedrich-Ebert-Stiftung (Berlin: Friedrich-Ebert-Stiftung, Forum Berlin, 2013), 327–357, ISBN: 978-3-86498-522-5, https: //ub01.uni-tuebingen.de/xmlui/ bitstream/ handle/ 10900/64182/10031.pdf?sequence=1&isAllowed=y.
[3] Catherine Appleton, "Lone wolf terrorism in Norway," The International Journal of Human Rights 18, no. 2 (February 2014): 127–142, https://doi.org/10.1080/13642987.2014.889390, https://doi.org/10.1080 %2F13642987.2014.889390; Christensen, Fimreite, and Lægreid, "Crisis Management–The Case of Internal Security in Norway."
[4] Christensen, Fimreite, and Lægreid, "Crisis Management–The Case of Internal Security in Norway"; Svein Vigeland Rottem, "The Political Architecture of Security in the Arctic–the Case of Norway," Arctic Review on Law and Politics 4, no. 2 (2013): 234–254; Hans Mouritzen, "The Nordic–Baltic Area: Divisive Geopolitics at Work," Cambridge Review of International Affairs 19, no. 3 (September 2006): 495–511, https://doi.org/10.1080/09557570600869556, https: //doi.org/10.1080%2F09557570600869556; Øystein Tunsjø, "Geopolitical shifts, great power relations and Norway's foreign policy," Cooperation and Conflict 46, no. 1 (March 2011): 60–77, https://doi.org/10.1177/0010836710396784, https://doi.org/10. 1177%2F0010836710396784.

in the Arctic and in international settings will be delineated.

## Geography of the Country & Geopolitical Importance

As one of the northernmost countries in Europe, Norway shares its borders with the Norwegian and Barents Seas and neighbouring countries of Russia, Sweden, and Finland. The Barents Sea has been regarded as a critical strategic passageway since World War I, as supplies and support have historically been sent by Russia along the Barents Sea.[5] Additionally, as tensions rise in the Arctic region, Norway's access to these passageways can be advantageous in maintaining security and securing intelligence.

Further, Norway is one of few countries that are seated along the Arctic and, therefore, continues to levy great geopolitical importance.[6] Interestingly, while Norway is a founding member of the North Atlantic Treaty Organization (NATO), it remains independent from the European Union (EU); previous attempts to join the EU in 1972 and 1994 ultimately[7] failed as the country's hesitance to submit itself, entirely, to its allies'political agenda(s). Nevertheless, the symbiotic relationship between Norway and the EU continues, as Norway operates as an informal partner to its Arctic neighbours in the EU.

The Svalbard region, an archipelago north of mainland Norway, has particular importance to the country's geopolitical influence. This region (formerly 'Spitsbergen') became part of Norway after enacting the Svalbard Treaty in 1925.[8] This Treaty also established the first formal regulations on

---

[5] Rolf Tamnes and Kristine Offerdal, Geopolitics and security in the Arctic: Regional dynamics in a global world [in en] (2014), isbn: 9781315813455.

[6] Tunsjø, "Geopolitical shifts, great power relations and Norway's foreign policy"; Valery Konyshev and Aleksandr Sergunin, "The Arctic at the crossroads of geopolitical interests," Russian Politics & Law 50, no. 2 (2012): 34–54; Mouritzen, "The Nordic–Baltic Area: Divisive Geopolitics at Work"; Rottem, "The Political Architecture of Security in the Arctic–the Case of Norway"; Marina Caparini, Kari Marie Kjellstad, and Trine Nikolaisen, A Stocktaking of Norwegian Engagement in Security Sector Reform [in en], technical report 11 (Norwegian Institute of International Affairs: Department of Security and Conflict Management, 2011), 89, https://www.files.ethz.ch/isn/133045/SIP11-Caparini%20et%20al-NUPI %20 Report.pdf; Maria Morgunova, "Why is exploitation of Arctic offshore oil and natural gas resources ongoing? A multi-level perspective on the cases of Norway and Russia," The Polar Journal 10, no. 1 (January 2020): 64–81, https://doi.org/10.1080/2154896x. 2020.1757823, https://doi.org/10.1080 %2F2154896 x.2020.1757823; Anne Heyerdahl, "From prescriptive rules to responsible organisations – making sense of risk in protective security management – a study from Norway," European Security 32, no. 1 (May 2022): 147–169, https://doi.org/10.1080/ 09662839. 2022. 2070006, https://doi.org/10.1080 %2F096 6 2 8 39. 2022.2070006. 7. Mouritzen, "The Nordic–Baltic Area: Divisive Geopolitics at Work."

[7] Andreas Østhagen, "Managing Conflict at Sea: The Case of Norway and Russia in the Svalbard Zone," Arctic Review on Law and Politics 9, no. 1 (2018): 100, https://doi.org/10.23865/arctic.v9.1084, https://doi.org/10.23865%2Farctic.v9.1084.

[8] Østhagen, "Managing Conflict at Sea: The Case of Norway and Russia in the Svalbard Zone"; Andreas

the inhabitation and use of the region.[9] Under the Svalbard Treaty, foreign nationals faced new employment and housing taxes specific to this region, as well as extreme limits on any (non-Norwegian) military presence. As a part of the "High North," the Svalbard region offers invaluable economic and military footholds to Norway. Svalbard rests between the Norwegian, Barents, and Greenland Seas and the Arctic Ocean. Not only is this region rich in its fishing industry and offshore natural resources,[10] but it also provides an area for Norwegian and allied forces to monitor and quickly respond to Russian (or other combatant countries) actions.[11] Similarly, negotiations between Russia and Norway concerning the Varangerfjord area have strengthened Norway's strategic positioning. During their 2004 delimitation settlement, Norway's territorial seas were extended to 12 nautical miles (from the four nautical miles originally negotiated with the Soviet Union in 1957) and now maintains a 24 nautical mile contiguous zone along the Russian coast.[12] Therefore, rights to these waters permit closer monitoring of activity along the Pechengsky District of Russia and shortens weaponry range (e.g., artillery range) demands for Norwegian border defence.

Iceland and Denmark have also been involved in land negotiations with Norway. These territories could extend Norway's existing continental shelves and increase Norway's access to natural resources and fisheries. Delimitations concerning the "Banana Hole," the waters that exists in the space between Norway's coastline (and Svalbard), Iceland, and Denmark's Faroe Islands were now determined to be international waters, negating sovereignty claims (as exclusive environmental zones (EEZ) cannot extend beyond 200 nautical miles).[15] During the 1980s, Denmark and Norway had a dispute over the land

Østhagen, OttoSvendsen, and Max Bergmann, Arctic Geopolitics: The Svalbard Archipelago [in en], technical report (Center for Strategic and International Studies, September 2023), https://www.csis.org/analysis/arctic-geopoliticssvalbard-archipelago.

[9] Østhagen, "Managing Conflict at Sea: The Case of Norway and Russia in the Svalbard Zone"; Morgunova, "Why isexploitation of Arctic offshore oil and natural gas resources ongoing? A multi-level perspective on the cases of Norway and Russia"; Rottem, "The Political Architecture of Security in the Arctic–the Case of Norway."

[10] Julie Wilhelmsen and Kristian Lundby Gjerde, "Norway and Russia in the Arctic: New Cold War Contamination?,"Arctic Review on Law and Politics 9 (2018): pp. 382–407, issn: 18916252, 23874562, https://www.jstor.org/stable/48710573; Østhagen, "Managing Conflict at Sea: The Case of Norway and Russia in the Svalbard Zone"; Rottem, "The Political Architecture of Security in the Arctic–the Case of Norway"; Mouritzen, "The Nordic–Baltic Area: Divisive Geopolitics at Work"; Nina Græger, "Norway in a Transatlantic Tight Spot Between US and European Security Strategies?," Security dialogue 36, no. 3 (2005): 412–416; Tunsjø, "Geopolitical shifts, great power relations and Norway's foreign policy"; Østhagen, Svendsen, and Bergmann, Arctic Geopolitics.

[11] The Norwegian Government's Arctic Policy [in en-GB], Publisher: regjeringen.no, January 2021, https://www. regjeringen.no/en/dokumenter/arctic_policy/id2830120/.

[12] The Loophole and the Banana Hole [in en], May 2012, https://www.barentswatch.no/en/ articles/the-loophole-and-the-banana-hole/.

between Greenland and Jan Mayen (a small island bordering the Norwegian and Greenland Seas). Ultimately, this area was split between the two counties, according to coastal distances, resulting in Norway having 57% of the disputed area and Denmark receiving the remaining 43%. These delimitations are seemingly an amicable resolution between Denmark and Norway.

### Historical Interaction in the Arctic Region

Historically, Norway has been, and continues to be, neutral in international conflicts.[13] A sizable portion of its historical interactions in the Arctic have been rooted in its military alliances with its allies. During both World Wars and even during their occupation by German forces in the 1940s,[14] Norway prioritized its domestic safety while quietly supporting its allies.

In the wake of World War II, substantial efforts within the Arctic countries were launched to create security unions specific to the region (including the U.S. and Soviet Union).[15] However, while these self-initiated efforts failed, Norway, shortly thereafter, became a founding member of NATO in 1949.[16] Importantly, Norway's traditionally neutral foreign policy was built into Norway's primary role as a sort of "peacekeeping" member of NATO. Due to its size and relatively weak front lines, NATO membership has proven to be invaluable in maintaining its legitimacy as a geopolitical power in the Arctic. Even though Norway kept close political ties, it was a country that was excluded from most security analyses throughout the Cold War era; Norway was neither a member of the EU nor did it share a border with the Baltic Sea. During the Cold War, the Baltic Sea was a critical area within the Cold War context.[17] While comparable in size and positioning, Denmark and Finland eclipsed Norway in their ability to negotiate with the Soviet Union: Denmark's longstanding control over the Baltic's straits[18] and Finland's shared borders with the Soviet Union and the Baltic Sea became important frontiers of the Cold War. However, despite weighted considerations,

---

[13] Tor Dagre, "The History of Norway.," Millenium, 1999, Mouritzen, "The Nordic–Baltic Area: Divisive Geopolitics at Work"; Tunsjø, "Geopolitical shifts, great power relations and Norway's foreign policy."
[14] Dagre, "The History of Norway."
[15] Mouritzen, "The Nordic–Baltic Area: Divisive Geopolitics at Work."
[16] Mouritzen.
[17] Tuomas Räsänen and Simo Laakkonen, "Cold War and the Environment: The Role of Finland in International Environmental Politics in the Baltic Sea Region," AMBIO: A Journal of the Human Environment 36, no. 2 (April 2007):229–236, https://doi.org/10.1579/0044- 7447(2007)36[229: cwatet]2.0.co;2,
https://doi.org/10.1579%2F00447447%282007%2936%5B229%3Acwatet%5D2.0.co%3B2.
[18] Kurt B. Jensen and Royal Danish Navy, "The Baltic Sea in the Post — Cold War World," Naval War College Review 46, no. 4 (1993): 29–41, issn: 00281484, 24757047, http://www.jstor.org/stable/44642522.

Norway remained inextricable from the NATO northern operations and interests.[19]

Remaining true to its nature, Norway cooperated with its allies' military objectives when agreeing to store military equipment and supplies in the country, starting in the 1950s.[20] In particular, NATO during this time sought to strengthen "flank forces" in the north, so that Central Europe could be readily protected from enemy advances.[21] Shortly thereafter, Norway garnered international attention by participating in Co-located Operating Bases (COB) with the United States starting in 1974. This COB was initiated mainly to address the need for air support. Norway's military prowess emanates from its navy. With its airspace protected, Norwegian Naval forces are free to continue monitoring and reporting on Russian maritime activity.[22] The decision to participate in the COB was met with mixed reactions as military activity in Norwegian territory has been legally restrained (since 1949) but also (hesitantly) desired as Soviet military forces continued to test socio-political boundaries.[23] These decisions have been important to security in the Arctic as they demonstrate Norway's willingness to cooperate in allied military operations and contribute to security maintenance.

Meanwhile, Norway maintained its apolitical relationship with the Soviet Union through its shared economic (and Norway's environmental) interest in fisheries. While physical security has The Joint Fisheries Commission was established in 1976 between the two nations and focuses on the scientifically sustainable hatching and catching of native fish species (e.g., the Skrei, Haddock, Capelin, and Greenland Halibut). This inclusion of environmental and food source considerations, to security efforts, demonstrates the thoroughness of Norway's security plans. Norway is unique as it has both freshwater and saltwater fish. These fish have become one of the country's top exports, having earned over 14.40 billion kroner (NOK) or $8.08 billion (USD). This Commission is one of the principal examples of successful Arctic collaborations.[24] At the end of the Cold War, this longstanding relationship between Russia and Norway allowed for booms in travel and

---

[19] Tamnes and Offerdal, Geopolitics and security in the Arctic: Regional dynamics in a global world.

[20] Græger, "Norway in a Transatlantic Tight Spot Between US and European Security Strategies?" 25. Tamnes and Offerdal, Geopolitics and security in the Arctic: Regional dynamics in a global world.

[21] Tamnes and Offerdal, Geopolitics and security in the Arctic: Regional dynamics in a global world.

[22] Tamnes and Offerdal.

[23] Tamnes and Offerdal, Geopolitics and security in the Arctic: Regional dynamics in a global world; Leif Christian Jensen, International relations in the Arctic: Norway and the struggle for power in the New North (Bloomsbury Publishing, 2015).

[24] Rottem, "The Political Architecture of Security in the Arctic–the Case of Norway"; Græger, "Norway in a Transatlantic Tight Spot Between US and European Security Strategies?"

tourism between these nations.[25] Additionally, the Search and Rescue Cooperation between the Soviet Union and Norway bound these seafaring nations until the mid-1990s.[26]

During this time, Norway also solidified its economic importance to the Arctic region by establishing its exclusive economic zone (1977) and fisheries protection zone (1977).[27] The exclusive economic zone (EEZ), however, has become a point of contention among other Arctic countries. As suggested by its title, the EEZ authorizes Norwegian forces to police this area's use economic or otherwise. Russian and Icelandic actors have expressed discontent with the EEZ, claiming that there has been discriminatory sanctioning against their fishing vessels. Despite these conflicts, the United Nations Law of the Sea Conventions and the Commission on the Limits of the Continental Shelf have extended Norway's claims to the continental shelf in 2006 and 2009. This is especially important when considering that Norway's territorial waters (i.e., its exclusive economic zone) are six times that of its land mass.[28]

While Norway has openly opposed major conflicts (including the Iraq War, stating that the War was a direct violation of international law), other members of the Arctic have begun to recognize the importance of the Barents Sea in the looming conflicts with China and Russia. Beginning with NATO's involvement in the 1999 Kosovo War, Norway has become an untapped defensive front. However, with apparent hesitance to involve itself in military conflicts, the likelihood that Norway will actively engage in future conflicts is questionable. It would be more likely that Norway follows its pattern of silent support, lending its support to its allies with supplies and access to strategic positionings.

## Relations with Other Arctic Countries

Examinations of Norway's modern relations with other Arctic countries largely focus on Norway's cooperation with the UN. Unsurprisingly, Norway has become an integral part of international peacekeeping efforts such as the United Nations (UN) Crisis Prevention Bureau and UN security sector reform efforts.[29] Additionally, Norway has spearheaded many

---

[25] Jensen, International relations in the Arctic: Norway and the struggle for power in the New North.

[26] Østhagen, "Managing Conflict at Sea: The Case of Norway and Russia in the Svalbard Zone."

[27] Østhagen, "Managing Conflict at Sea: The Case of Norway and Russia in the Svalbard Zone."

[28] Rottem, "The Political Architecture of Security in the Arctic–the Case of Norway."

[29] Caparini, Kjellstad, and Nikolaisen, A Stocktaking of Norwegian Engagement in Security Sector Reform.

environmentally-conscious programs, such as efforts to minimize the rapid melting of regional sea ice, something that has even been adopted into security policy.[30] Further, the UN Sustainable Development Goals are highlighted throughout Norway's Arctic policy strategies.[31]

Norway has also become an important actor in the Arctic Council. First established in 1996, the Arctic Council includes Norway, Canada, the United States, Denmark, Russia (i.e., the five nations that directly border the Arctic Ocean), Iceland, Finland, and Sweden. The Arctic Council has become a venue for Arctic countries to collaborate on environmental protections (e.g., Assessment of Oil and Gas Program in 2007), scientific advances, and pressing political matters.[32] In this way, the Arctic Council serves as an important avenue for Norway to participate in advances in research, policy, and "security" operationalized as environmental justice.[33] In May of 2023, the Chairship of the Arctic Council was transferred from the Russian Federation to Norway.[34] In their transference, Norway has expressed its intent for the Arctic Council to focus on environmental protections for its inhabitants, implementation of sustainable technologies, and empowering indigenous Arctic movements and voices.[35] Specifically, as the acting Chair, indigenous Arctic peoples' education, food and work opportunities and healthcare system will be the focus of Norway's indigenous aid in the Arctic Council.[36] In the two years as acting Chair, increased involvement and participation of indigenous folks in Arctic decision-making will also be strived for.

Of particular interest, the once apolitical relationship between Norway and Russia became rocky, at best, even before the Ukraine crisis. While Norway's EEZ has been an established and recognized part of Norway's territorial waters, Russian actors have continued to challenge restrictions imposed on them. Around the Spitsbergen region of the EEZ, Russian fishers have

---

[30] Rottem, "The Political Architecture of Security in the Arctic–the Case of Norway"; Østhagen, "Managing Conflict at Sea: The Case of Norway and Russia in the Svalbard Zone."

[31] The Norwegian Government's Arctic Policy.

[32] Alf Håkon Hoel, "The legal-political regime in the Arctic," in Geopolitics and security in the Arctic: regional dynamics in a global world, ed. Kristine Offerdal and Rolf Tamnes, Routledge global security studies (Abingdon, Oxon; New York, NY: Routledge, 2014), 49–72, isbn: 978-0-415-73445-5; Michael Wenger, Norway's strategy for the Arctic Council – and then what? [In en-US], March 2023, https://polarjournal.ch/en/2023/03/30/norways-strategyfor-the-arctic-council-and-then-what/.

[33] Hoel, "The legal-political regime in the Arctic."

[34] Emilie Canova and Pauline Pic, The Arctic Council in Transition: Challenges and Perspectives for the new Norwegian Chairship [in en], June 2023, https://www.thearcticinstitute.org/arctic-council-transitionchallenges-perspectives-new-norwegian-chairship/; Wenger, Norway's strategy for the Arctic Council – and then what?

[35] Canova and Pic, The Arctic Council in Transition.

[36] Wenger, Norway's strategy for the Arctic Council – and then what?

repeatedly been arrested for their attempts to fish the area illegally.[37] This tension is exacerbated by the environmental concerns that Norway prioritizes. International fisheries are assigned (fishing) quotas that are supported by environmental scientists protecting conservatory efforts. According to Norwegian estimates, Russian fishermen have illegally harvested over 100,000 tons of fish annually (from 2002 through 2005) from protected waters.[38] This overfishing has also caught the attention of the United Nations Convention on the Law of the Sea (LOS, which is responsible for regulating the international fishing efforts of migrating fish), which 165 nations (excluding the United States of America) have previously ratified.

Despite these conflicts, Norway still makes strides to create utilitarian partnerships. Started in 2006 and implemented in 2013, the Vardø Vessel Traffic System (VTS) and its Russian counterpart (the Murmansk) created a shared information network between the countries to promote safe travels along the Murmansk and North Norwegian coast.[39] Information concerning high-risk vessels and anticipated travel plans (e.g., what ports a vessel will stop at or anchor near) are processed into a joint traffic management system. After its implementation, the VTS has collaborated with the Norwegian Coast Guard to monitor illegal fishing practices. Additionally, in 2013, the Barents Ship Reporting System (BSRS) was created in response to some of the shortcomings of the VTS; the BSRS requires that all ships deemed risky must report their travels from Lofoten (a stretch of islands located in Northern Norway that neighbours the Norwegian Sea) Norway to Murmansk, Russia.[40] However, the interaction between Russia and Norway dramatically changed after Crimea's annexation.

## Military, Economic, & Political Importance for Arctic Region

### Military Importance

Since 1953, Norway's military force has been maintained through a system of universal conscription of Norwegian adults.[41] The Norwegian Armed Forces contains 13 operating units and, in 2021, had a force of 17,185 employees

---

[37] Østhagen, "Managing Conflict at Sea: The Case of Norway and Russia in the Svalbard Zone."

[38] Østhagen, "Managing Conflict at Sea: The Case of Norway and Russia in the Svalbard Zone."

[39] Østhagen.

[40] Østhagen.

[41] National Military service in Norway [in en], March 2023, https://www.norway.no/en/ latvia/norway-latvia/news-events/national-military-service-in-norway/.

and 9,888 conscripted personnel.[42] The Norwegian military force is largely an institution of naval security and domestic safety. Therefore, a heavy emphasis has historically been placed on Norway's Navy and Coast Guard. The Norwegian Navy operates 1,302 vessels (e.g., frigates and submarines), and the Coast Guards, a smaller unit of the Norwegian Navy, maintains 15 naval vessels and has completed 3,455 operations in 2022.[43] Norwegian forces are more often deployed in response to situations such as natural disasters, border security, and seafaring-related complications.[44]

Additionally, Norwegian military forces often offer support and supplies to allied forces in conflict(s).[45] While peacekeeping and security have been the priority for Norwegian military operations, the Ukraine crisis has forced Norway to evolve. As poignantly noted by the Norwegian Joint Headquarters Commander, Lieutenant General Rune Jakobson, Norway's security has had to shift from "believing in peace forever, to having to revitalize all planning."[46] As 80% of Norway's territory and one-third of its maritime zones are located in the Arctic's "high north," security in the region is imperative. Leaders of the Norwegian military, including the former Chief of Defense, Sverre Diesen, have highlighted the differential risk of Norway, compared to other NATO members, as the proximity to danger (in the face of military conflict) differs greatly; thus, military leaders have urged Norway to increase its efforts of military self-reliance.[47]

However, the recent aggressive actions of Russia have begun to test the durability of the region's security.[48] Russia's annexation of Crimea in March of 2014 upended the once amenable relationship between Russia and Norway. After 2014, high tensions prompted Norway and its allies to begin to initiate changes in their security policies. During this time, defence strategy releases from the respective countries'departments of defence offer insight into shifting narratives, where Norway's Ministry of Defense exponentially references Russia in their security briefs, while Russia has almost completely stopped referencing Norway. Despite this, Russia's Ministry of Defense (in

---

[42] Armed Forces in numbers [in en], August 2021, https://www.forsvaret.no/en/aboutus/armed-forces-in-numbers.

[43] Norwegian Coast Guard [in en], 2022, https://www.forsvaret.no/om-forsvaret/organisasj on/sjoforsvaret/kystvakten.

[44] Rottem, "The Political Architecture of Security in the Arctic–the Case of Norway."

[45] Caparini, Kjellstad, and Nikolaisen, A Stocktaking of Norwegian Engagement in Security Sector Reform.

[46] Håkon Lunde Saxi, "Alignment but not Alliance," Arctic Review on Law and Politics 13 (2022): pp. 57.

[47] Rottem, "The Political Architecture of Security in the Arctic–the Case of Norway."

[48] Andreas Østhagen, "Norway's Arctic policy: still high North, low tension?" [In en], The Polar Journal 11, no. 1 (January 2021): 75–94, issn: 2154-896X, 2154-8978, https://doi.org/10.1080/2154896X.2021.1911043, https://www.tandfonline.com/doi/full/10.1080/2154896X.2021.1911043.

2017) acknowledged the Svalbard region as a potential venue for conflicts with international forces.[49] This danger is further exacerbated by the (likely) strengthening of China and Russia's military and political cooperation.[50] Considering the presence of Chinese and Russian warships along the Alaskan coast in recent years, this does not appear to be an empty threat.[51]

In response, a renewed emphasis is being placed on the "Arctic" in maintaining safety and stability. After NATO revisited its defensive plans concerning Norway, Norway initiated its own plans, called the "Arctic Guard," revamping its existing military operations and strategies.[52] Of interest, the effects of global warming have a direct impact on Norway's military operations: ice that once provided natural barriers may open new avenues of access.[53] Furthermore, while Norway is not using its military to pressure a Russian ceasefire, it has become a home to many asylum seekers and a strategic home base for allied forces.

Sharing a border with northeastern Norway, Russia's Kola Peninsula has become one of the most militarized places in the world.[54] In response, Norway has made strides to increase its military prowess: not only has Norway increased its federal budget concerning naval operations, but it has also launched new frigates equipped with high-tech strike missiles and has purchased 48 American Joint Strike Fighter Aircrafts.[55] Increased Russian military presence has prompted Norway to lean on its NATO allies. Norway has long been reluctant to greenlight a more permanent presence of international military forces in their borders. Norway is a premiere strategic location, as it is one of the few spaces where successful long-range missile strikes against Russia can be launched.[56] Further, due to Norway's proximity to the Arctic Sea, its international allies would be allowed quick implementation/launching of submarines, surface warfare vessels, or strategic bombers.[57] Despite Norway's hesitance, since 2017, United States Marine Corps members have been stationed in Norway. This foreign military presence has only increased since the 2018 military exercise conducted by 36

[49] Østhagen, "Managing Conflict at Sea: The Case of Norway and Russia in the Svalbard Zone."

[50] Østhagen, Svendsen, and Bergmann, Arctic Geopolitics.

[51] Østhagen, Svendsen, and Bergmann.

[52] Saxi, "Alignment but not Alliance."

[53] The Norwegian Government's Arctic Policy.

[54] Saxi, "Alignment but not Alliance."

[55] Konyshev and Sergunin, "The Arctic at the crossroads of geopolitical interests."

[56] Konyshev and Sergunin.

[57] Njord Wegge and Sigbjørn Halsne, "Introduction: Security and Military Power in the Arctic," Artic review on law and politics 13 (2022): 32–33.

Russian warships in the Barents Sea.[58] Additionally, collaborations between allied defence representatives and Norway have increased. In 2020 and 2021, military cooperation agreements (officially declaring their resolve to strengthen operational cooperation) were signed between the Ministers of Defense of Norway, Sweden, and Finland.[59] Importantly, Norway has continued to offer aid to Ukraine. In 2022, Norway publicly vowed to send humanitarian aid to Ukraine after Russia's invasion from 2023 through 2027.[60] Norway's acting Prime Minister, Jonas Gahr Støre, has also shared that over 7.3 billion kroner will be sent to Ukraine in support.[61] A multitude of arms and equipment have also been sent to Ukrainian fighting forces, such as artillery rounds, national advanced surface-to-air missile system (NASAMS) firing units, and tanks.[62] In addition to its financial and military support, Norway has also continued to accept Ukrainian asylum seekers.

## Economic Importance

Norway has had a historically strong economic system, something reflected in recent economic estimates. In August 2023 alone, Norway produced 140.3 billion (NOK) in exports, 1,020,532 (NOK) in gross domestic product per capita (GDP) and has an unemployment rate of about 3.5% of the working-age population.[63]

As previously mentioned, a sizable portion of Norway's economic system rests on fishing. In fact, Norway has the fifth largest merchant fleet in the world, something which international powerhouses, such as China, rely on.[64] However, Norway's economic system is primarily centred around its natural gas and oil production. About 14 percent of Norway's gross domestic product, not including capital produced in the service sector, can be traced to its oil and gas production.[65] Norway is one of the few countries that both produces and exports natural gas and oil and has access to the Atlantic Ocean (i.e., a key avenue of trade).[66] While Norway has only begun to prioritize its

---

[58] Rottem, "The Political Architecture of Security in the Arctic–the Case of Norway."

[59] Saxi, "Alignment but not Alliance."

[60] Matthaios Melas, "The Arctic as a geopolitical bond among the European Union, Norway & Russia," The Arctic yearbook 20 (2016): 326–337.

[61] Gwladys Fouche, "Norway plans $7 bln in aid to Ukraine over five years" [in en], Reuters, February 2023, chap. Europe, https://www.reuters.com/world/europe/norway-plans-7-billion-aid-ukraine-over-five-years2023-02-06/.

[62] Arriving in Norway, https://www.ukrainianembassy.no/en/arriving-in-norway.

[63] Official Statistics [in en], https://www.ssb.no/en/economic-and-financial-data-for-norway.

[64] Tunsjø, "Geopolitical shifts, great power relations and Norway's foreign policy."

[65] Morgunova, "Why is exploitation of Arctic offshore oil and natural gas resources ongoing? A multilevel perspective on the cases of Norway and Russia."

[66] Morgunova.

offshore oil production since 2005, it has become the third-largest exporter of natural gas and oil in the world[67] and supplies about one-quarter of all natural gas used by EU countries.[68] Norway closely follows the likes of Saudi Arabia and Russia in exportation rates. Most of Norway's oil and gas operations are either in the Barents Sea (i.e., the Snøhvit and Goliat fields) or the Halter Banks of the Norwegian Sea (i.e., the Skuld oil field). Both the Snøhvit and Skuld offshore fields are operated by Equinor (formerly Statoil), the largest oil and gas operator in the country.[69]

While a leading supplier of natural gas and oil, Norway's concerns over environmental consciousness and sustainable energy sources have left many with questions about the country's future of fossil fuel use. This shift in policy comes at the heels of a 2009 agreement among NATO members to prioritize "soft security" (i.e., strategic planning addressing socio-political repercussions of climate change and other man-made disasters).[70] Outside of strictly environmental concerns, the disruption of large chunks of ice (due to climate change) has done serious damage to the structure of drilling platforms of offshore rigs, suggesting additional (economic) incentives to address the effects of climate change.[71]

## Political Importance

As a country, Norway is known for its decentralized government and citizens' trust/perceived legitimacy of their government.[72] This is likely due to cultural norms, ties to one's community, and familiarity and locality of

---

[67] Melas, "The Arctic as a geopolitical bond among the European Union, Norway & Russia"; Morgunova, "Why is exploitation of Arctic offshore oil and natural gas resources ongoing? A multi-level perspective on the cases of Norway and Russia."

[68] Morgunova, "Why is exploitation of Arctic offshore oil and natural gas resources ongoing? A multi-level perspective on the cases of Norway and Russia."

[69] Dag Harald Claes and Arild Moe, "Arctic petroleum resources in a regional and global perspective," in Geopolitics and security in the Arctic:Regional dynamics in a global world, ed. Kristine Offerdal and Rolf Tamnes, Routledge global security studies (Abingdon, Oxon; New York, NY: Routledge, 2014), 112–135, isbn: 978-0-415-73445-5.

[70] Konyshev and Sergunin, "The Arctic at the crossroads of geopolitical interests"; Per Lægreid and Synnøve Serigstad, "Framing the field of homeland security: The case of Norway," Journal of management studies 43, no. 6 (2006): 1395–1413; Tunsjø, "Geopolitical shifts, great power relations and Norway's foreign policy."

[71] Melas, "The Arctic as a geopolitical bond among the European Union, Norway & Russia"; Tunsjø, "Geopolitical shifts, great power relations and Norway's foreign policy."

[72] Christensen, Fimreite, and Lægreid, "Crisis Management–The Case of Internal Security in Norway"; Rojan Tordhol Ezzati and Marta Bivand Erdal, "Do we have to agree? Accommodating unity in diversity in post-terror Norway," Ethnicities 18, no. 3 (2018): 363–384; Øyvind Østerud and Per Selle, "Power and Democracy in Norway: The Transformation of Norwegian Politics 1," Scandinavian political studies 29, no. 1 (2006): 25–46; Jacob Aars and Anne Lise Fimreite, "Local government and governance in Norway: stretched accountability in network politics," Scandinavian Political Studies 28, no. 3 (2005): 239–256.

government actors.[73] This prioritization of local autonomy has been a formal aspect of Norwegian politics since 1837.[74] Generally, Norway is regarded as a politically left, egalitarian country, reflected in its foreign and domestic policies. As previously noted, Norway remains a non-member of the EU. However, in actuality, Norway wields a notable influence in the EU system, has applied many EU-mandated policies to their government's operations, and currently holds the Chairship position in the influential Arctic Council.[75] Aligning with its "peacekeeping" role, a sizable portion of Norway's foreign policy is operationalized as lending support and aid. An example of this can be found in Norway's Ministry of Defense's (MOD) support of the West Balkans from 2010 through 2014. A large percentage of the MOD's budget was used in a two-prong socio-political strategy in the West Balkans.[76] While prioritizing its allies such as Serbia, Bosnia-Herzegovina, and Macedonia, Norway first lent military aid (i.e., intelligence and arms) to civilian forces seeking to implement democratic institutions.[77] Additionally, secondary goals like strengthening military education and training, and integrating reform efforts to lay the groundwork for peacemaking were also included in Norway's strategic support.[78] In this way, Norway operates more as a silent (political) partner to its international allies.[79]

However, of concern, the resurgence of a far-right wave that has swept Europe has also hit Norway. Xenophobia and Islamophobia have begun to pick up a concerning level of domestic support.[80] The seriousness of this

[73] Jonas Stein, Marcus Buck, and Hilde Bjørnå, "The centre–periphery dimension and trust in politicians: the case of Norway" [in en], Territory, Politics, Governance 9, no. 1 (January 2021): 37–55, issn: 2162-2671, 2162-268X, https://doi.org/10.1080/21622671.2019.1624191, https://www.tandfonline.com/doi/full/ 10.1080/21622671.2019.1624191; Øyvind Østerud, "Introduction: The peculiarities of Norway," West European Politics 28, no. 4 (September 2005): 705–720, https://doi.org/10.1080/01402380500216591, https://doi.org/10.1080%2F01402380500216591.
[74] Østerud, "Introduction: The peculiarities of Norway."
[75] Rieker, "Norway and the ESDP: Explaining Norwegian Participation in the EU's Security Policy"; Nikolai George Lewis Holm, Linn-Marie Lillehaug Pedersen, and Elisabeth Pettersen, "Youth, gender, and perceptions of security in Norway," International Journal of Adolescence and Youth 25, no. 1 (2020): 421–434, https://doi.org/10.1080/02673843.2019.1669060, eprint: https://doi.org/10.1080/ 0267 3843. 2019.1669060; Hoel, "The legal-political regime in the Arctic"; Wenger, Norway's strategy for the Arctic Council – and then what?
[76] Caparini, Kjellstad, and Nikolaisen, A Stocktaking of Norwegian Engagement in Security Sector Reform.
[77] Caparini, Kjellstad, and Nikolaisen.
[78] Caparini, Kjellstad, and Nikolaisen.
[79] Caparini, Kjellstad, and Nikolaisen.
[80] Gabriella Elgenius and Jens Rydgren, "Frames of nostalgia and belonging: the resurgence of ethno-nationalism in Sweden," Publisher: Routledge _eprint: https://doi.org/10.1080/14616696.2018.1494297, European Societies 21, no. 4 (2019): 583–602, https://doi.org/10.1080/14616696.2018.1494297, https://doi.org/10.1080/14616696.2018.1494297; Fangen and Carlsson, "Right-wing extremism in Norway: Prevention and intervention"; Heyerdahl, "From prescriptive rules to responsible organisations

phenomenon is not lost on the country, as the devastation of the July 22, 2011, terror attacks perpetrated by the far-right terrorist, Anders Behring Breivik, remains a haunting reminder of the poisonous seeds of hate.[81]

## Norway & its Expectations from the Arctic

Overall, Norway has become an integral actor in the Arctic region. Its geopolitical importance should not be overlooked simply due to its propensity for peacekeeping. Its strategic stronghold in the Barents Sea and Arctic region creates a direct line for opposition to combatant international forces. This has become especially important when considering Russia's initiation of an aggressive war against Ukraine and its citizens. While Norway has typically opted for more passive roles in international conflicts, it could be a fatal mistake for the enemies of Norwegian forces to conflate this with feebleness. As exemplified by its comprehensive approach to security, Norway is ready, and able, to quickly respond to threats.

While Norway had maintained a civil relationship with its controversial neighbour, largely over their shared economic interests (i.e., natural gas, oil, and fishing), Norway's prioritization of human rights and peacemaking, as a security strategy, has allowed its allies premiere access to surveil Russia. While Norway is not a member of the EU, its membership in NATO has created a close allyship with other countries in the Arctic. Outside of the socio-political ties, Norway relies on its NATO allies for military support. Norway's security and defence policies rely on allied military support. Thus, in times of conflict, such as the current crisis in Ukraine, Norway has continued to exemplify its role as a silent force of support.

## Conclusion

To overlook Norway's importance to the Arctic region is to overlook a quiet powerhouse. It has proven itself to be a formidable actor in the Arctic 8. Historically, Norway has worked to strengthen its domestic operations while offering its support to fellow Arctic countries. Norway's unique location has offered premier access for its allies to its coastal waters and Russia, which has

---

– making sense of risk in protective security management – a study from Norway"; Magnus Ranstorp, "'Lone Wolf Terrorism'. The Case of Anders Breivik," *Sicherheit und Frieden (S+ F)/Security and Peace*, 2013, 87–92; William M. Lafferty and Oddbjorn Knutsen, "Leftist and Rightist Ideology in a Social Democratic State: An Analysis of Norway in the Midst of the Conservative Resurgence," *British Journal of Political Science* 14, no. 3 (1984): 345–367, issn: 00071234, 14692112, http://www.jstor.org/stable/193957.

[81] Stian Bromark, *Massacre in Norway: The 2011 terror attacks on Oslo and the Utya Youth Camp.* (Potomac Books, an imprint of the University of Nebraska Press, 2014), isbn: 9781612346694.

developed exponentially into a threat to its NATO allies and EU (informal) partners.

Over time, Norway has expanded its territorial waters, allowing for additional strategic positionings and increased economic opportunities. Access to the Barents and Norwegian Seas and the Arctic Ocean has allowed Norway to develop a flourishing maritime force. However, despite its heavy emphasis on naval and domestic defence forces (including a military conscription system), Norway heavily relies on its NATO and international allies for support and military power. While a founding member of NATO, Norway has never joined the EU, despite multiple attempts, it is influenced by and influences EU policy and practice. Additionally, since its foundation, it has been a member of the Arctic Council and currently holds the chairship position; this position will enable Norway to advance socio-political matters important to the nation and its fellow Arctic countries. In addition to its political strength, Norway has developed a booming economic system thanks to its fisheries and the later discovery of offshore natural oil and gas. Norway's oil and gas industry has become critical to countries in the EU. Domestically, Norway has one of the highest rates of public trust in government and largely relies on a decentralized system of democracy. However, the looming threat of far-right extremism (exemplified in the 2011 terror attacks), that has swept across Europe poses a domestic threat that requires continued monitoring.

In short, Norway is a country rich in resources and geopolitical importance. As a member of the Arctic region, Norway's silent strength should not be misconstrued as passivity. With the growing tensions in Russia and China, Norway offers a strategic stronghold in the Arctic region and one that will be geopolitically advantageous in the emerging conflict landscape.

## References

Aars, Jacob, and Anne Lise Fimreite. "Local government and governance in Norway: stretched accountability in network politics." *Scandinavian Political Studies* 28, no. 3 (2005): 239–256.

Appleton, Catherine. "Lone wolf terrorism in Norway." *The International Journal of Human Rights* 18, no. 2 (February 2014): 127–142. https://doi.org/10.1080/ 13642987. 2014. 889390. https://doi.org/10. 1080%2F13642987.2014.889390.

*Arriving in Norway*. https://www.ukrainianembassy.no/en/arriving-innorway. *The Loophole and the Banana Hole* [in en], May 2012. https://www.barents watch.no/ en/ articles/the-loophole-and-the-banana-hole/.

Bromark, Stian. *Massacre in Norway: the 2011 terror attacks on Oslo and the Utya Youth Camp*. Potomac Books, an imprint of the University of Nebraska Press, 2014. ISBN: 978 1

612346694. https://ezproxy.shsu.edu/login?url=https:// search.ebscohost. com/ login.aspx?direct=true&db= cat00667a&AN=sam.TSCEBC1656604&site=eds-live &scope=site.

Canova, Emilie, and Pauline Pic. *The Arctic Council in Transition: Challenges and Perspectives for the new Norwegian Chairship* [in en], June 2023. https://www.thearcticinsti tute.org/arctic-council-transition-challenges-perspectives-new-norwegian-chairship/.

Caparini, Marina, Kari Marie Kjellstad, and Trine Nikolaisen. *A Stocktaking of Norwegian Engagement in Security Sector Reform* [in en]. Technical report 11. Norwegian Institute of International Affairs: Department of Security and Conflict Management, 2011. https://www.files.ethz.ch/isn/133045/SIP11-Caparini%20et%20al-NUPI%20 Report.pdf.

Christensen, Tom, Anne Lise Fimreite, and Per Lægreid. "Crisis Management–The Case of Internal Security in Norway," 2007.

Claes, Dag Harald, and Arild Moe. "Arctic petroleum resources in a regional and global perspective." In *Geopolitics and security in the Arctic: regional dynamics in a global world*, edited by Kristine Offerdal and Rolf Tamnes, 112–135. Routledge global security studies. Abingdon, Oxon; New York, NY: Routledge, 2014. ISBN: 978-0-415-73445-5.

Dagre, Tor. "The History of Norway." *Millenium*, 1999.

Elgenius, Gabriella, and Jens Rydgren. "Frames of nostalgia and belonging: the resurgence of ethnonationalism in Sweden." Publisher: Routledge _eprint: https://doi.org/10.1080/14616696.2018.1494297, *European Societies* 21, no. 4 (2019): 583–602. https://doi.org/10.1080/14616696.2018.1494297. https://doi.org/10. 1080/14616696.2018.1494297.

Ezzati, Rojan Tordhol, and Marta Bivand Erdal. "Do we have to agree? Accommodating unity in diversity in post-terror Norway." *Ethnicities* 18, no. 3 (2018): 363–384.

Fangen, Katrine, and Yngve Carlsson. "Right-wing extremism in Norway: Prevention and intervention." In *Right-wing extremism in Europe: country analyses, counterstrategies and labor-market oriented exit strategies*, edited by Ralf Melzer, Sebastian Serafin, and Friedrich-Ebert-Stiftung, 327–357. Berlin: Friedrich-Ebert-Stiftung, Forum Berlin, 2013. ISBN: 978-3-86498-522-5. https://ub01.uni-tuebingen. de/xmlui/bitstream/handle/ 109 0 0/64182/10031.pdf?sequence=1&isAllowed=y.

*Norwegian Coast Guard* [in en], 2022. https://www.forsvaret.no/ omforsvaret/ organisasjon/sjoforsvaret/kystvakten.

Fouche, Gwladys. "Norway plans $7 bln in aid to Ukraine over five years" [in en]. *Reuters*, February 2023. https://www.reuters.com/world/europe/norway-plans-7-billion-aidukraine-over-five-years-2023-02-06/. *The Norwegian Government's Arctic Policy* [in en-GB]. Publisher: regjeringen.no, January 2021. https: //www.regjeringen. no/ en/ dokumenter/arctic_policy/id2830120/.

Græger, Nina. "Norway in a Transatlantic Tight Spot Between US and European Security Strategies?" *Security dialogue* 36, no. 3 (2005): 412–416.

Heyerdahl, Anne. "From prescriptive rules to responsible organisations – making sense of risk in protective security management – a study from Norway." *European Security* 32, no. 1 (May 2022): 147–169. https://doi.org/10.1080/09662839.2022.2070006. https://doi.org/10.1080%2F09662839.2022. 2070006.

Hoel, Alf Håkon. "The legal-political regime in the Arctic." In *Geopolitics and security in the*

*Arctic: regional dynamics in a global world*, edited by Kristine Offerdal and Rolf Tamnes, 49–72. Routledge global security studies. Abingdon, Oxon; New York, NY: Routledge, 2014. isbn: 978-0-415-73445-5.

Holm, Nikolai George Lewis, Linn-Marie Lillehaug Pedersen, and Elisabeth Pettersen. "Youth, gender, and perceptions of security in Norway." *International Journal of Adolescence and Youth* 25, no. 1 (2020): 421–434. https://doi.org/10.1080/ 02673843.2019.1669060. eprint: https://doi.org/10.1080/ 02673843.2019.1669060. https://doi.org/10.1080/02673843.2019.1669060.

Jensen, Kurt B., and Royal Danish Navy. "The Baltic Sea in the Post — Cold War World." *Naval War College Review* 46, no. 4 (1993): 29–41. ISSN: 00281484, 24757047. http://www.jstor.org/stable/44642522.

Jensen, Leif Christian. International relations in the Arctic: Norway and the struggle for power in the New North. Bloomsbury Publishing, 2015.

Konyshev, Valery, and Aleksandr Sergunin. "The Arctic at the crossroads of geopolitical interests." *Russian Politics & Law* 50, no. 2 (2012): 34–54.

Lægreid, Per, and Synnøve Serigstad. "Framing the field of homeland security: The case of Norway." *Journal of management studies* 43, no. 6 (2006): 1395–1413.

Lafferty, William M., and Oddbjørn Knutsen. "Leftist and Rightist Ideology in a Social Democratic State: An Analysis of Norway in the Midst of the Conservative Resurgence." *British Journal of Political Science* 14, no. 3 (1984): 345–367. ISSN: 00071234, 14692112. http://www.jstor.org/stable/193957.

Melas, Matthaios. "The Arctic as a geopolitical bond among the European Union, Norway & Russia." *The Arctic yearbook* 20 (2016): 326–337.

Morgunova, Maria. "Why is exploitation of Arctic offshore oil and natural gas resources ongoing? A multilevel perspective on the cases of Norway and Russia." *The Polar Journal* 10, no. 1 (January 2020): 64–81. https://doi.org/10.1080/ 2154896x.2020. 1757823. https://doi.org/10.1080%2F2154896x. 2020.1757823.

Mouritzen, Hans. "The Nordic–Baltic Area: Divisive Geopolitics at Work." *Cambridge Review of International Affairs* 19, no. 3 (September 2006): 495–511. https://doi.org/10.1080/09557570600869556. https://doi.org/10.1080%2F09557570600869556.

*National Military service in Norway* [in en], March 2023. https://www. norway.no/en/latvia/ norway-latvia/news-events/national-military-service-in-norway/.

*Armed Forces in numbers* [in en], August 2021. https://www.forsvaret.no/ en/about-us/armed-forces-in-numbers.

Østerud, Øyvind. "Introduction: The peculiarities of Norway." *West European Politics* 28, no. 4 (September 2005): 705–720. https://doi.org/10.1080/01402380500216591. https://doi.org/10.1080% 2F01402380500216591.

Østerud, Øyvind, and Per Selle. "Power and Democracy in Norway: The Transformation of Norwegian Politics 1." *Scandinavian political studies* 29, no. 1 (2006): 25–46.

Østhagen, Andreas. "Managing Conflict at Sea: The Case of Norway and Russia in the Svalbard Zone." *Arctic Review on Law and Politics* 9, no. 1 (2018): 100. https://doi.org/10.23865/arctic.v9.1084. https://doi.org/10.23865%2Farctic.v9.1084.

. "Norway's Arctic policy: still high North, low tension?" [In en]. *The Polar Journal* 11, no. 1 (January 2021): 75–94. ISSN: 2154-896X, 2154-8978. https://doi.org/10.

1080/2154896X.2021.1911043.
https://www.tandfonline.com/doi/full/10.1080/2154896X.2021. 1911043.

Østhagen, Andreas, Otto Svendsen, and Max Bergmann. *Arctic Geopolitics: The Svalbard Archipelago* [in en]. Technical report. Center for Strategic and International Studies, September 2023. https://www.csis.org/analysis/arctic-geopolitics-svalbard-archipelago.

Ranstorp, Magnus. "'Lone Wolf Terrorism'. The Case of Anders Breivik." *Sicherheit und Frieden (S+ F)/ Security and Peace*, 2013, 87–92.

Räsänen, Tuomas, and Simo Laakkonen. "Cold War and the Environment: The Role of Finland in International Environmental Politics in the Baltic Sea Region." *AMBIO: A Journal of the Human Environment* 36, no. 2 (April 2007): 229–236. https://doi.org/10.1579/0044-7447(2007)36 [229: cwatet] 2. 0.co;2. https://doi.org/10.1579%2F0044-7447%282007%2936%5B229%3Acwatet%5D2.0.co%3B2.

Rieker, Pernille. "Norway and the ESDP: Explaining Norwegian Participation in the EU's Security Policy." *European Security* 15, no. 3 (September 2006): 281–298. https://doi.org/10.1080/09662830601097413. https://doi.org/10.1080%2F09662830601097413.

Rottem, Svein Vigeland. "The Political Architecture of Security in the Arctic–the Case of Norway." *Arctic Review on Law and Politics* 4, no. 2 (2013): 234–254.

Saxi, Håkon Lunde. "Alignment but not Alliance." *Arctic Review on Law and Politics* 13 (2022): 53–71.

*Official Statistics* [in en]. https://www.ssb.no/en/economic-and-financialdata-for-norway.

Stein, Jonas, Marcus Buck, and Hilde Bjørnå. "The centre–periphery dimension and trust in politicians: the case of Norway" [in en]. *Territory, Politics, Governance* 9, no. 1 (January 2021): 37–55. ISSN: 21622671, 2162-268X. https://doi.org/10.1080/ 21622671. 2019.1624191. https://www.tandfonline.com/doi/full/10.1080/21622671.2019.1624191.

Tamnes, Rolf, and Kristine Offerdal. Geopolitics and security in the Arctic: Regional dynamics in a global world [in en]. 2014. ISBN: 9781315813455.

Tunsjø, Øystein. "Geopolitical shifts, great power relations and Norway's foreign policy." *Cooperation and Conflict* 46, no. 1 (March 2011): 60–77. https://doi.org/10.1177/ 0010836710396784. https: //doi.org/10.1177%2F0010836710396784.

Wegge, Njord, and Sigbjørn Halsne. "Introduction: Security and Military Power in the Arctic." *Artic review on law and politics* 13 (2022): 32–33.

Wenger, Michael. *Norway's strategy for the Arctic Council – and then what?* [In en-US], March 2023. https://polarjournal.ch/en/2023/03/30/norways-strategy-for-thearctic-council-and-then-what/.

Wilhelmsen, Julie, and Kristian Lundby Gjerde. "Norway and Russia in the Arctic: New Cold War Contamination?" *Arctic Review on Law and Politics* 9 (2018): pp. 382–407. ISSN: 18916252, 23874562. https://www.jstor.org/stable/48710573.

# CHAPTER 7

# ICELAND'S ARCTIC POLICIES

## Jared R. Dmello[1] and Bianca Acosta[2]

Iceland is a diverse country with a celebrated history. First settled by immigrants of Norwegian and Celtic descent in the late 9th and 10th centuries and the only Arctic State to not have an indigenous population,[3] Iceland is home to the world's oldest and continuously functioning legislative assembly, known as the Althingi, which was established in 930 A.D.[4] Benefiting from a robust tourism industry and recent construction growth, Iceland's economic position is on an upward trajectory. Similarly, the population is experiencing a slight growth as of 2023 and consists of highly diverse in terms of religion. Iceland currently has a frozen accession application to the European Union but is an active member of the Schengen Area.

Iceland's northernmost community, Grimsey Island, lays within the Arctic Circle, located approximately 40 kilometres off its northern coast, though most of the territory is in the sub-Arctic.[5] A nation committed to international sustainable goals, Iceland maintains the highest percentage of renewable energy across countries, averaging approximately 85% of the nation's energy coming from domestic renewable sources and almost 90% of Icelandic homes being heated by geothermal water sources.[6] While some would argue that Iceland's geopolitical importance has dramatically waned since the end of the Cold War, new geo-strategic interests in the Arctic space, such as the many discussed elsewhere in this volume, actually enhance the country's position. In fact, its recognition as a coastal state has re-imagined Iceland's potential as a geopolitical stakeholder, resulting in widespread transitions to police and practice to embrace the country's status as an "Arctic Coastal State" from both political elite, such as the Icelandic Foreign Ministry and Parliament, as well as in the popular discourse of everyday Icelandic

---

[1] Senior Lecturer of Criminology, University of Adelaide, jared.dmello@adelaide.edu.au, ORCID: https://orcid.org/0000-0001-8805-1061.
[2] Student Researcher, Sam Houston State University
[3] "Iceland." Arctic Council. https://arctic-council.org/about/states/iceland/
[4] "Iceland." Central Intelligence Agency. https://www.cia.gov/the-world-factbook/countries/iceland/.
[5] Arctic Council, n.d.
[6] Ibid.

citizens.[7] This chapter examines Iceland's Arctic policy and its interactions in the region as a part of the geopolitical chess of international affairs.

**Map 1.** Iceland and the Arctic.[8]

**Iceland's Arctic Policy**

Pursuant to Parliamentary Resolution 24/151 which solidified country's Arctic policy, the Althingi entrusted the Icelandic government with nineteen areas for consideration and engagement within the Arctic space. Then Minister for Foreign Affairs and International Development Cooperation, Gudlaugur Thór Thórdarson, noted his earnest desire that the implementation of the new policy would "strengthen Iceland's position and participation in Arctic cooperation."[9] Each item is addressed below, with the exact language from the resolution being reproduced in bold, followed by a discussion of its importance:

---

Klaus Dodds and Valur Ingimundarson. "Territorial nationalism and Arctic geopolitics: Iceland as an Arctic coastal state." The Polar Journal 2, no. 1 (2012): 21-37.

[8] Aurora Expeditions (2022). "Where is the Arctic?". https://www.auroraexpeditions.com.au/ blog/ where-is-the-arctic/

[9] Government of Iceland, "Iceland's Policy on Matters Concerning the Arctic Region: Parliamentary Resolution 25/151" (Government of Iceland: Ministry of Foreign Affairs, October 2021), https://www.government.is/library/01-Ministries/Ministry-for-Foreign-Affairs/PDF-skjol/Arctic%20Policy_WEB.pdf, page 2.

1. **To actively participate in international cooperation on matters concerning the Arctic region, based on the values that have guided Icelandic foreign policy, including peace, democracy, human rights and equality.** This objective directly contradicts claims that Iceland's geopolitical position was diminished at the end of the Cold War,[10] because it shows the Althingi's intent to continue advancing Icelandic influence in international affairs while advocating for its priorities. This is not surprising given Iceland's priorities and accomplishments during its Chairship of the Arctic Council, during which the Arctic Human Development Report (AHDR), which sought to re-imagine and enhance the cultural, social, and economic dimensions of the Council's work, was approved as a priority project.[11]

2. **To continue to support the Arctic Council and to promote it as the most important forum for consultation and cooperation on matters concerning the region.** From a theoretical perspective, this component is important, as it indicates Iceland taking a collectivist approach to security over that of a state-centred political realist framework.[12,13] Given the key geographical role of the country as a gateway between East and West, this tenet demonstrates Iceland's commitment to considering proposals and actions from a regional perspective.

3. **To promote a peaceful resolution of disputes that may arise in the Arctic region, as well as respect for international law, including the United Nations Convention on the Law of the Sea and international human rights treaties.** Unsurprisingly, this component aligns with past policy. For example, Iceland remained neutral in World War I, following the approach taken by Denmark, which retained its rule over the area. A commitment to peace and enhanced human rights is also enshrined in other unions for which Iceland is a member, such as the United Nations, as well as other bodies, such as the European Union, to which Iceland has pending applications.

4. **To make sustainable development a guiding principle, based on the United Nations Sustainable Development Goals.** Iceland's

---

[10] Daniel Kochis and Brian Slattery, "Iceland: Outsized Importance for Transatlantic Security" (Heritage Foundation, June 2016), https://www.heritage.org/global-politics/report/iceland-outsized-importance-transatlantic-security

[11] Arctic Council, n.d.

[12] Charles A. Kupchan and Clifford A. Kupchan. "The promise of collective security." International security 20, no. 1 (1995): 52-61.

[13] J. J. Mearsheimer (2007). Structural realism. International relations theories: Discipline and diversity, 83, 77-94.

commitment to implementing the UN's SDGs extends far beyond its Arctic policy. The country has continuously engaged in practices to enhance its sustainability. As previously mentioned, Iceland is already a global leader in renewable energy with the vast majority of homes powered by geothermal water sources. Knox-Hayes and colleagues found that Iceland's commitment to sustainability is tied to institutional structures and pro-sustainability values that manifest throughout the various echelons of the country.[14]

5.  **To focus on countering climate change and responding to its negative effects in the Arctic region.** Earlier chapters in this volume have extensively discussed the disastrous impact of climate change on the Arctic region, noting the rapid acceleration of temperature increase occurring in the region vis-à-vis other geographic locations. Research has shown that climate change results in negative change in the economy,[15,16] tourism,[17,18] and security.[19] Thus, it's not surprising that Iceland, like other countries, is seeking to prioritise efforts to slow climate change.

6.  **To put environmental protection first, including the protection of the biota and biodiversity of the Arctic region.** Research has found Iceland to be home to a vast array of flora and fauna;[20] connecting with the previous tenet and the country's promotion of sustainability, it is natural to also priories the importance of protecting the country's biodiversity. During its previous Chairship of the Arctic Council, Iceland emphasised a focus on "funding activities aimed at preventing and mitigating pollution in the Arctic, and develop a set of guidelines for the Instrument in close cooperation with the Nordic Environment

---

[14] Janelle Knox-Hayes, Shekhar Chandra, and Jungwoo Chun. "The role of values in shaping sustainable development perspectives and outcomes: A case study of Iceland." Sustainable Development 29, no. 2 (2021): 363-377.

[15] R. S. Tol. (2018). The economic impacts of climate change. Review of environmental economics and policy.

[16] Olivier Deschênes, and Michael Greenstone. "The economic impacts of climate change: evidence from agricultural output and random fluctuations in weather." American economic review 97, no. 1 (2007): 354-385.

[17] D. Scott, Gössling, S., & Hall, C. M. (2012). International tourism and climate change. Wiley Interdisciplinary Reviews: Climate Change, 3(3), 213-232.

[18] L. Hein, Metzger, M. J., & Moreno, A. (2009). Potential impacts of climate change on tourism; a case study for Spain. Current Opinion in Environmental Sustainability, 1(2), 170-178.

[19] Andrew Silke, and John Morrison. "Gathering storm: An introduction to the special issue on climate change and terrorism." Terrorism and Political Violence 34, no. 5 (2022): 883-893.

[20] K. Meißner, Brix, S., Halanych, K. M., & Jażdżewska, A. M. (2018). Preface—biodiversity of Icelandic waters. Marine Biodiversity, 48, 715-718.

Finance Corporation (NEFCO) and the Arctic Council's Arctic Contaminants Action Program (ACAP) Working Group."[21]

7. **To safeguard health of the marine environment, including taking preventive action against the threats posed by ocean acidification and all kinds of ocean pollution.** This tenet also aligns with the broader themes of sustainability and planetary healthy. For example, Pérez and colleagues found that warming contributes up to 50% of increases in acidification,[22] demonstrating the interconnectedness of these various tenets of Iceland's Arctic policy.

8. **To focus on reducing the use of fossil fuels in the Arctic region, including by ceasing the use of heavy fuel oil in shipping, improving access to renewable energy sources and supporting measures that ensure an energy transition.** This aligns with Icelandic policy beyond the Arctic and the country's commitment to reduce greenhouse gas emissions by a "significant amount in the following five major sectors by 2030: energy production and small industry (to achieve 67% GHG emission reduction), waste management (to achieve 66% GHG emission reduction), ships and ports (to achieve 42% GHG emission reduction), land transport (to achieve 21% GHG emission reduction), and agriculture (to achieve 5 % GHG emission reduction)."[23] As mentioned above, this is not a new initiative for Iceland, given its massive successes in the space of innovating sustainable energy.

9. **To look to the welfare of the inhabitants of the Arctic region, including their opportunities to earn a living and their access to digital communications, education and health care services, to support the rights of Indigenous Peoples and equality for all, as well as efforts to protect the cultural heritage and languages of the Arctic peoples.** Given Iceland's history of imperial rule and documented lack of indigenous populations within its own borders,[24] this speaks to the country's broader commitment for a holistic approach to the Arctic as a region. Yet, this tenet creates a stark contrast to

---

[21] Arctic Council, n.d.

[22] F. F. Pérez, Olafsson, J., Ólafsdóttir, S. R., Fontela, M., & Takahashi, T. (2021). Contrasting drivers and trends of ocean acidification in the subarctic Atlantic. Scientific Reports, 11(1), 13991.

[23] A. A. Alola, & Adebayo, T. S. (2023). Analysing the waste management, industrial and agriculture greenhouse gas emissions of biomass, fossil fuel, and metallic ores utilization in Iceland. Science of The Total Environment, 887, 1-11, p. 2.

[24] Arctic Council, n.d.

domestic affairs, where Iceland has been criticised for relying on third party entities to provide welfare services for its population.[25]

10. **To utilise possible economic opportunities in the Arctic region with an eye to sustainability and responsible use of resources.** This priority item is a popular trend across Arctic countries, as shown elsewhere in this book. Iceland is engaging in the same decision-making calculus as the other stakeholders, acknowledging both the current and the future opportunities the Arctic region can bring. Factors such as new sea routes for trade and transportation, energy opportunities, and defence, are all key components of Iceland's consideration of future economic opportunities.

11. **To further trade and cooperation on commerce, education and services in the Arctic region, especially with Iceland's nearest neighbours in Greenland and the Faroe Islands.** Similar to the above point, active and responsible engagement in the Arctic provides Iceland the opportunity to leverage partnerships to enhance its own well-being and strategic position while contributing to broader initiatives.

12. **To work towards stronger monitoring and safer transport by sea and air, including by improved connectivity and a tighter network of satellite systems, e.g. for satellite navigation.** From a security perspective, this priority is critical and is likely deeply rooted in Iceland's historically significant geopolitical role. Given its close proximity to both the United States and Russian Federation's strategic interests, Iceland is in a position to help its allies monitor active and emerging strategic threats, particularly those that could occur in the Arctic area. Given the pivot from traditional security threats (i.e. military invasions) to a need for a more multi-faceted security approach (encompassing water, food, health, etc.), Iceland has developed robust cooperation agreements with other entities, such as the Arctic Council, the UN, and the European Union,[26] providing it with options for assistance should a future threat emerge.

13. **To increase search and rescue capabilities, as well as response to accidental pollution incidents, e.g. by establishing a regional search and rescue cluster in Iceland, and further strengthening**

---

[25] Ólafsson, Stefán. "Normative foundations of the Icelandic welfare state: On the gradual erosion of citizenship-based welfare rights." In Normative Foundations of the Welfare State, pp. 226-248. Routledge, 2007.

[26] Gustav Petursson, "Cooperation in the High North: the case of Iceland." Nordia Geographical Publications 40, no. 4 (2011): 77-86.

**international cooperation.** Another tenet of good citizenship, this priority represents Iceland's commitment to being a positive stakeholder in the region. As new avenues for exploration and trade emerge, particularly through the melting ice caps providing emergent sea lanes, the need for emergency assistance capabilities will also increase. This priority item indicates Iceland's commitment to ensuring well-being of those engaging in work within the Arctic region.

14. **To guard security interests on a civil basis, grounded in the National Security Policy, thoroughly monitor security developments in cooperation with the other Nordic nations and our NATO allies, oppose militarisation and purposefully work towards maintaining peace and stability in the area.** This priority item connects the various components of Iceland's national and international security policies. Ultimately, Iceland is indicating a commitment to peace while ensuring a civil plan is in place should hostilities occur in the region or if one country seeks to militarise the region. Given recent hostilities and aggressions in the Ukraine by the Russian Federation, countries prioritising an opposition to military engagement in the Arctic could prove to be an important investment in the future.

15. **To look positively upon the growing interest in matters concerning the Arctic region from parties outside the region, provided that they respect international law and the status of the eight Arctic States and conduct themselves in a peaceful and sustainable manner.** This represents a commitment to global stewardship that encourages responsibility usage of the Arctic space beyond just those nations that border the Arctic Circle. Note that this priority effort emphasises both *peaceful* and *sustainable*, indicating that Iceland intends to ensure that future engagement by any stakeholder must adhere to these principles.

16. **To bolster Iceland's standing and image as an Arctic State by developing local knowledge and expertise on matters concerning the Arctic, and to increase support for centres of education, science and discussion.** This tenet relates back to long-term investment in education and training. To better plan for the future, there is a need to support educational opportunities and research for sustained innovation.

17. **To support international scientific cooperation in the Arctic region and facilitate the dissemination of scientific findings, and**

to boost national research activities, including by forming an Arctic research programme. The operationalisation of this policy can be seen through the extensive research efforts already being undertaken in the Arctic space. For example, work on climate change, biodiversity, energy, and more, have all utilised Iceland as case studies and stakeholders within the country have participated as research partners and collaborators.

18. **To build upon the success of the Arctic Circle and create a future framework for it by establishing a non-profit foundation that will operate an Arctic centre in Iceland.** This penultimate priority item ensures a lasting commitment with sustaining funding mechanisms to ensure the country's ability to continue being a leader in the Arctic space.

19. **To further strengthen the position of Akureyri as the centre of Arctic matters in Iceland, including by supporting education and research bodies and knowledge centres and by strengthening local consultation and cooperation on matters concerning the Arctic region.** Finally, this priority ensures that the various stakeholders have a platform to interact and engage with one another on critical issues to ensure responsible governance and cooperation within the Arctic region.

## Relations with Other Arctic Countries

Iceland is a strong partner in the global space. It has engaged in a variety of partnerships with global entities. For example, the country is a party to all major UN human rights conventions and is often a co-sponsor for related resolutions.[27] It also has served a strategic ally for the West in past conflicts, specifically during the Cold War, with positions enabling it to serve as a balance against the then-Soviet Union.

However, Iceland also maintains active territory disputes. For example, it has long been in conflict with Denmark over the Faroe Islands' fisheries median line boundary within 200 nautical miles and with Denmark, the United Kingdom, and Ireland over the Faroe Islands continental shelf boundary outside that boundary.[28] In 2019, Iceland, Denmark, and Norway signed delimitation agreements for the continental shelf, an area known as the

---

[27] Government of Iceland. (n.d.). "Iceland and the United Nations." https://www.government.is/diplomatic-missions/permanent-mission-of-iceland-to-the-united-nations/iceland-and-the-united-nations/

[28] GlobalSecurity.org (2024). "International Disputes). https://www.globalsecurity.org/ military/ world/ war/disputes-i.htm

"Banana Hole,"[29] which was subsequently ratified by all parties halting the ongoing conflict. The resulting agreement is shown in Map 2 below.

**Map 2.** Demonstrating the 2019 Delimitation Agreements between Norway, Iceland, and Denmark.[30]

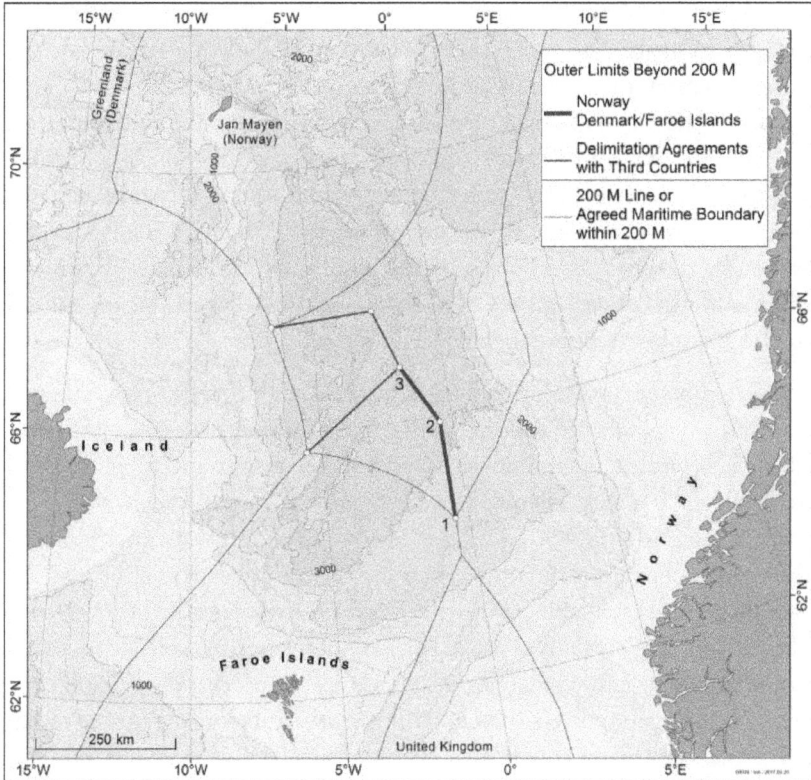

Source: *Alex Marsh (2022)*

## Future of Arctic Participation

Iceland has an extensively documented history of democratic processes, regional and international geopolitics, and commitments to sustainability and environmentalism. This background gives Iceland a wealth of experience for contributing to the broader Arctic region. Given its longstanding role as a territory ruled by foreign monarchs, Iceland has demonstrated a strong

[29] A.N. Honniball (2019). "Iceland/Norway/Denmark (The Faroe Islands): Three Maritime Delimitation Agreements Signed." De Maribus. https://demaribus.net/2019/10/31/iceland-norway-denmark-the-faroe-islands-three-maritime-delimitation-agreements-signed/
[30] Alex Marsh (2022). "More to Maritime Boundaries: The Extended Continental Shelf." Sovereign Limits. https://sovereignlimits.com/blog/more-to-maritime-boundaries-the-extended-continental-shelf

commitment to transparency, democratic faith, and ensuring all voices will be heard. This can be seen through several of the articulated priorities of Iceland's Arctic policy, such as the commitment to well-being, particularly of the Arctic's indigenous peoples. The country's pioneering efforts as a global leader in sustainable energy production and consumption also equips it to assist other stakeholders in the region to achieve their sustainable development goals. The geographic positioning of the country also equips it to serve as a monitor against potential hostilities and militarisation by a variety of actors, including historical aggressors, such as the Russian Federation, and emerging threats posed by state and non-state actors. Ingimundarson notes that "the Arctic has been projected as a symbol of Iceland's renewed geostrategic promise following the end of the Cold War and the US military withdrawal;"[31] thus, assertions of the country's weakened geostrategic position are inaccurate because they do not adequately account for the role of Iceland as a key Arctic stakeholder.

While Parliamentary Resolution 24/151 establishes a framework committing Iceland to a lot of contributions to the Arctic region based primarily on a collectivist approach that emphasises regional security and well-being, on the state-level, the country will also benefit greatly. Of note, as new sea routes emerge resulting from changing ice levels, the country is geographically positioned to benefit from those new economic revenues. Similarly, as a global leader in sustainable energy, Iceland will likely be able to leverage an exchange of energy resources as well as the knowledge to replicate its system for other benefits, either tangible (i.e., goods and resources) or intangible (i.e., defence or cooperation assistance). Chinese overtures in the Arctic sphere and Iceland's engagement with Beijing could also be indicative Iceland trying to capitalize on the increasing global visibility and economic opportunities perceived by a vast number of countries that the Arctic may hold, while working to leverage its own strategic position and enhance Reykjavík's sustainability goals.[32]

Overall, Iceland is a country filled with opportunity for the Arctic region, informed by a long and rich history. While the Althingi have passed an ambitious policy for the Arctic based on collectivist needs, Iceland also must balance its domestic priorities to ensure citizen satisfaction and trust in government. For example, while the country is a leader in sustainable energy

---

[31] Valur Ingimundarson, "Framing the national interest: the political uses of the Arctic in Iceland's foreign and domestic policies." The Polar Journal 5, no. 1 (2015): 82-100.
[32] Jesse Guite Hastings, "The rise of Asia in a changing Arctic: a view from Iceland." Polar Geography 37, no. 3 (2014): 215-233.

and prioritises environmental issues within Parliamentary Resolution 24/151, Iceland has also been severely criticised by its citizens, particularly through the art scene.[33] Likewise, the country's commitment to promoting overall well-being in the Arctic, specifically for indigenous populations, does not align with domestic policy that relies heavily on exporting welfare services to non-governmental entities.[34] As Iceland continues its engagement within the Arctic space, it will be imperative for the government to balance between collective and state priorities. Enhancing regional security bolsters Iceland's own strategic position, but it cannot come at the cost of domestic sacrifice.

## Bibliography

Alola, A. A., & Adebayo, T. S. (2023). Analysing the waste management, industrial and agriculture greenhouse gas emissions of biomass, fossil fuel, and metallic ores utilization in Iceland. *Science of The Total Environment, 887,* 1-11.

Arctic Council. (n.d.) "Iceland." https://arctic-council.org/about/states/iceland/.

Aurora Expeditions (2022). "Where is the Arctic?". https://www.aurora expeditions. com.au/blog/where-is-the-arctic/

Central Intelligence Agency. "Iceland." https://www.cia.gov/the-world-factbook/ countries/iceland/.

Deschênes, Olivier, and Michael Greenstone. "The economic impacts of climate change: evidence from agricultural output and random fluctuations in weather." *American economic review* 97, no. 1 (2007): 354-385.

Dodds, Klaus, and Valur Ingimundarson. "Territorial nationalism and Arctic geopolitics: Iceland as an Arctic coastal state." *The Polar Journal* 2, no. 1 (2012): 21-37.

GlobalSecurity.org (2024). "International Disputes). https://www.globalsecurity.org/ military/world/war/disputes-i.htm

Government of Iceland. (2021, October). "Iceland's Policy on Matters Concerning the Arctic Region: Parliamentary Resolution 25/151." https://www.government.is/ library/01-Ministries/ Ministry-for-Foreign-Affairs/PDF-skjol/Arctic %20Policy_ WEB.pdf

----- (n.d.). "Iceland and the United Nations." https://www.government.is/diplomatic-missions/permanent-mission-of-iceland-to-the-united-nations/iceland-and-the-united-nations/

Gremaud, A. S. N. (2017). Icelandic futures: Arctic dreams and geographies of crisis. Arctic environmental modernities: From the age of polar exploration to the era of the anthropocene, 197-213.

Hastings, Jesse Guite. "The rise of Asia in a changing Arctic: a view from Iceland." *Polar Geography 37,* no. 3 (2014): 215-233.

Hein, L., Metzger, M. J., & Moreno, A. (2009). Potential impacts of climate change on tourism; a case study for Spain. *Current Opinion in Environmental Sustainability, 1*(2), 170-

---

[33] A. S. N. Gremaud. (2017). Icelandic futures: Arctic dreams and geographies of crisis. Arctic environmental modernities: From the age of polar exploration to the era of the anthropocene, 197-213.
[34] Ólafsson, 2007.

178.

Honniball, A. N. (2019). "Iceland/Norway/Denmark (The Faroe Islands): Three Maritime Delimitation Agreements Signed." De Maribus. https://demaribus.net/ 2019/10/31/iceland-norway-denmark-the-faroe-islands-three-maritime-delimitation-agreements-signed/denmark-the-faroe-islands-three-maritime-delimitation-agreements-signed/

Ingimundarson, Valur. "Framing the national interest: the political uses of the Arctic in Iceland's foreign and domestic policies." *The Polar Journal 5*, no. 1 (2015): 82-100.

Knox-Hayes, Janelle, Shekhar Chandra, and Jungwoo Chun. "The role of values in shaping sustainable development perspectives and outcomes: A case study of Iceland." *Sustainable Development* 29, no. 2 (2021): 363-377.

Kochis, Daniel and Brian Slattery. (2016, June). "Iceland: Outsized Importance for Transatlantic Security," Heritage Foundation. https://www.heritage.org/global-politics/report/ iceland- outsized-importance-transatlantic-security

Kupchan, Charles A., and Clifford A. Kupchan. "The promise of collective security." *International security* 20, no. 1 (1995): 52-61.

Marsh, Alex. (2022). "More to Maritime Boundaries: The Extended Continental Shelf." Sovereign

Limits. https://sovereignlimits.com/blog/more-to-maritime-boundaries-the-extended-continen tal-shelf

Mearsheimer, J. J. (2007). Structural realism. International relations theories: Discipline and diversity, 83, 77-94.

Meißner, K., Brix, S., Halanych, K. M., & Jażdżewska, A. M. (2018). Preface—biodiversity of Icelandic waters. *Marine Biodiversity, 48*, 715-718.

Ólafsson, Stefán. "Normative foundations of the Icelandic welfare state: On the gradual erosion of citizenship-based welfare rights." In *Normative Foundations of the Welfare State*, pp. 226-248. Routledge, 2007.

Pérez, F. F., Olafsson, J., Ólafsdóttir, S. R., Fontela, M., & Takahashi, T. (2021). Contrasting drivers and trends of ocean acidification in the subarctic Atlantic. *Scientific Reports, 11*(1), 13991.

Petursson, Gustav. "Cooperation in the High North: the case of Iceland." *Nordia Geographical Publications* 40, no. 4 (2011): 77-86.

Scott, D., Gössling, S., & Hall, C. M. (2012). International tourism and climate change. *Wiley Interdisciplinary Reviews: Climate Change, 3*(3), 213-232.

Silke, Andrew, and John Morrison. "Gathering storm: An introduction to the special issue on climate change and terrorism." *Terrorism and Political Violence* 34, no. 5 (2022): 883-893.

Tol, R. S. (2018). The economic impacts of climate change. *Review of environmental economics and policy.*

# CHAPTER 8

# POLICIES OF DENMARK TOWARDS THE ARCTIC REGION

Veysel Babahanoğlu[1] and Elif Miray Yazıcı[2]

The Arctic region stands out as a region of increasing geopolitical and geostrategic importance in the international power struggle. This region attracts the attention of many countries in terms of the energy resources it harbours and the struggle for sovereignty over the new sea routes that have emerged/continue to emerge due to global warming. Denmark is one of these countries. As one of the influential actors of the Arctic because of its policies, Denmark has geopolitical importance for the region.

Denmark's Arctic policies are largely determined by its relations with other countries operating in the region. In this context, Denmark, as a member of the Arctic Council, contributes to the governance of the region in cooperation with other members. In particular, relations with Arctic countries such as Russia, the US, Canada and Norway stand out as a critical factor affecting the balances in the region. Denmark's relations with Russia play a critical role in maintaining regional stability. The United States of America (U.S.), on the other hand, is in close contact with Denmark for its interests in the Arctic region and develops various areas of cooperation. Among these areas, the military bases established in Greenland after the Second World War stand out. As a matter of fact, these bases shape Denmark's Arctic policies. Similarly, Denmark develops various relations with Canada and Norway, which are also Arctic countries, in line with common interests. The relations with these two countries cover many areas of cooperation such as management of the region, environmental protection, fisheries and energy resources. Moreover, historical and geographical affinities with Norway contribute to the evolution of bilateral relations into areas of cooperation rather than conflict.

Denmark realizes its presence in the region through Greenland, Faroe Islands and Hans Island. In addition to being the largest island in the world,

[1] Dr., Duzce University, E-mail: veyselbabahanoglu@duzce.edu.tr, Orcid: https://orcid.org/0000-0003-3734-7430
[2] Independent Researcher, E-mail: elifmirayyazici@gmail.com, ORCID: https://orcid.org/0000-0002-0348-2653.

Greenland plays an important geopolitical role in the Arctic region with its rich natural resources and strategic location. Greenland, which has been embroiled in disputes over sovereignty and ownership for many years, has a central position in Denmark's Arctic policies. Especially with the discovery of energy resources and minerals, Greenland's increasing geopolitical importance draws attention. Similarly, the Faroe Islands, which are an important part of Denmark's Arctic presence, come to the fore with economic activities such as fishing and seafood trade. Hans Island, on the other hand, stands out as a conflict area within the scope of the long-standing territorial dispute between Denmark and Canada. However, this dispute was resolved with a compromise between the parties.

Denmark shapes its Arctic policy with a sense of balance, seeking to increase areas of cooperation. Focusing on the region's rich energy resources, minerals and economic opportunities such as fisheries, Denmark also attaches importance to the protection of the environment and cultural values. This study provides an in-depth perspective on Denmark's Arctic policies, foreign relations, presence and strategies in the region.

## Denmark's Foreign Policy: Relations with Arctic Countries

Denmark's foreign policy is based on the principles of peace, democracy, human rights, security and sustainability. As a member of the European Union (EU), it contributes to EU policies and security issues, and as a member of NATO, it plays an important role in transatlantic security issues. Denmark contributes to projects on international peace, security, crisis resolution and humanitarian aid. In particular, the Danish Development Agency (Danida), which operates under the Ministry of Foreign Affairs, provides significant support to international humanitarian aid projects. Issues such as energy efficiency, climate change and environmental protection have an important place in Denmark's foreign policy. Denmark has become an important actor for the future of the region, especially with its stance and commitment to preserving the unique ecosystem of the Arctic and ensuring its environmental sustainability. It contributes to the sustainable future of the region by acting in cooperation with other Arctic actors. This attitude, which shapes Denmark's foreign policy, makes the country a respected and influential actor in the international arena.

Thanks to its strategic location between the Baltic Sea and the North Sea, a strong economy, and political stability, Denmark emerges as a prominent player in international relations. Despite becoming an EU member in 1973,

Denmark maintains the privilege of shaping its own policies on matters like defense, the justice system, and currency. However, it generally aligns itself with the EU's strategies and policies in the realms of politics and economics. Following the 2022 referendum, in which Denmark decided to join the EU's defense policy, its relations with the EU have further strengthened.[3] The decision is believed to be influenced by the Russia-Ukraine War. As one of the founding members of NATO, Denmark actively contributes to the alliance's defense and security policies. Simultaneously, as a member of the United Nations (UN), it plays a significant role in promoting international peace, human rights, humanitarian aid, and sustainable development. In this context, Denmark's key components of foreign policy are its membership in the EU, NATO, and the UN.

Denmark aims to take an active role in Europe by supporting the EU while also seeking to establish a close relationship with the United States, ensuring U.S. support against potential security threats. However, its support for U.S. security policies, as witnessed in cases like Afghanistan and the Iraq War, is in contrast to the peaceful cooperation policies adopted by EU members. Denmark endeavours to maintain this balance between the EU and the U.S. while striving to pursue an effective security policy.[4] Therefore, Denmark's foreign policy is shaped with the aim of safeguarding its national interests and establishing a strong presence on the international stage. Factors such as the increasing military influence of Russia and the growing importance of the Arctic region in the international arena significantly impact Denmark's security policies. Furthermore, the country places a strong emphasis on trade agreements with global markets to foster economic growth and enhance societal well-being. At the heart of these endeavours, Denmark embraces a foreign policy built on universal values encompassing international peace and security, human rights, freedom, democracy, justice, equality, development, climate, and the environment. It actively engages in international organizations to support the diplomatic and cooperative resolution of global issues based on these values.

Denmark's role in the Arctic region is primarily shaped through Greenland. Greenland contributes to regional cooperation as a member of the Arctic Council. Particularly, Greenland holds strategic significance in areas such as

---

[3] John Henley, "Denmark votes overwhelmingly to join EU's common defence policy", The Guardian, 2022, https://www.theguardian.com/world/2022/jun/01/denmark-votes-on-joining-eus-common-defence-policy, (Access Date: 18.10.2023).
[4] Anders Wivel, "Between Paradise and Power: Denmark's Transatlantic Dilemma", Security Dialogue, 36/3 (2005), pp. 419-420.

the extraction of natural resources, the security of sea routes, and environmental protection. Consequently, Denmark's relations with major Arctic actors, including Russia, the United States, Canada, and Norway, are vital for regional security and cooperation. For instance, access to energy resources is a critical issue that has a significant impact on the geopolitics of the Arctic region.

## Denmark's Relations with Russia in the Arctic Region

One of the actors Denmark maintains close relations within the Arctic region is Russia, which boasts the longest coastline among the countries bordering the Arctic Ocean. Approximately 64% of Russia's territory is situated in the Arctic. This rate corresponds to 50% of all the northern regions of other Arctic countries, from which 85% of Russia's natural resources are extracted.[5] After the dissolution of the USSR, the Arctic region took a back seat as the newly formed Russian Federation focused on re-establishing its relations with the West and former Soviet Bloc nations. However, since the late 1990s, particularly under the leadership of Vladimir Putin, the Arctic region has gained increased strategic importance.[6] In 1997, as a member of the Arctic Council established in 1996 to address the region's interests and challenges, Russia signed the United Nations Convention on the Law of the Sea (UNCLOS).

Denmark and Russia share similar goals concerning Arctic conservation, climate change mitigation, ecosystem sustainability, scientific research, and regional development. One significant point of dispute among Russia, Denmark, and Canada revolves around the sovereignty claims over the strategically vital Lomonosov Ridge, which holds substantial reserves of energy resources, minerals, and seafood. The Lomonosov Ridge, which demarcates the Arctic Ocean into Eurasia and Amerasia Basin, extends from Russia's New Siberian Islands to Greenland and Canada's Ellesmere Islands.[7] Russia argues that the Lomonosov Ridge and the Alpha-Mendeleyev Ridge are geologically continental extensions of Siberia. Moreover, it claims that the said area, including the Barents Sea, the Bering Sea and the Sea of Okhotsk,

---

[5] K. Nadezhda Kharlampyeva, "The Transnational Arctic and Russia", Energy Security and Geopolitics in the Arctic Challenges and Opportunities in the 21st Century, Ed. Hooman Peimani, World Scientific Publishing Co. Pte. Ltd., 2013, p. 96.

[6] Roderick Kefferpütz, "On Thin Ice? (Mis)Interpreting Russian Policy in the High North", CEPS Policy Brief No. 205, 2010, p. 3.

[7] Mel Weber, "Defining the Outer Limits of the Continental Shelf across the Arctic Basin: The Russian Submission, States' Rights, Boundary Delimitation and Arctic Regional Cooperation", The International Journal of Marine and Coastal Law 24/4 (2009), p. 658.

is within its jurisdiction. Therefore, in 2001, it was the first state to apply to the Commission on the Limits of the Continental Shelf (CLCS) for the extension of its continental shelf.[8] The Commission rejected Russia's application citing insufficient scientific evidence. Russia's continental shelf claims also faced opposition from the United States, Canada, and Denmark. In response, Russia shifted its focus towards data collection efforts in the region and organized an expedition named "Arctica 2007" in 2007. During this expedition, two submarines descended to depths of over 4200 meters and placed a Russian flag made of titanium on the seabed.[9]

Russia's efforts to establish sovereignty over the region have spurred other countries into action. In response to this, Denmark has also launched studies to demonstrate that the Lomonosov Ridge is an extension of Greenland, rather than Russia.[10] As a result of these efforts, Denmark also presented its extended continental shelf claims to the commission in 2014. Russia, seeking to bolster its claims, has increased its military presence in the region. Meanwhile, Denmark closely monitors these developments to safeguard its national interests and security. Denmark's NATO membership prominently enhances its position in terms of regional security and defence. Particularly, Russia's military operations in Ukraine in 2022 have solidified the belief that the post-Cold War era of low tension and cooperation has come to an end. This significant development has also influenced Denmark's stance. Denmark unequivocally condemned Russia's actions in Ukraine and made substantial changes in its security and energy policies. Within this context, Denmark has expressed its commitment to adopt more aligned policies with NATO and the EU in the realm of collective security and defence, as well as reducing its reliance on Russian energy sources.[11] Russia's escalating military presence in the Arctic has the potential to generate future tensions between NATO and Russia. In response, Denmark is in the process of developing a new security strategy and fostering cooperation to safeguard its interests in the Arctic region.

Arctic relations between Denmark and Russia exhibit a complex interplay of both cooperation and competition. While strategic interests and mutual

---

[8] Betsy Baker, "Law, Science, and the Continental Shelf: The Russian Federation and the Promise of Arctic Cooperation", American University International Law Review, 25/2 (2010), p. 258.

[9] Kefferpütz, "On Thin Ice?", p. 4

[10] Vsevolod Gunitskiy, "On Thin Ice: Water Rights And Resource Disputes In The Arctic Ocean", Journal of International Affairs, 61/2 (2008), p. 266.

[11] Reuters, "Denmark to Boost Defence Spending and Phase out Russian Gas", https://www.reuters.com/ world/europe/denmark-vote-joining-eus-defence-policy-this-year-danish-media-2022-03-06/, 2022, (Access Date: 19.10.2023).

claims can lead to disagreements between the two nations, both countries must acknowledge the imperative of cooperation for regional stability and security. Within this context, relations should be guided by diplomatic mechanisms and international law.

## Denmark's Relations with the U.S. in the Arctic Region

In 1867, the United States acquired the territory of Alaska, which has a coastline along the Arctic Ocean, from the Russian Empire for $7,200,000 gaining direct access to the Arctic region.[12] Alaska's geopolitical position offers the U.S. the opportunity to protect and develop its military, economic, and diplomatic interests in the region. However, for a considerable period, the Arctic region failed to gain a prominent place in U.S. domestic and foreign policy. This changed in 2007 when Russia planted its flag in the Arctic waters and criticized the U.S. for lagging behind Russia in the Arctic race.[13] These developments have prompted the U.S. to pay closer attention to its activities in the Arctic region and to play an active role in the area.

The first official document in which the U.S. defined itself as an Arctic State and laid out its policies in the Arctic region was National Security Presidential Directive 66 (NSPD-66), issued by the George W. Bush administration in 2009.[14] In 2015, during the Obama administration, a call for international cooperation to combat climate change led to the organization of the "Global Leadership in the Arctic Cooperation, Innovation, Engagement, and Resilience Conference (GLACIER)". However, Russia and China did not sign the GLACIER declaration.[15] Donald Trump, elected in 2016, took a negative stance on climate change. The May 2019 Arctic Council meeting concluded without a joint declaration as the U.S. delegation, for the first time, rejected the concept of climate change.[16] However, the Arctic Strategy published by the U.S. Department of Defense in 2019 points to the growing presence of China and Russia in the Arctic region as a factor threatening U.S. global power. Therefore, the U.S. aims to strengthen its military presence in the region, increase cooperation with regional countries and seize economic

---

[12] David Hunter Miller, "Political Rights in the Arctic", Foreign Affairs, 4/1 (1925), p. 58.

[13] Lassi Heininen, Arctic Strategies and Policies: Inventory and Comparative Study, Akureyri: The Northern Research Forum & The University of Lapland, 2012, p. 53.

[14] The White House, "NSPD-66/HSPD-25", https://irp.fas.org/offdocs/nspd/nspd-66.htm, 2009, (Access Date: 19.10.2023).

[15] Heather A. Conley, and Matthew Melino, "The İmplications Of US Policy Stagnation Toward The Arctic Region", Center For Strategic And International Studies (CSIS), 2019, p. 3.

[16] Michael Paul, "Polar power USA: full steam ahead into the Arctic", Stiftung Wissenschaft und Politik (SWP), German Institute for International and Security Affairs, 42 (2019), p. 2.

opportunities in the Arctic.

Greenland holds significant strategic importance for the United States. As an autonomous territory under Denmark, it occupies a crucial role in U.S. military, national security, and economic interests due to its unique location between the North Atlantic and the Arctic Ocean, along with its rich natural resources. The centrepiece of the U.S. military presence in Greenland is the Thule Air Base, originally constructed during World War II to safeguard Denmark from potential German threats. This airbase not only enhances the U.S. footprint in the Arctic region but also serves as a deterrent against major global players such as Russia and China. Notably, in 1946, then-President Harry Truman even proposed the purchase of Greenland from Denmark for a sum of 100 million dollars.[17] 73 years later, in 2019, Donald Trump similarly announced that he wanted to buy Greenland from Denmark.[18] All of this demonstrates how important Greenland is for the US. While Russia poses military threats in the Arctic, China seeks to influence the region through economic aid and projects. The U.S. aims to keep Greenland in close proximity as a response to its biggest global competitors. Therefore, it seeks to collaborate with Denmark to intervene in China's projects in Greenland.[19] In this context, the U.S. is seeking to uphold its interests in the Arctic region through its close relationship with Denmark. Denmark, on the other hand, is concerned about ensuring U.S. support against potential threats amid the competition among powerful actors in the region. This situation underscores the mutual interests of both countries.

As major coastal states in the Arctic, Denmark and the U.S. have significant interests in the region, including its natural resources, maritime trade routes, and security. Both countries are founding members of the Arctic Council, established to address critical regional issues. The strategic position of Greenland and the U.S.'s Arctic interests have further strengthened the relationship between these two nations. This close collaboration between Denmark and the U.S. is not only vital for the future of the Arctic region but also for the broader balance of international relations.

The geopolitical dynamics of the Arctic region are highly intricate and

---

[17] Kristian H. Nielsen, "Transforming Greenland: Imperial formations in the cold war", New Global Studies, 7/2 (2013), p. 133.

[18] Martin Pengelly, "Trump confirms he is considering attempt to buy Greenland", The Guardian, https://www.theguardian.com/world/2019/aug/18/trump-considering-buying-greenland, 2019, (Access Date: 19.10.2023).

[19] Drew Hinshaw and Jeremy Page, "How the Pentagon Countered China's Designs on Greenland", Wall Street Journal, https://www.wsj.com/articles/how-the-pentagon-countered-chinas-designs-on-greenland-11549812296, 2019, (Access Date: 24.10.2023).

constantly evolving. The increasing interest of major players like Russia and China in the Arctic has the potential to intensify regional competition. Therefore, Denmark and the United States are continuing their cooperative policies in the region, working within the framework of international law to uphold Arctic stability.

## Denmark's Relations with Canada in the Arctic Region

Canada has the second-largest Arctic coastline after Russia. Throughout its history, Canada has laid claim to sovereignty over Arctic lands and waters and has consistently asserted these rights.[20] Canada acknowledges the Arctic as an integral component of its territorial integrity. In other words, Canada sees the Arctic not only as a geographical location but also as part of its national territorial integrity. This underscores Canada's rights and claims to sovereignty in the Arctic, emphasizing the significance of these regions to its national identity and security. Canada's dedication to the Arctic reflects the strategic and national importance of this geographic area.

Canada maintains a relationship with its close neighbour Denmark in the Arctic that encompasses both competition and cooperation. The major point of contention between the two countries revolves around the sovereignty rights to Hans Island. This island is situated between Canada's Ellesmere Island and Denmark's Greenland territory. The Hans Island dispute is a diplomatic tension marked by both nations responding with symbolic gestures, such as leaving their flags and bottles of liquor on the island. This symbolic conflict has humorously been dubbed the "Canada-Denmark Whiskey Wars" in the media. The long-standing Hans Island dispute between Canada and Denmark was resolved through a diplomatic agreement in 2022.[21] This agreement is expected to further strengthen relations between the two countries. Currently, Canada and Denmark cooperate in areas such as climate change, protection of indigenous communities and ecosystems, scientific research, and sustainable development within the framework of the 1996 Ottawa and 2008 Ilulissat Declarations to protect their common interests in the Arctic and secure the future of the region.[22]

In addition, Canada and Denmark, as two neighbouring countries with

---

[20] Matthew Carnaghan and Allison Goody, Canadian Arctic Sovereignty, Ottawa: Parliamentary Information and Research Service, 2006, p. 7.
[21] Peter Beaumont, "Canada and Denmark End Decades-long Dispute Over Barren Rock in Arctic", The Guardian, https://www.theguardian.com/world/2022/jun/14/canada-denmark-end-decades-long-dispute-barren-rock-arctic-hans-island, 2022, (Access Date: 20.10.2023).
[22] Embassy of Denmark in Canada, "The Arctic", https://canada.um.dk/en/the-arctic, 2023, (Access Date: 20.10.2023).

common interests in the Arctic, are likely to cooperate more in the field of security and defence in the face of Russia's increasing military presence in the region and the competitive environment involving other actors. Indeed, in 2022, Canada and Denmark issued a joint declaration stating that the relations between the two countries will deepen, and they will cooperate in many areas, including the Arctic region.[23]

## Denmark's Relations with Norway in the Arctic Region

Norway holds a significant position in terms of energy resources due to its oil and natural gas reserves in the North Sea. These energy resources have established Norway as a major natural gas exporter. Additionally, fishing, mining, and maritime transportation are also vital sources of income for the Norwegian economy. Therefore, the abundant resources and opportunities offered by the Arctic region are crucial for Norway's economic growth.

During the Cold War, Norway was the only NATO country that shared a land border with the USSR. This formed the basis of Norway's Northern policy.[24] In this context, Norway adopts a balanced and peaceful foreign policy while increasing its defence capacity to protect its national security and regional stability. Within the framework of this foreign policy, the end of the Barents Sea dispute with Russia in 2010, which had occasionally led to diplomatic tensions, is considered an important step in terms of regional stability and cooperation.[25]

Norway is a country that actively supports regional cooperation and maintains close relations with other countries in the area, Denmark being one of them. Denmark and Norway share deep-rooted historical and cultural ties and are both founding members of the Nordic Council and the Arctic Council. Their common objective is to resolve disputes in the Arctic region through diplomatic means, with the goal of ensuring security and stability in the area. Although a dispute over the sovereignty of the Banana Hole area in the Norwegian Sea arose among Norway, Denmark, and Iceland, the parties reached an agreement on the delimitation of the continental shelf in 2006

---

[23] Government of Canada, "Canada-Kingdom of Denmark joint statement on bilateral cooperation", https://www.canada.ca/en/global-affairs/news/2022/06/canada-kingdom-of-denmark-joint-statement-on-bilateral-cooperation.html, 2022a, (Access Date: 20.10.2023).

[24] Andreas Østhagen, "Norway's Arctic policy: still high North, low tension?", The Polar Journal, 11/1 (2021), p. 82.

[25] Tore Henriksen and Geir Ulfstein, (2011). "Maritime Delimitation in the Arctic: The Barents Sea Treaty", Ocean Development & International Law, 42/1-2 (2011), pp. 1-21.

through cooperation.[26]

In the Arctic, Denmark and Norway aim for the sustainability of the region by cooperating on traditional issues such as climate change, energy resources, and maritime trade routes, as well as on green technology, clean energy, and environmental protection.

## Denmark's Presence in the Arctic Region

Denmark plays a distinctive role in the geopolitical struggles of the Arctic region due to its possession of overseas territories like Greenland and the Faroe Islands. Denmark's specific geopolitical challenges and areas of conflict in the Arctic encompass Greenland's quest for independence, the delineation of maritime boundaries, the melting of glaciers and environmental threats, geopolitical competition, and environmental conservation efforts, as well as the situation of the Faroe Islands. Although Greenland is an autonomous region within the Kingdom of Denmark, it has persistently strived for independence. Furthermore, disputes with Norway and Canada over the delimitation of borders in the Arctic Ocean have the potential to impact control over sea routes and access to energy resources. Additionally, the environmental threats posed by melting glaciers and rising sea levels in Greenland due to climate change are of concern. Meanwhile, the strategic importance of energy resources and sea routes in the region influences Denmark's geopolitical interests.

The Faroe Islands, functioning as an autonomous region under Danish sovereignty, are a part of Denmark's relations. The Faroe Islands are marked by their aspirations for maintaining autonomy and striving for economic independence. This complexity in the autonomy issue contributes to the intricate relations between Denmark and the Faroe Islands. Consequently, the situations in Denmark's various overseas territories in the Arctic region can be considered as factors that further complicate the geopolitical dynamics in the region and Denmark's role in the area.

Another dispute for Denmark in the Arctic is the demarcation of borders with Canada. There is disagreement over where exactly the borders are located in areas such as the Hans Islands (also known as Kalaallit Nunaat in Greenland) and Peary Land (North Greenland), which are part of Canada.

---

[26] Government.no, "Agreed Minutes on the Delimitation of the Continental Shelf beyond 200 Nautical Miles between the Faroe Islands, Iceland and Norway in the Southern Part of the Banana Hole of the Northeast Atlantic", Regjeringen.no, https://www.regjeringen.no/en/dokumenter/Agreed-Minutes/id446839/, 2006, (Access Date: 21.10.2023).

The disagreement over the delimitation of these borders is a result of strategic and economic interests, particularly regarding resources under the Arctic Ocean and control of sea lanes. Therefore, Canada and Denmark have negotiated under international law and treaties to resolve the maritime boundaries of these territories. For example, Canada and Denmark signed an agreement in 1973 to demarcate the border west of Greenland. However, there is still disagreement on exactly how to draw the boundaries in the Arctic Ocean. Such delimitation disputes reflect geopolitical struggles between countries in the Arctic region, where access to energy resources, sea routes and geographical boundaries play an important role. However, it is worth noting that usually such disputes are attempted to be resolved peacefully and are handled in accordance with international law.

## Greenland

The relationship between Denmark and Greenland has become more complex after Greenland was granted broad autonomy. Greenland's autonomy gives it more control over its resources and the management of its internal affairs. There are also political movements in Greenland seeking independence. At the same time, Greenland has a position that increases the geopolitical importance of the Arctic region. Factors such as melting glaciers, the opening of new sea routes and access to energy resources make Greenland the centre of international attention. Discussions on the future of the Arctic region have the potential to influence the fate of Greenland.

Greenland officially became a colony of Denmark in 1721. However, this geographical union didn't immediately translate into a political one. Until World War II, Greenland was governed as a closed colonial economy with minimal contact with the outside world. Even Danes who weren't part of the state bureaucracy had to apply for special permission to visit the colony, including journalists. It was only during World War II that Greenland's administration was temporarily consolidated under a single council. The outbreak of the war was crucial in significantly expanding Greenland's external relations. Shortly after Denmark was occupied by Germany in 1940, Greenland initiated attempts to trade with the U.S. This allowed the U.S. to establish a series of military bases in Greenland in exchange for material deliveries and the purchase of cryolite, crucial for aluminum production. This agreement also ensured the continuity of Danish sovereignty after the war. However, Greenland, upon returning to Danish rule, had different objectives. In 1953, a constitutional amendment terminated Greenland's colonial status. While there were indeed significant differences between

Denmark and Greenland, Greenland achieved legal equality.[27]

Two of the most contentious political issues between Greenland and Denmark involve the exploitation of oil and minerals, as well as security and foreign policy. During World War II, the U.S. established several bases around Greenland. In this context, particularly during the Cold War, the Thule Air Base held utmost strategic importance for the U.S. Strategic Air Command. One of the most significant political scandals in the relationship between Greenland and Denmark occurred in January 1968 when a U.S. B-52 bomber crashed near Thule Air Base. The plane was carrying four hydrogen bombs. At that time, Denmark did not permit nuclear weapons on its territory, including Greenland and the Faroe Islands. Consequently, the Danish government could not acknowledge that it had been clandestinely informed about the regular transportation of nuclear weapons by U.S. bombers landing at Thule.[28]

Greenland is considered successful in enhancing its foreign policy sovereignty by capitalizing on the increasing international geostrategic interest in the Arctic region. This situation further solidifies Denmark's reliance on Greenland's geographic location and its affiliation to Denmark to maintain its status as an Arctic state. As a result, Denmark benefits from the Arctic's recent ascension to one of the top five priorities in security and foreign policy. While this dependence provides Greenland with an "Arctic advantage" during negotiations with Denmark, it simultaneously transforms polar activities into strategic arenas for sovereignty games, aimed at reshaping the boundaries of Greenland's international autonomy without Danish intervention. These sovereignty games expand Greenland's capacity to maneuver within the existing legal framework in foreign policy, bolster its international standing, and attract foreign investments. Furthermore, they underpin efforts to achieve full Westphalian sovereignty as a state.[29]

Transitioning from the Cold War to Global Warming, Greenlanders are experiencing increased international interest in their island, especially since Greenland took over full management of its natural resources in 2010 under

---

[27] Jeppe Strandsbjerg, "Making Sense of Contemporary Greenland: Indigeneity, Resources and Sovereignty", Polar Geopolitics? Knowledges, Resources and Legal Regimes, Ed. Richard C. Powell and Klaus Dodds, Massachusetts: Edward Elgar Publishing, 2014, pp. 264-265.

[28] Poul Villaume and Thorsten Borring Olesen, I Blokopdelingens Tegn: Dansk Udenrigspolitiks Historie Vol 5: 1945-1972, Kobenhavn: Danmarks Nationalleksikon, 2005, pp. 635-648.

[29] Marc Jacobsen, "Greenland's Arctic advantage: Articulations, Acts and Appearances of Sovereignty Games", Cooperation and Conflict, (2019), p. 1.

the 2009 Autonomy Act. As part of both the "Arctic Eight"[30] and the "Arctic Five,"[31] Greenland, which together with Denmark covers 2,166,086 km² with less than 57,000 inhabitants, finds itself in the middle of a geopolitical power play. Greenland has enough natural minerals to attract everyone. For this reason, the island has become an international meeting place, presenting both opportunities and challenges for the people of Greenland on the path to becoming a sovereign state.[32]

Greenland gained its autonomy in 2009, just as the Arctic was starting to attract global attention. This is not the beginning of the statehood process, but it is viewed as a crucial step in a long journey toward increased sovereignty and independence. However, Greenland's most significant challenge in this process is to achieve economic independence and become a respected sovereign player in the international system that can hold its ground against other regional actors like Norway, Canada, Russia, and the United States. After almost 300 years of economic and political dependence on Denmark, economic independence now appears to be within reach in the foreseeable future. Nevertheless, the growing international interest in the Arctic as a whole, along with Greenland's small population, increases the challenges for developing a robust state apparatus with the necessary institutional framework.[33]

Greenland's national security is provided by Denmark. The Denmark Navy protects Greenland's coastline. Although Greenland would like to conduct its own foreign relations, it does not currently have the capacity to do so. Given international tensions, this goal may be further postponed in the future. Greenland's biggest destabilizing factor is climate change. Greenland is a member of the Inuit Circumpolar Council (ICC) along with Canada, Alaska and Russia. This situation always calls for active cooperation for common interests. For now, however, the ICC's connection with Russia is "on hold". The ICC is a permanent participant in the Arctic Council. It sends delegates to the COP meetings, the UN's annual conference on climate change. It also draws attention to the need to limit climate change at UN meetings. Greenland is believed to have significant mineral resources such as

---

[30] The Arctic Eight, established the intergovernmental Arctic Council with the Ottawa Declaration in 1996 to promote environmental protection and sustainable development. The member countries of the Arctic Council are Russia, U.S., Canada, Denmark, Iceland, Norway, Sweden, and Finland.

[31] The Arctic Five, consisting of countries with a direct coastline along the Arctic Ocean, includes Russia, U.S., Canada, Norway, and Denmark (Greenland).

[32] Nils Wang and Damien Degeorges, Greenland and the New Arctic: Political and Security Implications of a Statebuilding Project, Copenhagen: Royal Danish Defence College, 2014, p. 4.

[33] Nils Wang and Damien Degeorges, "Greenland and the New Arctic", p. 4.

rare earth elements and uranium. While China seeks access to these resources, Greenland is cautious. For example, China wanted to build a large airport in East Greenland. However, Greenland rejected this proposal due to concerns about loss of sovereignty. It has, however, formally agreed to hand over to Greenland the management of the military base that the United States built in Greenland during World War II.[34] As geopolitical tensions increase, Denmark's responsibility for security and defence has the potential to lead to disagreements among the constituent elements of the Kingdom.

Denmark plays a multifaceted role towards Greenland and is often criticized for acting as if it knows what is good and bad for Greenlanders. This is also the case with Greenland's NATO membership, which could change when Greenland seeks independence. Greenland would then have the freedom to determine its own preferences in defence matters. However, an independent Greenland would need assurances from another power to defend its vast territory. Denmark has a strong security-based interest in keeping Greenland within the "Kingdom". At this point, Copenhagen realizes that it needs Greenland's strategic territory to maintain its position in the Arctic Council. Even more important from a geo-strategic point of view is the fact that Copenhagen has consistently used the presence of the Thule Air Base in Greenland to "buy political influence in Washington". Therefore, in a politically unstable Arctic, the risk of a foreign power taking over Greenland is a real possibility for Denmark, which is aware of how fragile its dominance in Greenland actually is. Denmark is therefore committed to any regional cooperation that does not directly oppose American interests or Danish sovereignty over Greenland.[35]

## Faroe Islands

The Faroe Islands consist of 18 small islands located northwest of the Shetland Islands, southeast of Iceland and southwest of Norway. The population of these islands is made up of settlers of Viking origin.[36] The Faroe Islands are a Danish territory where sheep outnumber people. Historically, Denmark had to give independence to Norway in 1814. In 1917, it had to sell the Virgin Islands colonies to the United States. Denmark therefore maintained three overseas outposts: Iceland, the Faroe Islands and

---

[34] Adele Buckley, "Destabilization of the Arctic", Journal of Autonomy and Security Studies, 7/2 (2023), p. 138.
[35] Koen Verhelst, A Geopolitical Gem: How Greenland can be a Test Case for a more Ambitious EU, Discussion Paper C279, Bonn: Center for European Integration Studies (ZEI), 2023, p. 8.
[36] Christian Rebhan, North Atlantic Euroscepticism: The rejection of EU membership in the Faroe Islands and Greenland, Tórshavn: Fróðskapur – Faroe University Press, 2016, p. 26.

Greenland. Iceland gained independence in 1944. Following the Second World War, the Faroe Islands were granted self-government by the Home Rule Act of 1948. The Faroe Islands and Greenland differ in many ways. For example, the population in the Faroe Islands is mainly of Danish and Norwegian origin. There is no indigenous population in the Faroe Islands. Greenland, on the other hand, has an indigenous population of Inuit.[37]

The Faroe Islands is an autonomous territory with its own local government and parliament. This autonomy includes the power to control its own local government and economy. Denmark's strategic location in the North Sea and the Atlantic Ocean makes its relationship with the Faroe Islands important. Because of its geographically strategic location, the Faroe Islands cooperate closely with Denmark on defence and security issues. Furthermore, the economy of the Faroe Islands is based on the trade of seafood, especially fisheries and aquaculture. Therefore, the maritime and fisheries sectors increase the economic importance of the Faroe Islands. The Faroe Islands are also home to a people who preserve their own cultural identity. Faroese and Danish, the local languages, are spoken by the inhabitants. As an autonomous region under the Kingdom of Denmark, the Faroe Islands can act partially independently in international relations. However, it is dependent on Denmark in certain areas such as defence and foreign policy.

The 1948 Home Rule Act divides the future relations between the Faroe Islands and Denmark into two areas: special areas and common areas. Special areas are matters over which the Faroe Islands government can claim control at will. Common affairs can only be taken over by the Danish government after negotiations and subsequent approval. Apart from the Home Rule Act, there are core areas such as the court system, currency, defence and foreign affairs. These areas are considered subjects of the kingdom and therefore cannot be taken over. Overall, the home rule system creates an independent system of internal government. When the Faroe Islands parliament takes over an area, that area is subject to the laws and government of the Faroe Islands. The first law passed by the Faroe Islands parliament is a Government Act. This was followed by the takeover of key political and economic areas such as taxation and fisheries.[38] By 1973, the Faroe Islands decided not to follow Denmark's accession to the EU and join the European Economic Area. Although the Faroe Islands have signed their own bilateral agreements with

---

[37] Rebecca Adler-Nissen, "The Faroe Islands: Independence Dreams, Globalist Separatism and The Europeanization of Postcolonial Home Rule", Cooperation and Conflict, 49/1 (2014), p. 56.
[38] Gestur Hovgaard and Maria Ackrén, "Autonomy in Denmark: Greenland and the Faroe Islands", Collection Monografías Cidob, (2017), pp. 71-72.

the EU, they do not have the status of an EU overseas country and territory like Greenland. Therefore, the issue of the Faroe Islands'EU membership is still uncertain. In the mid-1990s, the decline of fish stocks in local waters led to a severe economic crisis, unemployment, and the emigration of 10% of the population to Denmark. This crisis was also an indicator of the Faroe Islands'need for autonomy and economic independence.[39]

The Faroese independence movement has been opposing Denmark's authority over the islands for decades. The movement emerged as a product of a romantic nationalist awakening in the 1880s, but early nationalists focused on promoting a Faroese identity within Danish sovereignty. The struggle for independence is a more recent phenomenon. Today, the independence movement and most of the the Faroe Islands'population (whether pro-independence or not) have a globalist orientation but are also committed to traditional lifestyles such as bird hunting and pilot whaling. Today, an important element of Denmark's post-colonialism is how it handles international criticism of the Faroe Islands'fishing and hunting. Seeking to establish itself as a progressive ex-colonizer, Denmark tries to balance the two global discourses of animal welfare protection and environmental friendliness while defending the "original cultural habits" of the former colonies.[40]

Entering the new millennium, the Faroe Islands faced a challenging process of declaring independence. In March 2000, they initiated independence talks with Denmark. Moreover, the Faroe Islands even took this issue to the United Nations. However, the UN recognized it as Denmark's internal matter.[41] Although a new referendum was planned for May 26, 2001, it was cancelled due to disagreements and concerns that Denmark would cut off financial aid. At that time, the democratic process toward independence was defined to include four stages: (1) agreement on general political objectives; (2) preparation of relevant reports and discussion papers; (3) negotiations between the Faroe Islands authorities and the Danish authorities; and (4) parliamentary approval and a popular referendum. The proposed independence process set a timetable for the Faroe Islands to assume responsibility for all areas currently administered by Denmark under the

---

[39] Adam Kočí and Vladimír Baar, "Greenland and the Faroe Islands: Denmark's Autonomous Territories from Postcolonial Perspectives", Norsk Geografisk Tidsskrift–Norwegian Journal of Geography, 75 (2021), p. 196.

[40] Rebecca Adler-Nissen, "The Faroe Islands", p. 56

[41] Kári à Rógvi. "The Land of Maybe. A Survey of Faroese Constitutional History", The Right to National Self-Determination: The Faroe Islands and Greenland, Ed. Sjúrður Skaale, Leiden: Brill-Nijhoff, (2004): 16.

Home Rule Act by no later than January 1, 2012, except for a few areas closely tied to sovereignty.[42] Nevertheless, the concerns of the Faroe Islands and their cancellation of the planned referendum are quite understandable. Because at the time, Denmark Prime Minister Poul Nyrup Rasmussen made statements indicating that full independence for the Faroe Islands also implied full economic responsibility.[43]

The Faroe Islands'efforts towards independence were not resolved until 2005. In 2005, the Faroe Islands gained more autonomy through the "Takeover Act," and in the same year, Denmark and the Faroe Islands signed an agreement strengthening authority in foreign policy matters. However, overall responsibility for the foreign, security, judicial, and monetary policies of the Faroe Islands still rests with Denmark.[44] However, national security, in particular, is still considered a sensitive issue. This is because the Faroe Islands are located in the strategic waters of the "GIUK Gap,"[45] which refers to the oceanic areas between the mainland of Greenland, Iceland, and the United Kingdom. The importance of this strategic link between the Arctic Seas and the Atlantic Ocean was especially evident during World War II when the Allies supplied the Soviet Union.[46]

As of the current point in response to the demands for independence, the Faroe Islands have their own local government and parliament, but constitutionally, they remain an autonomous region under Denmark. The Faroe Islands are governed by a law known as the "Home Rule Act," which grants the Faroe Islands broad autonomy. However, they maintain their allegiance to Denmark in certain areas such as foreign policy, defence, judiciary, and monetary policy. Although the Faroe Islands have the right to regulate their internal affairs, they represent Denmark in international relations. This arrangement creates a balance that preserves the Faroe Islands'independence while ensuring cooperation with Denmark. The Faroe Islands have their own local government and parliament but are constitutionally subordinate to the Kingdom of Denmark.

In addition to the independence debate, the Faroe Islands are striving to build a sustainable economy and are aiming to play a more active role in

---

[42] Maria Ackrén. "The Faroe Islands: Options for Independence", Island Studies Journal, 1/2, (2006): 227-228.
[43] Rebecca Adler-Nissen, "The Faroe Islands", p. 63.
[44] Adam Kočí and Vladimír Baar, "Greenland and the Faroe Islands", p. 197.
[45] The abbreviation GIUK is derived from the first letters of the names Greenland, Iceland and the United Kingdom.
[46] Klaus Dodds and Mark Nuttall, The Scramble for the Poles: The Geopolitics of the Arctic and Antarctic, Cambridge: Polity Press, 2016, pp. 107-108.

international relations. Economic discussions in the Faroe Islands often revolve around economic sustainability and the provision of aid from Denmark. However, their heavy dependence on exports of fish and related products is the primary factor negatively impacting their economy. Although the Faroe Islands have high hopes for oil and gas extraction, preliminary studies have not yet yielded commercially viable discoveries. Therefore, the development of sectors such as tourism and aquaculture are seen as the most promising path to follow before deriving wealth from fossil fuels. Today, the Faroe Islands receive over 100,000 tourists annually and consistently rank among the most renowned destinations resisting the influence of mass tourism.[47]

## Hans Island

If global warming continues to increase the temperature of the Arctic Seas, more of the Arctic region will be ice-free in the long term. The prospects for exploiting natural resources and controlling the Northern Sea lanes have reignited countries'territorial claims in the region. Canada and Greenland, which is an autonomous territory of the Kingdom of Denmark like the Faroe Islands, have had disputes over their respective claims to a small rock in the Arctic called Hans Island. One cannot underestimate the significance of this small piece of land, as it has given rise to prolonged tensions and disputes between Canada and Denmark.[48] In essence, the dispute concerning Hans Island is a long-standing territorial disagreement between Canada and Denmark. The island has been a battleground for claims of sovereignty by both nations, each asserting its ownership of the island. While Denmark argues that Hans Island is geologically linked to Greenland, Canada does not accept this perspective and maintains that the issue of the island's status remained unresolved without a precise border delineation.[49] Due to the intricacies of geographical, historical, and political factors, this dispute remained unresolved for an extended period. However, ultimately, negotiations between the two countries led to an agreement, resulting in the demarcation of Hans Island. This development can be seen as a significant stride forward in terms of the future of regional relations and cooperation.

Hans Island is situated in the middle of the Nares Strait, a 22-mile wide,

---

[47] Adam Koči and Vladimír Baar, "Greenland and the Faroe Islands", pp. 197-198.
[48] Franciska Jecs, "Maritime Delimitation Dilemmas Over Hans Island Between Canada and Denmark", Publicationes Universitatis Miskolciensis, Sectio Juridica Et Politica, 39/2 (2021), pp. 25-26.
[49] Christopher Stevenson, "Hans Off!: The Struggle for Hans Island and the Potential Ramifications for International Border Disupute Resolution", Boston College International & Comparative Law Review, 30/1 (2007), p. 265.

bitterly cold waterway that separates Canada from Greenland, an autonomous region of Denmark. The island falls within the 12-mile territorial boundary of both shores, allowing both parties to make claims to the island under international law. In 1973, Canada and Denmark made attempts to establish a definitive boundary for Hans Island in the strait, but they couldn't come to an agreement on how to proceed. Consequently, they set the issue aside for future resolution. However, the tranquil diplomatic waters were stirred in 1984 when Canadian soldiers visited the island, planted their nation's flag, and left a symbolic mark - a bottle of Canadian whisky. Denmark's Minister for Greenlandic Affairs, unwilling to accept this, soon arrived on the island. He replaced the provocative Canadian symbols with the Denmark flag, a bottle of Denmark whisky, and a note that read, "Welcome to the island of Denmark."[50]

The Hans Island, which is smaller than some of the icebergs in the region, is essentially a barren rock covering 1.3 square kilometres. The island was discovered by Denmark in 1853, and it was named after the explorer who found it. At that time, it was considered an extension of Greenland. During World War II, the island was used by Canadian scientists and soldiers, while in subsequent years, Canada began claiming that the island had separated Heyfrom Canada, expressing its intention to use it permanently. In the early 1980s, the Canadian government granted permission for the Dome Petroleum Company to establish a scientific camp to study the impact of sea ice and icebergs. In response to this, Denmark's jets started flying over the island in 1983, and for the first time in 1984, Denmark raised its Denmark flag on the island. That same year, Canadian soldiers took down the Denmark flag and raised the Canada flag in its place.[51]

In the context of the Hans Island dispute, despite the existence of a bilateral delimitation treaty ratified by both Canada and Denmark, the treaty has not defined the border of Hans Island. Additionally, the application of the uti possidetis doctrine is not feasible because the region encompassing North Greenland, Hans Island, and Ellesmere Island has never been under the exclusive control of a single nation. However, both countries have presented some evidence of "customary use of the disputed territory" or "effective control over the disputed territory," which constitutes the third determinative

---

[50] Dan Levin, "Canada and Denmark Fight Over Island With Whisky and Schnapps", The New York Times, https://www.nytimes.com/2016/11/08/world/what-in-the-world/canada-denmark-hans-island-whisky-schnapps.html, 2016, (Access Date: 10.10.2023).
[51] Michael Byers, International Law and the Arctic, New York: Cambridge University Press, 2013, pp. 10-16.

factor in resolving the dispute. Given the island's diminutive size and its remote location from the mainland of both Canada and Denmark, it is understandable that neither party has established a permanent settlement on Hans Island. Nevertheless, both states have taken various measures to establish effective control over the island. For instance, Canada has aimed to demonstrate effective control through military missions and a commitment to expand operations on Hans Island. Simultaneously, Denmark has sought to demonstrate effective control by maintaining military oil depots in Greenland and ensuring standard air surveillance over the disputed territory. While both states possess some evidence of effective control, it remains uncertain whether this evidence is sufficient to establish effective control over the territory for either party.[52]

While there are no known deposits of oil, natural gas, gold, or other minerals on Hans Island, it is speculated that the seabed beneath the surrounding waters may contain such natural resources. As global warming has warmed the Arctic seas, the waterways between Canada and Greenland have become navigable for longer periods of the year. Countries have taken advantage of this opportunity to explore potential oil and gas reserves. At this point, Denmark granted a license for oil exploration on its side of the Davis Strait. Interestingly, the company that acquired this license was EnCana Corporation, a Canadian company.[53]

With all of this, the parties have reached a compromise on the border dispute that has been ongoing for more than 50 years. On June 14, 2022, Canadian Foreign Minister Mélanie Joly and Danish Foreign Minister Jeppe Kofod, along with Greenland's Prime Minister Múte B. Egede, signed an agreement in Ottawa. This agreement reconciles maritime boundaries on the continental shelf within 200 nautical miles, including the boundaries on Hans Island, and the continental shelf beyond 200 nautical miles, including the Lincoln Sea. This agreement ensures access and free movement throughout the entire island while preserving the traditional, symbolic, and historical significance of Hans Island for the Inuit in both Kalaallit Nunaat, particularly in Avanersuaq, and Nunavut. This agreement is regarded as a historic milestone in the relations between friendly neighbours and is the result of years of negotiations. The efforts made to achieve this outcome demonstrate their leadership in the region and their commitment to resolving disputes peacefully and in accordance with international law. The land border on Hans

---

[52] Mahatab Uddin, "Hans Island: How to Resolve the Dispute?", Current Developments in Arctic Law, 4 (2016) pp. 31-32.
[53] Christopher Stevenson, "Hans Off!", pp. 267-268.

Island reflects the strong historical and cultural ties between the communities of Canada and Greenland. This paves the way for increased cooperation and a closer partnership between them.[54]

The agreement to divide Hans Island and establish boundaries for the disputed maritime territories holds not only symbolic value but also significant practical importance for the parties involved. The negotiated agreement is particularly significant for the Inuit settlement of Ausuittuq in Canada and Qaanaaq in Greenland, contributing to the groundwork for increased and more extensive cooperation between Canada and Greenland. The objective of future intergovernmental collaboration and mobility is explicitly embedded in the agreement. The demarcation occurs shortly after Canada declared its intent to rekindle Arctic cooperation in projects that do not involve the participation of Denmark (Greenland) and Russia. In a time when the international legal order is under substantial pressure, and concerns are growing about the extent to which states will adhere to their obligations under international law, the demarcation agreement between Canada and Denmark (Greenland) showcases the strong determination and commitment of Arctic states to uphold their obligations in line with the Law of the Sea and the 2008 Ilulissat Declaration.[55]

## Denmark's Arctic Policy

Denmark, a small European country, is an influential player in the Arctic region through its connection with Greenland, the world's largest island. This connection grants Denmark the opportunity to have a voice in various Arctic matters based on its sovereignty in the region. Moreover, it significantly contributes to Denmark's access to the Arctic's abundant natural resources and economic prospects. As a result, Greenland plays a pivotal role in Denmark's Arctic policies. With a landscape mostly dominated by glaciers, Greenland has a relatively small population. Due to its unsuitable conditions for agriculture, the primary sources of income are hunting and fishing. Given its climatic challenges and geographical characteristics, Greenland depends on external support in various domains. Denmark offers economic,

---

[54] Government of Canada "Canada and the Kingdom of Denmark, Together With Greenland, Reach Historic Agreement On Long-Standing Boundary Disputes", https://www.canada.ca/en/global-affairs/news/2022/06/canada-and-the-kingdom-of-denmark-together-with-greenland-reach-historic-agreement-on-long-standing-boundary-disputes.html, 2022b, (Access Date: 10.10.2023).
[55] Signe Veierud Busch, "The last bottle of the Whisky-War: A commentary on the boundary delimitation agreement on disputed areas between Canada and Denmark (Greenland)", The blog of the Norwegian Centre for the Law of the Sea, https://site.uit.no/nclos/2022/06/14/the-last-bottle-of-the-whisky-war-a-commentary-on-the-boundary-delimitation-agreement-on-disputed-areas-between-canada-and-denmark-greenland/, 2022, (Access Date: 10.10.2023).

administrative, security, environmental, and cultural assistance to Greenland.[56] This represents an important step towards reducing Greenland's dependence on Denmark. Greenland's rich natural resources and minerals attract the attention of other countries. In the face of instability in the Arctic region and the risk of Greenland seeking independence or the possibility of a powerful actor taking control of Greenland, Denmark is pursuing a strategic policy to ensure that the region remains under its control. Therefore, Greenland holds great significance in Denmark's Arctic policy. However, it's important to note that Greenland is a means to achieve Denmark's strategic objectives rather than a direct goal. Greenland's strategically vital position serves as a strategic bargaining tool that Denmark uses to strengthen its relations with the U.S.[57]

Denmark has published two strategy documents for the Arctic region in 2008 and 2011. The most recent one is the "Denmark, Greenland and the Faroe Islands: Arctic Strategy of the Kingdom of Denmark 2011-2020" published in 2011. This document describes Denmark's strategic objectives for the Arctic region, including Greenland and the Faroe Islands. According to this document, issues such as protecting the sovereignty and territorial integrity of the region, combating climate and environmental problems, protecting biodiversity, economic development and trade, energy resources, maritime activities, mining, scientific research, welfare of local people, sustainable development should be addressed based on international law and through cooperation.[58]

The Arctic region's wealth of energy and mineral resources has been a major driving force behind its rise to global prominence. Interest in the region's energy resources truly began to surface in 2007-2008.[59] In 2008, the United States Geological Survey (USGS) indicated that the Arctic could potentially hold 90 billion barrels of oil, 1.669 trillion cubic feet of natural gas, and 44 billion barrels of liquid natural gas.[60] After the discovery of unexplored energy

---

[56] International Labour Organization "Act on Greenland Self-Government (Act no. 473 of 12 June 2009)", https://www.ilo.org/dyn/natlex/natlex4.detail?p_isn=110442&p_lang=en, 2009, (Access Date: 24.10.2023).

[57] Jon Rahbek-Clemmensen, "Arctic-vism" in Practice – The Challenges Facing Denmark's Political-Military Strategy in the High Nort", Arctic Yearbook 2014, Ed. In L. Heininen, H. Exner-Pirot and J. Plouffe, 2014, pp. 400-401.

[58] Ministry of Foreign Affairs of Denmark "The Arctic", https://um.dk/en/foreign-policy/the-arctic, 2023, (Access Date: 29.10.2023).

[59] Arild Moe, "Russia and the Development of Arctic Energy Resources in the Context of Domestic Policy and International Markets", The Arctic and World Order, Ed. Kristina Spohr and Daniel S. Hamilton, Brookings Institution Press, 2020, p. 119.

[60] Kenneth J. Bird, Ronald R. Charpentier, Donald L. Gautier, David W. Houseknecht, Timothy R. Klett,

resources, interest in the region has significantly escalated. Consequently, the Arctic region has become a critical area, not only for the countries within the region but also for the economic prospects of foreign nations. According to the distribution of undiscovered hydrocarbon reserves among the Arctic coastal states, Denmark, via Greenland, possesses 18% of the oil and 8% of the natural gas.[61] Greenland is also abundant in minerals such as uranium, iron, lead, zinc, and diamonds. Denmark has entrusted the operation of many of these mines to foreign investors. For instance, the Isua iron mine was initially operated by the British company London Mining Greenland. However, following the company's bankruptcy, the mine was acquired by the Chinese company General Nice in 2015. China's presence in the region has raised significant concerns in the U.S. Greenland, for various reasons, revoked the company's license.[62]

Although China wants to establish close relations with Greenland and provide Greenland with substantial financial support, Denmark uses its veto over China's activities in Greenland. Denmark intervenes in Greenland's internal affairs on the grounds of international security. This intervention is based on its close relationship with the United States and the concern of losing its influence in the region by losing Greenland.[63] In conclusion, Denmark is an important actor in the region as the owner of some of the rich energy resources and minerals in the Arctic region. It wants to maintain its control over its energy and mineral resources in the region through Greenland. Therefore, although it supports Greenland's autonomy, it does not hesitate to intervene in Greenland's internal affairs to protect its interests in the region. This is an important element reflecting Denmark's role and strategic interests in the Arctic.

Global resource depletion and the presence of resources in the Arctic region due to climate change are indicative of a significant transformation. As glaciers melt, oil, natural gas, and precious minerals become more accessible. Additionally, the increasing diversity and stocks of fish in the Arctic Ocean hold great importance for the fishing industry. These developments

---

Janet K. Pitman, ... and Craig R. Wandrey, Circum-Arctic resource appraisal: Estimates of undiscovered oil and gas north of the Arctic Circle (No. 2008-3049), US Geological Survey, 2008.

[61] Lassi Heininen, Alexander Sergunin and Gleb Yarovoy, "Russian Strategies In The Arctic: Avoiding A New Cold War", Valdai Discussion Club, http://valdaiclub.com/a/reports/ russian_strategies_ in_ the_arctic_avoiding_a_new_cold_war/, 2014, (Access Date: 29.10.2023), p. 11.

[62] Mining Technology "Greenland cancels General Nice's Isua iron-ore project licence", https://www.mining-technology.com/news/greenland-cancels-general-nice-isua-iron-ore-project-licence/, 2021, (Access Date: 29.10.2023).

[63] Matzen, Erik. "Denmark spurned Chinese offer for Greenland base over security: sources", Reuters, https://www.reuters.com/article/cnews-us-denmark-china-greenland-base-idCAKBN1782EE-OCATP.

unequivocally underscore the immense economic value of the Arctic region. Consequently, the Arctic region has become a focal point for both the Arctic littoral states (such as Russia, the USA, Canada, Denmark, Norway) and non-Arctic actors (like China, the EU, NATO, the UK, India, South Korea). In this context, Denmark aims to bolster its position and influence as an active participant in the Arctic region.

The increasing significance of the Arctic region has spurred Arctic countries, particularly Russia, to take a more active role in the realm of security and defense. As a result, Denmark is making strides in the field of defense and security in the Arctic region, primarily in Greenland and the Faroe Islands. In this context, the Danish government has presented a defense agreement proposal to the parliament, encompassing an investment of 143 billion Danish Kroner. The aim is to fulfill the expectations of NATO and other allies in the region and bolster the country's security.[64]

Denmark also believes that NATO's presence in the Arctic region could be perceived as a security threat by Russia, potentially leading to increased military concentration in the area. Therefore, Denmark opposes its presence in the Arctic.[65] Safeguarding its sovereignty and security in the Arctic region is considered one of Denmark's primary responsibilities. As a result, the Danish Armed Forces regularly conduct surveillance and inspection activities in the region to protect the sovereignty and ensure the security of Greenland and the Faroe Islands.[66] The number of air bases, radar systems, submarines and missiles in the Arctic region is increasing every year. This situation shows that military competition in the region is increasing, and new dynamics are emerging in international relations. This increasing military presence in the Arctic region poses the risk of small countries like Denmark being caught between the great powers. Therefore, Denmark attaches much more importance to Arctic cooperation to protect its national security and prevent conflicts in the Arctic region.[67] In this context, Denmark aims to protect not only its national security but also regional stability and cooperation in the Arctic region.

Denmark adopts a policy that approaches climate and environmental issues in the Arctic with sensitivity. This policy aims to protect economic activities

---

[64] Hilde-Gunn Bye, "Denmark to Strengthen Defense in the Arctic and the Baltic Sea", High North News, https://www.highnorthnews.com/en/denmark-strengthen-defense-arctic-and-baltic-sea, 2023, (Access Date: 24.10.2023).

[65] Jon Rahbek-Clemmensen, "Arctic-vism", p. 404.

[66] Ministry of Foreign Affairs of Denmark "The Arctic".

[67] Jon Rahbek-Clemmensen, "Arctic-vism", p. 402.

in the region, such as fishing and hunting, as well as the cultural values of local communities. Fishing is a critical economic sector for Greenland and the Faroe Islands. It is, therefore, very important that these resources are sustainably protected. Denmark aims to preserve the cultural identity of local communities by focusing on the environmental and economic sustainability of the Arctic region. Denmark recognizes that the Arctic has a unique ecosystem and prioritizes the sustainable management of this region.[68]

Denmark's Arctic policy is centred around preserving its sovereignty and security in the Arctic region. However, it also aims to strategically harness the rich reserves of oil, natural gas, minerals, mineral resources, renewable energy, fishing, and other economic opportunities in the region. It carries the objective of safeguarding the vulnerable nature of the Arctic and the well-being of local communities. Denmark closely monitors the changing dynamics of the Arctic region and adopts a peaceful, cooperative, and diplomacy-based approach based on international law. Denmark's Arctic strategy will evolve in line with future power dynamics, with the goal of becoming an effective actor in both regional and international arenas.

## Conclusion

The Arctic region is a geography of geopolitical importance for the world. Denmark is positioning itself as an influential actor in this region. Denmark's Arctic policies aim to balance various factors by considering the dynamic balances in the region. Denmark realizes its presence and influence in the Arctic region mainly through Greenland and the Faroe Islands. The Arctic region's rich energy resources, trade opportunities and sea routes turn it into a geopolitical battleground. In this context, especially Greenland is of great strategic importance for Denmark. Therefore, Denmark's Arctic policies are based on its relations with these regions. Denmark uses the region's rich energy resources and trade potential as a strategic tool. At the same time, the responsibility to protect the environment and the welfare of local communities also comes to the fore for Denmark. In this context, it can be said that Denmark adopts a balanced and sensitive approach to environmental threats in line with the principles of sustainability in the region. At the same time, this balanced approach reflects the complexity of Denmark's Arctic policies.

The melting of glaciers, the discovery of new energy resources, the opening of sea trade routes, and the competition among actors seeking to establish a

---

[68] Ministry of Foreign Affairs of Denmark "The Arctic".

presence in the region are making the Arctic region more complex. Denmark is following a careful strategy to adapt to these changing dynamics and to remain an effective actor in the region. Denmark's strategy is crucial for maintaining the stability and prosperity of the region. Future Arctic dynamics could further complicate conflicts of interest and security issues in the region. How Denmark adapts to these changing dynamics and the role it assumes in the region will greatly influence the fate of the Arctic region.

Denmark pursues a policy in the Arctic region that encompasses climate and environment, economic opportunities, and security. This policy is a balanced approach aimed at both safeguarding Denmark's national interests and promoting regional cooperation. The Arctic region is a place of uncertainty, with intense international attention and growing competition. Denmark takes an active role in ensuring the security and sustainability of the region amid these uncertainties. In the face of changing dynamics and challenges in the Arctic region, Denmark will continue to pursue an effective and balanced policy to maintain its presence as a strong actor. Denmark's stance in the Arctic not only serves its own interests but also plays a critical role in the stability and prosperity of the region.

## Bibliography

Ackrén, Maria. "The Faroe Islands: Options for Independence", Island Studies Journal, 1/2, (2006): 223-238.

Adler-Nissen, Rebecca. "The Faroe Islands: Independence Dreams, Globalist Separatism and The Europeanization of Postcolonial Home Rule", Cooperation and Conflict, 49/1, (2014): 55-79.

Baker, Betsy. "Law, Science, and the Continental Shelf: The Russian Federation and the Promise of Arctic Cooperation", American University International Law Review, 25/2, (2010): 251-281.

Beaumont, Peter. "Canada and Denmark End Decades-long Dispute Over Barren Rock in Arctic", The Guardian, https://www.theguardian.com/world/2022/ jun/14/ canada-denmark-end-decades-long-dispute-barren-rock-arctic-hans-island, 2022, (Access Date: 20.10.2023).

Bird, Kenneth J., Charpentier, Ronald R., Gautier, Donald L., Houseknecht, David W., Klett, Timothy R., Pitman, Janet K., ... and Wandrey, Craig R. Circum-Arctic resource appraisal: Estimates of undiscovered oil and gas north of the Arctic Circle (No. 2008-3049), 2008, US Geological Survey.

Buckley, Adele. "Destabilization of the Arctic", Journal of Autonomy and Security Studies, 7/2, (2023): 128-143.

Busch, Signe Veierud. "The last bottle of the Whisky-War: A commentary on the boundary delimitation agreement on disputed areas between Canada and Denmark (Greenland)", The blog of the Norwegian Centre for the Law of the Sea, https://site.uit.no/nclos/2022/06/14/the-last-bottle-of-the-whisky-war-a-commentary-on-the-boundary-delimitation-agreement-on-disputed-areas-between-canada-and-denmark-greenland/, 2022, (Access Date: 10.10.2023).

Bye, Hilde-Gunn. "Denmark to Strengthen Defense in the Arctic and the Baltic Sea", High North News, https://www.highnorthnews.com/en/denmark-strengthen-defense-arctic-and-baltic-sea, 2023, (Access Date: 24.10.2023).

Byers, Michael. International Law and the Arctic, New York: Cambridge University Press, 2013.

Carnaghan, Matthew and Goody, Allison. Canadian Arctic Sovereignty, Ottawa: Parliamentary Information and Research Service, 2006.

Conley, Heather A., and Melino, Matthew. "The İmplications Of US Policy Stagnation Toward The Arctic Region", Center For Strategic And International Studies (CSIS), 2019.

Dodds, Klaus and Nuttall, Mark. The Scramble for the Poles: The Geopolitics of the Arctic and Antarctic, Cambridge: Polity Press, 2016.

Embassy of Denmark in Canada. "The Arctic", https://canada.um.dk/en/the-arctic, 2023, (Access Date: 20.10.2023).

Government of Canada. "Canada and the Kingdom of Denmark, Together With Greenland, Reach Historic Agreement On Long-Standing Boundary Disputes", https://www.canada.ca/en/global-affairs/news/2022/06/canada-and-the-kingdom-of-denmark-together-with-greenland-reach-historic-agreement-on-long-standing-boundary-disputes.html, 2022b, (Access Date: 10.10.2023).

Government of Canada. "Canada-Kingdom of Denmark joint statement on bilateral cooperation", https://www.canada.ca/en/global-affairs/news/2022/06/canada-kingdom-of-denmark-joint-statement-on-bilateral-cooperation.html, 2022a, (Access Date: 20.10.2023).

Government.no. "Agreed Minutes on the Delimitation of the Continental Shelf beyond 200 Nautical Miles between the Faroe Islands, Iceland and Norway in the Southern Part of the Banana Hole of the Northeast Atlantic", Regjeringen.no, https://www.regjeringen.no/ en/dokumenter/Agreed-Minutes/id446839/, 2006, (Access Date: 21.10.2023).

Gunitskiy, Vsevolod. "On Thin Ice: Water Rights And Resource Disputes In The Arctic Ocean", Journal of International Affairs, 61/2, (2008): 261–271.

Heininen, Lassi. Arctic Strategies and Policies: Inventory and Comparative Study, Akureyri: The Northern Research Forum & The University of Lapland, 2012.

Heininen, Lassi; Sergunin, Alexander and Yarovoy, Gleb. "Russian Strategies In The Arctic: Avoiding A New Cold War", Valdai Discussion Club, http://valdaiclub.com/a/reports/russian_strategies_in_the_arctic_avoiding_a_new_cold_war/, 2014, (Access Date: 29.10.2023).

Henley, John. "Denmark votes overwhelmingly to join EU's common defence policy", The Guardian, https://www.theguardian.com/world/2022/jun/01/denmark-votes-on-joining-eus-common-defence-policy, 2022, (Access Date: 18.10.2023).

Henriksen, Tore and Ulfstein, Geir. "Maritime Delimitation in the Arctic: The Barents Sea Treaty", Ocean Development & International Law, 42/1-2, (2011): 1-21.

Hinshaw, Drew and Page, Jeremy. "How the Pentagon Countered China's Designs on Greenland", Wall Street Journal, https://www.wsj.com/articles/how-the-pentagon-countered-chinas-designs-on-greenland-11549812296, 2019, (Access Date: 24.

10.2023).

Hovgaard, Gestur and Ackrén, Maria. "Autonomy in Denmark: Greenland and the Faroe Islands", Collection Monografias Cidob, (2017): 69-76.

International Labour Organization. "Act on Greenland Self-Government (Act no. 473 of 12 June 2009)", https://www.ilo.org/dyn/natlex/natlex4.detail? p_isn=110442& p_lang=en, 2009, (Access Date: 24.10.2023).

Jacobsen, Marc. "Greenland's Arctic advantage: Articulations, Acts and Appearances of Sovereignty Games", Cooperation and Conflict, (2019): 1-23.

Jecs, Franciska. "Maritime Delimitation Dilemmas Over Hans Island Between Canada and Denmark", Publicationes Universitatis Miskolciensis, Sectio Juridica Et Politica, 39/2, (2021): 25-37.

Kefferpütz, Roderick. "On Thin Ice? (Mis)Interpreting Russian Policy in the High North", CEPS Policy Brief No. 205, 2010.

Kharlampyeva, K. Nadezhda. "The Transnational Arctic and Russia", Energy Security and Geopolitics in the Arctic Challenges and Opportunities in the 21st Century, Ed. Hooman Peimani, World Scientific Publishing Co. Pte. Ltd., 2013: 95-126.

Koči, Adam and Baar, Vladimír. "Greenland and the Faroe Islands: Denmark's Autonomous Territories from Postcolonial Perspectives", Norsk Geografisk Tidsskrift–Norwegian Journal of Geography, 75, (2021): 189-202.

Levin, Dan. "Canada and Denmark Fight Over Island With Whisky and Schnapps", The New York Times, https://www.nytimes.com/2016/11/08/world/what-in-the-world/canada-denmark-hans-island-whisky-schnapps.html, 2016, (Access Date: 10.10.2023).

Matzen, Erik. "Denmark spurned Chinese offer for Greenland base over security: sources", Reuters, https://www.reuters.com/article/cnews-us-denmark-china-greenland-base-idCAKBN1782EE-OCATP, 2017, (Access Date: 29.10.2023).

Miller, David Hunter. "Political Rights in the Arctic", Foreign Affairs, 4/1, (1925): 47–60.

Mining Technology. "Greenland cancels General Nice's Isua iron-ore project licence", https://www.mining-technology.com/news/greenland-cancels-general-nice-isua-iron-ore-project-licence/, 2021, (Access Date: 29.10.2023).

Ministry of Foreign Affairs of Denmark. "The Arctic", https://um.dk/en/foreign-policy/the-arctic, 2023, (Access Date: 29.10.2023).

Moe, Arild. "Russia and the Development of Arctic Energy Resources in the Context of Domestic Policy and International Markets", The Arctic and World Order, Ed. Kristina Spohr and Daniel S. Hamilton, Brookings Institution Press, 2020: 119-142.

Nielsen, Kristian H. "Transforming Greenland: Imperial formations in the cold war", New Global Studies, 7/2, (2013): 129-154.

Østhagen, Andreas. "Norway's Arctic policy: still high North, low tension?", The Polar Journal, 11/1, (2021): 75-94.

Paul, Michael. "Polar power USA: full steam ahead into the Arctic.", Stiftung Wissenschaft und Politik (SWP), German Institute for International and Security Affairs, 42, (2019): 1-4.

Pengelly, Martin. "Trump confirms he is considering attempt to buy Greenland", The Guardian, https://www.theguardian.com/world/2019/aug/18/trump-considering-buying-greenland, 2019, (Access Date: 19.10.2023).

Rahbek-Clemmensen, Jon. "Arctic-vism" in Practice – The Challenges Facing Denmark's Political-Military Strategy in the High Nort", Arctic Yearbook 2014, Ed. In L. Heininen, H. Exner-Pirot and J. Plouffe, 2014: 399–414.

Rebhan, Christian. North Atlantic Euroscepticism: The rejection of EU membership in the Faroe Islands and Greenland, Tórshavn: Fróðskapur – Faroe University Press, 2016.

Reuters. "Denmark to Boost Defence Spending and Phase out Russian Gas", https://www.reuters.com/world/europe/denmark-vote-joining-eus-defence-policy-this-year-danish-media-2022-03-06/, 2022, (Access Date: 19.10.2023).

Rógvi, Kári á. "The Land of Maybe. A Survey of Faroese Constitutional History", The Right to National Self-Determination: The Faroe Islands and Greenland, Ed. Sjúrður Skaale, Leiden: Brill-Nijhoff, 2004: 13-48.

Stevenson, Christopher. "Hans Off!: The Struggle for Hans Island and the Potential Ramifications for International Border Disupute Resolution", Boston College International & Comparative Law Review, 30/1, (2007): 263-275.

Strandsbjerg, Jeppe. "Making Sense of Contemporary Greenland: Indigeneity, Resources and Sovereignty", Polar Geopolitics? Knowledges, Resources and Legal Regimes, Ed. Richard C. Powell and Klaus Dodds, Massachusetts: Edward Elgar Publishing, 2014: 259-276.

The White House. "NSPD-66/HSPD-25", https://irp.fas.org/offdocs/nspd/nspd-66.htm, 2009, (Access Date: 19.10.2023).

Uddin, Mahatab. "Hans Island: How to Resolve the Dispute?", Current Developments in Arctic Law, 4, (2016): 30-33.

Verhelst, Koen. A Geopolitical Gem: How Greenland can be a Test Case for a more Ambitious EU, Discussion Paper C279, Bonn: Center for European Integration Studies (ZEI), 2023.

Villaume, Poul and Olesen, Thorsten Borring. I Blokopdelingens Tegn: Dansk Udenrigspolitiks Historie Vol 5: 1945-1972, Kobenhavn: Danmarks Nationalleksikon, 2005.

Wang, Nils and Degeorges, Damien. Greenland and the New Arctic: Political and Security Implications of a Statebuilding Project, Copenhagen: Royal Danish Defence College, 2014.

Weber, Mel. "Defining the Outer Limits of the Continental Shelf across the Arctic Basin: The Russian Submission, States'Rights, Boundary Delimitation and Arctic Regional Cooperation", The International Journal of Marine and Coastal Law, 24/4, (2009): 653-681.

Wivel, Anders. "Between Paradise and Power: Denmark's Transatlantic Dilemma", Security Dialogue, 36/3, (2005): 417-421.

# CONCLUSION

This book represents the result of a collective initiative to further investigate the role of the Arctic in broader security and socio-political contexts. As mentioned at the onset, the initial purpose was to emphasise that the Arctic is a large and promising area for future growth. However, as the various scholars associated with this research effort further explored their substantive areas, it became clear that to enhance the efficacy of this volume, it needed to instead encompass the large body of work already examining the Arctic sphere while contributing to these discussions by centring our analysis on the geography and geopolitics of the region. Early on, the various scholars also recognized the importance of history in this effort, as each of the stakeholders'pasts impact decision-making and actions undertaken within the Arctic sphere.

Gone are the days where the Arctic is viewed as an impenetrable mass of ice. Instead, the region is now a vibrant sphere of geopolitical importance. Research in this volume emphasises how emerging sea routes through the Arctic circle result in renewed opportunities for economic growth, trade, and broader transport for stakeholders and the global community more broadly. Research focusing on energy has demonstrated how this characteristic will likely be a primary driver for future decision-making and strategy, similar to efforts being seen in other areas of the world. Indeed, energy is integrally tied to domestic production, citizen satisfaction, and national defence. The chapter on climate change captures the multi-faceted challenges that global warming poses to state, regional, and global security, noting that heating occurs at a faster rate in the Arctic sphere.

After presenting the broadly encompassing areas impacting the Arctic, notably energy, transportation, climate change, and geopolitics, we then turn to individual country-level analyses for the Arctic Circle stakeholders. Within these contributions, scholars evaluate national-level strategies for engaging in responsible conduct and governance over the Arctic region. In some cases, we see overlapping synergies of priorities. For example, most of the countries discussed make mention to sustainability, environmentalism, and opportunities for economic growth. Yet, we also see deviations between countries. For example, the United States and the Russian Federation, the political entities that drove international relations during the Cold War, vary in their own approaches and priorities for the region. Of note, geographic size does not necessarily equate to power and dominance within the Arctic space. In the Arctic Circle, all stakeholders provide valuable contributions to the region, which helps add to the dynamics of a more collective partnership agreement.

This volume provides new insight into the geopolitical considerations of the region. While these contributions are important to the broader discussions about the Arctic north, the work is far from over. Further research can and should empirically evaluate the many factors that impact Arctic security and well-being, building on existing efforts occurring in disciplines spanning the social and natural sciences, as well as the humanities and the arts. Future technologies and innovative disruptions at the state-level, such as continued military developments, changing governmental ideations, various threats posed by non-state actors, and natural considerations, such as health pandemics, could impact efforts within the Arctic space. In combating these emergent threats, it is essential to first contextualize the Arctic Circle as a dynamic and evolving space in its own right and to leverage the strong collective and strategic partnerships developed amongst the region's stakeholders in collaboration with the global community.

www.ingramcontent.com/pod-product-compliance
Lightning Source LLC
Chambersburg PA
CBHW030353270326
41926CB00009B/1087